PRAISE FOR R~~~~

Fifty-Six Counties

"Russell Rowland is a whirlwind of a writer, clothed in the stark colors of Montana's mountains and sky, her high plains and her deep true rivers. *Fifty-Six Counties: A Montana Journey* is astounding in beauty and vitality, interwoven with great wisdoms about human shadow and human light, touched by divine notions of the sacredness that binds all people, and graced with a hard-won and ultimately natural sense of illumination. In writing the book, Rowland says he wanted to tap 'into the spirit of Montana...to explore its heart.' The result is something soulful, defiant, and revolutionary. He is fiercely devoted to the atonement and beauty that are the hallmarks of all great works of art. Rowland names our collective loneliness, but does so with a fierce and tender devotion to the mothers and fathers of all races, all cultures. His unique, person-to-person path through the history, present, and future of Montana is a vision both elegant and muscular, rich with the scents of forest and arid lands, violence and community, ranch life and city life, conservation and industry and ore. *Fifty-Six Counties* is animated by the numinous even as it humbles us, makes us more sane, and draws us into a new and invigorating experience of the essence of life. This is a book for Montana, for the nation, and for the world."

> — Shann Ray, author of *American Masculine*, *Balefire*, and *American Copper*, and winner of the American Book Award, the High Plains Book Award, and the Spur Award

"I can't wait for others to discover this book. Thoughtful, wise, funny, sincere, and *deep*: those are the words that come to mind when reading this treasure. Rowland is a humble observer, but he's also willing to dig deep and bravely, offering astute reflections on the state, its resources, its peoples, its history, and its charm and its dangers. This book does not blink or turn away from the harder issues, nor does it refrain from celebrating all that deserves adoration. In a voice all his own, Rowland proves to be warm and personable, and yet cutting and real—basically, one couldn't wish for a better guide to the state of Montana. This book is utterly unique. A gorgeous accomplishment."

> —Laura Pritchett, author of *Stars Go Blue*, and winner of the High Plains Book Award and the PEN USA Award

"Everything about Montana is big: its proverbial sky, its mountains, its wide open spaces. And yet, Russell Rowland has managed to capture all that grand landscape--and the people who inhabit it--into the intimacy of a single book. *Fifty-Six Counties* is a remarkable book: a macro-focused narrative using a wide-angle lens. If you have room for only one book about Montana on your shelf, make it this one."
—David Abrams, author of *Fobbit,* a *New York Times* Notable Book

In Open Spaces

"This heartfelt exploration of the lives and hard times of a prairie ranch family fairly pulses with the intrigues of existence. Russell Rowland has given us a vivid and distinctive piece of homespun to take its proper place in the literary quilt of the West."
—Ivan Doig, author of *This House of Sky*

"Charged with dramatic tension—a joy to read."
—Ha Jin, author of *Waiting*

"[An] outstanding debut...Rowland's examination of family dynamics is poignant and revealing."
—*Publishers Weekly* (starred review)

"A family epic that has a muted elegance....A gracefully understated novel."
—*New York Times Book Review*

"*In Open Spaces* is as good as it gets....a powerful book."
—C. J. Box, author of *Open Season* and *Savage Run*

High and Inside

"Richly and intimately told, *High and Inside* is a raucous tragicomedy, infused with the desire we all feel in the face of our greatest mistakes: to somehow win redemption, no matter how large our flaws."
—Kim Barnes, author of *In the Kingdom of Men*

"At times funny, at times tragic, often wise and always moving, this wonderful novel is a grand slam of indelible characters and infectious drama, and a flat-out great read."
—Alan Heathcock, author of *VOLT*

FIFTY-SIX COUNTIES

A MONTANA JOURNEY

RUSSELL ROWLAND

Bangtail Press

The counties of Montana, with county seats

ISBN-13: 978-0-9961560-2-8

Manufactured in the United States of America

An excerpt from the poem "The Necessary Bullet," by M. L. Smoker, reprinted from *Another Attempt at Rescue*, © 2005 by M. L. Smoker, by permission of Hanging Loose Press.

Cover photograph of author by Wendy Elwood.

Published in the United States by

Bangtail Press
P. O. Box 11262
Bozeman, MT 59719
www.bangtailpress.com

To my mother, Lorene Rowland,
with love and thanks for dropping me in Montana

CONTENTS

ACKNOWLEDGMENTS

This book owes a great deal to four people in particular. The first is my uncle Lee Arbuckle, who first suggested this idea soon after my first novel came out. For reasons I'll explain later, the idea got shot down then, but I was never able to completely dismiss it, and eventually I realized that it was something I really wanted to do.

That's where person number two came into the picture. After Bangtail Press published *High and Inside,* I was knocking around ideas with my editor, and a few of them sort of stuck and a few of them bounced off, but the minute I mentioned this one, he said without hesitation that he would love to publish a book like this. And then the idea was off and running.

I owe a huge debt to everyone who contributed to the Kickstarter campaign that raised more than $7,000 to cover the cost of my trip around the state. I would not have been able to afford this without your help, but more importantly, it made me realize how much people really wanted to read a book like this. It was a wonderful boost of confidence and a validation that I wasn't wasting my time.

The third person—and this is more for overall support over a long period—goes to Mom, who has been my biggest fan.

I also owe a huge thank you to Wendy Elwood for her wonderful photographs and companionship through the writing of this book.

I would also like to thank all the people who offered their homes, their food, and their hospitality, and their wisdom during my travels. You know who you are, and this project would not have been possible without your help. I would name you all but I'm sure I'd forget a couple, and then I'd offend someone.

And finally, to Montana, for all of its wonderful richness and variety. Its people are the best I've met, and I've been plenty of good places.

Russell Rowland
Billings, Montana
February 4, 2016

INTRODUCTION

I have a secret to share with you. It's about this whole Montana mystique. The magic of this place. I have lived in twelve different states in the past thirty years, and I have always been amazed by how people respond when they hear I'm from Montana. Not always, of course. Some people can't even place Montana. They sometimes know it's near Canada. And many others see it as just another small part of that big empty space between New York and California. But I often come across people who say, "Oh, I *love* Montana."

"Have you been there?" I ask.

"No, but it looks so beautiful in the pictures! I've always *wanted* to go!"

And of course there are the inevitable questions, sometimes entirely baffling. A friend of mine was recently asked, "Do you have grocery stores there?"

Montana is a place whose vast expanses are really impossible to comprehend until you've been here. I was recently talking to someone who works at the wind farms in Wheatland County and he told me about the owner of the company coming out to visit the work site.

"He said he would just catch a cab from the airport in Billings. I said, 'I don't think you want to do that.' So he asked me whether there was a train, and I said, 'No, tell you what, I'll just come and pick you up.' He was blown away by how isolated this place is."

Another friend tells a story about when they first moved to Montana, and they had to drive to Great Falls for business. "This guy was giving me directions, and he said to turn left at Eddie's Corner, and I asked him what that was, and he said, 'Oh, it's just a gas station,' and I thought, 'Wait…I'm driving over 200 miles to get to this town and I'm supposed to pick out one gas station to know where to turn?' But of course when I got to Eddie's Corner, it made complete sense."

For decades, the West, and Montana in particular, has developed a reputation as a place where you can go to start over, to create a whole new persona or become the person you always envisioned. It's the kind of place where a week-long trip to one of our more picturesque locales fuels the imagination. The fresh air, the huge sky, and the wide open space instills in you a belief that anything is possible. It's a place where starting over can move from a concept to a reality in the course of a walk around Bozeman or a drive along Flathead Lake.

But here's the secret: The secret is that we Montanans are completely bipolar. That's right. Up and down like a goddamn bucking horse. Not all of us, of course. But as a state. As one big entity, we are completely manic-depressive. Why do I say that? Well, in February 2014, Gallup did a survey to determine the "Happiest States in America," and Montana finished number one. Number one! That's the image most people have, right? That's the idea you get when you visit this place. People are friendly as hell. They really *do* seem happy. You rarely get that shiver up your neck where this friendliness seems to be hiding some slimy ulterior motive. People in Montana let you go first because it doesn't *matter* whether they get to go first. They smile at you on the street because there's no good reason *not* to.

But here's the other side of it. That same year, 2014, several studies listed Montana in the top three for suicide rate. And for the last forty years, we have been in the top five every single year. What? What the hell does that mean? How is that possible? How can a place that is the happiest in the whole country…what?

Well, that is one of the many things I want to address in this book. For one thing, there is an inherent pressure when you live in Montana to be happy. Seriously—if you can't be happy living here, what's wrong with you? But of course it's way more complicated than that.

Much of the explanation goes back to the very beginning, when Montana first came into being, or at least the current form of Montana, when it was "settled." From the start, the narrative about our history has been altered or often completely rewritten in order to support the actions of certain people or certain groups of people. From the start, those who wrote our history were so intent on shining a bright light on Montana that they ignored many of the pertinent facts. Particularly the shadows.

And perhaps the most troubling aspect of this phenomenon is that many of those who wrote or made movies about the West, and particularly about Montana, did not even live here. From the time Owen Wister came out with *The Virginian,* which is considered the first great "Western," writers have been presenting the stereotypical Westerner as stoic, self-contained, multi-talented, and completely cool under pressure. But Wister was a lawyer from back East, a law school friend of Teddy Roosevelt's who came West a few times as a rich tourist.

The American West was built around misconceptions. Misconceptions and misdirection. And although most of us who live here know this by now—especially after decades of wonderful historians and journalists digging deep enough to tell the real story—many of these misconceptions still persist. Not only here, but worldwide. Because they have become an important part of the American culture. They still justify certain behaviors. They romanticize the idea that men who ride into town and take care of business are the kind of men we need. The number of American presidents and other world leaders who have posed on horses, or in various "Western" activities, is hilarious, and frightening. From Reagan chopping firewood to Putin sitting shirtless in the saddle, leaders have found ways to align themselves with the old John Wayne mentality. And it seems to work. It tells the public, "I am a man of action; I can handle an axe. And I look good on a horse."

Look at Teddy. He was actually known as The Cowboy President. And he not only relished that image but perpetuated it. Partly because it was based on fact. Because he lived it for a few years. But there was a dark side to Theodore Roosevelt's time out West, and that contradiction fits right in with our whole bipolar history. Roosevelt moved here and built a cattle ranch when he was still in his twenties, after he lost both his wife and his mother on the very same day, in the same house, from completely unrelated ailments. He spent the next several years immersing himself in a world of physical labor. Raising cattle and hunting like a fiend (the number of animals Roosevelt killed in his time out West is estimated in the thousands). It doesn't take a professional to figure out that there was at least some element of escapism going on there. Roosevelt never mentioned his wife's name (Alice) again as long as he lived, even in his autobiography. So you could say it worked for him. But none of us will ever know how much pain he buried over those tragic events. It could very well be what drove him to accomplish as much as he did. It is well documented that he was a man who couldn't sit still.

WHEN I MOVED BACK TO Montana in 2007, I realized two very important things. The first was that, after twenty-five years away, I was exceedingly grateful to be home. In the time I had been away, it had become apparent to me that Montana is one of the few places in this country that inspires a powerful sense of identity and an undying sense of loyalty in its people. It was not unusual during that twenty-five-year period for me to meet someone, and after talking for just a few minutes, to have a strong instinct about them, only to find out that they were from Montana. These meetings were inevitably followed with a big smile and a comment such as "I knew there was something I liked about you."

The second thing I realized was that I did not know my state nearly as well as I thought I did. After a few years back, it became clear that if I intend to keep writing about this place, I need to get to know it better. Several years ago, my uncle, Lee Arbuckle, had suggested a book idea to me. He said, "Why don't you visit every county in Montana and write about your travels?" I was dating an editor at the time, and when I told her about the idea, she shook her head and said, "Nobody would buy that." So I dismissed the idea then, but it would not go away. It kept coming back, and everything about it appealed to me.

When I suggested it to Allen Jones, my editor at Bangtail Press, he didn't even hesitate to say yes. And his confidence in the idea, before I had written a word of this book, inspired me to dive in. Over the period of almost two years, I visited all fifty-six counties, talked to hundreds of Montanans about what's happening around our state, and read nearly one hundred books to try to understand how we got here. This book is the result of that effort. I had no idea what I was looking for on this journey, but the further I delved into the project, the more I realized that one thing I wanted to accomplish was to explore the connection between our past and our present.

Many wonderful journalists and historians have told this story before, and this is intended as just one more contribution to the growing narrative of this place. It is just one man's take on the contradictions and complexities that are Montana. Because a story this big and complicated needs to be told over and over again.

CHAPTER ONE
Law and Order

*"When plunder becomes a way of life for
a group of men living together in society,
they create for themselves in the course
of time a legal system that authorizes it
and a moral code that glorifies it."*
—Frédéric Bastiat

The job of rewriting our past started from the beginning, with the first book ever published in Montana, *The Vigilantes of Montana*. Thomas Dimsdale, who was the editor of the *Montana Post* in Virginia City, wrote this book just after some very interesting events unfolded around him. The book reads like an article from the local sports page, as if Dimsdale was celebrating the heroic feats of the high school football team.

Although much has been written about these events—my own personal favorite being *A Decent, Orderly Lynching* by Frederick Allen—their importance cannot be overstated. Dimsdale was a colorful writer, and by all accounts a fine reporter, but he also had to live in the same community as the vigilantes, during a time when everyone was walking those dusty streets in complete fear. Between the Native Americans and the road agents that finally inspired the vigilantes to action, and finally the vigilantes themselves, people never knew when they might be attacked, pulled aside and questioned, beaten, or strung from a tree.

Dimsdale seems to have been convinced that he was reporting the events in an unbiased manner, but he had little chance of *not* being biased toward the vigilantes; when it came right down to it, his life depended on it. Those who spoke out against them—and that included two of the most prominent lawyers in the region, James Thurmond and H. P. A. Smith— often found themselves chased out of town by threats of death. A few years after being exiled, Thurmond filed a defamation suit against one of the founders of the Vigilante Committee and would win a settlement of $8,000 in a Utah court. These guys didn't like anyone pointing out when they were in the wrong, and they were often in the wrong. Toward the end of their reign, a man was hung just for expressing his disapproval of their activities. And they continued their campaign despite direct orders from federal judges to cease and desist.

Today, at first glance, it is impossible to imagine that the sixty-mile stretch between Bannack and Virginia City could inspire the kind of greed that led to dozens of men being hung. There is nothing the least bit remarkable about the area where Bannack sits now, which no doubt explains why nobody lives there anymore. But for several years this area was the number-one destination for people moving West. It's even harder to imagine when you consider that most of these pioneers traveled thousands of miles, mostly by horse and wagon, and often on foot. Before there were actual roads.

It is impossible to imagine until you understand the reason. Which was, of course, gold. In May 1863, a small group of grubby miners found gold in Alder Gulch, near where Virginia City and Nevada City sprang up, and word spread so quickly that the population of these three towns (Bannack being the third), which were then part of the Idaho territory, swelled to around ten thousand people in the next three months. The following year, prospectors pulled $10 million worth of gold from the creeks and rivers between Bannack and Virginia City, an astonishing sum for that time, approximately $230 million in today's money. Over the next five years, the amount extracted from the mines in that area was estimated to be between $30 and $40 million.

But one of the more interesting aspects of that period is how many different groups of people converged on this place at the same time. When we think of the native population that was already there, many people just think "Indians." But it was much more complicated than that; there were many different tribes. It had only been thirty years since President Andrew Jackson initiated the Indian Removal Act, a blatant combination of coercion, bribes, and massaging of laws wherein thousands of Native Americans were forced to leave the regions where they had lived for generations (leading to, among other horrible events, the Trail of Tears). The Dakota War, where the US Cavalry clashed with the Sioux in the Black Hills, had just taken place a year before the Alder Creek Gold Rush, and the Sand Creek Massacre was just around the corner. A good percentage of these Natives had been directed toward what is now Montana, and they were not happy about it. Each tribe had been designated their own territories, which was determined by the government with little thought to these peoples' needs. And although they had developed a mutual respect for each other's territories, many of these tribes hated each other and often battled. So there was already a volatile atmosphere that permeated this part of the country. People were already living in constant states of danger and fear.

Add to this an incredible variety of people who flocked to the West with the news of gold. The Western films like to portray most of the pioneers as good family folk just wanting to get their hands on a nice piece of land to build a life for themselves, and of course there was that demographic. But that was not the typical resident of Montana in the 1860s.

Most of the early white folks that came to Montana were single men who were looking to get rich. They were deserters from the military or disgruntled Civil War veterans, particularly from the South, who were pissed off that they'd lost the war. They were men with criminal records or men who were trying to escape families that didn't want them around. They were men who had failed in their search for gold in California but hadn't given up on the dream. They were from Germany and Ireland and the Scandinavian countries. They were from China.

The old movies like to portray all of the inhabitants of the West talking with the Western drawl we have all come to associate with John Wayne and other Western stars. But it probably sounded a lot more like modern-day San Francisco, with every language and accent imaginable. And with it, every cultural and ideological concept imaginable. The possibilities for conflict were endless.

On top of that, the conditions of the time also have to be considered. The old Western movies, and even photographs from that time, present the West in sepia tones that seem quaint and romantic from here, like a costume party. But the influx of that many people, in such a short amount of time, in a place that had no water or sewage or waste system, must have made for interesting living conditions. Garbage and sewage alone provided a persistent, horrible odor. And because it was mostly men, it was inevitable that the services of ladies were soon made available, as well as copious amounts of liquor.

People tend to assume that most of these men were rough and crass and only cared about such things as drinking, fighting, and prostitutes, but there is plenty of evidence to the contrary. *The Diary of Ichobod Borror,* written by a prospector who moved to Virginia City from Ohio in 1864, reveals a spirit of camaraderie among the prospectors that is surprisingly tender at times. At several points in Borror's account, he talks about how lonely he is when his partners are off working in other areas of the state. There are even entries that describe men standing in a group and weeping openly because one of their friends has decided to go back home. That's not a scene you'd ever see in a John Ford movie.

What's also remarkable is how many people who would go on to become major influences in our state's history showed up in Bannack or Virginia City during this short, volatile period. There was the young Canadian fur trader Johnny Grant, who developed an innovative way to build a cattle herd, trading one healthy cow for two of the bedraggled cattle that people had pushed into Montana. Grant would go on to start the Grant-Kohrs Ranch near Deer Lodge. Grant's eventual partner in that venture, Conrad Kohrs, a German immigrant who spent much of his life working as a seaman, also found his way to Bannack, which is where he and Grant first became acquainted. Kohrs would eventually be recruited by the vigilantes to take part in one of their raids, a decision that was made for him, and the cost of which he was still bitter about when he wrote his memoirs decades later.

There was a resourceful young woman of nineteen named Libby Smith who arrived in Virginia City in 1863 with her brother. Libby was working as a cook for a freighting wagon that delivered another load of people hoping to strike it rich. Libby eventually married one of the vigilantes and started a ranch near Choteau, where she became known as the Cattle Queen of Montana.

Granville Stuart, who some refer to as Mr. Montana, spent many years in the Bannack area after moving there with his brother, James, in the late 1850s. The Stuarts were among the original prospectors in the area but they had little luck, so they moved to what eventually became Deer Lodge. But when the big strike happened in 1863, the Stuarts moved back to Bannack to establish a butcher shop to provide food for the multitudes of hungry young miners. After the gold rush played out, Stuart returned to Deer Lodge where he became an active businessman, community leader, and politician.

One of the more puzzling figures to come to the area was our first territorial governor, Sidney Edgerton. Edgerton was appointed by President Lincoln to serve as Chief Justice of what was then the Idaho Territory. He settled in Bannack in the winter of 1863, waiting for the warmer weather so he could make his way to Lewiston, Idaho, the territorial capital. Despite his position, Edgerton's involvement in the events that soon followed was mostly one of complete *in*action.

Edgerton was so single-minded about becoming the first governor of the territory (he later made a special trip to Washington to lobby for this position), that perhaps out of fear of political backlash, he made no effort to take any action or show any alliance during the years that the vigilantes were doing their business. When Edgerton was approached about charging someone with a crime or arranging for a trial, he gave the excuse that he had not been officially sworn into office. It's possible that Edgerton was an early example of why Montanans often show such exasperation with people in government.

John Bozeman followed Stuart from Deer Lodge to Bannack in 1863 and would eventually build the trail and the town that bore his name before dying under mysterious circumstances.

Another future governor of the state became a prominent figure because of his efforts to establish some order in this chaotic place. Samuel Hauser emerged from this period as one of the few with a solid perspective on what was happening and how to profit from it. Hauser financed the first smelter in Montana after silver was discovered near Argenta, just a few miles from Bannack. He later founded banks in Virginia City and in Helena, became involved in the cattle business, and earned tremendous respect for his business acumen and fair dealings.

And finally there was a tiny, ambitious Irishman that showed up in Bannack and, although he didn't strike it rich, made a modest amount of money from the placer mines. But his ability to make shrewd use of this small amount of money would eventually make him one of the wealthiest men in the world. That man, of course, was William Andrews Clark.

The fact that so many of the people who shaped the future of our state were there during this crucial phase of our history still influences the way Montanans look at business, government, and law enforcement, as well as many other aspects of communication and community. Many of us tend to look at our history through a Vaseline-smothered lens of nostalgia.

We like to picture these figures as rational, morally upright people who handled things much better than we do today. And when you focus on the people who managed to come out of that period as leaders of their communities, it's understandable that people would see them that way.

But there were thousands of others who did *not* strike it rich. Not enough attention has been paid to the fact that scores of men lived in this place that were barely able to accommodate their most basic needs for food, shelter, medical care, and sex. We don't consider the possibility that many of these men, who had just lived through one of the bloodiest wars in history, may have been suffering from some kind of mental disorder as well. Post-traumatic stress disorder may not have had a name yet, but it must have been rampant among these Civil War veterans, as well as those who were forced into action against the Native Americans. Based on the number of saloons that thrived in the area, there was probably a very high percentage of alcoholics. And wife-beaters. We don't like to think about it, but there was probably a lot of rape going on.

Dimsdale and others present this period as one of great social order, but when you read Frederick Allen's account, it sounds a lot more like a bizarre combination of *Peyton Place* and Keystone Cops, with men getting their noses bent out of shape and overreacting left and right to slights and perceived hurts.

So what happened? Yes, I was just about to get to that.

When thousands of men show up in one place and are all after one thing, there is some predictable chaos involved. Imagine just the simple act of trying to provide housing and supplies for so many people in an area that was almost completely inaccessible. Men lived in tents, or dugouts, or tiny self-constructed shacks. Resourceful shop owners charged ridiculous fees for supplies that these men needed to carry out the business of trying to strike it rich. Shovels cost as much as ten dollars. The fight for some of the most necessary supplies, like flour, sometimes got ugly. At one point, all of the flour in the area was gathered up in one place so people couldn't hoard it anymore. And of course most of these men did not find gold. The sense of desperation must have hovered over these towns like an odor.

So crime was rampant, with no structure provided to deal with it. The Idaho Territory had just been established a few months before the strike happened, but Congress had adjourned before assigning anyone to enforce law and order in the region. The biggest targets for the road agents were the miners returning from their work day, or those who had managed to make a strike and had to deliver their goods to the bank. Men tried to hide their good fortune, but in a place where good fortune was scarce, that was difficult.

By Dimsdale's account, over one hundred people had been killed by the time the vigilantes finally decided to do something about the situation. Frederick Allen did extensive research, scouring through records and newspapers from the time, and he came up with a much different total. In fact, he only counted eight. But in spite of the discrepancy, the issue was clear: People were afraid to travel along the roads. People did not feel safe, and something had to be done.

There's more than a little irony surrounding the two murders that finally led people to take some action. The first was a stereotypical barroom showdown between two former associates who ended up shooting each other, one fatally. The two men had arrived in Bannack together less than a year earlier, and the one who survived was a man named Henry Plummer. Plummer was a dapper fellow who carried himself well and showed considerable charm. He had a checkered past, though, and the man he killed, Jack Cleveland, was part of that past, and may have died because Plummer was afraid of what Cleveland might reveal to others. But Cleveland was a rough customer, not as likable as Plummer, and most of those who knew both men believed that Plummer shot Cleveland in anticipation of Cleveland shooting someone else, including Plummer himself.

The second shooting involved an ex-con named Charles Reeves, who also had a history with Plummer. Reeves had arranged to marry a young woman from the local Bannock tribe, a peaceful people who were well respected by the locals. But Reeves liked his whiskey and had a reputation for abusing his women. His bride returned to her tribe one night reporting that Reeves had beaten her, and when Reeves came to retrieve her, he was turned away.

Later, drunk and furious, Reeves and two friends returned and surrounded one of the teepees, riddling it with bullets, killing three Indians and a white fur trapper who had wandered over to see what the commotion was about. The outrage over this crime might surprise people who think that everyone was living under the "only good Indian is a dead Indian" philosophy. The fact was a good many people were working hard to maintain good relations with the Natives, and the Bannocks were considered especially amiable at the time.

The most bizarre part of the story comes when these three men decided to leave town to try to avoid the wrath of the local community. Reeves knew Plummer from their days in California, and the men stopped to invite Plummer to join them in exile. Plummer was apparently worried enough about his own fate that he went along, so he was with them when a small posse tracked the men down and brought them in. It was on their return to town that Plummer discovered how much people were on his side. His case was quickly dismissed.

But the other three men were brought to trial for murder. A judge and jury were spontaneously assembled, as was the custom in this chaotic place. One of the men was acquitted when they determined that he had not fired his gun. The other two were found guilty but the jury was too afraid of repercussions to sentence them to death. So the two guilty men were instructed to leave the area and not return.

Here, the story gets stranger. It happened to be the dead of winter, so although the men did leave town, the conditions were such that they couldn't travel very far. Soon afterward, the townspeople learned that the men were holed up in a cabin with little food, nearly frozen to death, so they were allowed to come back. The end result of all of this was that nobody paid any consequences for these crimes, which added to the sentiment that something had to be done.

One might assume that Henry Plummer came out of this experience with some degree of caution. That he might want to lay low. But hard feelings had developed between him and Hank Crawford, a local butcher who had voluntarily taken on the role of sheriff during these events. Crawford made an attempt to collect compensation for court costs, including confiscating the guns of the four men who had been tried. Plummer took offense to this, especially considering he'd been acquitted. Although he got his gun back, the feud was in full blossom.

According to most accounts, Crawford generated the majority of the animosity, mostly out of fear. Crawford had very little experience with the law, and Plummer's reputation and cool demeanor apparently had Crawford convinced that Plummer was going to gun him down just out of principle. In today's world, the two men might have met and worked it out, with the help of a mediator, or over a few drinks. Instead they circled each other like alpha dogs for a few days.

One morning, Plummer blatantly planted himself on the main street of town, his foot propped on a wagon wheel and a rifle resting on his arm. Crawford was inept with a gun, and rather than risk a showdown, he decided on a sneak attack, and sighted his own rifle on Plummer from behind, then shot him. The bullet entered Plummer's elbow and traveled down to his wrist, shattering bones along the way. Plummer whirled and shouted at Crawford to shoot again, which Crawford did. But he missed.

Crawford was ostracized for shooting a man in the back, a serious violation of unwritten frontier law, and he ended up leaving town, moving to Fort Benton and never returning.

After this incident, the community decided that they needed some structure, and they held elections to choose a judge and sheriff. Just weeks after he had been tried for murder, Plummer threw his hat in the ring for the job of sheriff, and perhaps because they felt the need for someone who would take action (aside from the incident with Crawford, it was a well-known fact that Plummer had killed at least three other men, although they were all determined to be self-defense), he won the election.

The events of the next few months are unprecedented in American history. Within months of Plummer's appointment as sheriff, the amount of robberies on the roads leading to and from Bannack and Virginia City rose, and he did little to investigate or charge anyone, even when rumors flew about who was involved. He hired questionable characters as deputies, many from his past, and made little effort to explain behaviors that were at the very least odd if not extremely suspicious.

It was only a matter of time before leaders in the community drew the conclusion that there was an organized group of men carrying out these crimes, and that Plummer was somehow involved, possibly even the leader. Meanwhile, Plummer continued to present the same suave demeanor, causing people to question their own instincts even when they were sure he was involved. He was living in the same house with Francis Thompson, a man who would become one of the co-founders of the Montana Historical Society, and who considered Plummer to be a good friend. And right up to the end, Thompson was unsure how he felt about the charges against Plummer.

The event that finally tipped the public opinion was the discovery of the body of a young man named Nicholas Tieboldt. Tieboldt had been hired by William Clark (not *the* William Clark) to buy some mules, and when Tieboldt didn't return, his disappearance became a source of concern. A few days later, his body was accidentally discovered by a hunter, William Palmer, not far from the house of a rancher named George Ives. Palmer approached the house to get help moving the body and was surprised when two men who worked for Ives, George Hilderman and "Long John" Franck, refused to help him.

This particular William Clark had been part of a vigilante movement in California a few years earlier. When he learned what happened to his young charge, Clark gathered several men who had been considering a similar organization and they formed a posse to track down Hilderman, Franck, and Ives.

After riding all night, without thinking to bring provisions, the posse found a group of men near Ives's house, and discovered Franck among them. The posse was hungry and cold and wet, having crossed a creek on their travels, and many of them, probably fueled by whiskey as well, called for the immediate execution of Franck, an act that would have dramatically altered the course of the next few months. But a young rancher named James Williams intervened, providing a voice of reason among these angry, bloodthirsty men.

Although Williams was only twenty-seven, much younger than many of the men involved, he had a presence about him and a sense of calm that apparently won the others over. He would later hold an important role of leadership within the group. That night, he convinced them to allow him and another man to question Franck before they decided what action to take. Although the men were tired and impatient, they agreed and, after intense questioning, Williams was able to coax a confession from Franck—not that he had killed Tieboldt but that George Ives did, and that Ives was in fact hiding not far away from where they were.

With Franck's help, the posse captured Ives and again called for immediate action. They were again persuaded by Williams and a growing cadre of supporters that they needed to calm down, follow proper procedure, and take the men in.

In the course of developing a brand new region, in an atmosphere that was already volatile, the line between chaos and civilized behavior was thin and constantly moving, and there were several moments over the next several days where events nearly tipped into mob rule. The fact that they didn't was thanks in large part to Wilbur Sanders, a man who was on his way out of town when the Ives trial was about to begin. Some of the locals realized that Ives had cornered every lawyer in the region except Sanders and hired them to defend him, so there was no one left to act as prosecuting attorney for this important trial. They begged Sanders to take on the role, and at first he was wary. Like James Williams, Sanders was young, only twenty-nine. He was the nephew of Sidney Edgerton, the judge who had somehow avoided taking on the role of judge since his arrival in Montana. Ives proved to be a very popular figure and the sentiment around the community was decidedly mixed about his guilt. Sanders knew he would be stepping into a very combustive situation. But he also recognized the importance of having someone take on this role, so he agreed to do it.

The decision about how to run the trial reads like a chapter from *Lord of the Flies*. There was great debate about whether to hold a jury trial or to simply have the crowd vote on a verdict. Somehow they reached a consensus that makes almost no sense, where they would have two twelve-man juries, one from Nevada City and one from Junction, a nearby mining camp. The two juries would provide their recommendation but ultimately it would be the crowd vote that determined the outcome.

The proceedings threatened to become more of a farce when "Buzz" Caven, who had been appointed sheriff of Virginia City and was known to be friends with Plummer, interrupted to insist that his community also be allowed to provide a jury. Caven was an imposing man, and when he stood toe to toe with Sanders, challenging him to defy this suggestion, Sanders knew he faced a crucial moment. Caven even had his list of twelve men, which he held in Sanders's face, asking whether he had an issue with any of these men.

Sanders knew that things could tumble out of control based on the way he responded to this question, and he decided on a firm reaction. He told Caven that he did not know any of these men personally, but from what he'd heard he had no desire to know them either. It was a courageous stand, a statement that could have thrown the entire crowd into revolt, and Sanders knew it. But enough of the crowd agreed with him to vote against the third jury.

The rest of the trial would be considered a mockery by

today's standards. As a crowd estimated at nearly two thousand people shouted their comments throughout, people approached Sanders and others, spreading rumors of Ives's other crimes, including robbery and murder. Although there was no proof of any of it and no evidence to support the fact that he had killed Tieboldt, the rumors fueled a growing anti-Ives sentiment. The case itself was mostly based on the testimony of Franck, an unpopular character toward whom the crowd took an instant dislike. But Franck gave a detailed account of what had occurred that day, and it fit with the facts.

As Franck and other witnesses visited the stand, the men who had stories to tell of Ives's other crimes continued to circle the crowd, getting people riled up and swaying their judgment against Ives. That evening, after the testimony had been presented and people came together to discuss the case, the group of men who would become known as the Vigilance Committee gathered and gave Sanders their assurance that, if he got Ives convicted, the punishment would be carried out immediately. They wanted to avoid another situation where crowd sentiment prevented such punishment.

The next day, with great tension throughout the crowd, the final arguments were presented, and the two juries, twenty-four people, retired to discuss their verdict. The deliberations lasted only a half hour, and when they returned, they announced that twenty-three of the twenty-four had voted for a guilty verdict. The lone dissenter would have been, and should have been, enough to demand more deliberation, something Sanders did not want. So he knew that he had to act quickly or risk losing control of the situation. He stood and demanded an immediate vote from the crowd, who roundly voted Ives guilty. Sanders followed with a demand that they render the sentence as well, and before the defense lawyers could respond, the judge agreed. Within minutes, George Ives was condemned to die from hanging.

Ives, ever the smooth manipulator, responded with a calm and calculated move. He approached Sanders, offering his hand. And as they shook, he told him that he was a gentleman and considered Sanders a gentleman as well. And that if he was in Sanders's position, he would be willing to give him what Ives was about to ask for himself, which was another day to say goodbye to his wife and daughters.

Sanders knew it would be difficult to say no to this man without appearing incredibly calloused. But he was saved by a shout from the crowd that became Montana legend. A short, energetic miner and merchant named Nathaniel "X" Beidler, who would go on to become a central figure in the vigilante movement, even after it had supposedly ceased its activities, yelled out, "Sanders! Ask him how long he gave the Dutchman!"

The crowd responded wildly, and after they gave Ives enough time to write a letter to his family, he was hung. But not without a bit of further drama. After Sanders, in a moment of overzealousness, demanded that Ives's belongings be sold to cover the court costs, one of Ives's lawyers took offense to such a heartless suggestion in the face of his execution and stood to confront Sanders.

Sanders had been worried enough about the day's events that he had tucked two pistols in the pockets of his jacket, and as the lawyer approached, Sanders reached into his pockets and gripped the pistols, ready to act if necessary. But in his nervousness, Sanders pulled the trigger on one of the firearms and nearly shot himself in the foot.

The defense lawyer thought for a moment that Sanders had fired at him, and he stepped forward and gripped him by the jacket, but some of the men surrounding the two grabbed them and pulled them apart.

Ives stood on a wooden box and, when asked if he had any final words, he shocked the crowd and named another man, Alex Carter, as the actual killer, a claim that would later condemn *that* man to death at the hands of the Vigilance Committee.

BECAUSE THERE WAS A trial, Ives is not counted among the victims of the vigilante movement, but this was the beginning of what would amount to the executions, most of which were completely spontaneous, of anywhere from twenty-one to fifty-seven men (the latter is Frederick Allen's count, based on events over the next several years that involved various members of the group). Plummer and his two deputies were hanged just three weeks after the Ives trial. A total of twenty men, including Plummer, were hung during the month of January 1864 alone.

Among many Montanans, and many people around the country, the vigilantes are considered heroes for their efforts to restore order in a place where the community was about to be overrun by complete chaos. It's difficult to argue with that opinion when you consider where things were headed. It's difficult to argue against the fact that something had to be done.

But the long-term effects of this period are worth exploring further, because there are echoes that linger in our short history even now.

The most significant byproduct of these events was quite predictable based on the old absolute power corrupts absolutely bromide. It's easy to make a case that the early actions of these men were justified.

But it's alarming to observe how quickly their actions accelerated. Just one day after Henry Plummer and his two deputies were hanged, the mob surrounded the dilapidated cabin of a Mexican man named José Pizanthia. Pizanthia's crime, it seems, was being generally unlikeable. The worst crime on record for Pizanthia was breaking the window of one of the local taverns with the butt of his pistol. But the committee decided unanimously that Pizanthia was a nuisance, and so just hours after the entire community had witnessed the hanging of the three top law enforcement officers of the area, an army of men surrounded Pizanthia's shack and called for him to surrender.

It's not hard to imagine what must have been going through Pizanthia's mind. He knew he was screwed, so he started shooting. He struck one man, mortally wounding him, and what followed was one of the more gruesome executions recorded in Montana's history. The men procured a howitzer, which is basically a cannon, from none other than Sidney Edgerton, who seemingly continued to turn a blind eye to the events swirling around him. They set up the gun and fired three rounds into Pizanthia's house, hoping he was still inside. The first two did not detonate, but the third exploded. Inside, they found Pizanthia lying on the floor, wounded but still alive. And they proceeded to empty six shots into him.

They then tied a rope around his neck and dragged him to a pole, where they hung him up and filled his lifeless body with another 100 rounds of ammunition. The viciousness of their attack is hard to comprehend, but it can perhaps be explained.

These men had just hanged three men who had held their community hostage for several months, creating an atmosphere of fear and anxiety that could probably be compared to a war zone. It's easy to imagine how the resolution of this situation made these men temporarily drunk with power, if not a few other spirits, and they simply went nuts with the momentum and took it out on someone they could all agree was disposable. The fact that Pizanthia was a minority is unlikely to be a coincidence.

Dimsdale's account of this incident is dismissive. He even refers to Pizanthia as "the greaser."

Although there weren't very many victims over the next year who were as innocent as Pizanthia, the standards that were initially laid out in the bylaws—murder, armed robbery and horse thieves were supposed to be their sole targets—were constantly compromised, with one man hung for being a pickpocket, and the aforementioned man executed for voicing his disapproval of their actions. The vigilantes ignored written instructions from a federal judge to stop their activities, and paid no price for this defiance. On two occasions, they went out of the territory and brought men back to Montana to hang them, without the cooperation of the other territory's authorities.

There are many examples throughout history where men have decided that the greater good is more important than following the law. And there are many excellent examples in which the results of these actions have led to important social change. In fact, many important social changes were started by people breaking laws that were morally or ethically misguided. As Martin Luther King, Jr. stated in his brilliant "Letter from a Birmingham Jail," "One has not only a legal but a moral responsibility to obey just laws. Conversely, one has a moral responsibility to disobey unjust laws. I would agree with St. Augustine that 'an unjust law is no law at all.'"

But there are also many examples in which people have determined a greater good based on their own misguided interpretation of what is moral or ethical. Men like Joseph McCarthy. The Ku Klux Klan. Richard Nixon, who said in an interview with David Frost that if the president does something, it is not illegal. And the Bush administration, who decided that torture was acceptable just because they said it was, despite clear laws against it.

The Vigilance Committee applied a similar approach to their actions after the death of Plummer and his gang. They felt empowered by the support they received from their neighbors, even after the infrastructure was established and the prudent act would have been to step back and let that structure do what it was designed to do. It's easy to imagine how hard that must have been. When you look at the makeup of this group, many of the men involved were undistinguished. So being part of the vigilantes may have been the highlight of their lives. Like athletes who are past their prime, the notion of giving up the source of their shiniest moments of glory was probably difficult to swallow.

AS A SECOND EMERGING theme, this period established a pattern of, and perhaps even a romance with, a boom-and-bust economic structure, a paradigm that naturally creates situations where all of the elements of a society are suddenly stretched beyond their natural boundaries. In many ways, Montana is perfectly suited to this economic model because we are so incredibly rich in resources. Over the next several decades, aside from briefly producing the most gold in the country, Montana would have a run at being the largest producer of copper in the world (Silver Bow County), and would, for a time, be home to the largest silver mine in the world, near Philipsburg (Granite County). Granite County also, for a time, produced 90 percent of the manganese used for batteries in America. There was a period, during World War II, when Big Horn County (Hardin) had the biggest wheat farm in the world, the Campbell Farming Corporation. Today, counties in Montana are the largest producers of durum wheat (Sheridan County) and malt barley (Teton County) in the United States.

And of course, at the moment, one of the largest oil fields in the world, the Bakken, lingers just below the surface of Montana. I will explore these industries in detail later, but, for the moment, I want to focus on how often we as a state have relied on industries like this to provide our people with jobs, and some of the by-products of that pattern.

For one thing, if you look at the towns where most of these "booms" occurred, they are classic studies in what the trickle-down theory of economics looks like in real life. One look at Bannack and Virginia City today and you'd never guess that millions of dollars were pulled from the waters and hills surrounding these towns. Bannack is completely deserted, with about twenty buildings preserved as a state park. You can stand in the building where Plummer shot Cleveland and in the spot where he and others were hung. All by yourself.

Virginia City has become a charming but blatant tourist trap. The tour that takes you through town shows a place where pretty much everyone lives off tourism. The tour extols the virtues of the vigilantes and demonizes those who were executed, avoiding any mention of the gray areas that are the most interesting part of the story. Tourists apparently prefer their stories cut and diced into bite-sized morsels.

Broadus, Montana, which hosted another huge oil boom in the 1960s, boasts one singular symbol of the millions of dollars that were pumped from the ground: a massive, state-of-the-art courthouse that looks completely out of place in this dying little town. There is a bumper sticker in a Broadus bar that states it quite plainly: "Dear God—Please bring us another oil boom and we promise we won't piss it away this time."

And of course there's Butte, which I will explore in detail in a later chapter.

All of these places have one thing in common: Most of the men and women who benefited most from these booms left at the first chance. The people who went on to become prominent citizens from the Bannack gold rush were not the miners themselves. They were men like Samuel Hauser, who opened the bank. They were men like Johnny Grant, who started raising cattle to feed the working class.

Whether those who profited most from the gold itself blew the money on gambling and bordellos or whether they went on to greener pastures, it was apparently not in their best interests to invest in the place that provided them such tremendous wealth. And this has held true time and again, with a few stellar exceptions.

The most egregious example, though, has to be the aforementioned William Clark, a man who became a multi-millionaire and then left Montana for good, building a huge mansion in New York City and famously saying that he owed the people who had made him wealthy nothing. Mark Twain, who came and performed in Butte and spent time with Clark, said of him:

> He is as rotten a human being as can be found anywhere under the flag; he is a shame to the American nation, and no one has helped to send him to the Senate who did not know that his proper place was the penitentiary, with a ball and chain on his legs. To my mind he is the most disgusting creature that the republic has produced since Tweed's time.

When Huguette Clark, Clark's last surviving child, died in 2011, she was worth approximately $320 million. And she made no effort to reach out to Butte, the town that had provided her with the money to maintain several mansions all over the country for decades. This despite the fact that there is an open pit in Butte that is essentially a cesspool of toxic materials. Some people would (and do) argue that the wealthy have no obligation to do anything philanthropic with their money, and that's certainly true. But when you know the story of the lengths Clark went to in order to avoid paying taxes and to avoid taking responsibility for the damage his company caused, it makes his neglect of his hometown particularly troubling.

Part of the issue that has come up time and again with these various industries is that the working classes of Montana have been so thrilled to have work that they don't put much thought into the long-term effects of the industry, not to mention the need for an infrastructure that would prevent some of the problems that inevitably arise. There is a long history of Montanans ignoring warning signs that they should probably hold the people in charge accountable for their actions.

One great example was the early days of the copper mines and the smelter in Butte and Anaconda. William Clark and Marcus Daly, before they became mortal enemies, managed to bully the Montana legislature, or perhaps grease their palms, to get a law passed that incorporated an obscenely tiny tax rate for mining. For decades, the biggest money-making industry in our state paid a tax rate that was a fraction of what farmers, ranchers, and timber companies paid. And because almost all of the major newspapers were owned by the company, they were able to provide constant propaganda to support their claim that they couldn't afford to pay more. They certainly had the support of their workers, who were mostly silenced by the threat of losing their jobs.

So an early pattern developed in which Montanans were ripped off by corporate carpetbaggers and resented the hell out of them after it was over, despite the fact that we didn't see it coming and didn't force the kind of infrastructure that could have prevented it. It's happening again in the Bakken, and again, I will go into more detail on that later.

ANOTHER THEME THAT EMERGES from the story of Bannack and Virginia City, and perhaps this is not that unique to

Montana, is the human penchant for group identification at
the expense of others, what psychologists might call "moral
exclusion." And of course this started from the very beginning
as well.

It's alarming to read the words of many of the leaders from
that time, men who were in charge of the "Indian problem."
Most of these men were convinced that the Indians needed to
be wiped out completely. And they were also convinced that if
we got rid of most of them, the others would eventually either
die off or leave. But what is perhaps even more disturbing was
how the Vigilante Committee became instrumental in determining who was considered acceptable company in their community. Aside from the unfortunate Mr. Pizanthia, it appears
that race played almost no role in their decisions.

Good people like James Thurmond and H. P. A. Smith (the
lawyers who were scared out of town) were made to feel unwelcome simply because they had the courage to speak their
minds about what was happening.

In the book *The Copper Chorus,* author Dennis Swibold explored the incredible story of how widespread the influence
of the Anaconda Company, and later the Amalgamated Copper Company, were in the newspaper business in Montana.
As I mentioned, these companies owned most of the major
newspapers in the state, which probably doesn't surprise most
people if they're thinking about the days of the Copper Kings.
But what people may not realize is that this continued until as
recently as 1959, when Amalgamated finally sold its papers to
Lee Enterprises.

As a result, Amalgamated often used its influence to sway
public opinion toward certain groups of people in Montana.
During World War I, the anti-German sentiment in Montana
became so volatile that German newspapers, of which there
were several around the state, were forced out of business.
German books were banned in the schools. Entire communities with a high German population packed their things and
moved to Canada. Cartoons in these newspapers depicted
Germans in ways that would be appalling to today's citizens.

A German farm family, near Livingston, the Urbachs, were awakened in the middle of the night by a loud explosion. Mr. Urbach woke up to find his wife dead next to him. And he became so distraught that he slashed his own throat. The crime was never solved.

In Anaconda and Butte, the construction of the railroads brought a large Chinese community. But once the railroad was completed and people decided the Chinese were taking away too many *good* jobs from the whites, a town-wide shunning was quietly instituted, fueled by a vote by the unions to fine anyone five dollars for doing business with a "Chinaman." Within a few years, the Chinese population had dwindled to nothing.

For a state that is considered friendly and welcoming, the truth is that most communities in Montana are even today still selective about who is welcomed. It is perhaps a symptom of small towns throughout America, but it also contributes significantly to this dark side of Montana. The suicides. The high rate of alcoholism. One look at the reservations and you have a stark example of how people in the West view minorities. If they keep to themselves, we might tolerate them. But that doesn't mean we like it.

TODAY, BEAVERHEAD AND MADISON Counties cover the area where the Bannack/Virginia City gold rush combusted and flamed out. The three towns that provided much of the drama of Montana's early years now serve as three very different examples of how we view our past.

Many of the buildings in Bannack have been preserved, and it is now a state park, but it is not a place where you would suddenly find yourself. Like so many of the small towns in Montana, you have to be going to Bannack to get to Bannack. It lies in one of the more stunning valleys in the state, just south of Beaverhead National Forest and a few miles off of Highway 278, which takes you through the Big Hole Valley, with the emphasis on *Big*.

Bannack is a husk of a town now, the buildings propped up

for display, most of them completely empty. It's easy to imagine a strong wind lifting this tiny little ghost town into our famous Big Sky and scattering it across the Big Hole, making it more forgotten than it already is. In fact, a flood in 2014 nearly wiped out many of the buildings, and it took the hard work of the Bannack Association, a group dedicated to keeping the town alive, and the generous donations of many people, to get those buildings put back together again. If it wasn't for the Bannack Association, these buildings would fold in on themselves like so many of the barns that line the highways of Montana.

But this town now provides a stark example of what boom and bust economies look like. Bannack went from being the capital of the Idaho Territory to a ghost town in just a matter of decades. It went from being the most popular destination in the West for about a year to being virtually forgotten.

Nevada City has also preserved a number of its original buildings, and it has imported many other historic buildings from around the state, arranging them in a semblance of what the town looked like at its peak. Unlike Bannack, most of the buildings in Nevada City are furnished, not only with period furniture but with the instruments and décor of various businesses. There are even a couple of businesses still operating in Nevada City, including an excellent bakery and a small hotel. So this cluster of buildings provides a much more authentic feel of what it was like in those early pioneer days.

But Virginia City has gone in another direction. Virginia City is the Hollywood version of Montana. Visiting Virginia City to get a feel for the history of Montana is like riding the Matterhorn at Disneyland and claiming you went on a mountain climbing expedition. It is an amusement park made up of every bad cliché about the West. Like Deadwood, South Dakota, Virginia City provides a version of the West that people *want* to see.

At the same time, Virginia City is still part of Montana, so there are nuggets. In the midst of all this crass commercialism are signs of Montana pride and authenticity. Like Cindy, the clerk at the local pharmacy where I bought two books. Cindy, like many of the merchants in Virginia City, was dressed in a period costume: a brown dress with a high neckline and belted waist with a bow in the back, with lace covering the front.

Cindy grew up in Bozeman and had no desire to go back. In her view, Bozeman is a better example of crass commercialism. But digging a little further, I discovered a deeper wound. Cindy's father once owned a butcher shop in Bozeman, and when a member of her family took it over, he was unable to keep it going. Drinking, it seems, got in the way.

Cindy got teary-eyed telling me this story. It was a surprising show of emotion in the middle of the morning, in the middle of a store, and I wanted to let her know how much I appreciated her honesty. So I came back later with a copy of one of my books.

Cindy was remodeling one of the famous bordellos in town, a tiny building called "The Brick." They cited this building later when I was on a tour, and I found it amazing that anyone would make an effort to restore the place. There was nothing to it. But to Cindy, it was part of history, and to her, history was clearly important.

One thing you quickly discover if you travel around Montana is that Montanans are completely devoted to their history. The volunteers in every museum I visited, and I didn't miss many, present their wares like delicate glass sculptures. They want you to understand how important *their* town is to *them*. But in a town where you would expect one of the more fascinating museums in the state, Virginia City's museum instead features a space that is about three-quarters devoted to souvenirs. To merchandise. And bad, inaccurate merchandise at that. In a state where people have taken advantage of our resources time and again throughout the decades, even our history isn't sacred. Virginia City is a place where history is for sale.

CHAPTER TWO
Boom and Bust

"History doesn't exactly repeat itself,
but it certainly does rhyme."
—Mark Twain

In 1972, K. Ross Toole, one of the premier Montana historians, came out with *Twentieth-Century Montana: A State of Extremes.* This concise account of our history lays out very simply how corporations have taken advantage of our resources through the decades, as well as how they made little attempt to conserve or restore what was there to begin with. But Toole was more than a student of the past. He was also a visionary, and at the end of this book he cites *The Montana Economic Study* conducted by the Bureau of Business Research at the University of Montana in 1970.

This study revealed some frightening trends, including a steady decline in Montana's standing on the list of average per-capita personal income. In 1950 Montana actually ranked 8 percent higher than the national average in this category. But by 1968 we were 14 percent below average. Montana also showed a much slower rate of growth than our neighboring states at that time.

But the most troubling part of the study was the assessment by these expert economists that Montana's decline in personal income would continue at a faster rate than our neighboring states, and for one simple reason: because we were not making enough of an effort to diversify our economy. The major sources of income at the time of the study, outside of agriculture (which has been and still is our number-one industry) were logging, mining, and railroads. And there was little indication that our cities or our government were making much of an effort to expand our horizons.

Toole went on to suggest that Montanans are not the kind of people who accept defeat, so I think it's safe to suggest that he intended to pass along this information as more of a warning than as a prophecy. But forty-some years later, it's interesting to study what's happening now and determine who paid attention. In my travels, I observed over and over again (especially in the eastern part of the state), a stubborn determination to hang on to old ideas, old ways of making a living. And it was often, but not always, those areas of the state that were most reluctant to change that were suffering the most.

Beaverhead County and Madison County are two examples of a running theme in Montana's early development. When you build a community around a resource that is finite and that resource runs out, what do you do next? The mines in these two counties were tapped out within just a few years of their explosive beginnings. So the people who stayed, as I heard in a recent radio interview about another state, experienced "an involuntary diversification" of their economy.

From the time the first gold was discovered in what would become Montana, people have come here for one thing, and then found themselves stranded. They came for nuggets and ended up with crumbs. They came for thick fields of grass and ended up with a mouthful of dust. When you look back on those early days, it's amazing to think that many of these people who came with the hope of striking it rich in the gold mines managed to cobble together a living at all.

The people who stayed, the ones who became the ancestors for those of us who are here now, had to have been incredibly resourceful to figure out a way to make a living in a place that had no built-in infrastructure, very few established places of business, very little opportunity to ship products, and very few costumers for whatever products they did produce.

Some of the other examples of county seats that owe their existence to mining are Philipsburg, Kalispell, Helena, White Sulphur Springs, Great Falls, Lewistown, Columbus, Red Lodge, and, of course Butte and Anaconda. With the exception of Columbus, which has the most productive mine in the state right now, most of these towns were forced to alter the focus of their economy when the mines got tapped out.

In the case of Beaverhead County, while the miners were slogging away on the riverbeds, a few enterprising souls realized that these people needed to be fed, and started bringing cattle and sheep into the area. I will be going into more detail about the history of agriculture later, but just to summarize, many of the people who first started raising crops and livestock in Montana had little or (more likely) no experience in agriculture. That inexperience led to many years of misguided or sometimes outright ignorant abuse of the land. And some of the damage that was done in those early years was irreversible.

But from the beginning, there were also those who recognized that there are ways of both utilizing *and* conserving what little water and natural feed were available. Jim Hagenbarth's family has been raising sheep in the southeast corner of the state since the 1870s, and Hagenbarth's grandfather was one of the first to notice and to voice concerns about the way the grazing land was being used in the area. He even led a group of ranchers who contacted Theodore Roosevelt to voice their concerns. Unfortunately, it wasn't until 1934 that any legislative action was taken to address the issue of abusing public lands. So for nearly fifty years, out of a combination of ignorance, desperation, and perhaps simple greed, sheep and cattle growers allowed their animals to graze to their hearts' content, sometimes doing permanent damage to the soil.

Despite the mismanagement that was so prevalent in those early years, ranching and farming eventually became the primary industries in Montana.

But the factor that has perhaps most influenced the ag industry has been the scarcity of water. It took most of the early settlers by surprise. Beaverhead County falls near the bottom of the list for average rainfall in Montana. So on top of the usual issues of disease, the elements, accidents, and the unpredictability of market prices, the farmers and ranchers of Beaverhead County have had to learn to make do with rainfall that barely exceeds ten inches a year.

One of the most common misconceptions about rural life is that farmers and ranchers live a simple life. That they are simple people. That anyone with the proper resources can come out West and buy land, livestock, or seed and start a farm or a ranch. If you ever sit and talk to a rancher or farmer, however, you quickly realize that there is nothing simple about these practices. Listen to a farmer or rancher talk about the art of finding the right balance of rotating crops, leaving some of the land fallow, finding new ways to utilize what little water is available, and figuring out how to provide enough feed for their sheep or cattle, and you realize that these people are scientists in the bodies of defensive backs. It's hard to imagine a profession that requires a more complete balance of knowledge, curiosity, innovation, open-mindedness, and physical labor. It's small wonder the American farmer/rancher is a dying breed. There are few things harder, with less guarantee of a payoff, than running your own farm or ranch.

So Beaverhead County went from relying on one of the most volatile, unreliable sources of income you can possibly imagine—mining—to something that is only slightly more reliable, in agriculture. And this is true of so many counties in Montana. Our history is one built on some of the shakiest economic structures you can imagine. So many people here never know, one month to the next, whether or how they're going to be able to feed their families.

This uncertainty has had two very powerful influences on Montanans. First, those who survived the early years had to be among the toughest, most versatile group of people in the history of our country. Not only did many of them establish a life for themselves in a landscape that was presented to them as way more productive than it actually was, but they did it during a time when just getting supplies was a constant challenge, with roads that were barely carved out of wilderness, and nothing more than horses and wagons, or an occasional steamboat, to haul their freight.

The negative side of this is that it generated an almost Darwinian community dynamic. Not always, of course. It has become quite common to talk about those early years in Montana as a time when people would drop everything to help a neighbor, and to a certain extent that was true. It was common practice for neighbors to help new folks build their houses and barns, to lend a hand at branding and calving and harvest time. There is a wonderful anecdote in an early memoir called *Cow Range and Hunting Trail* where Malcolm Mackay and a friend get stuck in a blizzard and find their way to the only building in sight, a tiny little cabin inhabited by a family of four. It's clear from the time they enter that this family is barely getting by, and the family's initial response to these strangers is one of abject fear. But once they realize that Malcolm and his friend are simply lost travelers, they offer to feed and shelter them for the night. The two men notice that there is only one bed in the tiny cabin, so when it's time to retire, they pack their things and prepare to head for the barn, where they will be less of a nuisance. But the family insists on making a bed for them on the floor. Stories like this abound in memoirs and histories from Montana.

But there was a dark side to the rural communities that we are always hesitant to acknowledge, and I think it can be attributed in part to these early days when the chances of survival were so small. There must have been an incredibly strong feeling that if you didn't make it, you were on your own. There was a spirit of cooperation to a point, but the people who were getting by were just barely getting by, so it wasn't as if they had a lot to give in terms of helping out. One of my relatives told me a story about a neighbor who went through a rough period, and I asked whether people reached out to him. His response was telling. He basically said no without coming right out and saying no, but it was clearly not because of a lack of compassion. The man was self-destructive, drinking too much, and neglecting the basic duties of his profession. And this would have been at a time when there wasn't help available for that kind of affliction. The current pulled him under.

There is a strong sense in Montana that you need to take care of yourself no matter what. If you don't do that, people are likely to let you suffer the consequences. It makes sense to some extent, but until recently, the concept of depression, or mental illness, hasn't even been on the radar as the cause of this kind of behavior. So a lot of people have been abandoned through the decades because they didn't seem to care, and in a place with so few people, being snubbed can bring on an incredible sense of loneliness. It's hard to imagine being more isolated.

So early Montana was a strange combination of *Mayberry R.F.D.* and *Lord of the Flies.*

I was surprised when I studied the statistics for suicide rates around the state. When I first heard that the suicide rate in Montana was one of the highest in the country, I jumped to a conclusion that I imagine a lot of people do. I assumed it could be attributed to the fact that Montana has seven Indian reservations. And the reservations do indeed have a higher suicide rate than the rest of the state. But on the average, the rate is only higher by about 5 percent per capita. The fact is, many of the counties with the highest suicide rates are nowhere near the reservations. And, as it turns out, Beaverhead and Madison are two of them. They consistently fall in the top ten counties with the highest suicide rates in Montana.

Lynn Weltzien is the director of the Campus Counseling Program at the University of Montana Western in Dillon, and she has studied the high rate of suicide in this area extensively. Lynn has determined that much of this trend can be attributed to those early days. A legacy that started back when survival was brutal and unpredictable. Attitudes that contribute to suicide can be prevalent in a community not because they want their residents committing suicide, of course, but because they have a long history of people who live with a feeling of hopelessness and overwhelming fear. The kind that paralyzes you. The economic landscape of this part of the state contributed to that early on, and probably still does. Much of it can also be explained by the isolation. Beaverhead County is the largest county by area in Montana. The average number of people per square mile in Montana is 6.8, compared to 87.4 in the rest of the country. Beaverhead County has 1.4 people per square mile. That's a lot of open space. But more importantly, that's a real lack of available company.

"There is a prevalent and proud 'western' culture and attitude among the Caucasian majority in Montana—'we can take care of ourselves.' This is especially true when it comes to asking for help for depression or anxiety. We see asking for help as a weakness and we are being a burden to our families," Weltzien said.

Oh, and she also mentioned the booze. The story of alcohol runs through our history like a river, just as it did in the best Montana novel ever written, its current providing a soothing and mostly harmless backdrop until it pulls someone under. According to Lynn, "Montana is near the top in the nation in alcohol-related deaths, underage drinking, binge drinking, and consumption per capita."

Other factors are a lack of availability of mental health services, and the availability of guns. Research indicates that a home with a firearm has twenty times the risk of having a suicide.

"Limited access to mental health resources and easy access to guns contribute, but in our opinion these could be overcome if we could let go of the idea that mental illness equates to a burden to our families and should be dealt with in the same way as a lame horse."

AGRICULTURE HAS ALWAYS BEEN a volatile business, and it has become even more so in the modern age. And Beaverhead and Madison are great examples—along with Carbon County (Red Lodge), Flathead County (Kalispell), Granite County (Philipsburg), and Park County (Livingston)—of places that have abandoned the idea that they have to rely on the old ways. Instead, these counties have embraced tourism as a major source of income, some more effectively than others. According to Lynn's husband, Alan Weltzien, a professor of English in Dillon, Beaverhead County still resists promoting itself as a tourist destination, despite the many wonderful resources it offers.

I have known Alan for a few years, and always appreciate his take on Montana because he came here as young man but has made it a point to study Montana closely. I value the opinion of someone who grew up somewhere else but who has come to both appreciate and question his feelings about this place. I met Alan at the new brewery in town, Beaverhead Brewery, where he introduced me to the owner, a young man who came from an old Beaverhead ranch family—someone who has adjusted to the new ways, although he still works on the ranch as well.

Weltzien is tall, slender, with a strong jaw, a radio announcer's voice, and an earnest, intent manner. He grew up in the Pacific Northwest but has lived in Montana for a very long time, and has become the state's expert on one of the more under-appreciated Montana writers, a Beaverhead County resident named Thomas Savage. Savage left Montana as a young man, but it clearly never left him, as most of his novels take place in Montana. And it's easy to see why Weltzien finds his work interesting, not to mention relevant.

In Weltzien's own words, "I like him because he's a strong novelist whose sardonic commentary appeals deeply to me. He is deliberately harsh about any sort of parochial pretensions, in Horse Prairie, Dillon, and elsewhere. Parts of him despised all matters Montanan, yet that's not the whole story at all. Against the hate remained a love, of sorts."

Savage was born in 1915 and later admitted to being gay, so it's easy to imagine how he must have felt growing up in a region where the pressure to hide such tendencies would have been strong. It would have been a matter of survival. So it's not surprising that he spent most of his life on the East Coast, in Maine and Massachusetts. Most of the people in Beaverhead County have never heard of Savage, which is part of what makes living there an interesting challenge for Weltzien. The one writer that captures the area, in his view, isn't even appreciated there. "So I have never really felt like I belong here either," he said. Weltzien himself talks of leaving Montana pretty much every time I talk to him, but you know, there's something about this place.

FOR EVERY PERSON THAT realizes that tourism could make a strong contribution to the economic growth in Montana, there are three who want Montana to remain a well-kept secret. (Just for the record, this data is completely made up.) But despite Alan's contention about Beaverhead County, there does seem to be more of an effort there to promote tourism than there is in some of the counties I visited.

Of course all of these above-mentioned counties, with the exception of Granite, share a common benefit, which is that they serve as gateways to the state's two major national parks, Yellowstone and Glacier. They have been blessed with the luck of the draw in terms of location, location, location. But there are other places that have just as much to offer in terms of pure dramatic scenery and excellent hunting, fishing, and hiking. A lot of these places stubbornly cling to the notion that they are going to get back to what brought them to life in the first place. Dillon's second largest source of income, after government employment, is no longer agriculture. It is now retail/food service. They are blessed with some of the best fishing and hunting in the state, which brings in a significant amount of business.

Madison County, where Virginia City is the county seat, still relies on agriculture for about 10 percent of its economy, but it's clear at a glance that its primary source of income is tourism. Madison County has become a popular destination for retirees as well, as indicated by the fact that it ranks in the top ten of per capita income in the state.

Red Lodge, which once relied almost exclusively on mining, is now near the top of the most popular tourist destinations in the state. Carbon County boasts one of the most incredible stretches of highway in the United States with the Cooke City Highway, also known as the Beartooth Highway, a winding road that hugs the side of the Beartooth Mountains in a way that makes uneasy travelers queasy. But it provides a breathtaking view of the valley where Red Lodge and its fewer than two thousand inhabitants reside. Charles Kuralt, who traveled all over the country with his CBS television show *On the Road*, called this "America's most beautiful drive."

The story of how this stretch of highway came to be is one of the better examples of how the foresight and determination of one man can alter the future of a single town. In his outstanding book of essays, *Stories from Montana's Enduring Frontier: Exploring an Untamed Legacy,* John Clayton recounts the story of Dr. Johann Carl Frederick, the man who came up with the proposal to build the Beartooth Highway. In 1924, long before people were thinking about Montana as a destination for tourists, Frederick met with a group of leaders in the Red Lodge community and presented an idea for saving the economy in Red Lodge.

Frederick's idea may have been laughed out of the room if anyone else had proposed it. But Frederick was highly respected by almost everyone in the community. He was a doctor who often "forgot" to charge for his services. He was known to join every club that was available, a man who loved his community and its people. After living in nearby Bearcreek for many years, Frederick moved to Red Lodge and ran for mayor on the platform that, although prostitution and gambling were illegal, they were vital to the community. He won.

So when Frederick suggested that they carve a road leading nowhere along the edge of the Beartooth Mountains, the other men in the room were willing to listen. Frederick was not the first to suggest this route but he was the first to push it from the idea phase to an actual plan. And when Red Lodge needed an economic boost, he convinced community leaders to seek federal funds to get the road built.

The road eventually provided access to Yellowstone Park, and it has proven to be a consistent draw for tourists ever since. Carbon County also contains Red Lodge Mountain, one of the best ski hills in the state, especially east of the divide. Red Lodge Mountain draws huge crowds every winter, and although it's not considered as challenging as Big Sky, Bridger Bowl, or Big Mountain, it still provides fine skiing, not to mention a spirited night life.

But Carbon County has a very familiar history. First, it was part of an area originally signed over to the Crow Tribe in an 1851 treaty. Rich coal reserves were discovered in 1866, however, soon followed by the discovery of gold in 1870. By 1880 a new treaty had given the region over to settlers. And then, while the county was originally built on the backs of miners, the mines eventually closed. Those early days were wild, with the town growing to as many as five thousand people by the early twentieth century. Saloons, gambling, bordellos, and fighting were rampant in Red Lodge. But the mines suffered during the Depression, and then the worst coal mining disaster in Montana occurred in 1943, with seventy-four men killed when an explosion ripped through the Smith Mine, near the town of Bearcreek. That was pretty much it for the local mining.

ABOUT TWENTY MILES OUTSIDE of Red Lodge, Jael Kampf escorted me into a log cabin so small I had to duck to enter. The cabin looked like every image of a log cabin that a person could conjure from the early twentieth century, with thick log walls, a hardwood floor, and a fireplace with another thick log serving as the hearth. But this one was special. Branded into the hearth were the initials of the most famous artist the West has ever produced, along with his signature steer skull. This tiny building was, in fact, called the Charles Russell Cabin, and it was part of the Lazy EL, Jael's family ranch. According to family lore, the brand in the hearth came about after Russell and Jael's grandfather had a few whiskeys and then started "decorating."

There is an interesting relationship between the West and people with considerable wealth, going way back to the beginning. To many of this class, the West has served as something of a playground, and not always in the most positive sense of the word. A good example of that would be Sir St. George Gore. Between 1854 and 1857, Gore came out West and hired an entourage of more than forty people, including Jim Bridger, for a hunting expedition. By the end of that three-year hunt, Gore had killed an estimated 4,000 buffalo, 1,500 elk, 2,000 deer, 1,500 antelope, 500 bears, and hundreds of other creatures. Most of these animals were left to rot in the prairie. The expedition cost Gore approximately $250,000; it is still considered the most expensive hunting expedition to ever visit the West.

Gore's excessive slaughter of the local wildlife angered both the Native Americans and the settlers, many of whom relied on wild game for food. But he also broke so many of the codes of the local culture by showing such blatant disregard for nature and by wasting so much of what he killed that by the time Gore was ready to leave the area, the locals were anxious to get rid of him. Gore had made arrangements to sell his equipment and supplies to the American Fur Company, which had provided Gore with most of his crew. But Gore was so angry with the offer they made that he went on a drunken rampage during which he ended up burning everything he owned, including all of his journals from the trip, his passport, and all of the official papers he brought with him. And his bank notes. So in a bit of karmic justice, Gore had to spend the next year sleeping on the ground and foraging for food just like everyone else as opposed to luxuriating in his massive private tent with a feather bed and French rugs.

On the other end of the spectrum is a whole different breed of wealthy who discovered the West and considered it to be a place that was worthy of respect and honor. Jael Kampf's great-great-grandfather, Donald Mackay, was one of the founders of the New York Stock Exchange. Donald had a son named Malcolm who was the restless sort. A man who would not have found a life working in offices, bantering about money markets, to be a satisfying one. When Malcolm was introduced to the West at sixteen, he vowed to come back, and he saved up for three years to return in 1901. After acquiring a few cattle with a friend, Charlie Wright, he convinced his father to invest in a cattle ranch in Montana, and his father reluctantly agreed, providing him $10,000 to start the Rosebud Cattle Company. Malcolm's memoirs reveal a man who was completely comfortable with life on the prairie, talking about sleeping on the ground and fighting the elements as if they were part of a great adventure rather than a hardship.

Unfortunately for Malcolm, after he had firmly established the ranch, his father fell ill and died, and Malcolm was persuaded to take over his father's business on the stock exchange. Sadly, Malcolm himself died at a young age, and the ranch was then left to his own son, Bill Mackay.

Bill was in college when his father died, during the Depression, so he was tempted to sell the ranch rather than take it over. But Bill must have had some of his father's devotion to this place because he decided against selling, and he was able to keep the ranch productive enough to support his family, primarily by raising sheep and cattle.

Today, the Lazy EL is much like many family ranches in Montana. There are thirty-three stockholders, and only the person who runs the ranch is able to make a living from its operations. But with that many people involved, there has been much dispute about how to best utilize their resources. Jael ran the ranch for several years and hers is a story that needs to be told, a story that reflects how little some things have changed in the West.

Jael is a tiny woman with a huge presence. She speaks with authority, laughs loud and long, and favors big hats with a flat, wide brim. She was a track and basketball star in high school and still has the figure of an athlete. She lost her father when she was eleven and determined at that young age to never be a burden to her mother. She went on to study Religious Studies at Yale, with an emphasis on the Lakota Sundance, and her interest in that subject led her to spend a great deal of time on the Lakota reservation in South Dakota, where she met and married Gerald Sherman, a Lakota man.

When Jael took over the ranch, her uncle Bill had already started to make the transition from a working ranch to a recreational business. They started by partnering with a neighbor to guide hunting trips and eventually started offering weeklong stays for "city slickers" to come and get a taste of the cowboy life.

Jael's experience of running a ranch as a woman is telling. "For all the years I ran the ranch, other ranchers would stop by and direct their questions to my ranch hands, never to me," she said.

But perhaps the most telling event was one where a local rancher, an older man that Jael had great respect for, stopped by to congratulate her for telling off another local. Jael wasn't sure whether to be pleased or disturbed, mainly because she had no idea what he was talking about. Plus the man he was referring to was another man she considered an ally. What was he talking about? She wondered whether she had inadvertently done something to hurt the man's feelings and realized later that it was the kind of thought process that would probably never even occur to a man. "I think most men would have been pleased to have someone tell them they were proud of them for telling someone off. For a woman, it's a chance of creating a new enemy, someone who might hurt your relationship with others.

"I finally realized he was talking about a discussion we had one day, where I disagreed with this man and told him so. And I couldn't help but laugh, because it wasn't even that big of a deal. But it also made me realize how differently I am viewed in that world. Or maybe it's the same, where I earn respect by acting more like a man."

After many years fighting the battle to be taken seriously in a world that is still very much dominated by men, she became weary of the fight and handed over the position of running the ranch to someone else.

But her passion for this ranch and for this region was still evident and strong. In her words, "Family members love the ranch. It reconnects us with our roots, with open space, with each other. And it is a stunning property. I hate to say it, but it's a legacy ranch, one of the cherished and historic places. Who wouldn't love it?"

Red Lodge also fights its own unique battle for a strong identity, as it has become a popular destination for people who want a taste of the West. So among the events that take place here are the Beartooth Rally and Iron Horse Rodeo (a smaller version of the Sturgis Rally), the Rendezvous at Red Lodge, which is a gathering of people who embrace the old "mountain man" lifestyle, and The Festival of Nations, a tradition since the 1800s featuring music, food, and culture from many different nations. It tells you a little bit about the direction things are trending that this last event has slowly dwindled in attendance while the rally draws bigger crowds each year.

PHILIPSBURG HAS SLOWLY DEVELOPED into a smaller version of Red Lodge, with a main street that features many of the same types of shops with original Montana art as well as the famous Yogo Sapphires. You can even "mine" a sapphire for a small fee. Not that far from Philipsburg was a silver mine that was the largest in the world for a very brief period in the late nineteenth century. Like Carbon County, mining provided most of the jobs and income for this tiny county in its early years. But once the mines closed, the population here began to rely mostly on agriculture.

Granville Stuart and his brother James were early influences on this area, and when the silver mine was opened here in the 1860s, James Stuart decided to open the first substantial lumber mill in Montana. The town was actually named after Philip Diedesheimer, the engineer who designed the mill. It's easy to understand why they chose his first name as opposed to his surname. Diedesheimerburg doesn't have quite the same ring to it. When that mine failed in 1872, James Stuart was forced to close the mill, and he died just a few years later.

Mining was not over with by a long shot, though. A man named Charles McClure became the superintendent of a small silver mine called The Hope Mine in 1877, and McClure proved to be an astute businessman, as well as a man who put much of what he earned back into the area. Within a few years, two of the more successful mines, one of them being McClure's renamed Granite Mine, merged to form the Granite Bi-Metallic Mine, which is the mine that became the world's largest silver mine. For decades, mining was the main source of income for the county, but the last mine in this county closed in 1971, forcing the locals to turn their attention back to agriculture.

But Philipsburg is an example of a phenomenon that I encountered time after time in the smaller counties in Montana. The largest source of jobs in Granite County is the government. Retail services have risen, and construction is providing more jobs than it once did, but the majority of income comes from either state, federal, or county jobs. And yet, like alcoholics who resent the codependent people who support them, the sounds that often accompany the word "government" among people in Montana contain a special brand of bitterness.

I decided early on that I needed to try to understand where this bitterness comes from, and I came up with some interesting conclusions. There's no question that the places I encountered the harshest anti-government sentiment were the towns that were really struggling. But it was clear that many of these people were simply looking for someone to blame. Because Montanans have always had such incredible pride in their work ethic and in their ability to adapt, it's easy to imagine how people could become overwhelmed with confusion when things take a turn for the worse. And it's also natural to look for a scapegoat. And what's easier than a one-word, all-inclusive entity like "government." The fact that statistics simply do not support this opinion is not important. It's inconvenient, but when you live around so many like-minded people, it's easy to ignore the facts.

I'm not saying most of the people of Philipsburg displayed this kind of bitterness. But there was a hint of it here, just as there was in many of the smaller towns I visited.

As I MENTIONED EARLIER, part of the reason Philipsburg has a more positive energy than many of these smaller towns is it has become more and more popular as a tourist destination. That is surely due in part to The Sweet Palace, one of the largest candy stores in the country. The building that houses this amazing shop looks like an old hotel, with a pressed metal ceiling and a balcony that lines the entire upper floor. They make taffy in the front window for anyone who's interested in watching, and they also have someone in the middle of the store making fudge, in case you're not tempted enough by the finished product.

Philipsburg also features a new business that has become common in many small towns—its own brew pub, Philipsburg Brewing Company. This phenomenon started soon after Montana voted to offer brewery licenses, partly as a response to the rising cost of liquor licenses. The brewery license allows brew pubs to serve certain amounts of their beer on premises. Within a few years of its inception, in 1997, the number of breweries, and consequently, brew pubs, skyrocketed. While I was in Philipsburg, the brew pub was packed every night, with crowds spilling out into the street.

But my favorite experience in Philipsburg was my night at the Quigley Cottage, a bed and breakfast run by a retired couple, Dave and Davee Letford. I had the whole place to myself, and I felt like royalty. When she found out I was working on a book, Davee led me to a cozy little reading area with shelves lined with books about the history of Montana and particularly of that area. I spent that evening sitting quietly in this little nook, soaking in the history.

And when I rose the next morning, I stumbled out to the same area, which was just off the dining room, expecting nothing more than your average breakfast. I was in for a surprise.

First Dave led me to the dining room table, where a place was very formally set just for me. He served me excellent coffee and fresh-squeezed orange juice, and brought out a basket with bread he had made that morning. While Davee rattled around the kitchen, Dave soon emerged with what looked like an ice cream sundae, which he set in front of me. It turned out to be steel-cut oatmeal, adorned with pecans, peaches, cinnamon, brown sugar, and a small scoop of vanilla ice cream on top. This alone would be enough for breakfast on a normal day. But Davee was just getting started.

After I finished my oatmeal, she sent Dave out with a plate crammed with food. Bacon, eggs over easy, just as I asked, of course, and fried potatoes with sliced avocado on the side. It's far and away the best breakfast I've ever eaten in my life. And on top of everything else, I had a very pleasant visit with the Letfords. They had been an average working-class couple before deciding to retire and open their bed and breakfast.

They have lived in Philipsburg about forty years. Long enough to be considered locals, they joked. They opened Quigley Cottage in 2002 after Davee retired from a career in respiratory care at the local hospital and a short stint running a Victorian Tea Room in Philipsburg. They were a few years ahead of their time in that endeavor. Dave had been working in the oilfields in Alaska for many years and continued to do so while building the B&B. He retired to work full time at the B&B in 2007. They consider the business a great adventure. "We meet so many interesting and inspiring people," Davee said. "We intend to keep doing this as long as we are able."

That night I watched a fabulous band from Kalispell play samba music out on the street of Philipsburg to celebrate the summer solstice. I knew very little about Philipsburg before coming here, but it turned out to be one of the highlights of my trip.

ANOTHER SURPRISE WAS LEWISTOWN (Fergus), which lies smack dab in the middle of the state. I had never been to Lewistown and had never heard much about it, so I had no idea what to expect. What I found was a town that was much bigger than I anticipated, at almost six thousand people, making it the sixteenth-largest town in the state.

Lewistown is on ground that was part of the Blackfeet Nation until gold was discovered. In 1874 the army built a fort at the site to provide protection for travelers, and it was named Fort Lewis, after Meriwether. But perhaps the most surprising fact about Lewistown is that it was first settled by the Métis, a race of people that descended from Native American women and French fur trappers in Canada in the early nineteenth century. It was not at all unusual in the early days when the West was "settled" for white men to marry Native American women, in part because they were the only women around. But many of these marriages, such as that between Granville Stuart and his wife Awbonnie (which produced eleven children), lasted a long time. Intolerance for interracial marriages became an issue in later years, and in fact marriage between a white and black person was illegal for a time, but marriage between whites and Natives never was. But I came across many stories of people being snubbed because of their choice of spouse.

After the Métis established the town in 1879, gold was discovered in the nearby Judith Mountains, bringing yet another rush of fortune-seekers. But this particular rush was short-lived, leaving a whole host of young men who needed work. So the area developed a strong foundation of businesses. The town was big enough to garner a $10,000 grant to build a Carnegie Library in 1905, but that project turned out to create something of a controversy. Local contractor T. J. Tubb went way over the budget on the construction of the building, to the point where they had to stop and raise enough money to cover the final stages of the project. It took three years, and when they finally opened in 1908, they still didn't have the money for furniture or electricity.

The building is beautiful, though, one of the many examples in Lewistown of a strong history of talented stonemasons. The hills and mountains surrounding Lewistown—and there are five ranges—are rife with sandstone, and several of the most impressive buildings in town are made from that material. I met a man named Ray who was a third-generation stonemason. Ray was in his eighties, and he walked with the posture of a man whose bones have borne many tons of stone. He was long retired, but he named many buildings that were built by him or his father or grandfather, who emigrated to Lewistown from Yugoslavia in 1905. Ray also listed a number of businesses that are gone now—businesses that used to form the foundation of the Lewistown economy.

At one time there were two refineries, a concrete plant, a flour mill, and of course the railroad. All long gone. Ray said the biggest employer in town now outside of the county offices would probably be Albertsons.

The day I pulled into Lewistown just happened to be the beginning of the Montana Cowboy Poetry Gathering, an event that is held every August and attracts hundreds of cowboy poets, many from surprising places. I heard poets from California and New Mexico, and some of the work was hilarious and moving. People in Lewistown are proud to say that this is the second-oldest cowboy poetry gathering in the country, just one year behind the National Cowboy Poetry Gathering in Elko, Nevada.

I heard rumors that there was another event taking place in Lewistown that same weekend, the Christian bikers' convention. I was never able to find out the name of the bikers' club, nor did I see any evidence of it, but I secretly wished for a showdown between the cowboy poets and the Christian bikers.

Bucolic is a fabulous word, and it could easily be overused when describing places in Montana, but it applies to Lewistown. The houses are cozy, the setting gorgeous with the mountains all around. The people are friendly and smile easily, and there's a creek that runs under Main Street. That's right, you can actually ride an inner tube *under* the main street in Lewistown, although I didn't learn this until later so I didn't get a chance to try it.

A barista who moved here from Chicago said she had to sleep with the radio on for the first few weeks she was here because it was too quiet. One lady said that she wished they could fill more of the stores along Main, but her friend asked, "Why? Have you been in the ones that they have now?" And they both laughed.

Lewistown seems to be one of those places that is happy just the way it is. There doesn't seem to be a lot of discontent here, or any desire to become something more than they are now. And of course there's something peaceful about a place like that. It made me want to come back.

IF THERE ARE TWO counties in Montana that attract more immigrants from other states than any other, it would have to be Park (Livingston) and Flathead (Kalispell). In the early days, Park County was yet another to emerge from local mining operations. Fifty miles south of Livingston, and just two miles from Yellowstone Park, the town of Aldridge grew up around a company called the Montana Coal and Coke Company, which provided the ideal blend of coal and coke needed to run the smelter in Anaconda. The town reached a population of eight hundred, but within fifteen years the coal was tapped out, and the town fell into the healthy list of long-forgotten Montana towns.

But it could be that one of the more noteworthy stories from Livingston's early days is that of the Murray Hotel. A woman named Josephine Kline was the brainstorm behind this landmark. Kline decided to combine two buildings—an old hotel called the Elite, and an office building called Livingston Enterprises—to form a larger hotel. She retained the name Elite, and enlisted the family of future US Senator James Murray to help finance the venture. The hotel's early success was due in large part to the introduction of the railroad, and for many years it thrived, making Josephine Kline one of the most successful businesswomen in Montana. Or it might be more accurate to say "legitimate" businesswomen, as there are stories of many madams around the state who were highly regarded and very influential in their communities.

But being a woman in the business world was not easy in those days. Just about every book about the history of Montana mentions very few women. It was a time when a woman had to be exceptional to overcome the resistance—or outright animosity—of the good ol' boy network. In the 1920s

James Murray, who was a rising star in the political world, inherited $10 million from an uncle, and soon after that he and his family foreclosed on Josephine Kline, squeezing her out of the business. The details of how and why this came about have been lost to time, but it's not hard to imagine how it could be another example of a successful businesswoman being labeled as "difficult" after dealing with her male counterparts for decades. Only the participants in that venture know for sure. Josephine Kline fought this move in the courts until 1934 and was unable to retain ownership.

Today the Murray Hotel is a landmark, and Anthony Bourdain, who travels all over the world with his television show "Parts Unknown," recently named it one of his top ten favorite hotels in the country.

LIVINGSTON FLOURISHED FOR A long time on the income generated by the mines and the railroad, but it was one of those places that had an aura about it early on. A place where people went to get a flavor of the West. A ranch called the OTO, which is one of several to claim to be the first dude ranch in Montana, started serving customers in 1912 with the stereotypical amenities we have come to associate with dude ranches. Horseback riding, of course, was the main offering. But Dick and Nora Randall also led their guests on short hikes and fishing and hunting expeditions. They sold the ranch in the 1930s, and it closed in 1939.

But a precedent was established, and several other similar facilities opened up in the county through the years. The proximity to Yellowstone Park, as well as Chico Hot Springs, a resort featuring natural hot springs, made this area especially desirable to world travelers who wanted to get a taste of the West. And if they were ambitious enough to drive a couple hundred miles, they could also take in another of the most popular tourist destinations in Montana, known then as the Custer Battlefield.

John Fryer, who owns one of the oldest establishments in Livingston, Sax & Fryer, said that Livingston "has always been a transient town." Sax & Fryer, which started as a department store but now focuses mostly on books, was started in the 1860s, and John's great-grandfather bought into the business in the 1890s. The family has owned the store ever since. John, who is in his eighties, has lived in Livingston his whole life, except for a ten-year stint in New York, where he suggests he might have spent a little too much time enjoying the nightlife before his father convinced him to come home and help with the business.

John Fryer is stunningly handsome even at his age, with bright blue eyes that have a permanent twinkle. Knowing the reputation Livingston has for attracting celebrity visitors, it's easy to imagine that he has some amazing stories to tell about the nightlife. But it was clear that he had no inclination toward this kind of talk. He was a gentlemen, and answered such questions with nothing more than a wry smile and a nod. "Yes, we had a lot of fun around here," he said.

William Hjortsberg, a novelist and screenwriter who moved to Livingston in the 1970s, had quite the opposite attitude toward talking about the past. Hjortsberg, affectionately known as "Gatz," knew all of the celebrity crowd that made Paradise Valley home in the seventies and eighties. I have been a fan of Hjortsberg's for many years, especially an obscure book of contemporary fairy tales he published in the eighties called *Tales and Fables.* So I was nervous when I met him and his wife Janie (a very talented painter) at Gil's for dinner. But Gatz is one of these people who puts you immediately at ease, with his squinty smile and his loud, warm laughter. He has one of those faces that invites honesty, locking into you with an expression of expectation and anticipation. He's like a big kid, really. I felt as if I could tell him any story that came to my head and he would be delighted by it.

Gatz wrote a massive biography, *Jubilee Hitchhiker: The Life and Times of Richard Brautigan,* about the San Francisco beat writer who bought a cabin in Paradise Valley in the seventies so he could drink and fish all day. Brautigan happens to be the first famous writer I ever met when one of my best friends from high school, Steve Klingman, was hired to work for Brautigan in the summer of 1979. Steve's job was basically to chop wood, make sure the whiskey supply never ran out, and accompany Richard to his daily fishing holes.

Sadly, Mr. Brautigan's drinking got the best of him and he committed suicide in 1984 in California. But he was more than gracious when I met him, even though I was starstruck and too nervous to talk. Steve and I stopped in unannounced one evening, and Brautigan had guests for dinner. I didn't know who any of these people were, but it's entirely possible that Gatz was there, maybe even Tom McGuane. Brautigan suggested that we join them, but of course that would have been too weird. It already felt surreal for two young kids from Podunk, Montana to be standing in the middle of a bunch of famous people, as if a world we had never ever come close to had been dropped into the middle of our humble little state. Livingston still feels that way sometimes, with its cadre of celebrities buying cabins nearby and coming to town for dinner and a few drinks.

Hjortsberg told me an amazing story about his experience writing a screenplay for *A River Runs Through It,* a story that puts a certain famous movie star in a bad light, and I again felt as if I'd stepped into a world that was out of my sphere of experience. Part of me wanted to ask more about the people Gatz has rubbed shoulders with, but it honestly didn't feel right. It didn't feel like Montana. Maybe it's my own humble beginnings, but somehow it felt as if I were eavesdropping on a world where I didn't belong. So as much as I loved talking to Gatz, I couldn't bring myself to press him for the dirt. I preferred to continue thinking of Livingston as a charming little burgh with a few high-priced galleries and an aura.

IN KALISPELL I SPENT several hours in a senior center visiting with a group of women who had just finished their exercise class. I'm not sure I've met a happier group of ladies, and it made me suspicious at first. But the longer I talked to them, the more I realized that these women seemed to be honestly content. Every question I asked them about the area brought a positive response. Kalispell is a wonderful place! Oh no, they've never had any issues with people moving in from out of state! I started to wonder whether the whole group hadn't dipped into a stash of happy pills of some kind. *Stepford Wives* came to mind.

But although most of these women were about twenty years younger than my grandmother would be, they made me think of her and her generation. My grandmother was a ranch wife, a woman who was widowed three times, twice by the time she was thirty-five. When my real grandfather died at the age of thirty-six, dropping dead from a heart attack while loading grain, she was left with four kids under the age of ten.

Thankfully, just a few years later she met the man I would come to know as my grandfather, a rancher from Carter County named Frank Arbuckle. They were married, and Frank took her family into his home as if they were his own.

But as far back as I can remember, my grandmother was a picture of optimism. Even living out in the middle of nowhere, fifteen miles from Alzada (a town of just a few dozen people) and sixty miles from any town of size, she maintained a sense of style and positivity. I did not see my grandmother in slacks until she was in her seventies. And never jeans. I will always think of her in a print dress with an apron, striding out to the chicken house to gather eggs or to chop the head off that night's dinner.

These women in the Kalispell Senior Center reminded me of her with their persistent joy. But it is an image I have come to mistrust over the years. Not the optimism. I admire optimism. But after reading as much as I have about the history of the West, I don't believe this relentless presentation of happiness. I think many women from my grandmother's generation were forced to present this image because the truth would prove to be way too inconvenient in a world where everyone was doing all they could to survive.

My Grandpa Arbuckle was a straightforward, witty man with few of the stereotypical qualities people imagine from a Montana rancher. I never saw him talk down to anyone, including my grandmother, nor did he have any tendency toward macho posturing. He was a wonderful communicator, and I suspect that if he ever had conflict with other men in the area, he handled it through conversation. So he wasn't the type to bully my grandmother into being quiet about whatever fears or insecurities from which she may have suffered.

It was a product of that time that women who complained were a burden. Because everyone was in the same boat. I saw this in the group of women in the Kalispell Senior Center. Each time I asked them a question, they directed me to a particular woman. "She's been here longer than any of us," they kept telling me. "She's the one you should be talking to."

But each time I looked to her for an answer to my question, I saw a look of panic in her eyes, as if the last thing she wanted was to be tagged as the spokesman. There was an Asian woman at the end of the table, and I secretly wished that I could separate her from the rest of them to find out *her* story. I suspected that if anyone could give me a real look at the inner workings of this community, it would be someone who had experienced it as an outsider. She looked to be Japanese, and I was dying to know whether she was a war bride or perhaps someone who spent time in an internment camp.

But because I have so little experience as a journalist (wait, none!) I didn't have the skill to approach her without feeling conspicuous about it.

A HALF HOUR LATER, I WAS in a coffee shop called Norm's News, which my friends at the senior center recommended as another good resource for history about the region. I invited myself to sit at a table of men about the same age as the women I just visited, and the reception couldn't have been more different.

For the first time in my life, the word *writer* brought a chilly response, and I wondered what it was that these men suspected. Although they did welcome me to sit at the table and poured me a cup of coffee, their responses to my questions were also quite the opposite from those of their neighbors at

the senior center. I asked pretty benign questions, about how
they liked the area, and how they ended up here. There was
a clear leader of the group, and it seemed as if the others all
waited for him to take on his role, looking at him each time I
posed a question. And each time they looked to him, he met
me with an odd look, as if he wasn't sure whether to trust me.
I never quite found my footing with these guys, although they
did disclose that they were all in business of some kind. One
was a banker. Most of the others owned various types of businesses. One was an architect.

Their responses were so different from what I'm accustomed
to from Montanans that I puzzled over it for days afterward. It
was hard to understand. Toward the end of the conversation,
the men tossed out a couple of political comments. It doesn't
matter what they said, or whether I agreed with them, but
what made me uncomfortable was the casting of blame. It was
that same familiar tendency of focusing on a singular entity
or person as the cause of their problems that I saw briefly in
Philipsburg.

It's an aspect of Montana culture that baffles me,
especially considering our history. What most people probably
don't realize is that there are few states in the Union that have
benefited more from government assistance. From the time
the US government granted James J. Hill millions of acres to
build the Great Northern Railroad, much of Montana's development has come as the result of government largesse. During
the Depression, many Montana families, especially in Butte
and Anaconda, were able to survive only because of the help
they received from the US government.

In 2000, government subsidies to farmers in Montana exceeded $500 million, which accounted for one-third of the
state's agricultural income.

So this narrative about the government interfering with
Montana's productivity doesn't hold water. Plus it's pretty
hard to sympathize with people in the Flathead Valley, especially rich guys. How much better can it get? They live in
one of the most picturesque places in the country. Flathead

County has one of the highest rates of economic growth over the past twenty years in Montana. Much like Bozeman, they have found ways to compensate for the decline of logging and mining by providing an idyllic setting for companies that can function anywhere.

I came away from Kalispell thinking about my conversations with these two groups of people and wondering how they reflected the gender differences in Montana. When reading about the history of our state, it is hard to overlook the influence of women on Montana's culture, going back to Bannack, where the arrival of more civilized women—women who wanted a comfortable place to raise children—was a huge factor in creating a demand for some kind of action.

There is perhaps no county that is more familiar with how far a town can go awry than Flathead, where the infamous town of McCarthyville saw nearly two hundred deaths as opposed to a single birth in their two-year existence in the early 1890s. It is probably not a phenomenon unique to Montana, but it's clear when you read our history that women played a key role in demanding some kind of order as well as in creating a sense of community. Time and again you find stories of the women organizing theater companies, music groups, women's clubs, schools, and any number of community activities. While the men dealt with the day-to-day struggle of finding a way to keep the family farm or the hardware store viable, it fell on the women to keep up the family spirits.

My grandmother played the piano at community dances for decades, never learning to read music but relying on her innate ability to hear a song and pick out the chords and melody after a few times through. She served as a symbol of this responsibility to keep up the family's spirits, and one could argue that it served her and her family well. When she was in her seventies, my grandparents were driving home late one night when they encountered a rancher who was pulling a stacker behind his pickup, on his way home. The stacker was backward, so the teeth were facing behind, and he had no lights on the rig, so my grandfather, who was an excellent driver, did not see him until they were right on top of the machine. Several of the teeth penetrated the front of their car, and one of them pierced my grandmother's leg, breaking it in several places. Doctors told her she would never walk again, but within a year she was on her feet, cooking and cleaning and back on the dance floor. I was a teenager at the time, and completely incapable of comprehending the enormity of this accident, much less how impressive her recovery was. But this was who she was. And it makes me wonder about the women who didn't have that kind of grit and determination. I think it's safe to say that the pressure they were under to keep the household going, as well as bolster the confidence and optimism of the rest of the family, was more than any one person should have to endure. And for many, it was too much.

NORM'S NEWS TURNED OUT to be one of the few places where I didn't feel welcome during my travels, and it left me with conflicted feelings about Kalispell, a place I've adored since I spent a couple of weeks there visiting my friends, the Wilkersons, when I was sixteen.

I thought a great deal about these men over the course of the next few months, because my first inclination was to be completely offended by their attitudes. To think that they were acting like typical entitled white guys, looking for something to complain about despite the fact that their lives appeared to be going very well. But I realized I better rethink this or I could be in trouble. Because this was one of the first stops on my journey, and I was likely to come across more people who think this way. So I took these men with me, and I vowed to try to understand where this sense of dissatisfaction comes from. Why do we see so much of it in this place that is considered one of the best places in the world? It was a phenomenon I really wanted to understand.

One last thought about Kalispell: I love the fact that one of the most successful show business people to come out of Montana—a list that includes Gary Cooper, Myrna Loy, and David Lynch—is Michelle Williams, who grew up in Kalispell.

I love it because she is incredibly versatile. In one of her early roles, Williams showed a gift for goofy humor as one of two teenagers who inadvertently uncover the Watergate scandal in a movie called *Dick,* named for Richard Nixon. Williams has earned three Oscar nominations, for *Brokeback Mountain, Blue Valentine,* and *My Week with Marilyn.* But Williams seems not to have forgotten her roots, as her role in a gritty pioneer drama called *Meek's Cutoff* indicates. Much like *Brokeback Mountain,* where she plays a harried young mother and wife of Heath Ledger's character, there is nothing glamorous about Williams in *Meeks' Cutoff.* She appears more than comfortable in roles that show her in a less-than-flattering light, a quality I would love to attribute to her upbringing.

ONE TOWN THAT HAS found its own way to survive, and doesn't really fit easily into any category, is Hamilton, in Ravalli County.

The first thing you need to know about Hamilton is that, like Anaconda, it exists because of the ambition of one man, Marcus Daly. When Daly opened his copper smelter in Anaconda, it soon became the biggest in the world, and Daly realized that he was going to need a source of timber to support this venture. He found an ideal spot for this resource just across the mountains, where he started a whole new town. Rumor has it that this move was also fueled by a strong desire to protect his own family. While the workers in Anaconda and farmers in the surrounding areas protested loudly and even filed lawsuits about the effects of the smelter on their air and water, Daly beat them back with his legal clout, while at the same time moving his family to a place where the air and water were pristine.

In 1886 Daly bought one of the largest farmhouses in the area, owned by Anthony Chaffin, and remodeled it to accommodate his large family, as well as his wife's penchant for entertaining. The mansion was remodeled again in 1897, just a few years before Daly's death. And his wife remodeled the home twice more after his death, including the addition of a huge trophy room where Marcus Daly, Jr. could display the trophies from his hunting expeditions. The younger Daly died at the age of forty-eight while duck hunting, although many suspected that the report of a heart attack was a cover-up for suicide.

Although Marcus Daly, Sr. practiced questionable tactics to obtain his wealth, he was also a man of considerable charm and generosity, and the people of Hamilton still celebrate Marcus Daly Day every year. It's difficult to find anyone who will speak badly of the man in this town. But it takes nothing from what he accomplished, or the people he helped, to point out that the way his family flaunted their wealth was obscene and deprived the people who helped him achieve his status of their basic needs. And of course there were also the suspicious deaths of men who had the courage to fight for labor rights. I point this out not to besmirch Mr. Daly's reputation, but because it is a recurring theme in the history of Montana and one that is relevant today.

Like many of the Montana towns that are doing relatively well, Hamilton is a lovely mix of the old and new, with many buildings in the downtown that have been preserved from the early twentieth century, but also an impressive choice of restaurants featuring an international flavor, including a sushi place, a restaurant called Taste of Paris, and a wonderful bistro called Bouilla. Hamilton, like many of the smaller towns in Montana, also has its own brewery now, called Bitter Root Brewing. There is a sad sort of irony to the influx of more international cuisine in Montana considering that when the territory first came into being, there was probably more diversity than there has been since. Between the Chinese railway workers, the buffalo soldiers (former slaves who fought for the Union in the Civil War and ended up in great numbers in the West), and the widely diverse number of immigrants who made their way over from Europe, early Montana was a true melting pot.

IN A CONTEMPORARY COFFEE shop on Hamilton's main street, I met Peter Rosten and Susan Latimer, two terrific examples of modern-day Montanans. Peter and Susan have that easy affection of a couple that was meant to be together. They interrupt each other without any sense of tension or irritation and they share looks that are tender and even pretty adorable. For a couple in their sixties, they still act very much like teenage lovers. Peter is a former Hollywood producer, and he looks it with his hip glasses and his blond hair tied back in a ponytail. Peter moved to Montana not long after the turn of the century to get away from the insanity of Los Angeles and the film industry. He took a job as a ranch hand, and a couple of years later met Susan, a native of Montana who has an interesting past of her own. Susan, also blond, with an endearing gap in her teeth, was raised Mormon, the daughter of a polygamist father whom her mother eventually left. Her great grandparents homesteaded near Fort Benton around 1888 and founded a town called Loma.

Susan's grandmother lived with her family when Susan was a child, and she instilled in Susan a great appreciation for the land and also for how you treat people, "because you never know who you might need to help change your tire in the middle of the night."

"People kept their politics more private then," Susan said. "They were way more concerned with whether you were a good person."

Susan calls herself a conservative but made it clear that her definition of *conservative* is very different from those who have become associated with that word.

"A conservative cares for the land, conserves that which is good. I don't waste water, I don't believe in keeping it from my neighbors," she said. "We were taught things like—my uncle would never trap an unwanted animal anywhere near where his neighbor's dog might go because you would always want to conserve the goodwill among friends and neighbors. We were so proud of the stories of my great-grandfather founding the school in Loma and that even though he mostly paid for it, it was for all the kids. Education was so important. We were told that paying state taxes was a *good* thing because we were investing in colleges for kids in Montana. Paying it forward meant paying for other's future kids also, not with anger but with pride!"

Peter was born in Brooklyn, and his family moved to Los Angeles in 1954, where he spent most of his life. Peter became enamored with the film business, and after spending $1,000 on the film rights to a series of books called "A Pictorial History of Black America" he managed to raise enough money to produce a TV special called *The Greatest Story Never Told.* The show won a local Emmy award, and for the next few decades, Peter made a living producing television and film, peaking with his proudest accomplishment, a movie called *True Believer,* starring James Woods and Robert Downey, Jr. His first trip to Montana was in 1985, and "it left an indelible impression." So Peter bought a home near Hamilton in 1992, and after forty years in the entertainment business, finding himself less and less satisfied with the projects he was hired to do, he decided to move to Montana permanently.

There is an interesting parallel between Peter's story and that of the James Woods character, Eddie Dobbs, in *True Believer.* Woods plays a man who was once an idealistic young lawyer, fighting against the establishment for worthy causes. But when we meet him, he has become embittered, taking cases to defend drug dealers because it's easy money. Downey, Jr. plays a young man who comes to work for Dobbs because of his reputation from the early days, and when he finds him to be a completely different person, his disgust eventually leads him to guilt-trip Dobbs into taking on a case he would normally go nowhere near. Because it's Hollywood, of course, the case turns Dobbs around.

But in Peter's case, Susan seems to have played the Downey role in his own life. While working as a ranch hand, his boss, who was a friend of his, offered him a job managing the ranch, and Peter considered it briefly before realizing that he was getting too old to take on such a physically demanding job. But Susan encouraged him to try to figure out a way to use his training and experience to help people. She told him she thought it would help him feel more at home in Montana as well. What emerged is nothing short of miraculous.

Peter started by approaching the superintendent of schools in Corvallis and offering to teach an after-school class in film production. The superintendent, who later admitted he was nervous about the idea, agreed to allow it, but only if Peter would provide his own equipment. Oh, and teach the class without pay. So Rosten invested $10,000 of his own money, along with an odd collection of used equipment, and started teaching.

Ten years later, this program, which has become known as MAPS, for Media Arts in the Public Schools, has mentored hundreds of students in five different school districts: Corvallis, Hamilton, Stevensville, Darby, and Victor. As of 2015 the number of graduates who were part of the MAPS program was well over one thousand, and only a handful of them had failed to graduate from high school. In addition to being able to boast of reduced dropouts, they have also seen an increase in GPAs, increase in credits attained, and an increase in graduates going on to college. Rosten and his team have managed to form solid partnerships not only with the school systems but with local businesses. The kids don't have to pay to be part of the program, and they are also afforded opportunities to make money doing production projects.

In Rosten's own words: "MAPS Media Institute after-school program is a unique public/private partnership that combines arts education, job training and service learning. Our mission: to inspire, instruct and train our rural, economically disadvantaged and sometimes at-risk students in multiple media arts courses."

The program was named in 2014 as a finalist for an Encore Purpose Prize and was also named one of the top fifty after-school programs by the President's Committee on Arts and Humanities. Rosten was also recently named a member of the Montana Ambassadors. There is one major factor that Rosten considers most important to what they've accomplished: It's the focus on creativity. Rosten's own experience, stumbling into a creative profession when he was struggling to find a purpose for himself, led to a strong belief in developing creative energy, which has proven to be extremely effective. And he has passed this along to his students, many of whom have gone on to devote themselves to their own creative pursuits.

The thing that I find most striking about this venture by Peter and Susan is its contrast to the big mansion just across town. While Marcus Daly and his family used their enormous wealth to indulge themselves, with a few bones thrown to the locals to keep them from squawking, Peter Rosten has turned his modest means into an incredible resource for young people to learn valuable lessons.

HAMILTON IS A TOWN that reflects a strong future. It is home to two microbiological research and production facilities: Rocky Mountain Laboratories and a branch of the Corixa Corporation. Unlike many towns this size in Montana, it has shown an increase in population in the past ten years, and it's not hard to imagine why. Hamilton has obviously found a way to attract businesses, with its picturesque setting and a strong school system. The towns in Montana that seem to be doing the best are the ones that have embraced new possibilities. With tourism becoming the second-highest source of income in the state, there is a growing interest in the area as a place to live, or retire, or start a business. For decades, Montanans resisted that notion, and they often still do. It's not unusual to see a bumper sticker in Montana that says "Montana is Full." But the towns that have embraced people like Peter Rosten seem to be benefiting from their welcoming attitude.

I EXPERIENCED SOME BIG surprises, both good and bad, on my trip around the state. I was especially surprised when I began to research certain aspects of Montana's economy. You tend to draw certain conclusions about what towns and counties are doing well and which are not. So when I came across a chart that measured the highest per capita income among Montana counties and found Columbus (Stillwater) to be number one, I was surprised.

Surely it had to be a mistake. If it wasn't Sidney, or Bozeman, I expected that it would be Billings, or Missoula, maybe even Kalispell with their influx of rich outsiders. But Columbus? I didn't even expect that to be in the top ten. But that was before I knew about the Stillwater Mine.

Okay, the truth is I knew about the mine. But I had no idea about the influence or significance of the mine. The Stillwater Mine employs more than 1,600 people, mining primarily platinum and palladium. Both of these elements are used primarily to convert harmful gasses from engine exhausts into less toxic chemicals in catalytic converters. The Stillwater Mine is among the top four suppliers of these materials in the world, which has made it an extremely valuable resource not just to our state but to the national economy, as well as the environment. It is also our nation's sole provider of these two minerals.

But the main reason I didn't expect Columbus to be among the top economic generators in the state is because it is such an unassuming little town. The main street features the most basic businesses, with nothing flashy or high-end to indicate the presence of big money. There is a CrossFit gym and an Ace Hardware. But much of the lack of bigger businesses has to do with the fact that Billings is just forty-five miles along Highway 94 from here. There's no need for big department stores or specialty shops in Columbus.

Columbus has one interesting distinction, though, and I think it is probably a strong indication of the people that live here. The best funeral I ever attended was in Columbus. My friend Brian died a couple of years ago at the age of forty-two. Brian was a local hero, a kid who excelled at all sports but particularly football, for which he got a scholarship to Arizona State University. But since college, he had battled some demons.

Brian's death was not a pretty one. He drowned in his own vomit while passed out in his recliner, alone in his home. He had lost his job a few months before due to his drinking. His girlfriend was in jail. A few years before that, Brian had managed to put together several years of sobriety, and it was a joy to get to know him during that time. He took care of himself, losing weight and spending quality time with his son. He followed the Red Sox and the Fighting Irish as if his own fate was attached to theirs. He got the opportunity to travel to Boston and watch his favorite team in person. He told horrible jokes and teased everyone in a way that made us laugh at ourselves.

But after falling off the wagon, he had become bloated and morose. When he died, it had been just a few years since he got out of treatment a second time without being able to sustain any consistent sobriety.

But the funeral for Brian was a celebration like few I've ever seen. For one thing, I really appreciated the fact that the family did not dodge the issue of Brian's drinking. Just a few months earlier, I had been to a funeral for another friend of mine who had died due to complications from his drinking, and no one mentioned the subject. The funeral was a classic example of euphoric recall, where everything about him was noble and upright. I knew him well enough to know better, and I kept thinking that it was a shame they couldn't be honest, because his life, and his death, could have served as an example for others who might be following the same path.

That's what Brian's family did at his service, and while the first funeral was dry and sterile, Brian's was a smorgasbord of deep emotions. People told stories about him that were sometimes a little off-color but conveyed the infectious sense of fun that was a huge part of who he was. But they also talked about how he never managed to embrace just how much people loved him, a common trait among alcoholics. He was one of those people who drew people in and kept them close even at his absolute worst.

I left that church hoping that everyone there appreciated what a gift they had just witnessed—and that maybe a few even took his death to heart and considered the possibility that they might need to look at their own drinking. It seemed so much more likely that Brian did not die in vain. Sadly, I did not feel the same way about my other friend.

It also reminds me of one of my favorite jokes, about a guy

who goes to a funeral for a guy he didn't know that well. At the reception, he starts talking to two older gentlemen who were close to the deceased. "Drinking did him in," one of them said.

"Yep, he drank himself to death," the other echoed. "Couldn't break free of its grip right up to the end."

"Well, did anyone ever try to get him some help?" the guest asked.

To which the two men looked up in horror. "Oh no, he wasn't *that* bad."

IT'S NICE TO SEE A town like Columbus do well in a part of the state where there are a lot of towns that are struggling. This town started as a stagecoach stop by the name of Sheep Dip. The name was later changed—for reasons that hardly need to be explained—to Stillwater, but due to confusion with a town in Minnesota with the same name, it was again changed, this time to Columbus.

Before the mine came along, Columbus relied as much as most Eastern Montana towns on ranching, dry land farming, and the railroad. Also, like many counties in Eastern Montana, they experienced some tension between sheep ranchers and cattlemen. This was one of the few towns where the conflict became deadly when a sheepherder named Gottlieb Heide was murdered, back in the homestead days. Although Heide's murder was never solved, it was common knowledge among the locals that cattlemen were responsible. It's the kind of story that runs counter to the setting of this quaint, pretty little town. One can imagine people saying, "We never thought anything like that would happen here." With a quick look around, you can see why.

The Yellowstone River runs nearby, sprouting a lovely column of trees along its banks, and sandstone cliffs linger just in the distance. There is a curve that I always look forward to when I'm driving east toward Billings, where you catch a very quick glimpse of the river from a hill above. There's a bend in the river, going in the opposite direction from where the highway curves, and the cliffs rise up in the distance with a reddish hue that, if you catch it just right, reflect the sunlight, making them look more orange than red. It is one of my favorite views in all of Montana, despite the fact that it lasts just a matter of seconds. And like so many things about our state, this view gives me nourishment. It sinks into my skin like sunshine.

WHEN I PULLED INTO White Sulphur Springs and checked into the Spa Hot Springs Hotel, I was dismayed to see several dozen motorcycles parked in front. Convinced I was in for a long night, I lugged my bag to my room, changed into my swim trunks, and decided to test out the natural hot springs while it was still light out.

It was a warm, cloudless day, and I was able to soak in the pool for an hour or so before dinner. I found a restaurant not far from the hotel and ordered a burger. And while waiting for my food, in came a big group of the bikers I'd seen at the hotel. I watched them closely, thinking that it would be an opportunity to get a good measure of how much mayhem I could expect for the night.

And…they lined up at the counter, and one by one, ordered ice cream cones. Even better, the conversation that followed as they took their seats and started licking away at their respective cones went something like this:

"What did you order?"

"Cotton candy!"

"Isn't that what you ordered in Great Falls, too?"

"Yeah, I love cotton candy ice cream. What about you? What did you order?"

"Coconut…this is really good."

For the next thirty minutes, seven bikers carried on about ice cream and about riding bikes when they were kids. I didn't hear a swear word out of a single one of them, and when they were finished, they all graciously thanked the waiter, a young man who was clearly gay. No slurs, no sneers on their faces. I couldn't stop smiling at how judgmental my thoughts had been leading up to that moment. I wondered whether these were the mythical Christian bikers from Lewistown.

This is not just the beauty of Montana. This is the beauty of America. The unexpected. The surprises.

And I found another marvelous surprise in Meagher County, which at one time was the poorest county in the state. The surprise is that the county's fortunes changed largely due to one person, a woman named Sarah Calhoun. If you haven't heard of Sarah Calhoun, you've probably heard of her company, at least if you live in Montana. Sarah is the founder of a company with the fabulous name of Red Ants Pants. She is also the organizer of the Red Ants Pants Festival, an outdoor music festival that features mostly bluegrass and folk/country musicians like the Nitty Gritty Dirt Band, Merle Haggard, Emmylou Harris (is there a festival she hasn't taken part in?), and Keb Mo. The Red Ants Pants Festival, which takes place just outside of White Sulphur Springs, brings an estimated $3 million to the area in just three days, a staggering amount for any county in Montana, much less one with a population of less than a thousand people.

A few months after my initial visit to White Sulphur Springs, I came back to attend the festival, thanks to a press pass from Sarah. It was my first time to the festival, and knowing that it took place out in a field somewhere, I pictured Woodstock, Montana-style, which wasn't too far from the real deal. Hand-painted signs led us just a few miles outside of White Sulphur Springs to a makeshift parking lot that nearly required a four-wheeler to navigate. The rock pickers from Wheatland County might have come in handy.

The thing I loved most about Red Ants Pants was the atmosphere. It had the Woodstock vibe without the excess or the lack of services. There was a spirit of joy and camaraderie, which of course is not unusual at music festivals. But this one seemed more genuine somehow, with less chemical inducement, if you get my drift. The presence of children was a big part of that. Tattooed fathers held their kids in cowboy hats on their shoulders as they danced to the music of Hank Williams' granddaughter, Holly Williams. The organizers provided seemingly unlimited space for campers to park their RVs or pitch a tent. I did not camp, but those who did told me the crowd was laid-back and friendly. It's the kind of gathering that doesn't inspire the anxiety that can sometimes come from such large groups of people.

And the music was fantastic. Aside from Holly Williams, we heard The Red Mollies, a female trio from New Jersey (!) that plays a mean bluegrass/folk rock combination complete with a Dobro player who, if you closed your eyes, could have been an old cowboy with slicked-back hair and snaps on his shirt. She was good.

But the highlight came when Turnpike Troubadours reached the middle of their raucous hit song "Before the Devil Knows You're Dead" and the skies suddenly opened up, and hard drops of rain pelted us for a grand total of two verses and one chorus. The crowd got just wet enough to realize we were alive, and then the clouds floated away as if they had done their job. And they had. We had been baptized in the name of the Holy Rockabilly Father, and it was one of those moments where everyone looked at each other and smiled. We knew we had experienced something special.

THE BEST BY-PRODUCT OF the festival is the money that goes to the Red Ants Pants Foundation, a non-profit that supports women's leadership, working family farms and ranches, and rural communities. In just a few years, the Red Ants Pants Festival has become a major force not only in Meagher County but in the state. Calhoun was named Entrepreneur of the Year in 2011 by Governor Brian Schweitzer and was invited to take part in a White House forum on jobs and economic development after serving as a US delegate to the Asia Pacific Economic Cooperation Women in Business Summit hosted by Secretary of State Hillary Clinton in San Francisco.

And it all started when Sarah, who was raised on a farm in Connecticut, decided after years of wearing men's jeans that wore out quickly and didn't quite fit right, that she wanted to design work pants for women. Thanks in part to a chance meeting in a coffee shop in Bozeman with Richard Siberell, a designer for Patagonia, she was able to launch her company. And somehow, from the tiny town of White Sulphur Springs, it took off in ways that Sarah never imagined. "In Montana," she has said, "you can still be a pioneer."

The thing I admire most about Sarah is how she went about becoming part of her community in White Sulphur. Sarah knew from growing up in a rural community that if she showed up in this small town with an attitude of helpfulness and cooperation, she would have a much better chance of being accepted. "From the time I moved here, I spent a lot of time at the local bar, which is just a few doors down from my apartment. I offered to lend a hand at brandings, and I just made myself generally helpful."

The results are evident. Although Sarah only employs two full-time and two part-time workers at the shop, they mail their products all over the world. The pants are made in a factory in Seattle, but she has recently started offering aprons made by a woman who lives in White Sulphur Springs.

Of course the odds of a business doing this well from an isolated little burg like White Sulphur Springs are ridiculously low. Not everyone can expect this kind of success. But the thing that is so fitting about her story is that she was inspired by the book *This House of Sky* by Meagher County native Ivan Doig to dream that something like this could happen and that this was the best place to pursue that dream. There are elements of the fairy tale in her story, which has been true of most Montana success stories.

MEAGHER COUNTY IS ALSO home to the Smith River, one of the most treasured secrets in Montana. Because Montana is crisscrossed by so many beautiful rivers—the Yellowstone and the Missouri, the Clark's Fork, Gallatin and Madison, and the Powder (mile wide and an inch deep), Milk, Marias and the Tongue (and what fabulous names too, right?)—it's easy to see why most people have never heard of the Smith. Because those who know it hold it to their chests like four aces. Plus it has that name, as if it is part of the witness protection program.

The river's headwaters are in the Castle Mountains, directly east of White Sulphur, and it runs north into the Missouri, just outside of Great Falls.

Each year, the Smith offers 1,175 float permits, and 2015 they received more than 8,000 applications. The Smith is the only river in the state that has to limit its permits. Without the limit, the river would be thick with boats and rafts all summer long.

But the river has recently been brought out of hiding and into the national news, and it's a familiar story—in this case, one that centers around copper. A Canadian company, Tintina Resources, has announced plans to open a copper mine not far from the Smith River. Their mine would tap into the Johnny Lee Deposit, a rich vein that they estimate to be the source of about $2 billion worth of copper. The company proposes to open the mine in 2020, and they have predicted to bring as many as two hundred jobs to Meagher County, a development that would be a boon for a community that is still struggling to provide jobs, especially for its young people.

This proposal also brings up more of the same old issues. Although Tintina is offering assurances that they intend to do everything they can to prevent any damage to the area, this is a story that Montanans have heard often through the years. The process of copper mining always runs the risk of contaminating the local water source with a nasty chemical that comes when the rock holding the copper is exposed to the air. Tintina has employed geologists from Montana, people who would seem to have a vested interest, and they argue that this company is determined to do things differently. But according to a July 15, 2015 article in the *New York Times,* locals like Joe Sowerby, the owner of Montana Flyfishing Connections, are concerned ("Can Montana's Smith River Survive Local Mine?" *New York Times,* July 15, 2015).

"It's the questions they can't answer that bother me," Sowerby told reporter Christopher Solomon. Solomon went on to write, "What happens if caring locals...get pushed out of the company? (An Australian mining company, Sandfire

Resources, now owns 36 percent of the project.) What if they eventually want to expand the mine further? What if an accident happens? What if they can't control the acid drainage?"

Sowerby, who identified himself as a conservative on most issues, went on to say that he wasn't 100 percent against the mine, he was just 100 percent against degrading the Smith.

So Meagher County, and perhaps Montana in general, will once again be faced with the choice of whether the risk is worth the reward. Or will we have a voice in the matter? That's always the biggest question.

WHEN I WAS CHECKING out of the hotel the next morning, the clerk recommended that I talk to one of the women who was cleaning rooms, a woman whose family had a long history in White Sulphur Springs. I wandered along the row of rooms until I found a maid's cart halfway in and halfway out of one of the rooms. "Hello?" I called out.

"Can I help you?" The maid straightened up from making a bed. Her name was Harriett, and she had lived her entire life in White Sulphur Springs. She had kids who were grown and had moved on to other things, other places. "There used to be three mills here, and since they closed, there aren't any jobs for the young people," she told me. "The graduating class here is about half as big as it was when I was in school." I can't count how many times I heard this same story on my trip.

I told Harriett about my experience with the bikers, and she laughed. "They're always the best customers," she said. "The people driving the nice cars and wearing all the fancy clothes leave their rooms in a complete mess. The bikers are always very polite and clean."

Expect the unexpected.

THERE IS NO BETTER EXAMPLE in Montana of a town whose business community has embraced the diversity of industry than Bozeman. Recent statistics showed Gallatin County as number one in economic growth, even ahead of Richland County, which contains a portion of the Bakken oil field.

Gallatin County has shown a steady growth for years in large part because the community has made a concerted effort to make Bozeman a place that is attractive to progressive businesses. In other words, technology.

The advent of the Internet has been a huge factor in allowing places like Bozeman to attract the kind of business that can be conducted from remote locations. People who have a choice of locating their business anywhere in the United States are inclined to look at many factors, but two of the most pertinent are cost of living and quality of life. And although Bozeman comes in higher than many Montana towns in the former, it is still in Montana, where the cost of living is much lower than in most of the more industrial states.

Companies like Wisetail, which provides training programs for large corporations; Headwaters Economics, an environmental think tank; and RightNow Technologies, a customer service software company that was purchased by Oracle in 2011, have chosen Bozeman as their headquarters. On top of bringing business into the area, these companies also provide better-than-average pay (at least for Montana, which is far below the national average). In 2013 RightNow Technologies was ranked as the largest private employer in Montana, with 550 employees. Thanks in part to the strong engineering program at Montana State University, Bozeman also rates twice the national average per capita in businesses focusing on engineering and computer science. And the university has attracted hundreds of millions of dollars in grant and research money in recent years.

Bozeman also serves as a wonderful breeding ground for more innovative ideas, as evidenced by companies like Sci-Gaia. SciGaia was founded by Gary Gannon, a technology and software developer who moved to Bozeman about six years ago. Gary and his wife, Kelly, live a few miles outside of Bozeman in a small subdivision with an incredible view of the mountains. When Gary becomes interested in something, it consumes him, which explains the small greenhouse (two, actually), in his backyard, featuring an incredible crop of fruits and vegetables. Gary is equally passionate about all things economic, and when he explains them, his eyes become an even brighter blue. He's one of those guys who can make anything sound exciting, even if you don't have a clue what he's talking about.

Gannon was co-founder of UBmatrix, a company that specializes in XBRL-based software and data exchange, and while working to develop that company, he became involved in a consortium of business people who were interested in developing a revolutionary new method of measuring wealth. One of the other people involved in this group was Erik Thomsen, who once worked as an aggregation specialist at the World Bank, where he implemented a variety of socio-environmental-economic models. It was at World Bank that Erik worked with a man named John O'Connor, a pioneer in the field of economic theory.

O'Connor decided that the methods people have been using for centuries to measure the economic potential of a company, or any entity at all, was flawed because they really only took one factor into account—finances. O'Connor believed that a system needed to be developed that would measure other pertinent factors that could have an impact on the viability of any organization that deals with money.

So he developed a formula that considers four major categories and assigns a score for each to compile an overall measure of a company's potential. The first of the four categories is Economy, which includes whatever assets the company starts with, whether it be money, resources, or property. The second is Social, which considers how well the society around this entity is structured: Do they have strong health care, good schools, what is the crime rate, and so forth. The third factor is Natural, which covers the environment. As an example, Gary mentioned bees. He said that one of the things they measure with this method is what services might be provided by nature that don't exist in this area. So for example, if there are no bees, what is it going to cost to make sure that the plants that need to be pollinated get pollinated? And of course there are many

other environmental factors, such as what it's going to cost the
taxpayers to clean up an area that has been poisoned with asbestos for decades, or what it's going to cost to suck the toxins
out of a lake of chemical waste at the bottom of an open pit
mine. Minor details like these would count very much against
some entities, hypothetically, of course. The final category is
Human Resources, in which they measure how many people
in an area or a country or a company are educated, how many
have criminal records, the average ages, and so forth.

O'Connor's basic idea has been adopted by the World Bank,
as well as most major countries in the world. But Gannon and
Thomsen decided that the process could be taken one step further. In the World Bank model, right now there is simply a
spreadsheet, compiled by hours of laborious data gathering. It
also lacks a basic ingredient that Gannon considers the most
crucial one of the whole process, which he calls the *stock and
flow.*

Basically, stock and flow determines how these four entities
play off of each other. So, for example, if a state starts drilling
oil, this will affect each of the four categories, depending on
how the taxpayers, and the owners of the companies that do
the drilling, convert this resource. There will be money coming into the state, resulting in immediate economic growth.
The way that money is allocated is going to affect the other
three categories, whether it is used to build hospitals (social),
or schools (human resources), or whether a county decides to
simply put the money aside to raise more money, which builds
up the economic leg of the chair but will eventually have a negative impact on the other three. The other obvious by-product
of drilling is environmental, which would be determined by
how much of this money the company or the county or the
state decides to use for cleanup and restoration.

The World Bank first adopted a form of O'Connor's theory
in 1995, as part of its efforts to include environmental impact
on economic growth. By 2006, the World Bank had published
a report called "Where Is the Wealth of Nations," which described its revolutionary approach of measuring wealth by

breaking a country's assets into three categories—natural, produced, and intangible. The model has been adopted by several international organizations, including the UN-sponsored Millennium Ecosystem Assessment, the United Nations Environment Programme, and the United Nations Educational, Scientific and Cultural Organization (UNESCO).

Gannon is convinced that this revolutionary method of measuring wealth is much more applicable to the real world. Countries like Sweden, which gets the highest ratings on the World Bank model, have found a way to devote the right balance of their economic surplus to the resources that will give them long-term sustainability rather than simply focusing on building their wealth exponentially without regard for the health of their people or the land.

Gannon and his team at SciGaia are currently gathering the data for counties all over Montana to develop the first-of-its-kind software program designed specifically for a state. The project, Wealth of Montana, should be in place within the next couple of years, and Gannon is hopeful that once people understand the value of this approach, it will spread to other states and corporations. He has already met with representatives from Idaho to discuss implementation of the program there. It's hard to imagine a better place to develop this project than Bozeman, where quality of life doesn't have to be explained to anyone.

PERHAPS THE MOST INNOVATIVE and invigorating company that has taken root in Bozeman is Wisetail Learning Management Systems (LMS), founded by Missoula native Justin Bigart. Bigart is one of the most impressive people I met on my trip. He is built like a bike racer, and he looks at you with the expression of a man who is fit and serene, one of those disgusting fellows who does more than just talk about living a healthy life. He wears one of those fashionable mountain man beards, only it actually looks good on him. He's in his early thirties, but he could easily be mistaken for twenty-two.

When Bigart graduated from college in Missoula, he left

Montana with the expectation and hope that he would never live here again. He got a good job in an Internet startup in San Jose and settled into the lifestyle of the Bay Area. But it didn't take long for Justin to realize that he wasn't going to be happy in California. As someone who loves the outdoors, he missed Montana more than he expected. Plus he found himself increasingly disillusioned with a world where so much of the power lay in the hands of investment bankers. He saw too many companies that were beholden to those who provided the money to finance their ideas.

So Justin quite accidentally came up with a plan to start a company that combined the best of what Silicon Valley had to offer with the best of what Montana had to offer. It started when he and his wife moved back to Bozeman, and she started a yoga center and spa called Sage Spa Living. Justin created some software to help train her employees. This went so well that someone actually hired him to do the same thing, and before he knew it, he was in business.

The result was Wisetail, a company that creates individually designed training programs for companies that are interested in providing a positive and productive work environment for their employees. I found that the Wisetail offices very much reflected this combination of the two worlds. The office space itself was open, with a few dogs roaming around and many bikes parked out front. Conference rooms were all enclosed in glass so there was no place to isolate yourself from the rest of the company. It reminded me very much of the advertising agency I worked at in San Francisco in the 1990s, where we did ads for such brands as Levi's and AT&T. The whole vibe is one of casual confidence, a place where people know they are good at what they do but that they also love it.

Bigart employs twenty people, and he described his management style as "carrots versus sticks." In other words, incentives rather than punishment. There is no time clock, so people are expected to work their hours at their own pace and in the time that works best for them. He has not had to work hard to recruit people for the company. This philosophy also comes into play in the designs of their programs for the companies that hire them, most of which are hospitality-oriented, like restaurants and hotels.

After just six years, Wisetail's LMS is in use by about 100 companies, accounting for roughly 1 million people. Bigart said that being in Bozeman is the biggest advantage they have over their competitors, something that he didn't expect. In fact, for the first few years they were in business, they maintained a Palo Alto mailing address to indicate that they were a California company. But it soon became clear that, when companies found out Wisetail was actually in Montana, they found it to be a huge selling point.

It has also been a big advantage that Bigart started this company with no venture capital money. Bigart can no longer imagine starting his business the traditional way, any more than he can imagine doing business anywhere else.

BOZEMAN TRULY IS ONE of my favorite towns, and it has nothing to do with the fact that I was born there. Bozeman is one of those places that draws you in. Its proximity to the Bridger Mountains is perfect for people whose main attraction to Montana is the outdoors. For years, Bridger Bowl was the premier ski hill in the area until Chet Huntley, a Montana native and the co-anchor of the *Huntley-Brinkley Report,* opened Big Sky Resort in 1973.

And then there's the fishing. Just thirty miles northwest of Bozeman, the Madison, the Gallatin, and the Jefferson Rivers all converge near the aptly named town of Three Forks. These three rivers provide some of the best fishing in Montana, a secret that is no longer well-kept. People come from all over the world to cast their lines for rainbow, brown trout, and mountain whitefish, among others. The Gallatin is also known for some of the best whitewater rafting in the state, including a challenging section known as the "Mad Mile."

Okay, so that's the travel brochure version of Gallatin County. But what's it really like?

A friend of mine once told me it's like living in a J. Crew catalogue. Another friend told me that when she moved to

Bozeman, she quickly learned *not* to say that she was from New York but that she was from "a small farming town in upstate New York." I struck up a conversation with a young man in a coffee shop in Bozeman, and it turned out he was an aspiring writer. I told him I was also a writer, and that I was doing a reading at The Country Bookshelf, the local bookstore. I asked him for his last name so I could send him a friend request on Facebook. "Why?" he answered with the most smug expression.

So yeah, Bozeman can be pretty goddamn snooty; in fact, in Bozeman the only thing worse than being from California or New York might be telling them you're from anywhere else in Montana. On the one hand, I kind of admire them for it. They know it's one of the best places in the country and, for many of them, there's no reason to pretend otherwise. There's also no reason to provide a welcoming atmosphere when people are already dying to move there. The housing market in Bozeman is impossible. Prices are out of most peoples' range. So the friendly atmosphere you find in most Montana towns is a little chillier here. But it's still there. I've lived in cities, so I know real snobbery. Bozeman's snobbery is Montana-style snobbery. They can't really get mean about it because they are still Montanans at heart.

So if you're fortunate enough to find yourself in the midst of a bunch of people from Bozeman, you'll find the reception much less chilly. There's a scene from a Woody Allen movie, maybe *Hannah and Her Sisters,* where Woody's character is on the subway and the train he's on is a typical New York subway car, with graffiti and miserable people surrounding him, while the car that's going in the other direction hosts a lavish party, with chandeliers and people sipping champagne. That's a little bit of what it's like to be walking the streets of Bozeman by yourself, when you feel like you're on the typical subway car or attending a party of friends on the other. When you're in, it's fabulous. There are people here who have lived fascinating lives and are interested in all manner of the arts and literature. Bozeman is a desirable place to live for good reason. Just ask them.

So what is it about Bozeman? And it's not just me; I've heard this from people all over the state.

Well, I can only speak from my own experience; I'm not too proud to admit that most of it is flat-out jealousy. I actually had the good fortune of living in some of the most interesting cities in America, spending two years in Boston, thirteen years in San Francisco, four years in the Seattle/Tacoma area, and even a few months in Savannah, Georgia, which turned out to be one of my favorites. But all of these places, for their incredible cultural offerings and fine cuisine, were too big for a kid from Montana. Bozeman is like the Goldilocks town of America. It's just right. In every way. So there's that.

I think what makes their attitude annoying to me is that it goes against the unspoken code of Montana. My mom grew up on a ranch in the far southeast corner of the state, and my dad was from a dirt-poor working-class family in Casper, Wyoming. So I had it pounded into me from an early age that you do not put yourself above other people. We do not like big shots in Montana. I'm not saying this is right. It's just a fact—especially in the smaller towns in Montana—that if you put on airs, whether you're successful or not, you will not be popular with the locals.

I don't think there's any question that this attitude grew out of those early years, when almost everyone was in the same boat, just fighting like hell to get by. The odd dynamic that grew out of that period had two sides to it. First, there was the strong sense of community, the attitude that if a neighbor is going through a difficult time, everyone rallies. It's the attitude that recently blossomed in Jordan (Garfield County) when a young rancher, a father of seven girls, was killed unloading a piece of equipment. Friends of the family set up an online fundraiser and raised more than $130,000 to help his wife and family.

But there is also the dark side. There's the herd mentality that you feel when you walk into a café in any small town in Montana. It's the feeling that if they don't like you, they'd just as soon not have you around. And if you move here, you damn well better figure out the rules and stick to them, or you'll find yourself spending a whole lot of lonely nights.

As lofty as it can be, Bozeman doesn't project that sense of myopic xenophobia, and I admire them for it. Because I think that attitude has damaged a lot of people. Living in the middle of nowhere is hard enough without having neighbors who don't accept you. I think Bozeman has a pretty healthy image of itself, and why not? Better yet, why not admit it? It seems to be working for them. So the truth is, as much as I hate the snooty aspect of Bozeman, I would still choose it as one of my top five places to move. And not just in Montana. In the world.

CHAPTER THREE
Cowboys and Indians

*"Until the lion learns to write, every
story will glorify the hunter."*
—African proverb

This chapter originally began with a long explanation of how we have mistreated our Native American brothers and sisters. And then I realized (with a nudge from my editor), that I was either preaching to the choir or that I was preaching to people who really don't like this choir's music. Either way, I was preaching, and the last thing we need is one more white guy "telling it like it is" about Native Americans. Because of course I don't have a clue what it's like. Even after reading many books on the subject, and talking to many Native American friends, I can never really know what it's like to be Native American.

A NATIVE AMERICAN FRIEND of mine, Crystal Rondeaux-Hickman, recently went to one of the local drugstores with her daughter, who is about ten.

"There were two cashiers within view when we walked in, and they both ignored us, and then proceeded to position themselves so that whichever aisle we were in, they could watch us. One or the other was in sight the whole time we were in there. Neither of them ever greeted us, and neither of them asked if we needed any help."

Meanwhile, Crystal's husband David, who is white, entered the store about five minutes later, after he parked the car. David has long bushy hair, a full beard, and by his own admission, "I looked like I'd been out scrounging in the dumpsters that day. I think I even had food on my shirt."

One of the clerks cheerfully greeted him as soon as he entered, asked what he was looking for, and rather than simply tell him where to find it, took him directly to the item.

This story reminds me a little of a *Saturday Night Live* sketch in which Eddie Murphy made himself up as a white guy and experienced the world from that perspective for a day. Of course that sketch exaggerated the particulars, with one example being a banker pushing a pile of money across the desk and laughing as he told "white" Eddie he didn't have to worry about filling out any paperwork or paying the money back. Okay, that's extreme. But you get the idea.

Crystal's take on her pharmacy experience is sad and so very telling. "I thought about it later, because you know, things like this happen all the time. It wasn't anything new. But I thought about how often I have to make this choice of whether to say something, or whether to simply overlook their rudeness and act pleasant and gracious. It's not really even that much of a choice, but to have to think about it almost every day can get really old. And exhausting. And it's not something I experienced growing up, because we moved around to a lot of different countries when I was a kid because my dad was military. And in those places, being Native was celebrated!"

Her story made me ponder my own day-to-day experience, especially the fact that I never have to worry about this stuff. For the past fifty-eight years, I have gotten up every morning, and there has never been a single moment where I had to consider the possibility that I would have to go out into the world and deal with someone treating me badly just because of the way I look. I have rarely even found myself in a position of choosing whether to confront someone about being rude to me for no reason. And of course, I have never had to think about the fact that if I make a scene, there's a very good chance someone will call the cops. I'm an entitled white guy. Throwing a fit is part of how we get things done. Crystal doesn't have that same luxury. If she were to make a big deal out of the way they treated her, there's no guarantee she wouldn't find herself in handcuffs.

I also thought about Crystal's daughter, who is a smart, perceptive little girl, and how Native American kids learn at a very young age that they are not the same in this place. And to me, that is one of the saddest parts of the whole story. Because what has she ever done?

I'm reminded of a recent talk I watched online by Dr. Joy DeGruy, author of *Post Traumatic Slave Syndrome,* talking to a group of police officers about racism, and the second question she asked, after first asking whether they think there are white and black racists out there (yes, everyone agreed), was "What are some of the ways that white racism adversely affects the lives of black people?" and the answers came one after another. Next, she asked the same question: "What are some of the ways that black racism adversely affects the lives of white people?" and after a long silence, there was only one answer. "Fear."

The answer lies in the power. We white folks have a lot more influence, therefore more ways of affecting the lives of minorities with our racist attitudes. Those who don't have that kind of power can really only do one thing to adversely affect our lives. Get mad. And some people don't like that very much.

WHEN I WAS A SOPHOMORE in high school, I had an excellent English teacher named June Conaway, also known as Junie Moon. Junie Moon was a tiny woman, with a serious smoker's hack and a towering presence in the classroom. She once threw an eraser across the room and hit my sister smack in the head because my sister wouldn't stop talking. Junie Moon had that same passion for making damn sure we learned.

June gave us an assignment to read *Bury My Heart at Wounded Knee,* Dee Brown's excellent book about the history of Native Americans in the West. We were then supposed to form groups of three or four and give a presentation on the book. I was an A student in high school, but for some reason, I didn't get around to reading this book in time for the presentation. But just a few years before, my father had spent two years teaching school at St. Labre Indian School, on the Northern Cheyenne Reservation. My father told us a lot of stories about his experiences there, about how much he loved the people, but also how sad the conditions were on the reservation. So I figured I could improvise enough to fake my way through this presentation. Tell a few stories, voice a few opinions.

It did not go well.

June was very displeased with me and told me so privately but in no uncertain terms. And I had the feeling, even in my self-centered teenage mind, that I had missed more than an assignment. I had missed something important.

Understanding how this history has affected these people, and how it still affects them today, is a task that one chapter in one book will never come close to accomplishing. The more I learn, the more I don't know, and the more obvious it becomes that this situation has become incredibly complicated, tangled up in bureaucracy, mismanagement, political infighting (both between the tribes and the government, and within the tribes) and outright greed, among both Natives and non-Natives. I think it is way more important that we listen to what they have to say. But if there's one thing that did become clear during my travels, it is that this situation still affects everyone in Montana, whether they realize it, or want to believe it or not.

To break it down to its most basic elements, the narrative about Native American history started out with a story that was built on lies. And one of the biggest myths that came out of those lies was that the Indian Wars had anything to do with cowboys. For one thing, there was hardly a cow to be seen in this part of the West during the time of the Indian Wars. But more importantly, the people who were waging this war were not a bunch of cattlemen who banded together John Wayne–style and decided to defend their land. The movies have perpetuated this myth for so many decades that people still believe it, though, especially everywhere *but* the West.

What the Indian Wars were really about is the same thing almost every war in history has been about, which was land and money. Once the West was "discovered" and it became clear that there were untold resources here, the determination by the power elite, mostly back East, to take over this land grew in increments that quickly escalated. And each time a new resource was discovered, the presence of the Native American tribes quietly trying to earn a living on buffalo became more and more inconvenient.

The most egregious example of this dynamic was incited by the discovery of gold in the Black Hills in 1868, just a few months after the Lakota had signed a treaty with the US government concerning the Black Hills, which comprise a good portion of what is now South Dakota. According to Patricia Limerick, in her book *The Legacy of Conquest,* the hills were to be "set apart for the absolute and undisturbed use and occupation of the Indians." In this case, the Lakota tribe. One of the men who benefited most from that particular discovery was a colonel in the US Cavalry named George Armstrong Custer. Custer was charged with exploring rumors of rich sources of gold in the region, and when some of his men indeed discovered gold, his reputation as a rising star became just a little bit brighter. When word got back to the powers-that-be back East, they came up with a strategy to convince the Lakota to accept an alternative agreement.

So the government bullied the Lakota leaders into renouncing the land, and the treaty was abrogated in 1877. Limerick points out that one court later said, "A more ripe and rank case of dishonorable dealings will never, in all probability, be found in our history."

The Supreme Court agreed with that assessment, and in 1980, based on a land valuation of $17.5 million in 1877, awarded the Lakota tribe a $122.5 million settlement. The interesting part of that settlement is that the Lakota, who were only interested in getting their land back, have refused to collect this money. For one thing, the complications of who that money would go to, and how that would be determined, is considered a bureaucratic nightmare. So this money still stands in escrow, gathering interest.

We all know how the government manipulated the facts to justify breaking treaties and then eventually slaughtering thousands of Native Americans in order to get what it wanted. Eventually, the narrative shifted. But, as often happens, it was an overcorrection, so that for a time, all Native Americans were viewed as noble, spiritual people who value the land, while all whites got lumped into the category of the heartless bastards who stole it. Of course there is just enough truth to both of these narratives to keep people stuck in these perceptions. But the real truth of the matter is much more complicated. As my grandfather used to say, "Saints and sons-a-bitches come in all shapes and colors."

Demonizing everyone on either side does nothing to solve the problems that exist today, and although there are Native Americans who don't trust any white people, and vice versa, there is a growing desire on both sides to put the past in its proper perspective and find a way to coexist without the past determining how we treat each other.

What matters now is that the aftershock of these events, which after all only happened a few generations ago, are still deeply felt throughout the Native American community. The trauma that they suffered reverberates through each generation that follows, each time they are treated differently. And anyone who thinks they are not treated differently is ignoring the reality of the situation.

One of the most striking aspects of this whole series of events, at least to me, is how the Native American population in the West (actually, in all of America) had to completely change their approach to living in a society—and do it over the course of just a generation or two. When the whites arrived, the Native American population had been living in a world where the laws were not written down, where the land belonged to no one, where people roamed around or stayed put, based on traditions and instinct and spiritual inspiration. The Plains tribes had little notion of property lines or even permanent residencies. They roamed around freely when the need arose.

When the American government started to present them with options that were completely foreign to them, options like signing a piece of paper that surrendered whole swaths of land for the promise of food and supplies, they must have found it very confusing. Probably even amusing. One can almost imagine them sitting around the fire at night, discussing the fact that these people had just informed them that they wouldn't be able to go to certain areas. "How will they stop us, kill us all?" And laughter all around.

There are few written accounts from the perspective of the Native Americans who lived through this time, stories like *Black Elk Speaks* and *Plenty Coups: Chief of the Crows,* but all of them indicate this initial confusion about what was happening. Because they had no concept of owning land or of owning livestock, the whole foundation of this process made no sense. It wasn't because they were primitive, or stupid, as many people assumed then and still assume now; it was because their whole sense of a society was simply different.

The violent reaction that these people had when they finally realized what was really happening was completely human. Their livelihood was threatened, and eventually worse than that—it was taken away. They were pissed. Any of us would be pissed. But as with almost every war, the people they were pissed at were nowhere to be found. So it was the young families that came out here to try to earn a living, or the young soldiers who got sent here to defend some place they had no emotional investment in, who suffered the most. The damage to both sides of this conflict was immense, and it has never been adequately addressed for either side. The ancestors of the victims of this war have had that bitterness and anger passed down through the generations, and the effects are impossible to measure.

BECAUSE I FOCUSED ON the county seats on my journey around Montana, I didn't spend much time on the reservations during this trip. Only two county seats—Wolf Point and Polson—are on any of the seven reservations. However, I have spent time in many of these towns before and since. If you know anything about the history of this state, the Native American presence follows you everywhere, whether you're driving through the nondescript yellow hills of the Little Big Horn, the beautiful stretch along the Yellowstone that sheltered the original Crow Agency, or paying attention to the many names that carry the echoes of our history. There are a few amazing Indian names— Lame Deer, Heart Butte, Lodge Grass. But there are in fact many more places named after the men who carried out the worst atrocities ever on American soil. Custer, of course, Forsythe, Miles City, and Sheridan. It's akin to traveling through Germany and staying at the Himmler Hotel in the town of Goebbels.

ONE OF MY FIRST STOPS on my journey was Polson (Lake County), where I got the perspective of a non-Native who has lived on the reservation his whole life. Gil Mangels belongs to one of the early white farm families on the Flathead Indian Reservation, and although Gil says he and his family have always gotten along well with the Native Americans in the county, there is also a certain faction that does not want him and his family there. I discovered Gil inside a place called the Miracle of America Museum. His name tag identified him as "FOUNDER," and one look around indicated that this was a one-man operation.

Gil had hands as big as a soccer goalie's gloves, and he wore worn Wranglers with a threadbare flannel shirt. He looked to be in his late seventies or early eighties. Outside the Miracle of America Museum were several whimsical metal sculptures—a brightly painted pig, an absurdly long blue fish, and a hubcap-faced man with curly metal hair. I asked Gil whether he'd made these, and he nodded. My heart swelled a bit, because my father, who had died just a year before, had also been a metal sculptor, one who had made whimsical figures much like these. And this just happened to be Father's Day. I felt as if I had discovered Gil for a reason. A soulmate of sorts.

But these sculptures were just one small part of the Miracle of America Museum. Inside was a wonderland, full of thousands of items that my father would have loved.

Gil is a third-generation Montanan. His grandparents came to the Polson area straight from Germany and started farming, raising mostly potatoes or, as Gil said, "certified seed potatoes." I asked him what made their potatoes better than others, and he explained that, unlike many of their neighbors, he and his family got out there every day and pulled everything that wasn't a potato plant out of the ground. "I learned my work ethic from working on the farm," he said, and as is so often the case with people who really know the work ethic, there wasn't a trace of resentment or bitterness in his voice. I've always been suspicious of anyone who talks about how hard they worked with a sense of anger. I tend to believe they're either exaggerating or that they don't understand the value of work.

Gil's family's farm had mostly been sold off and, like much of this little valley, turned over to developers. "Polson is trying to be a tourist town," Gil said. "And they're starting to figure out that there are more things to bring people out here than just the lake and Glacier Park."

The museum, as well as the farm, are on the Flathead Reservation, and he reiterated the fact that his family had always worked hard to maintain a good relationship with the Native Americans. From his telling, most of the dealings he'd had with the tribe had been positive, but apparently there was a small contingency that was determined to get all whites off the reservation, including Gil. The confusing thing, according to Gil, was that so many Indians had intermarried that he didn't understand how they expected to determine who was white and who was Native.

After we visited for a while, I entered the museum, and I quickly realized that what I'd really entered was Gil Mangels' mind—his idea of what America is all about. And that idea obviously involved a certain ethic. This museum was a testament to men and women who labor for a living.

The outside portion of Miracle of America Museum resembled a small town that had survived a natural disaster. The grounds included a barbershop, a saddlery, a dentist's office, and a general store, all populated by mannequins in various states of disrepair, some missing hands or arms. Every single room in every single building was crammed with so much stuff that it would have been impossible to take it all in, even spending a week there. There was all manner of tools and machines for farming and ranching. Gil seemed to have a particular affinity for tractors. There must have been more than a hundred tractors spread throughout the grounds. Wagons. Sleighs. Mowers. Stackers.

One huge building was completely filled with old snow cats and snowmobiles, but it also included a random, lone piano in the corner. Another building housed old combines and a full-sized thresher. A soda fountain counter, complete with a mannequin soda jerk, filled one corner of the main building.

Although there seemed to be some slight sense of order to the layout, I suspected it would require considerable explanation from Gil to understand what it was. Gil had mentioned his late wife several times, and it was easy to imagine that the upkeep of the museum had become an overwhelming chore now that he was alone; there didn't appear to be anyone else who worked there. Another building contained a huge display of old cars from every era, all of which sported a thick coat of dust. Like so many of the people I talked to in Montana, Gil exuded a sense of hope that his luck was just about to turn, but there was little evidence to support this attitude. He personified the "always next year" mentality that carried many Montanans through the crippling depression that lasted ten years longer here than it did in most of America. Spending time around people like Gil Mangels, I wanted so badly for it to be true. He reminded me so much of my dad, who fought a brutal and losing battle with depression in his final years but continued right up to the end to *try* to appear optimistic.

When I drove away from this place, I thought back to two Christmases before, when my father first found out he had mesothelioma, or asbestos-related lung cancer. He declared to the family that his goal was to dance with my mom at her class reunion that summer. He posed wearing boxing gloves, with a goofy tough face that we had seen many times through the years. Three months later, he was gone. And now, a year later, I pulled over to the side of the road and cried, wishing I could tell my dad about this place. It was a place he would have loved.

It was several months later before I would start to piece together the Native American perspective about what's happening on the reservations around Montana. And I started with an old friend. Mandy Smoker Broaddus is the director of Indian Education for the State of Montana, a position she has held for ten years. I have known Mandy for several years through various writing projects, and I have tremendous respect for what she does in her job, as well as her talent as a poet. I was able to meet with her in Billings, where she was in town for a job-related conference. Mandy's job consists of two major elements. The first is the implementation of Indian Education for All. The most recent Montana constitution, adopted in 1972, states: "The State recognizes the distinct and unique cultural heritage of the American Indians and is committed in their educational goals to the preservation of their cultural integrity." We are the only state in America that has this provision in our constitution.

In 1999, the legislature transformed this promise into a law with passage of the Indian Education for All Act, which states that "(a) every Montanan, whether Indian or non-Indian, be encouraged to learn about the distinct and unique heritage of American Indians in a culturally responsive manner; and (b) every educational agency and all educational personnel will work cooperatively with Montana tribes or those tribes that are in close proximity, when providing instruction or when implementing an educational goal or adopting a rule related to the education of each Montana citizen, to include information specific to the cultural heritage and contemporary contributions of American Indians, with particular emphasis on Montana Indian tribal groups and governments." June Conaway would approve.

Every county in the state gets money as an incentive to make sure these topics are addressed, and it is Mandy's job to provide the materials for the schools and to monitor their progress. But she faces an interesting obstacle in that there is no accountability. There's no way of measuring or determining how well, or even whether, they are implementing the materials they've been provided. It is essentially an honor system, and although Mandy's office has several hundred pieces of curriculum available to those who want them, there are several counties that have made no effort to use these resources. And there's nothing her staff can do about it except call every once in a while to remind the school administrators that they've been provided funding for this purpose. There is no punishment if they don't.

The second part of Mandy's job is to make sure the Indian schools themselves are meeting the same standards of education as other schools.

"I am on the road a lot, and with a young son, I don't have a lot of energy even when I am home. So it can wear on you," she said. You would never know this from Mandy's appearance or demeanor, though, which may be one reason why she has been so successful at her job. In fact, just a few months after I met with her, Mandy was named 2015 Educator of the Year by the *National* Indian Education Association. She laughs easily, has a dazzling smile, and has a warmth that I can easily imagine is appealing to young people.

I asked whether enforcing the policies is a matter of being underfunded. "No, it's not the money as much as it is the attitudes and overall mood on the reservations that is so hard to overcome or change," she said. "Besides substance abuse, which is always a problem, there is a general hopelessness on the reservations that it's a constant struggle just to get the kids to believe there's any purpose to their lives." This naturally presents a huge challenge to teachers.

Mandy was born in Wolf Point (Roosevelt), on the Fort Peck Reservation, but soon after that, her family moved to Frazer, where she lived for the first eight years of her life. When she was eight, she went to live with her grandmother near Fresno, California, where her father grew up, and she spent the next ten years there. Mandy's dad is white, although from her appearance you would never guess she has any white blood in her at all. She is striking, with all the classic features of an Indian woman, including the high cheekbones and sleek black hair, which she has the habit of twirling into a tight little twist.

She went to college at Pepperdine, where she studied English and Education, getting her master's in the latter. But she said she always knew she was going to move back to Montana. Her family came back to Montana every summer, and she felt a strong connection to this state from the beginning. Her mother had eight siblings so she had a huge number of relatives on the Fort Peck Indian Reservation. "All but one of my mother's siblings are now dead, and so are half of my cousins…I used to have about forty cousins." This is the state of the Fort Peck Reservation today. Substance abuse, particularly meth, continues to undermine the Indian culture. And Mandy says that the Cobell settlement from a few years ago—in which Elouise Cobell, along with several other plaintiffs, filed suit on behalf of the Assiniboine tribe—has only perpetuated the problem.

Elouise Cobell was the treasurer for the Blackfeet Nation, and she founded the Blackfeet National Bank, the first national bank located on a reservation and owned by a tribe. Elouise won a MacArthur genius award for her work at the bank, which operated so efficiently that twenty other tribes joined and eventually formed the Native American Bank.

But it was while she was working as the treasurer for the Blackfeet Nation that Elouise began to notice discrepancies with the money that had been set aside in a trust for the tribe as well as for individual Native Americans. The government was supposed to be paying royalties on these funds, and they had failed to do so for a long time. Elouise tried for years to point these discrepancies out to someone, including the Bureau of Indian Affairs (which is notoriously bad about following up on such charges), but her efforts led nowhere. She finally filed a class action suit (Cobell vs. Salazar) in 1996. The suit demanded reforms in the accounting system, and after an extensive and thorough investigation, the government settled for a total of $3.4 billion. Elouise Cobell died in 2011, but needless to say, she left an imprint on Roosevelt County.

What's interesting about this suit is that it took someone who was successful in their field to get this accomplished. In other words, quite the opposite of a Native American trying to milk the system but, rather, someone who was fighting to enforce a policy that was implemented by the government. This is a common story among the tribes. In many cases, it is not their nature to look for free handouts so much as some form of justice for promises made in the past. But because of the unemployment and drug problems on the reservations, this kind of fast money can often provide more problems than solutions.

"It would have been really nice if they had put more of that money into improving the infrastructure on the reservation, but I understand why they didn't," Mandy said. "There were just too many people who insisted on their share. They were desperate. But it has just made the presence of drugs that much worse."

It's so bad, in fact, that gangs from California and other states have become a major presence on the Fort Peck Reservation, expanding their drug business because of the easy money. She is hopeful that once the money from this settlement dries up, people will be motivated to find a way to improve their lives again.

But in the meantime, Mandy is hard at work trying to improve the state of education all over Montana. And from all accounts she's doing an incredible job. Montana is the only state that has such an extensive Indian Education program, and with her staff of eight people she is able to accomplish a great deal. Of course, they are constantly busy and, as with any program of this ambitious nature, she could always use more staff.

I asked Mandy whether she ever runs into the problem of having people not take her seriously. She quickly nodded. "You get that look, you know, where it's clear that people have a preconceived notion of what you're going to be like, or what they're dealing with, and you just have to be prepared for it and make the effort to prove them wrong."

I told her that sucks, and she laughed.

"Yes, it's a burden," she said. "But it's the way it is. My dad always told me that you can't let those people get to you. You just have to show who you are, and of course it's twice as hard for me as it would be for other people, being both a Native and a woman, but that's just the way it is."

Mandy is an incredible poet, although with her job and a three-year-old son she has very little time for writing these days. But she writes as eloquently about this aspect of life on the reservation as any of her contemporaries. An example, from "The Necessary Bullet," from her collection *Another Attempt at Rescue:*

> can you hear the sound of old women clacking
> their old tongues to the roofs
> of their mouths in the dust?
> this is a prophesy so never
> ask the Indian whether she'd take
> the million dollars or the match.
> gasoline is on the shelves in all our houses.

Like so many Montanans, Mandy Smoker Broaddus finds a way to cling to some sense of hope that things will get better. Although her job brings her in contact with some of the most discouraging stories imaginable, and she gets overwhelmed with how much needs to be done, she has inherited the typical Montana attitude, where we see a bank of dark clouds as the promise of moisture.

Just this past year, the Wolf Point School District won a very important lawsuit involving the voting districts for the Wolf Point school board. For years, the districts had been organized so that there was a clear advantage to white candidates. People had been complaining about it for a long time, but as Mandy said, it was just one more thing that they felt like they had no control over and no way of addressing. But Scott Crichton at the ACLU became aware of the situation, filed a lawsuit, and won. Over the course of the next two years, the voting districts will be reconfigured to make sure that the board is adequately represented by Native members. It may seem like a small victory, but for Native Americans in Montana, every little step is an indication that they are still visible and alive in the conscience of Montana. It's an important element of restoring their sense of hope for a future where their children have a reason to put the effort into improving their lives.

MANDY SMOKER BROADDUS and Elouise Cobell certainly aren't the only women from Roosevelt County who have had an impact on Montana or on the Native American community.

In the early twentieth century, a young woman named Dolly Smith Cusker used to attend the Fort Peck tribal executive council meetings because her husband George was too drunk to go. Dolly quickly made an impression as someone who wasn't afraid to speak her mind. She became the first woman appointed to that board, where she was a strong advocate for finding solutions to the economic issues on the reservation. In 1932, she ran for the state legislature and got almost 100 percent of the votes in Roosevelt County, which had a 10-1 ratio of whites to Native Americans. She was twenty-three years old at the time.

A couple of years later, Governor Frank Cooney appointed Dolly as Montana's first coordinator for Indian welfare, and as part of that job she traveled to Washington, where she was instrumental in convincing Congress that Native Americans should receive equal treatment in regard to government relief during the Depression. At that time, they did not receive the same benefits as non-Natives. Dolly Smith Cusker, who later married a rancher named John Akers, remained active in politics throughout her life, accomplishing much while also making plenty of enemies on the way because of her forceful personality. She serves as a great example of a woman who probably got punished for acting too much like a man in a time and place where this kind of behavior was unacceptable. Perhaps the most telling fact about her is that Dolly was not an advocate for women's liberation because she felt it was too limiting.

ANOTHER STRONG FEMALE ROLE model among the Native American population is Janine Pease, who lives on the Crow Indian Reservation in Crow Agency. At first glance, Crow Agency is not a town that inspires thoughts of progress, but I found it difficult to talk to Janine without her optimism rubbing off. Although I interviewed her on the phone, I had met Janine several times at various events, and she is a tall, striking, confident woman of about sixty who has been a strong presence in the field of education.

The main thing she wanted people to know about what's going on with the Native community is that, since 1978, there have been seven reservation colleges created in the state of Montana, including Little Big Horn College, where she served as founding president. She estimated that there are about five thousand students in these seven colleges, which are accredited institutions that function independently of the state university system. The community college on the Flathead Reservation, Salish Kootenai College, alone boasts about a thousand students.

"This has been a well-kept secret, and it shouldn't be," Janine said. "Montana has the best Indian college system in the country and hardly anybody knows about it."

Janine believes education is a key to improving reservation economies, which she fully acknowledged are in need of help. She is also very encouraged by a recent piece of legislation that requires financial institutions to give Native American LLC businesses the same consideration for loans as other business propositions. For decades, it has been difficult for Native American businesses to get funding, and the effects have been evident on the reservations. But Janine is hopeful that this is going to change, given the training that many of the young people are getting from the new college system.

She is also optimistic about the growing Indian population in the counties where reservations exist. For many years, even the counties containing reservations had a majority of white residents. But in at least three of those counties—Big Horn, Roosevelt, and Glacier—the population is now over 50 percent Native American, and Janine thinks this is a good thing.

I asked whether the political representation among these counties reflected their populations, and she said, "No, not yet. But another well-kept secret in Montana is a longtime effort to challenge the voting districts in these counties so that they do not favor white candidates. The ACLU has been filing lawsuit after lawsuit since the 1980s to make sure the voting districts reflect a fair balance, and they've won in several counties, including Rosebud and Big Horn, where the county commissions now feature a fair balance of Indian members."

Although both of Janine's parents are native Montanans, Janine grew up in Washington State, where her parents were teachers. Her father was from Lodge Grass, and her mother is a Butte native, but they met at Linfield College in Oregon, where both of them studied education. Janine did not move to Montana until she was in her twenties, and I asked whether she thinks that growing up out of state, off the reservation, helped her to avoid the kind of scrutiny and criticism that many Native Americans talk about.

"I don't think so," she said, which surprised me until she explained why. "The thing is, growing up Indian is hard no matter where you are in America. Whether it's the reservation or some urban community, there are obstacles that most people don't have to think about."

RHONDA WHITEMAN WOULD MOST definitely support that opinion. Rhonda's parents grew up on the Crow Reservation, her father in Pryor and her mother in Lodge Grass. After the Whitemans got married, Rhonda's father started to get caught up in the drinking culture on the reservation. There were also other issues from both sides of the family, many related to alcohol. So the Whitemans decided that they needed a fresh start, and they moved to Billings, which is in fact only thirty miles from Pryor.

But it might as well have been a continent away. Mr. Whiteman soon found how strong the prejudice was when he tried to find a job in Billings. Although this was the 1970s, almost a century after the Indian wars, the doors were still closed to Native Americans, although of course nobody ever came right out and said so. But he was persistent, and a hard worker, and, most importantly, a reliable employee, and after years of taking whatever day labor he could get, he was able to land a full-time job at one of the refineries in Billings, a job he held until he retired.

The Whitemans built a nice life for themselves, and they maintained relationships with their relatives on the reservation, but not without a cost. Rhonda told me that because they had built this stable life for themselves, the suggestion that they should help out their relatives was strong. She remembers her own grandmother calling the family "apples," the popular derogatory term on the reservation referring to Natives who are red on the outside but white on the inside.

"That really hurt my parents because they were barely getting by, with three little kids. Just because they left the rez didn't mean they were making it rich."

She also said it was amazing to her how much different her life was from her cousins' on the reservation. She remembered attending a hearing for a relative one day with her sister. Sitting in the courtroom, they listened in on the conversations among their cousins, who sat behind them, sharing stories about the times they'd been in the same jail. Rhonda was grateful that her parents left the reservation, but through her relatives, she still experiences the pain of what is happening there.

"The hardest part is watching how everyone tears everyone down instead of building them up," she said. "Nobody encourages anyone. They cut each other down with humor, so it comes across as a joke, but you can tell they mean it, too." It brought to mind an analogy that you hear often among Natives—where you have a bucket of crabs, and when one crab tries to crawl out of the bucket, the others drag it back in.

It is this lack of hope that seems to be the hardest thing to overcome for the Natives I have met. The fight to be taken seriously in a world where that is never automatic is compounded by the fact that those in the world you left behind chastise you for trying to make a better life. Natives often find themselves feeling left out no matter where they go. Even those with the most positive attitudes, work ethic, and determination possible are fighting a battle most of us can't imagine.

The best story Rhonda told, though, was at least one small indication that when people stick up for themselves, good things can happen. Her mother owned some property out on the reservation, and for a few years she leased the land to a local farmer, who raised wheat. But the man who leased this land had gotten used to paying a lower rate than the market demanded, and when Rhonda's mother finally told him she was going to raise the price, he refused to pay it. So she told him he could no longer farm the land.

About two years later, the Whitemans, who lived quite a distance from the land, found out from a friend that the farmer was still raising wheat on their land. Rhonda's mother contacted the Bureau of Indian Affairs (BIA), but after waiting for months for them to do something, she decided to contact a lawyer. The lawyer told Rhonda's mother that they had a strong case, and that if she was willing to file a suit against both the BIA and the farmer, he estimated a settlement of around $500,000.

"My mom didn't want to ruin anybody's life, so she wasn't interested in doing that. Instead, she just contacted the farmer and told him that if he would turn the harvesting of the wheat over to her, she would not file suit. Of course he agreed."

Rhonda's favorite part of the story is when they went up to harvest the wheat, and her mother was driving their truck along the perimeter of the fields, watching the process. The farmer, who also showed up to oversee the process, yelled out to her, "You shouldn't be driving so close to the wheat…you might spark a fire or something."

"She just looked at him and yelled out, 'I'll go anywhere I like! It's my land! If it burns, it burns!'"

To MANY PEOPLE—and this isn't just true in Montana—Native Americans get lumped into a single category. Even people who realize there are many tribes don't always know that there are conflicts between the tribes, or even conflicts *within* certain tribes, so that the dynamics on a particular reservation can be complicated by events that are decades old. For example, many Crow warriors served as guides during the Indian Wars, and there are those among the other tribes that have never forgiven them for this.

And when the government doled out the land for the reservations, it was probably no accident that they located the Northern Cheyenne Reservation just east of the Crow Reservation, knowing that these two tribes had a long history of animosity. They did the same thing on the Flathead Reservation, throwing the Pend d'Oreilles and Salish tribes onto the same land knowing they were life-long enemies. But there are factions even within tribes, such as those within the Northern Cheyenne. Many of the ancestors of those who live there surrendered to the military during the Indian Wars, a fact that others still don't forgive. The attitudes among these people are often long held and deeply etched, so that grudges are passed from one generation to the next.

JOHN ROBINSON WAS elected as tribal chairman for the Northern Cheyenne tribe after serving as a tribal judge for many years, and he talks frankly about the difficulty of getting things done in the face of these long-standing conflicts.

I met John for lunch in downtown Billings after getting to know him a few months earlier. John is a dapper fellow, with slicked-back gray hair and a matching goatee. His blue

eyes indicate some white blood in his ancestry, and he tells
an amazing story of being kicked out of the Indian section
of a movie theater as a boy because they didn't believe he was
Indian, an incident that contributed to a long-standing sense
of confusion about where he fit in. But while John might have
taken advantage of his appearance to pass as white, instead
he always had a strong devotion to his heritage, a dedication
that led him to play a role in the occupation of Alcatraz in the
1970s.

"People think it was AIM [the American Indian Move-
ment] that organized that whole thing, but it wasn't," John
said. "There was a group of people from many different tribes,
and we called ourselves the Indians of All Tribes (IOAT). And
we worked very well together. It was a pretty amazing experience."

I myself was still a teenager during this occupation, which
started just before Thanksgiving of 1969, so I didn't remember that it lasted for more than a year and a half, and it ended
up being a very significant event in the growing awareness of
issues involving Native Americans and reservations over the
next several decades. John said he was also part of a small
group that went to Wounded Knee when things started to heat
up there in 1973. "It was pretty clear from the time we got there
that we were in over our heads," he said. "I was uncomfortable
right away. It just felt like we were pushing things too far." So
they left before the worst of that tragedy played out. But John's
activism has had a great impact on how he carried out his job
as judge and chairman.

"When I took over as tribal chairman, I wanted to create
more transparency," he said. "So I proposed that we set up a—"
John struggled with the modern terminology for a second,
smiling. "What's that thing called, where they have a camera
and people can watch..."

"Live streaming?"

He pointed at me. "Yes! So we set that up, and a lot of the
people on the council were very unhappy about that. I made
some enemies right off the bat. People also knew there were a

lot of political appointed department heads and key employees who had just been taking up space for years...they didn't really contribute in any meaningful way, so we managed to get rid of a lot of those people, which made me even more unpopular."

John felt good about the changes and optimistic that they would be able to make some progress with tribal politics. But his actions had created too much animosity, and a small group of opposition eventually voted him out of office over an incident where John fired the head of a center for abused and neglected children. John filed a report of child abuse, and he said it was investigated and confirmed. But the BIA claimed to have no record of it, which led John's detractors to call for a vote to oust him as tribal president less than a year after he took the job. When a hearing was held to discuss the incident, John offered to present the written evidence, but the council refused to hear it and called for an executive session. John was in the hospital undergoing an emergency appendectomy when the vote was held, and his request that they delay the hearing until he could be there to defend himself was ignored. After he was ousted, the director was given her job back, but she was fired ten days later, confirming what many suspected, that her case was used as nothing more than political leverage.

"Is this a common example of how things happen in tribal politics?" I asked John.

He quickly nodded, and the lack of hesitation told me a great deal. John speaks of these incidents with a surprising lack of bitterness just a couple of years later. But it's easy to imagine how frustrating it must be to believe he had good ideas to help the people in his community, only to be denied the opportunity before he even started to wear in his office chair.

A FEW MONTHS BEFORE I met John Robinson, I met a cousin of his when I was the commencement speaker at Miles Community College. One of the members of the Montana Board of Regents was a man with the fabulous name of Major Robinson. After visiting briefly with Major at the graduation reception, I interviewed him by phone a few weeks later. Major, who is named after his grandfather, spent the first fourteen years of his life in Lame Deer, which is also on the Northern Cheyenne Reservation, just twenty miles along Highway 212 from Ashland, where Major now owns his original family home.

Major was one of nine children, and his father always wanted his own ranch. When Major was a boy, his father bought some land near Ashland and started building a house. In the meantime, the Robinsons lived in a house in Lame Deer provided by the BIA, where his mother worked. The house had only three bedrooms, which made it awfully crowded for a family of eleven. So when his father finally (sort of) completed the house, when Major was fourteen, he said they couldn't have been more excited. "We thought it was a mansion," he said. "And the basement wasn't even finished. We had rooms downstairs that were only half done, but we couldn't have been happier."

Major and his siblings went to St. Labre Indian School in Ashland, so when they lived in Lame Deer, they spent the week in the dorms. The bus would take them to Ashland Monday morning and then they'd return to Lame Deer on Friday. So when they moved to the new house, they were thrilled to be able to be home all week.

Major left the reservation when he graduated, going first to Bozeman where he was accepted into the architecture program. But after a couple of years there, he had the opportunity to take a trip to New Mexico, and he fell in love with the area. He found out that the University of New Mexico in Albuquerque had a good architecture program, so he transferred there to finish his degree.

Major's life took an interesting turn when, after a couple of years working in Albuquerque, he moved to Los Angeles. It was there that his training led to some work in set design for a few movies and television shows and, eventually, for amusement parks. For ten years, Major worked at set design in Los Angeles, working for Disney as well as Universal Pictures, where he met his wife, who was in the same business. They were just friends at first, but after they worked together on a theme park called "Islands of Adventure," they realized there was more to their relationship and they got married.

Major moved back to the reservation in 1999 and established his own business, doing architectural work all over the state, as well as outside Montana. I asked whether he encountered much of the well-documented animosity from reservation members who resented his success, and he answered without hesitation that he had. But Major has a unique attitude and personality.

"I decided to deal with the people who expressed this animosity, which was often very nasty, by recognizing that most of them were probably hurting somehow," Major said. "I decided to show them through my actions that I was there for the long haul. That I wanted to become an integral part of the community, and that I wanted to do what I could to improve life for our people."

So he set out to do that, and he said that most of the people eventually came around, although of course there are always exceptions. But after spending time with Major, it's not hard to understand how he won people over. One quality that he shares with Mandy—and it's evident right away—is his dedication to his culture, his authentic interest in the welfare of the Indian people. It's more than just wearing your hair in a ponytail, which Major also does. It is more about action, and Major has proven without question that he is devoted to improving life for the people on the reservation.

Major started a group in Ashland for people with addiction problems, and he said it was heartening, after a slow start, to see people find some hope in the possibility of other choices. He was especially pleased to see how the younger people responded to this notion of different choices. But like Mandy Smoker Broaddus, he said the addiction problems are huge on the Northern Cheyenne Reservation. He reiterated that, at this point, drugs are way more of an issue than alcohol.

But in Major's view, the biggest problem facing the reservation now—and I heard this from others—is the lack of strong, consistent leadership. Major tells a story of getting involved with a project in Busby, which is about forty miles from Ashland, also on the Northern Cheyenne Reservation. They planned to build an alternative school and detention center in Busby, and Major was hired to design the building.

"People started telling me right from the beginning—this isn't going to happen," he said. "They told me it would never get off the ground, so there was no point in getting involved. I asked them why, and they said, 'That's just the way things are around here.'"

But Major wasn't willing to accept this, and he went to work, not just designing the building but promoting the need for it. "I wasn't happy about the detention center part of it," he said. "But people convinced me there was a need for housing for kids who were in troubled situations, so I bought into it over time. It took longer than I thought it would, but we got it done."

It's clear from Major's track record that overcoming the odds is one of the keys to his success. Major applied for a job working for the government as the Director of the Office of Indian Affairs. He didn't get that job on the first try, although he would be hired for that same position later, but the interview did lead to a job helping with business planning for tribes all over Montana. One of the things that makes Major so likeable is that he talks about his accomplishments with such a strong sense of humility. Like so many of the people who have had the most dramatic effect on Montana's history, Major's purpose shows through in everything he says, and it's way more focused on how he contributes to society than in what he has gotten out of it. Major has served on the Board of Regents for the Montana University system for the past five years, and he talks about running into some unpleasant resistance, both when he worked for the governor's office and when he first became a member of the board.

"They sort of presented me as a token 'successful Indian,' and that gets interesting reactions from some people," he said.

But again, Major worked to win them over by proving that he was in it for the right reasons and that he was willing to do the work.

Major is concerned about the reservation "because there is not nearly as much of a sense of community there. People used to get together whenever someone had a big job to do and help out. And now everyone is kind of left to themselves."

But he also thinks that if you put the effort into it, you can find the people who are dedicated to making things better. And he says that the Indian culture is still very much alive, although he worries that the younger generation has lost interest in keeping it going. "It's more about hip hop these days for the young kids," he said.

Major's story is interesting because he is such a dramatic exception to the rule of people who grow up on the reservation. And although his success can certainly be attributed to his hard work, there is also a degree of luck involved, in that he chose a profession that can be carried out anywhere, so that he was able to work both on and off the reservation. It also needs to be mentioned that, aside from his ponytail, Major doesn't immediately strike you as a Native American. He is lighter skinned, with less dramatic features than many Natives. He makes no effort to hide his heritage, but the point is that he would probably encounter less blatant, immediate racist reactions from people.

In an interesting update to Major's story, a few months after I interviewed him, he was offered a job in Orlando, Florida, where he has since moved with his family. So we have one more example of someone who brought his success story back to the reservation but couldn't resist the opportunity for better things.

Because for every Major Robinson, there are thousands of Elvis Old Bulls.

ELVIS OLD BULL BECAME a Montana legend after leading the Lodge Grass Indians basketball team to three straight state Class B titles from 1988 to 1990, earning the MVP award all three years. At the time, the population of Lodge Grass was a little over four hundred people, and the school boasted about a hundred kids, and yet they produced a basketball team that

averaged a phenomenal 95.5 points per game, playing what
has become known as "rez ball," a fast-paced, full-court press–
dominated style that simply wears opponents down. Sadly,
there is no footage of Old Bull's exploits, but those who saw
him play talk about the fact that he was never the fastest, nor
the best shooter, nor was he all that tall. He simply had a head
for the game, establishing state records (for all classes, not
just Class B) in free throw attempts (329) and eighth all-time
in assists, with 484, including a state-record 22 in one game.
Perhaps the best story about Old Bull involved a game against
Hardin, a much larger Class A school. The Indians were down
10 with 57 seconds left, and many Lodge Grass fans left the
building, only to find out the next day that Lodge Grass had
won the game, with Old Bull scoring 12 points while Hardin
scored 2 of their own to send the game into overtime.

I recently attended a tournament in my home town called
the All-American Indian Shootout, an event organized to feature some of the best reservation teams in the state. I'm sure
one reason the tournament was organized was to get away
from many of the well-known issues that happen with reservation teams, where the referees heavily favor white teams, or
the reservation teams are pitted against each other in the early
rounds of state tournaments so they cancel each other out. The
stories have been around for decades. So this tournament features only Indian teams, with only Indian refs. The best game
was between Old Bull's old school, Lodge Grass, and the team
from Pryor, the Plenty Coups Warriors.

The final score was 93-84. I checked the scores the next
day for the other high school games in the state, and most of
them showed scores in the fifties, with a few in the sixties. And
what amazed me most about this game was how incredibly
team-oriented these kids were. After hearing for years about
the "controlled chaos" of rez ball, I expected a freewheeling,
shooting-from-all-over-the-court style of play. But these kids
had clearly been very well coached. The passing, the spacing
on the floor, the set plays they ran time after time had me completely engrossed. They were amazing "team" basketball players.

Old Bull's story from there is a sad but common one. He never finished high school, and although several colleges showed interest, they didn't seriously pursue him because they so rarely do. Despite many players for reservation teams who had similar careers as Old Bull, only one really went on to make a name for himself at the college level. Jonathan Takes Enemy played for Rocky Mountain College in the early 1980s.

Shann Ferch, who writes fabulous books under the name of Shann Ray (his first novel, *American Copper,* is a must read, covering many of the most important contemporary issues in Montana), was a star basketball player in his own right. Shann's father coached at Busby, on the Northern Cheyenne Reservation, before he got a job coaching in Livingston, where he led that team to two state titles with Shann and his brother Kral among his star players. So Shann played with many of the Native American legends of the game, including Jonathan Takes Enemy, who was a year older.

Jonathan told Shann years later that the only way he could stay sober enough to play for Rocky was to leave the reservation, a sad commentary on the pressure among Native Americans. He now lives in Washington State, where he has a good job and a family.

Elvis Old Bull died in a car accident when he was forty-two, still living on the reservation.

IN THE SUMMER OF 2015 I organized a symposium in Billings with my friend Adrian Jawort, a Northern Cheyenne writer. Adrian was born and raised in Billings to a Polish father and a Northern Cheyenne mother, and although he never finished high school, he is one of the most knowledgeable people on Native American history I've ever met. Adrian has published two powerful anthologies of writing by indigenous people, called *Off the Path I* and *Off the Path II.* The first consists only of writers from Montana, but he got more ambitious with the second collection, inviting indigenous writers from New Zealand, Australia, and Hawaii.

The symposium Adrian and I organized lasted six hours,

with three panels: one focusing on the history, one on issues facing Native Americans now, and one focusing on solutions for the future. For a whole day, the attendees, which numbered over a hundred people, got to hear stories about what's happening today in Montana and what we might be able to do about it.

I came away from this event with several revelations, mostly concerning some misconceptions that I had and that I think a lot of people have. The first is that most Native Americans are still looking for some kind of free ride because of the fact that we wiped out most of their people and took away their land. One could argue that they would be totally justified in wanting this. But the simple fact is that many Native Americans have come to accept the reality of the situation. Returning the land would be the most just way of resolving what is an atrocious chapter in our history, but the chances of this ever happening are pretty much nil.

Another misconception is that reservation land belongs to the tribes, so that they have control over how it's used and what they do with it. This hasn't been true for a very long time, mostly due to a piece of legislation called the Dawes Act, passed in 1886.

The Dawes Act was one of those ideas that appeared to be well-meaning but was actually one more intentional effort to take more land from the Native American population. The idea was to parcel out the land on the reservations to individual Native Americans so that they would have an opportunity to control their own economic future. But the underhanded aspect of this seemingly generous offer was that by the time they assigned these small sections (most of them were between 40 and 160 acres) to the Natives, they offered up the rest of the reservation land to the highest bidder. Non-natives jumped all over this opportunity, and they also took advantage of the fact that the Native American culture gives little credence to owning land. So they offered to buy their small parcels, and many Native Americans sold without hesitation, thinking only of their immediate future.

Before the government put a stop to it—it only took them about fifty years—millions of acres of land that had been designated as reservation land was sold to either white landowners or to the government. From 1887 to 1934, land owned by Indians decreased from 138 million acres to 48 million acres.

Teddy Roosevelt is considered one of our greatest presidents, but for all his strengths, he was not a friend of the Indians, as his take on the Dawes Act shows. During his first inaugural address, Roosevelt stated his view that the Allotment Act was "a mighty pulverizing machine intended to break up the tribal mass."

CONTRARY TO POPULAR BELIEF, few Native Americans are calling for the return of this land. They recognize that their ancestors made these choices freely, however duped they may have been.

What they do want is way more practical—and pretty goddamn reasonable.

First, they want to be heard.

Second, they want a chance to be productive members of society.

And third, they want an apology.

STERLING HOLYWHITEMOUNTAIN IS a writer from the Blackfeet Reservation. He lives in East Glacier, where he teaches English and writing after completing a degree at the Iowa Writers Workshop, one of the top-rated graduate programs in writing nationwide. As is the case on most Montana reservations, the unemployment rate on the Blackfeet Indian Reservation is very high (it is almost 10 percent on the Northern Cheyenne Reservation and nearly as high on the others).

I met Sterling through Adrian Jawort when we all took part in a panel at the Montana Festival of the Book in Missoula, and he made an immediate impression with his confident, honest perceptions about what's happening on the reservation as well as in the rest of America in terms of Native Americans.

In an email interview, I asked Sterling what can be done

to improve conditions on the reservation, and his answer was lengthy but logical. "It's clear to me that it's very difficult for any human to feel good about him or herself when it's not possible to work for a living, when your only way to live is to be dependent on someone else for some kind of welfare. Humans need to work. It feels good to work and know that the work you've done is the means to your survival or your family's survival."

Sterling goes on to explain, "We're predisposed to feel good about hard work whose reward is material comfort—and I'm talking about material comfort in the most basic sense, in terms of food, shelter, and clothing. When we can't do that for ourselves, it does something to our psyches and our hearts, and it takes away from our basic dignity as people who stand on the earth. And of course economies in Indian Country are typically utterly fucked, if you'll forgive my language."

This is an opinion I have heard from many Native Americans. The old stereotype that most of them are just looking for their monthly check is highly exaggerated. Most Native Americans who get regular checks do so because of water or mineral rights that were part of the negotiations that put them on the reservations to begin with. So the money they get is usually not just a free handout for being Indian. Some tribes dole out a single payment to their tribal members when they turn eighteen, and it can sometimes be considerable. But as Adrian Jawort points out, "How many eighteen-year-old kids, no matter what race they are, are going to use that money for something useful? On the rez, it's even worse. They end up buying a new truck, or blowing it all on parties with their friends, or people talk them into loans. It's often gone in a matter of months."

Sterling expounds on this further. "So the problem with economy as we now know it (the buffalo were an economy, and that economy was destroyed by various American agendas) is that you can't make money without first having money. And most tribes or individual Indians don't have the kind of capital it takes to start businesses that make money. And so that money has to come from the outside. And the difficulty with that is that most investors—and I've seen this many, many times on our reservation, and assume it happens on other reservations all the time—don't want to invest money when they can't be guaranteed they will get a return on their investment. This then becomes an issue of tribal government, and tribal constitutions, and the fact that there aren't really any legal avenues to pursue in Indian Country if you invest money and something goes wrong. Where are you supposed to go? Tribal Court? There aren't enough safety mechanisms in place to make sure money doesn't just 'disappear,' or is misspent, etc. And no business man at any level is going to invest money in a situation like that."

Sterling's summary matched what I heard all over the state. And it fits with what I see every time I visit a reservation town. There are very few businesses. There was a really nice convenience store/gas station in Ashland for a few years, and it just inexplicably closed last year. They opened a huge facility just off the highway in Crow Agency that had a KFC, a convenience store, and about ten gas pumps. Just a few months ago, I pulled into the parking lot and everything was boarded up.

The old saying "This is why we can't have nice things" comes to mind.

Jawort has written extensively about the fact that when tribes do get money, especially for big projects, the job of managing that money, or organizing the projects, often goes to someone who is either unqualified for such a big job or is corrupt. Jawort wrote an article for *Indian Country* in 2013 that cites several examples, including:

> On the Crow Indian Reservation, seven were convicted in a double billing scheme totaling more than $500,000. And money was not the only cost as ultimately a priceless sacred bison site was dug up under the schemers' watch as they were in charge of the tribe's Tribal Historic Preservation Office.
>
> In north-central Montana's Rocky Boy Reservation, construction was halted for a $361 million water pipeline project after five indictments of tribal

members allegedly claimed $311,000 diverted from $33 million in stimulus money received via shell companies and money laundering, according to the *Missoulian*.

Further west on the Blackfeet Reservation, a $9.3 million Po'Ka Project designated to help at-risk youths through 2005-2011 became defunct after years of mismanagement, the *Billings Gazette* reported. There was allegedly $4.6 million lost over those years via doctored invoices to make it seem as if the program was still efficient, among other kickback schemes, according to Cotter.

Sterling says one of the main reasons reservations are so dysfunctional is because of the tribal system. "There is a huge issue of accountability on the part of tribal governments. This is perhaps the biggest problem I see, and I've seen it everywhere I've gone in Indian Country, and I hear it from everyone I've met who lives in Indian Country. This is directly related to the structure of many if not most tribal constitutions—any tribe with an IRA [Indian Reorganization Act] constitution has a council that has absolute power on their respective reservation. There is no separation of powers with any IRA tribe, and as a result the council acts as judge, jury, and executioner in all situations involving tribal politics. This is obviously a huge problem, because when you have a council that is utterly out of control, there is no system of checks or balances to stop them from continuing. They also appoint tribal judges, heads of tribal programs, etc. I don't need to explain why this is problematic."

Perhaps the most troubling part of the Native American situation is how hopeless people, both Native and non-Native, seem to feel about it. There is a sense that nothing can be done, or that no matter what people try, it will make no difference.

PATRICIA LIMERICK, AGAIN from *The Legacy of Conquest*, presents a compelling analysis about the difference between America's approach to its history with slavery and its history with the indigenous population. Her basic argument is this: Because the way we dealt with slavery had a forward narrative motion, we took it more seriously as a nation. In her words, "The Civil War, Reconstruction, the migration of blacks into other regions (besides the South), and the civil rights movement all guaranteed that the nation would recognize the significance of slavery." Even the name of the process had a more forward motion to it: Reconstruction.

On the opposite end of the spectrum, the government policy enacted to deal with the Native Americans was blatantly called The Indian Removal Act. The difference of how we saw these two issues is stated right in the names of these government policies: Emancipation versus Removal. As Jawort is fond of pointing out, the Declaration of Independence also set a precedent for how Native Americans are viewed when, just a few lines down from the famous statement "All men are created equal," Jefferson refers to the "merciless Indian savages."

When you compare the history of these two races, Limerick's theory makes a lot of sense. The Emancipation Proclamation was signed in 1863, granting freedom to the slaves. Obviously the story of what happened next is long and complicated, and people can and do argue to this day about the relative freedom that blacks share in American society. But it's impossible to deny that there has been a narrative arc to this story, that the discussion has continued, and that progress has been made. One only has to look at the White House to see a powerful symbol of that progress. Now imagine the chances of a Native American in that same position.

The Indian Removal Act was passed in 1830, and the next sixty years were a bloody battle, ending according to most historians with the massacre at Wounded Knee in 1890. Most of the discussion of what should be done with America's native peoples ended there. They were shuttled off, most often to the worst land in the West, and have lived in what is essentially forced segregation ever since. It is well documented that the men who engineered this plan expected those who survived the genocide to eventually either die off or give up and go somewhere else. So any thought of providing them with an opportunity to become productive, useful members of our communities was rarely part of the conversation, for decades. In the minds of many, because they had been "conquered," they were expected to go away.

Those who instituted these policies underestimated these people in a big way, and they also underestimated their commitment to staying in this place that was their home for centuries before the rest of us came long. They tried shipping generations of Native American children to boarding schools, where they beat the culture out of them. They tried outlawing such traditional cultural events as powwows and sundances. They tried for a short time to urbanize Native Americans, providing financial incentives for them to move to more urban areas.

Considering how much most people who move to Montana love it here, it should come as no surprise that the people who lived here for centuries also happen to like it here. But it is very inconvenient to those who expected them to give up or go away. Which means it is time to consider other possibilities. To me, the most obvious place to start would be to expand on an event that should have been held decades ago.

ON FEBRUARY 13, 2008, Australian Prime Minister Kevin Rudd issued a four-minute speech in Parliament that was an official apology to the indigenous peoples of Australia. It was the very first act of his term as prime minister, fulfilling a promise he made during his campaign.

The apology included the following:

> We apologise for the laws and policies of successive Parliaments and governments that have inflicted profound grief, suffering and loss on these our fellow Australians.
>
> We apologise especially for the removal of Aboriginal and Torres Strait Islander children from their families, their communities and their country.
>
> For the pain, suffering and hurt of these Stolen

Generations, their descendants and for their families left behind, we say sorry.

To the mothers and the fathers, the brothers and the sisters, for the breaking up of families and communities, we say sorry.

And for the indignity and degradation thus inflicted on a proud people and a proud culture, we say sorry.

The speech was seen by some as nothing more than an empty gesture, a pose. But Rudd pushed for legislation to back up his words. A *New York Times* article published six years later analyzed the effectiveness of Rudd's apology and pointed out that he had laid out an ambitious plan he titled "Closing the Gap," with six specific goals for the indigenous people of Australia. The six issues he targeted were "the gap in health, in housing, in educational opportunity and attainment, in employment. And the obscenity of the 17-year gap in life expectancy" (*The Australian*, February 6, 2009). The Coalition of Australian Governments followed this commitment by pledging $4.6 billion toward reform in these areas, and of course there was much political backlash and debate about where the money should go and who should have control over it.

Prior to Rudd, various prime ministers had refused to offer any such apology for a couple of reasons, including the fact that they had not been part of the atrocities committed, and because they were afraid of the financial obligations that might come with actually acknowledging such failures of the government.

Glenda McCarthy is a teacher in Billings who grew up in Australia and was there when this apology was issued. Glenda is a sprightly woman of fifty with blue eyes and auburn hair and a fabulous smile. She had done a lot of work with Aboriginal children as a teacher there and was very invested in that culture. I asked her what it was like. She said that she and her husband Kelly (who is now a state legislator, and whom she met while he was working in Australia) were on their farewell tour of Australia, and "I got a text message from my aunt. 'Are you watching this? It's so beautiful and I can't stop crying.'" I knew she must be referring to the apology so we drove into town and bought *The Australian* newspaper."

Glenda said that the results of the apology are hard to gauge. "There are ebbs and flows," she said, "but it seems to me that Australia is having the often painful public discussion necessary for any hope of healing and social justice. I take heart in reading Facebook posts from former students in Alice Springs. They work in education, community development, health care, and media. These were students who struggled through aspects of high school, I think for many of the same reasons other Indigenous students struggle: lack of connectedness and relevance. Now they are thirty-year-olds, strong in their cultural identity, with great professions, mortgages, and beautiful children."

Later that same year, in June, Prime Minister Stephen Harper of Canada performed a similar ceremony, offering a public apology for the years of abuse that were suffered by indigenous children in Canada at the hands of the Indian residential schools. These schools, much like the Indian schools in America, spent years trying to beat the Indian out of their students. Canada took this one step further by organizing the Truth and Reconciliation Commission, which did a six-year study of the abuses and then compiled a list of ninety-four recommendations for righting these wrongs. Included in this report were thousands of stories by the victims, including that of a young girl who was thrown in a cold shower every night, often after being raped, after she was snatched from her family home at the age of seven. A story from the 1930s, or perhaps 1940s? No. This was 1974.

Justin Trudeau, who was recently elected Prime Minister of Canada, has shown a strong commitment to carrying out these promises, which include an effort to extract some show of responsibility from none other than the Pope for the Catholic Church's role in these events. Trudeau, who is the son of former Prime Minister Pierre Trudeau, has been cautious about saying he will ask the Pope for an apology but promises to engage in a discussion about the issue.

Many people would be surprised to know that a similar apology was signed by President Obama in 2009. I know I was. But there's a good reason most of us have never heard about it. It's because the gesture was deeply buried in the 2010 Defense Appropriations Act, a bill that was signed in private, without fanfare. And it wasn't exactly specific in its wording: "We apologize on behalf of the United States to all Native Peoples for the many instances of violence, maltreatment, and neglect of Native Peoples by citizens of the United States" and "urge the President to acknowledge the wrongs of the United States against Indian tribes in the history of the United States in order to bring healing to this land."

They eventually held a public ceremony where this tepid statement was read at the Congressional Cemetery in Washington, with leaders from only five tribes present. It's clear that there is little desire in the US government to face the possible financial consequences that a real, specific apology would suggest. And as understandable as that may be, I think it presents a situation where little progress will be made until a sincere, meaningful apology is offered.

Ever since the BIA was established in the late nineteenth century, that organization, which currently costs taxpayers almost $3 billion annually, has been rife with corruption. In 2011, an investigation revealed that ten people, including Superintendent Florence A. White Eagle of the Fort Peck Tribe, had been running a scheme for ten years to embezzle money, totaling $1.2 million, from a BIA program intended to help tribal members secure loans for businesses on the reservation.

This is just one of many examples of misappropriation of BIA funds through the decades, including money that was supposed to go to a fish hatchery that was instead funneled into a housing development, money that was supposed to build roads that somehow never appeared, and, perhaps most troublingly, misdirected BIA moneys, through infamous lobbyist Jack Abramoff, to the election campaign for Montana Senator Conrad Burns.

But perhaps the most egregious in the BIA's long history of mismanagement are the dozens of examples of them offering access to Indian land to farmers, ranchers, and energy companies at a fraction of the market price. Their motivation for doing this isn't hard to imagine.

Assigning the management of Indian lands to a government agency seems a little bit like having a battered wife hand over her finances to her ex-husband after fighting for years to leave him. The relationship between abused and abuser, however well it started, eventually becomes heavily grounded in mistrust and resentment. I believe there are good people in the BIA, just like there are good people in all tribal governments. But the corruption and ineptitude of this system has corroded most of the good intentions.

It's easy to see how anyone involved in this process must look at the problems and wonder where to start. What can possibly be done to fix this mess? So the default theory seems to still be that if we just ignore the problems, they will eventually go away.

Meanwhile, it's still there. And like the mold that slowly grows behind the drywall in your house, we may not see it. And it might be a long time before it affects us, but over the long run, it's costing us all a lot of money. Avoiding the ugly fact that it's there is not working.

It seems to me that offering a public apology, no matter how small it may seem in the overall picture, would at least break through that wall so that we can get to the real stench of the issue. The first step toward solving a problem is always acknowledging that it exists. And although we have come a long way in terms of admitting what happened, that is not nearly as powerful and symbolic as a public, formal acknowledgment.

The irony of this whole situation to me is the fact that, from the time the pioneers and miners and trappers and, finally, farmers and ranchers came to this land, the Native Americans have warned us that if we abuse the land and its people, we will eventually pay.

THERE IS A SINGLE, poignant statement that sums up the Native American situation, and it comes from a very surprising source.

> We took away their country and their means of
> support, broke up their mode of living, their habits
> of life, introduced disease and decay among them,
> and it was for this and against this that they made
> war. Could anyone expect less?

The man who said this was General Phil Sheridan, who was considered the most ferocious Indian fighter in the West.

CHAPTER FOUR

Copper

*"It is well enough that people of the nation
do not understand our banking and monetary
system, for if they did, I believe there would
be a revolution before tomorrow morning."*
—Henry Ford

I'm accustomed to approaching Butte from the east (technically south) on Interstate 90, a beautiful drive any time of year although it can be treacherous in winter. The highway winds precariously through Homestake Pass, a steep climb and then a dramatic descent over the Continental Divide. When you approach from that angle, the town actually looks beautiful, partly because the Berkeley Pit is tucked away behind the mountains to your right.

But this was the first time I drove into Butte from Anaconda, which gives you a whole different view. A more realistic view, honestly. Between the heaps of slag just off the highway from Anaconda, to the panoramic view of this town that has taken a beating for a century and a half, the first impression you get from this angle is a town that shows its colors proudly. There is no pretense in Butte, Montana. Plus there is the small matter of the town suddenly dropping away to the south, as if a huge sink-hole suddenly appeared—which is pretty much what happened, except for the suddenly part.

The Berkeley Pit, in just the right light, looks disturbingly like scarred human flesh. As if a chunk of someone's leg has been gouged out and healed over without proper medical care. And yes, that's a blatant metaphor for what this hole represents for the town of Butte. It's hard to imagine another town in Montana, if not in America, where the residents have given so completely of themselves with so little return.

Butte is the closest I have ever seen to a town that looks as if it has been lifted directly from a Dr. Seuss book. It consists of a series of steep hills with houses that sometimes look as though they've been slapped together, perched precariously on these sharp angles so that any slight tremor would send them tumbling. All of it completely charming. And yet, in the midst of some of the most dilapidated houses, which despite their appearance are probably inhabited, you also find stunning pieces of architecture. As a matter of fact, there are almost six thousand structures in Butte and Anaconda that are listed in the National Register of Historic Places, more than any other town in America. Think about that for a minute. A town with a current population of just over 30,000 people has more historical buildings than any of the amazing cities in the country.

It's easy to imagine a delightful Seussian children's book about this place, with a pit that has swallowed up half of the town. It's almost comical, this massive hole that has grown over decades. Except that at the bottom of it lies a festering pool of toxic waste that has become an environmental puzzle to everyone. A lake, really, more than a thousand feet deep. For years, no one knew what to do about this pool of toxic waste, although there is finally a plan in place. There is even a website called Pitwatch dedicated to giving updates on the progress of this cleanup operation. Butte is a classic example of what happens when the awkward dance between commerce and conservation is dominated by commerce. There is no evidence here of trickle-down economics. But there is more than ample evidence of a greedy few packing their bags and leaving a mess behind.

In fact, as I drive around this town, especially up toward Walkerville, where the streets start to lose their senses—no matter which way I turn, I feel as if I am more lost than I was before—I get the strongest sense that a silly children's rhyme would be an insult to this place. That whatever Grinch lingered in the hills above this town stole more than the pretty packages under these peoples' trees, more than the baubles hanging from the branches, more than the trees themselves. These crooked streets have the feel of a place where tragic things happened. And of course, after hearing Butte's stories, you learn that the tragedy that has taken place in this town is way beyond anything you might imagine. You learn that the Grinches that created this place had hearts that were way more than three sizes too small.

Butte is a place that conjures up every possibility *beyond* the imagination, both good and bad. It is the kind of place where you can buy a latté at the Florence Coffee kiosk with *five* shots of espresso. It is the kind of place where you can smell violence and raucous laughter in the same whiff. There are thousands of miles of tunnels underneath this town—a recent study by the Montana Bureau of Mines and Geology confirmed the Anaconda Company's claim of over 10,000 miles of tunnels— where thousands of men worked and got hurt and fought the company and each other, sometimes to the death, from fire, from poison, from being buried. Or from simply breathing.

It's easy to imagine a place like this spawning a young man like Bobby Kneivel, who spent many nights in the Butte jail before developing a brilliant strategy to make money, by doing daredevil tricks on his motorcycle. Evel Knievel became the most famous Montana resident of his time, perhaps of all time. He was nicknamed by a jail guard when young Bobby spent the night in the pokey with a friend named William Knofel, who was nicknamed "Awful" Knofel. Kneivel soared over cars, then semi-trucks, breaking his own world record time after time, and eventually making the *Guinness Book of World Records* in that category as well as another, the most broken bones. Knievel is a perfect personification of Butte because he gave everything he had, body and soul, to making a living. He also did one of the more remarkable jobs of representing the darker side of Butte, living up to his reputation as a hard-drinking pill addict, a womanizer, and a brute, especially when he assaulted journalist Shelly Saltman with a baseball bat after Saltman wrote an unflattering biography about him. Knievel actually flew all the way to Los Angeles in order to carry out the assault, where Saltman suffered multiple broken bones and had to have several surgeries to repair his arm after trying to fend off the blows.

The story of Butte and Anaconda has no rival for the most compelling chapter in Montana's history. The people of Butte in particular know this and are often derided for being a bit too proud of it, but I think they have every right to be. It is a story that captures all the important elements of American history, and it does so over the course of just a few decades. For a town that never exceeded 100,000 people and for the most part has lingered closer to 40,000, Butte is, by its very presence, a massive town, representing everything that is the best and the worst of American capitalism.

THE NARRATIVE HERE PICKS up where Bannack and Virginia City left off, with many of the same themes. Unlike some resources that have made Montana great, like logging, crops, or livestock, minerals have a finite quantity. The old "non-renewable resource." So once the mines around Alder Gulch were tapped out, the prospectors did what prospectors do. They followed the rumors, branching out to other parts of the state. More gold was discovered near Helena, and prospectors tapped into a rich supply of silver near Philipsburg. Placer mining camps sprung up in places called Diamond Hills (Jefferson), Maiden (Beaverhead), Gilt Edge and Kendall (Fergus), Landusky (Phillips), Monarch (Broadwater), Barker (Judith Basin), Niehart (Cascade), and Castle (Meagher).

But it soon became evident to those with longer-term vision that none of these placer mines, where the minerals lie loose among the sand of a waterbed, were going to provide enough income to sustain any one place. The future, it seemed, was in quartz mining, which required much more capital. Montana needed a smelter to separate the mineral from the rock.

And more importantly, this new approach to mining meant a whole new kind of Montanan. Before mining took hold, the men—and it was mostly men—who were drawn to this country were primarily trappers and prospectors. The demographic of the Montana Territory in its early days was mostly that of wanderers, men with dreams of moving from one big strike to another. Most of them weren't inclined to stay put.

The placer mining camps were perfectly suited to men like this, with their temporary lodgings that left little time to bond with other people. From the beginning, one of the most striking things about the little towns that grew up around these camps was the enormous number of saloons. According to Richard Roeder and Michael Malone's *Montana: A History of Two Centuries*, a visitor to Virginia City in the early days of the Alder Gulch strike recorded "eight hotels, two churches, six billiard halls, four or five elegant gambling houses, three hurdy-gurdies or dance-halls, several bawdy houses, and innumerable saloons." In other words, too many to bother counting.

Just a few miles from Kalispell are remnants of a long-forgotten town named McCarthyville, a community so rife with murder and bloodshed that it imploded just a few years after it began. The town came into being in 1890 when an enterprising young man named Eugene McCarthy saw the need for railroad ties for the tracks headed that way, and he staked a claim for an area rich with timber. The town grew quickly, reaching its peak in 1891 when it housed about a thousand people, and boasted an astonishing thirty-two saloons. There was a makeshift hospital, run by a man who was actually a completely incompetent veterinarian. By the time the town died, only about three years later, close to two hundred deaths had been recorded, many at the hands of others. By contrast, within that same period, a single baby was born.

Most people know that those who "settled" this area were tough. But not enough attention has been paid to the long-term effects of this aspect of our history. There were enough refined, upright citizens around to keep Montana on its feet in those early days. But our heritage for the most part is built on the backs of men who liked to drink and gamble. Men who often left other places because those habits had gotten them into trouble. There's a reason that Montana still has one of the highest rates of alcoholism in the country. And it's no accident, of course, that I'm bringing this to your attention in the chapter about Butte, although I was surprised to learn that Butte's reputation for drinking is actually very much exaggerated.

So WHILE THE PLACER MINES began to play out, an interesting dynamic developed in yet another unlikely place. While the prospectors scrambled from Madison County to Lewis and Clark County to Meagher County and back, there were an enterprising few who started to buy up the interests that were failing. Just as anyone who dipped a pan into a creek bed knew about the small odds of pulling something from that mud, the entrepreneurs ran the risk that one of these failing enterprises was harboring some hidden treasure. They were prospectors with more to lose.

The names of those who gambled and lost—and there must have been thousands of them—are also mostly lost. But there were two who won, and won big.

In 1872 William Clark came to Butte after working for a few years as a banker in Deer Lodge. Clark had seen a number of foreclosures cross his desk, and seeing an opportunity, he began to use his earnings from Alder Gulch to buy the foreclosed properties. We'll never know what Clark's methods were for choosing his properties, but it soon became apparent that he had an eye for it. He even spent part of one year in New York, taking a class in mineral engineering at Columbia University to make more educated choices.

In 1876, an immigrant miner from Ireland named Marcus Daly also began buying up mines around Butte. At first both of these men were focused mostly on silver and gold, following the demands of the time. But there turned out to be a bigger fish in this pond, a massive vein of copper that Daly discovered in one of his mines. This discovery completely shifted the fate of our state and indeed of America itself.

According to a 2014 article from the *Engineering and Mining Journal*, from 1880 through 2013, Butte produced (recovered from its ores) more than 22 billion pounds of refined copper, 4.9 billion pounds of refined zinc, 854 million pounds of refined lead, 720 million ounces of refined silver, 2.9 million ounces of refined gold, 3.7 billion pounds of manganese, and 271 million pounds of molybdenum. The gross value of all of Butte's historic production, at today's metals prices, would be more than $101.6 billion. There is a reason this has been called the Richest Hill on Earth.

It's kind of fun to speculate about how different our history would be if it had only been Mr. Daly who was involved in the development of the billions of dollars' worth of copper that was extracted from the hills surrounding Butte and Anaconda. By all accounts, Daly was much more approachable, the one who seemed to show more interest in the people who worked for him. When he opened the smelter in Anaconda, he built a water and sewage system and financed the streets and lighting. He built a huge theater. Daly was known to buy a house for any woman who lost her husband in one of his mines.

But like most successful businessmen, he could also be ruthless, even before Clark became his bitter rival. At the Constitutional Convention in 1889, the two men worked together, first to get Clark appointed as the president of the convention and then to push through tax laws that favored the mining interests to an obscene degree. It took thirty years for the legislature to finally amend these laws. So for that thirty-year period, the industry that was driving our state, and bringing in the most money by a wide margin, paid a fraction of the taxes that farmers and loggers and ranchers paid.

But that was the entire honeymoon between Clark and Daly. For the next ten years, these two men went at each other with every resource they had, fighting over everything from the location of the state capital (a battle Clark won despite Daly investing an estimated $1.5 million toward promoting

Anaconda) to Clark's effort to bribe his way into the United States Senate, a move that appeared to be successful until Daly hypocritically had his people call for an internal investigation. Daly won that battle, but Clark managed to get to the Senate eventually. It's probably no surprise that Clark proved to be completely indifferent toward serving the people of his state.

There are many factors that came together to allow these men to waste millions of dollars fighting each other while the people who worked for them fought to make a living, working long hours in deplorable conditions with no medical coverage.

First, this was a time when the American megalomaniac was a celebrated figure. Names like Carnegie, Vanderbilt, and Rockefeller represented the success of American capitalism, and the majority of the people gave little thought or worry to how these men achieved their success. Clark in particular had no qualms about accumulating as much as he could. He once said that he owed nobody anything, and he stayed true to that principle to the end, removing himself from Montana as soon as he could comfortably do so without ever looking back.

It's not hard to imagine how a man as ambitious as Daly would get caught up in fighting with the only significant competitor he had in his own home state. But it's a nice fantasy to play with, imagining whether his softer hand would have led Butte and its people to a different outcome. It's also possible that having someone to compete with drove him to achieve what he did. We'll never know.

Another factor that Clark and Daly had working in their favor was the desperation of their workforce. Many of the men who found their way to Butte had spent years trying to make their mark in prospecting and just wanted some steady work. A paycheck. There was another group that came from overseas, especially from Ireland, where Daly recruited people to work in his smelter. The great potato famine was just a couple of decades past so the economy in Ireland was still on the mend. The idea of working in a gold mine? For an Irish guy? How could they pass that up? And of course most of these people did not have the means to return home if things didn't work out. They likely spent everything they had to come here. They were ripe to be treated badly. Although the promise of a steady paycheck lured many people to Montana, they were often misled about how lucrative the work would be, and there was nothing they could do about it except put their heads down and take what was offered.

It took years of horrible wages and completely unsafe working conditions before the people of Butte and Anaconda built up enough power to launch any kind of an effective union. For years, men died from fires, from collapsing tunnels, from scoliosis, and from simple things like elevators that had no sides so if they got their foot caught between the platform and the shaft, they likely not only killed themselves but everyone else on the elevator as well. People may wonder why it took them so long to fight back, and the answer is simple. Each time they tried, they were beaten into submission, sometimes even killed, as in the case of Frank Little, a union organizer who was lynched in 1917.

The third element that worked in Clark and Daly's favor was their control of the press. They each quickly realized the power of buying their own papers, as well as their own editors and reporters, and they brought in some of the best in the country. These men helped them make damn sure that any dissenting voices were dismissed in a very public way. There were few restrictions on the press at this time so the editors of these papers were merely mouthpieces for the corporations that owned them, with little regard for the truth.

The line that is often repeated about history is that it is written by the winners. Clark and Daly have dominated the story of Butte and of Montana from the time they hovered above us all. But for me, the question that needs to be asked now, more than a hundred years later, is what definition of winning do we want to apply to our story? How long are we going to consider the men who exploited their own people and put almost nothing positive back into the world as the winners? Because we do get to decide this stuff. Daly is often credited as "the winner" of the war of the copper kings, because he sold his Anaconda

Copper Company to Standard Oil for a hefty sum. But if he won the war, he paid a heavy price for it, as he was dead within a year of that deal.

Many people would look at Clark as a winner from the standpoint of pure capitalist economics. He became one of the richest men in the world, building himself a huge mansion in Manhattan and going on to spend the rest of his life developing one of the largest art collections in the country. But he was also a man who was universally reviled.

THERE IS A TENDENCY to lump the history of Anaconda with Butte's, as if there was no difference between what happened in these two towns. But as Laurie Mercier points out in her excellent book *Anaconda: Labor, Community and Culture in Montana's Smelter City,* there were some significant differences between the two towns that gave Anaconda its own distinct character.

Perhaps the most obvious differences were a result of the simple fact that Anaconda has always been much smaller than Butte. Both of these communities drew a large influx of immigrants in their early years, with Anaconda at one point showing roughly 40 percent of its population having been born on foreign soil. Because of Butte's larger population, many of the immigrants from specific countries developed their own small communities, many of which even had their own names, including Meaderville (largely Italian), McQueen (eastern Europeans, including Slovenians, Czechs, Hungarians, and Austrians), Fintown (can you guess?), and Dublin Gulch (yes, Irish). But for Anaconda, there simply weren't enough in each group to do that. So Anaconda developed an atmosphere of cooperation and community that was much more inclusive.

Part of this was also due to Daly. When he first opened the smelter, Daly not only built the sewer and water systems and the streetcars but he donated land for churches and opened a massive store called the Copper City Commercial Center, which sold groceries as well as hardware. Daly was determined to create a strong sense of community in Anaconda, an attitude he also carried over when he started the town of Hamilton.

Although the workers of Anaconda were ahead of their time in embracing labor unions, it became clear that "the company," as everyone called the Anaconda Company, would use whatever influence it had to prevent these unions from making real progress. Soon after the smelter opened, everyone realized that the smoke coming from the smelter's stacks had a profound effect on the local vegetation and livestock. So the local farmers' union filed a lawsuit against the company. At first the company tried to assuage the locals' fears by building a taller smokestack. But this had little effect, and the farmers continued to pursue the case until the company finally decided to bring out the big guns and put the matter to rest. They paid scientists to provide evidence disputing the farmers' claims. They even managed to get a professor from the University of Montana fired for testifying in support of the farmers. A judge eventually threw the case out. The company's influence could be felt all over the state as, at one time, three-fourths of the workforce in Montana worked either directly or indirectly for Anaconda Copper Company.

But thanks to that wonderful phenomenon wherein suppression sometimes brings out the best in people, Anaconda's population responded by forming tight bonds and developing the kind of resilience in which Montanans take pride. This might be more true than ever in the female population of that time. Before the unions were able to achieve some of the rights we now take for granted, women in Anaconda and Butte had to contend, every day, with the knowledge that a single dangerous act, a slip, a falling piece of machinery, one of the sudden fires that plagued their town—any one of these things— could not only render them widowed but also, because there were so few jobs for women, without any means of making a living. And there was no compensation for employees who were killed on the job. No Social Security. No pension. The pay during the 1920s in the smelter was twenty-nine dollars a week (for a seven-day week), so there wasn't a lot of opportunity to put money away for the proverbial rainy day.

The community rallied around these women in remarkable ways, supporting the boarding houses they created out of their family homes or frequenting the small grocery stores they opened (during the 1920s and 1930s, 40 percent of the grocery stores in Anaconda were owned by women). Women were not welcome in the smelters or the mines, with an abundance of men already in the employee pool, so they had to find their own creative ways of making a living. And they did.

But they were also a force in the community at large. They formed ladies' auxiliary clubs to support their union men and to back community causes. While the men focused on issues of the national level, the auxiliary clubs tended to be more concerned about the issues close to home.

Meanwhile, the smelter workers themselves had a hard time forming their own union, mainly because the company was so self-contained and so determined to make it difficult for them to do so. It wasn't until a few months after Daly died and after he had sold the company to Amalgamated that they formed their first union, in March 1901.

My favorite example of how this community worked together and supported each other takes place during the Depression, when the smelter was barely operating, and a huge percentage of the population was forced to rely on government assistance in order to survive. There are countless stories of one family sharing their first allotment of food with their neighbors, knowing that the others would follow suit when their turn came.

This sense of cooperation also came in handy during the many strikes and shutdowns that plagued this industrial town's first few decades of existence.

DRIVING THROUGH MODERN-day Anaconda—especially when you know its rich history—feels like coming late to one of the best parties ever. Most towns in Montana have a strong vibe, whether it's one of a strong sense of community or a strong sense of paranoia and distrust. In Anaconda, it's melancholy.

I heard a lot of laughter in Butte. But the faces that I encountered in Anaconda seemed resigned.

There are tremendous reminders here of what once was. There is a gorgeous old library, built with financing from the Hearst family. And there is the Washoe Theater, which doesn't look like much from the outside but has an absolutely stunning interior. On the side of one building, in huge letters, is an ad that reads "Rocky Mountain Beer: You work better refreshed!" a wonderful indication of the uneasy marriage between work and play in Anaconda.

But the Margaret Theater that Daly built for his wife is long gone, lost to fire in the 1930s. I got out to take a picture of the once-famous Montana Hotel, and a man walking by with his two young daughters said, "It's not like it used to be…just like everything else around here."

"What's different?" I asked.

"They tore the whole top stories off. Tore off the top of it."

He went on without another word, his head hanging. R. L. Polk & Co.'s Butte City Directory (1902) described the Montana Hotel as "the handsomest and most elegantly appointed hotel in the state, built in European style with strictly first class cuisine and service." The hotel boasted of being "thoroughly fire proof, and having running water, baths, steam heat, elevators, electric bells, fire alarms, open fire places, and all modern conveniences." In 1902, rooms started at $3.50 a day.

In one of the more risky efforts to rejuvenate a town, Anaconda took an old Superfund cleanup site, the location of the original Old Works smelter, and decided to build a world-class golf course. They hired Jack Nicklaus to design the course and flew him in for the grand opening. My friend John Sullivan laughed about how much publicity it drew to the community whenever Nicklaus came to town.

"They were trying to decide whether the black slag would work for the sand traps, so they flew Nicklaus in to hit some shots out of one of these traps filled with slag. So a whole ton of people gathered to see Nicklaus hit shots out of the trap. We're all standing in a huge crowd, and a helicopter comes in and lands, and Nicklaus gets out and hits a few shots out of the trap, nods, then gets back in the helicopter and flies off."

The golf course is fabulous. But the objective of bringing in more businesses, including a big luxury hotel, has not been successful.

I DROVE BACK AND FORTH between Butte, where I stayed with my friends John and Karen Sullivan, and Anaconda a couple of times to try to get a feel for the area. It is striking in a sad way how little vegetation there is on that twenty-five mile stretch. For decades, there has been a train connecting these towns, originally operated by the Butte, Anaconda and Pacific Railway. It was first built in 1892 and in 1913 became the first railway primarily used for freight to electrify. The train carried passengers until 1955, and I can just imagine the controversy it must have brought when they decided to change that policy. The railway ran on electricity until 1967, when it became more cost-effective to use diesel. The line still regularly carries freight.

But driving this short stretch of highway today—with the barren landscape, the impotent smoke stack to the south, and buildings that look either empty or under-maintained—makes me wish I'd had a chance to see what it was like in its heyday. No matter how much people were struggling then, you get the sense that there was never a dull moment in Butte or Anaconda in those days. And there are so many elements about Butte and Anaconda's history that have had a significant impact on Montana.

First is the drinking. Both of these towns prided themselves on making the effort to bring culture to this new frontier. Butte brought in performers like Charlie Chaplin, Mark Twain, and Enrico Caruso. But no amount of bunting or lace could disguise the fact that, in the early mining days, these were working-class, blue-collar towns. And more importantly, they were towns where people had very little money for the finer things in life. The company made sure of that. They paid them just enough to keep them from storming the castles but not enough to actually build anything other than a life of basic survival. It was common for a man to have another job because the smelter or the mines paid so poorly, not to mention the fact that they were constantly closing down or laying workers off.

There were two natural by-products of this atmosphere, both of which echo through the main streets of towns all over Montana to this day. The first is that the people had nowhere to go with the anger this kind of treatment produced. The company was masterful at using their newspapers to channel this anger at anyone but themselves. Whether it was union leaders or the government, or some vague foreign threat, there was never a shortage of targets that they could direct this anger toward to distract the workers from coming after *them*. If nothing else, these working men probably found an easy target in their own neighborhoods, where the people in management perhaps had a house with a bedroom for each child or an indoor toilet.

Sometimes tensions with the company led to fighting within the union itself. While in Butte, I went to hear a talk by local historian Richard Gibson describing the events leading up to the bombing of the Union Hall in 1914. According to Gibson, tension had been building within the Western Federation of Miners (WFM). For one thing, miners were upset that the union wasn't doing more about the fact that they were still being paid $3.50 a day, the same wage they had been earning since 1878, despite the fact that the price of copper had more than doubled. But there was also friction within the union concerning the use of dues to help support some striking miners in Michigan. Rumors of misappropriation of these funds were circulating, and the day before the WFM's annual parade, 1,200 miners walked out of the Speculator Mine.

On that day, June 13, the tensions boiled over into a riot, and union members took over their union hall. The acting mayor came down to try to talk some reason into the crowd, and he was thrown out the second-story window. Fortunately, he was not seriously hurt, and there were few other injuries that day. But it wasn't over yet.

A few days later, Charles Moyer, the president of the WFM, came to Butte to try to calm things down. He fired some of the more conservative union leaders and promised a new election, but the damage was already done. That same day, union members met and decided to form the Butte Mine Workers Union, with a vote of 6,348 to 243 in favor. Five days later, Moyer scheduled a meeting of the old union, and only about fifty men showed up, while a growing crowd gathered outside. The meeting went on for several hours, and as the tension outside built, probably fueled by a few bottles of Irish whiskey, a man who was mistaken for an outsider started to enter the building, and someone shot him. Members from the inside started firing into the crowd and ended up killing an innocent bystander.

That's when all hell broke loose, and the crowd decided to attack the Miner's Hall, dynamiting it several times until it was completely destroyed.

Richard Gibson is a very interesting fellow. He grew up in Flint, Michigan, a town not much different from Butte in terms of its blue-collar population, and a town that has also suffered from corporate neglect, as evidenced by their recent water crisis. Gibson got his degree in geology from Indiana University, which had a geological field station in the Tobacco Root Mountains, just an hour or so south of Butte. So he started coming to Montana in 1969, and after teaching at the field station for fourteen years, from 1989 to 2002, and living there from 1989 to 2003, he decided to leave that position, and he had two choices. "I could either move back to Denver, where I would have to work hard just to pay the rent," Gibson said. "Or I could move to Butte and live cheaply."

Since his arrival, Gibson's interest in the history of the town led him to volunteer for various historical activities, including tours, and eventually to start a blog called "Butte History and Lost Butte," based on a book Gibson wrote (*Lost Butte*) that features some of the more fascinating buildings in town. He is also working to catalog those nearly six thousand buildings, a project that is slow going. "None of this happened by design," Gibson said. "It really did just happen."

Gibson's take on the current status of Butte was that it is holding its own despite the virtual disappearance of mining operations. I asked Gibson about the Outlook Mine, an open pit copper mine that has gone against convention in Butte by banning unions. Instead, they pay a fair wage and provide good benefits and other incentives to keep their employees happy, and they pay close attention to environmental concerns. "Anyone who rejects their value to Butte isn't paying attention," Gibson said. "Yes, there are still plenty of environmental concerns, including dust and other things, but those are (I think) being dealt with. Vigilance is good, but Montana Resources (the company that was established in 1986 and opened the Outlook Mine) is a good citizen, in my opinion. As for the non-union nature of the present mine operation, who cares? As far as I can tell, the workers have benefits, salaries, and working conditions that are as good as possible, union or not."

Gibson said the backbone of Butte's economy today, though, are the small businesses owned by locals. And he believes they have huge potential for growth as a tourist attraction ("although we have to deal with this thing called winter"). I would have to agree with Richard on that count. Aside from all the amazing buildings, there is an excellent mineral museum at the Montana Bureau of Mines at the college, the World Museum of Mining, and the Mai Wah Chinese Museum, as well as many smaller tours.

Butte also happens to have one of the most amazing archives in the state. Half the building is one of the old firehouses, and a fabulous addition was built to match that section. It's impressive to look at but even more impressive to tour, as millions of newspapers, photographs, maps, and countless other documents are stored in rows of 1984-style file cabinets.

THE SECOND BY-PRODUCT of Butte's history—and it's something Gibson also talks about quite openly—is the culture of alcohol and gambling. The pressure of trying to make a living in such deplorable conditions, especially with so many of these people giving up so much to come here, had to have been enormous. And it had to have brought tremendous tension into their homes.

So they needed somewhere to bury themselves for a few hours, whether it was a bottle or a mound of soft flesh that wasn't going to demand anything more than a few bucks, or a spinning wheel that could put them in a daze for an hour or two. Gambling and alcohol and prostitution thrived in these towns, and it's not hard to understand why. The interesting thing about this subject in relationship to Butte and Anaconda is that you will never encounter the kind of defensiveness or denial you would expect from a place that has a reputation for alcohol consumption. No, these two mining towns embrace that reputation with a cheerful zeal. They make no apologies about it, and in fact are more likely to make fun of anyone who suggests it might be something to be concerned about.

But it's also true, when you look at the statistics, that Butte and Anaconda are no worse than the rest of the state in terms of alcohol consumption, binge drinking, or alcoholism. It has become more a case of people holding onto an old truth. As a state, we tend to rank high in these statistics no matter what county you're in.

And in the early years, it was clear that it was interfering with the mine workers' productivity and community. The Anaconda Company had to post signs warning their workers not to drink on the job. There was even a rumor among the miners that a few shots would loosen up the lungs so that it lessened the chances of getting sick from all the chemicals they were breathing. Many of the workers timed their trip home on the train so that they could stop in the pub and toss down two or three shots before the last train continued to their final stop.

It's NATURAL THAT THE history of this place would focus on the copper kings, but when you dig deeper, Butte has so much more to offer. In fact, it's amazing to think that these men have been gone for almost a hundred years and still dominate the story of Butte, not to mention Montana.

But it is the story of resilience and grit of the people of Butte that holds much more interest in today's Montana. With its strong Irish heritage, Butte stepped easily into the role of Montana's red-headed stepchild. I remember Butte jokes from early in my life. But like many Montanans, I knew very little about the place. The stereotypical image was that people from Butte loved to drink and they loved to fight. When their high school teams came to town, you never knew what to expect. They scared the hell out of us.

In light of their history, it's not hard to understand why.

There is an amazing story about John D. Rockefeller, who would eventually become part owner of the Anaconda Copper Company. When he discovered oil, he had only one option for transporting his product—along the railways owned by his arch-enemy Andrew Carnegie. These two men spent decades locked in a battle as to who was the richest man in the world, and apparently they were each willing to go to any length to win. When Carnegie tried to raise his shipping rates, Rockefeller came up with the brilliant idea of building pipelines to transport the crude. The downside of this plan was that it meant closing several of his refineries and thus putting thousands of his employees out of work—for months. Rockefeller didn't care. He was only concerned with outdoing his rival. This was the business environment that William Clark and Marcus Daly operated in, and the number of people who lost their lives or struggled to survive can't even be estimated.

The importance of Butte's labor movement to Montana history can't be overstated. Montanans are practical people. As a group we seldom embrace anything without clearly seeing the benefits. So the people of Butte did not rush into becoming a labor town without considerable thought. They knew they would pay a heavy price. They knew they would probably lose some lives if they threw themselves headlong into forming unions. But they were losing lives left and right as it was, and it finally got to the point where they weren't willing to pay that price any longer. The first strike, organized in 1878, started because of a reduction in wages from $3.50 to $3.00. The company eventually raised the rate back to the original, but it didn't change again for more than twenty years. The fight for a reasonable living wage was beaten back time after time by a company that had become powerful enough that it could simply shut down their mines and wait it out until the miners gave in.

During the 1950s, the demand for copper became so great that the company decided to come up with a more efficient way of extracting its precious commodity—by simply stripping away the ground above it. The Berkeley Pit grew slowly from that time forward until the inevitable happened and other countries, particularly Chile, were able to provide copper at a cheaper price. ARCO shut down the Amalgamated Mine in 1982, and the pump station was also closed down, leaving groundwater to gather freely in the base of the Pit. The Pit is now a mile and a half long, a mile wide, and over seventeen hundred feet deep, with an estimated 2.5 million gallons of water flowing into it every day. The water in the Pit contains arsenic, copper, cadmium, cobalt, iron, manganese, zinc, and sulfate, plus other inorganic constituents. The Pit is now the largest Superfund site in the country and, although there are plans to extract the toxic chemicals, it's going to take years.

In 1995 a flock of 342 snow geese flew into the Pit, and all died. ARCO, which still acted as custodian for the Pit, denied that the water was responsible, claiming it was an infection caused by a grain fungus.

KAREN AND JOHN SULLIVAN are a classic Butte couple. They both grew up there, where John's father worked in the mines, and Karen's father was the manager of the local Buttrey's grocery store. I have known Karen since high school, when her father's job moved the family to Billings, and I stayed at their home a few miles from the tiny town of Rocker for the three days I was in the area. John's mother lives just up the road, as does former governor Judy Martz. John and Karen both come from good Irish families. They root for Notre Dame, as well as the Celtics and Red Sox—a passion I share.

So we planned our schedule around the Red Sox games, and we laughed a great deal. John worked for the post office for many years, and he still does a rural delivery route in Basin, which is on Highway 15 toward Boulder. He has two fully grown stuffed bears in his living room. Two! And a picture of President Obama prominently featured on the wall next to them. While I was there, John was sporting a dirty cast with a lime-green lining on one wrist, the result of surgery, and when he got excited, he talked loud and fast, sometimes tripping himself up with an endearing stutter. Although the Sullivans made me laugh, they are also passionate about issues that matter to them.

"I was talking to this guy in a bar one time—rich guy, his dad owns one of the biggest companies in town," John said, "And maybe it was because he was drunk, but he told me something that made me sick to my stomach."

John leaned forward, his pointer finger protruding from that lime-green lining in his cast. "He says to me, 'You know what I think? I think people like us *should* have control over most of the money. Because we know how to handle it.' I just looked at him, and I've never wanted to punch someone so bad in my life. I had to walk out of there or I would have." He leaned back. "And you can imagine how hard it is for me to walk out of a bar." And he laughed loud and long.

Karen was hired as Butte-Silver Bow's health officer in December 2013. That previous November, a Butte teenager committed suicide over the Thanksgiving holiday. Another teenager committed suicide New Year's Day 2014 and yet another on January 7, 2014. After the third death, Butte-Silver Bow Chief Executive Matt Vincent called together a group of people, mostly representing various agencies, to consider what the Butte community reaction would be. That was the basis of the formulation of the Butte-Silver Bow Suicide Prevention Committee. Since that early group decided to take a public health approach to addressing the issue, Sullivan has facilitated the group. Butte had a fourth youth suicide April 5, 2015, an eighteen-year-old named Jake Heard, a friend of Sullivan's daughter Mary. Jake's death made this work much more personal for Sullivan.

The findings of Sullivan's group have been surprising. For one thing, these four kids did not fall into the category people would normally associate with suicidal teenagers. They were not considered outsiders or loners. They weren't victims of bullying. They were all very involved in their community, very active in their school. When they found Jake, the tuxedo he was planning to wear to the prom that evening was hanging on the doorknob in his bedroom. He had just talked to his principal the day before about how excited he was to have received a scholarship to college.

Sullivan points to several contributing factors, and the similarities to those listed by the study in Beaverhead County are disturbing. These are the leading factors, compiled by the Montana Department of Health and Human Services:

> Montana is a large frontier state with many isolated communities.
> There is a generational culture of acceptance of suicide as a viable option to resolve feelings of hopelessness, when one feels they are a burden to others.
> Ongoing stigma toward seeking mental health services and concerns of maintaining confidentiality in small communities inhibit individuals from seeking needed treatment. (People on the coasts talk openly about their therapists and their therapy sessions. Obviously, the opposite is true of Montana.)
> According to the U.S. Census Bureau, in 2010, 17 percent of the population, or 161,500 Montanans, lacked health insurance coverage, including more than 23,000 children. The Affordable Care Act will continue to improve this, and Medicaid expansion in Montana will help greatly.
> Montana has a high availability of lethal means, especially firearms, which increase the lethality of impulsive suicidal behaviors. In Butte-Silver Bow, 55.5 percent of adults have a firearm in or around

their home, much higher than the national average of 34.7 percent. In Butte-Silver Bow, in households with children, 71.4 percent have a firearm kept in or around the house, nearly twice the national finding.

Montana has high rates of alcoholism, underage drinking, and binge drinking, along with other drug addictions, including the current trend of methamphetamine use.

The up-and-down economic nature of the farm and ranch industry and the difficulty in attracting industry to provide a stable employment market in Montana are ongoing stressors.

An analysis of National Violent Death Reporting System (NVDRS) data revealed that suicide rates are higher among people who live at high altitudes than those living at lower elevations. Butte is at 5,505 feet in altitude.

There is a shortage of inpatient mental health treatment facilities and crisis stabilization beds in Montana. The availability of this resource is diminishing with the closure of inpatient psychiatric beds (there's no money to be made in this business).

The funding/reimbursement for outpatient services throughout the state is considered inadequate by many providers.

There is insufficient integration of traditional and culturally specific interventions, especially among Montana's Native American populations.

Montana has a severe shortage of psychiatrists, especially child and adolescent psychiatrists. There is, in fact, one psychiatrist east of Billings.

Montana has a shortage of psychiatric mental health nurse practitioners.

Montana does not recognize licensed marriage and family therapists (LMFTs) as a separate professional license. This further reduces mental health resources in the state. There are only two states in the nation that do not recognize LMFTs: Montana and West Virginia.

There is a shortage of physicians capable of providing
appropriate psychiatric medication treatments.
There is a shortage of postvention services available to
schools and communities concerning how they react
after a suicide has occurred.

Sullivan believes that the lower median income is a big factor in the high suicide rate for Silver Bow County. She also believes that the stigma about asking for help is a huge contributing factor among Montanans in general, and of course the lack
of available resources is an enormous issue. Among five bills
that were proposed this last legislative session to encourage
more attention to Montana's ranking, only one passed. And
that one was a watered-down version. Sullivan and her group
had recommended that teachers receive suicide prevention
training each time their certification is renewed. Although the
bill passed, most of the teeth was taken out when the legislature changed it to having teachers "encouraged" to get this
training.

Sullivan believes that the biggest factor for such a high suicide rate in Montana can be attributed to the economy. I was
surprised to see among her data that the percentage of suicides is about 85 percent men. Sullivan believes that between
the pressure among Montana men to be "the providers" and
the stigma about asking for help we have a ready-made atmosphere for men to decide that everything is hopeless. Add to
this the high alcoholism rate and the availability of guns, and
you have what one of Sullivan's fellow committee members
calls the Lethal Triad—drugs/alcohol, an upset individual,
and high availability to means.

I BELIEVE IT'S IMPORTANT to recognize the people from Butte's
past who lived hand to mouth, suffered innumerable indigni-
ties from their employees, and lost loved ones before demanding the kind of treatment they could and should have been getting all along. Clark and Daly, and later Standard Oil (which
bought the Anaconda Copper Company in the 1890s), could

have easily paid their workers a wage that would have allowed them to live comfortable lives, but they refused to even consider it.

So although the history of Butte is naturally centered around the copper kings, there are so many other interesting stories. I was pleased to watch a documentary that came out a few years ago called *Butte America* that never even mentioned the copper kings. It focused on the working people. So in that spirit, I'd like to put forth a few other names.

One of my favorite Butte personalities is a woman named Ella Knowles, who lobbied the Montana legislature in the late nineteenth century to allow women to become lawyers. She became the first female lawyer in Montana in 1889 and was eventually nominated to run for Attorney General, twenty-two years before women were allowed to vote in Montana. She was the first woman in the country to run for that office. She lost by just a few votes. Henri Haskell, the man who won the election, appointed her Assistant Attorney General and then married her. She was also the first woman elected as a delegate to a national convention. Unfortunately, Ella Knowles Haskell suffered from poor health, which had brought her West to begin with, and she died when she was only forty-one. But reading her story, it's hard not to think of Jeanette Rankin, who would become the first woman in Congress just a few years later. Rankin had her own connection to Butte when the Speculator Mine disaster occurred in 1917. When 168 men were burned to death in a fire, Rankin stepped in and tried to arrange a negotiation with the mine to get compensation for the families. But they refused to meet with her.

In 1905 a young lawyer was taking the train to Seattle when he stopped in Butte and got involved in a poker game, eventually losing everything he owned. He ended up setting up practice in Butte and went on to become one of the most active political leaders of his time. His name was Burton K. Wheeler. Wheeler was one of the few politicians of his time who stood up to the Anaconda Company, and he often paid the price for it. But he did not let this deter him from living by his conscience, which earned him four terms in the US Senate. Another statesman who had a connection to Butte was a young man who spent several years mucking ore in the mines. Mike Mansfield hadn't finished high school when he moved to Butte and took a job shoveling slag and ore for the next eight years. During that time, he met a schoolteacher named Maureen Hayes, who encouraged him to complete his education. Mansfield went on to become the longest-running Senate Majority Leader—and one of the most highly respected senators—in the history of the United States.

There is also one aspect of Butte that is little known, which is its literary history. My friend Aaron Parrett recently published a book called *Literary Butte* which chronicles a rich and varied bibliography of literary works that were either written by Butte's citizens or written about Butte. I won't summarize Parrett's extensive history here, but I do want to mention one story.

Mary MacLane was one of the first and most unlikely literary sensations from Montana. In 1902 she wrote a book that she wanted to call *I Await the Devil's Coming*. But her publisher convinced her that this title might affect sales, so it was released as *The Story of Mary MacLane*. Still, the provocative nature of the book, which talked very openly about her sexual desires, was enough to shock many readers, and the book was an immediate international sensation, selling 100,000 copies in the first few months.

MacLane also talked openly about the mixed feelings she had for her home town, calling Butte "so ugly that it is near the perfection of ugliness." But she followed that with this: "And anything perfect, or nearly so is not to be despised."

MacLane's writing was much more accomplished than those who dismissed it for its sexual frankness were willing to admit. She utilized the notoriety and wealth that came her way to spend several years in New York and other Eastern cities. But the interesting thing about her story is that she eventually tired of that life and returned to the place that made her famous. As is so often the case, a few years of hobnobbing with the social elite gave MacLane a greater appreciation for the down-to-earth people with whom she had grown up. In her later years, she wrote about her hometown with great fondness, saying, "I have none but a joyous hand for it. Butte is sordid, beastly and time-serving—but withal full of romance and poetry and the wideness of the West."

BUT THE TRUE HEROES of Butte's history are the working man and woman. What the people of Butte did for Montana was to establish our state as an industrial power. There was a time when the Anaconda Copper Company was the fourth-largest privately owned company in the country, and it was the men who burrowed into the earth day after day, breathing dust and gas and chemicals until their lungs were scarred, that made that company relevant. And right beside them, the women who managed to feed their families on a shoestring budget and started boarding houses or laundry services to keep the family fed.

Silver Bow County is one of the few counties in Western Montana that shows a drop in economic growth since 1970, and it's a significant drop. But unlike Anaconda, Butte does not have the feel of a city on the downhill slide. No matter how bad things get in Butte, they've seen worse. The people of Butte have learned to ignore the facts. They respond to bad news with a raise of a glass and a bawdy joke.

These two towns ended up relying a great deal on government assistance at various times during their history, and are therefore much less inclined to look down on people who do, something that cannot be said about many communities in Montana. There is a sense of acceptance toward others in Butte that is borne of experience, as well as the cultural diversity that has always been a prevalent part of this community.

More than anything, I believe that both Butte and Anaconda serve as the greatest example of a cautionary tale that we have in Montana, if not in America. Because seldom has there been a town where a single man so ruthlessly flexed his power in the faces of the people—and got away with it for decades.

CHAPTER FIVE

Trees

"Storms make trees take deeper roots."
—Dolly Parton

One of the most fascinating dynamics that shows its face over and over again in Montana's history is the conflict between environmentalists and big business. Although the issue has affected almost every corner of the state in one way or another, there are few areas in Montana where this conflict has had a more dramatic impact than the northwest corner, in Lincoln (Libby), Sanders (Thompson Falls), Mineral (Superior), and Missoula (Missoula) counties. Because so much of Montana, in terms of annual precipitation, is virtually desert, the areas that provided timber became vital in the early years, especially with two of our most crucial job providers—railroads and mines—depending so much on lumber. There are few states in the union that are big enough to provide such diverse resources as Montana. Aside from vast amounts of ore, we also have millions of acres of forest-land—94.11 million acres of forest, including 19.39 million acres of national forest. Driving the highway from Kalispell to Libby, where I'd never been before, I was surprised to find a part of the state that looked as if it had been cut like a piece of cake from the Pacific Northwest and dropped into the corner of our Montana-shaped plate.

It was pouring rain the day I made this drive, and to make it even more surreal, dozens of vintage Model A's appeared on the interstate, coming toward me in a steady thrum, like a blast from the days when this county was thriving. I felt as if I was traveling into history. Many of these cars had open cabs, and the drivers were exposed to this tremendous downpour as if they were trying to prove themselves as worthy descendants of those early settlers.

And there *was* a time when Lincoln County was thriving, with the high point being the 1970s when the lumber industry was still in its prime, the vermiculite mine employed more than two hundred people, and construction of the impressive Libby Dam on the Kootenai River provided hundreds of jobs, eventually forming Lake Koocanusa. It was probably hard for residents of Libby to imagine that, forty years later, they would be an afterthought, a withering flower in the midst of a place so rich with fertile soil and moist air.

When I asked about the cause of Libby's decline, I heard a familiar refrain.

"Environmentalists!" many of them cried, as if there was a single form that defined the term, some evil entity that converged on innocent victims and squashed their hopes and dreams. One pictured Godzilla in a tie-dyed t-shirt.

And indeed it's impossible to deny that people who have been conscious of the environment are partly to blame for the fact that there is so little work available in the area. There are few towns in Montana, if not America, that have been so deeply affected by environmental policies and, in turn, so closely scrutinized by the Environmental Protection Agency (EPA) and other such organizations.

But...there *was* that small matter of people dying. A lot of people. The count as of 2010 was 400 people, and that's just the ones who died directly from asbestos poisoning. Another 1,500 were found to have the fibers in their lungs. This in a town that has a current population of about 2,700 people.

One of the things that struck me immediately on this journey was that if I removed politics from a discussion—and believe me, in this volatile political climate, that wasn't always easy—but when I could, I found myself understanding peoples' opinions much better than I expected. Most Montanans are reasonable people, just trying to find their way. So the biggest mistake I could make when talking to someone was to assume from their appearance or from their profession or from the town where they lived that they were going to have a certain attitude or opinion. And of course, the pleasant surprise from that experience was that talking to people often changed my viewpoint.

But what it really made me realize is how often the two sides of a major issue tend to be much more in agreement than they think they are. For example, in the case of the mines and logging in Lincoln County, the people who had lost their jobs were angry at the environmentalists who they believed had brought their industries to their knees. So the fighting ended up being on the ground, between two groups of people who had very few resources and very small voices. Meanwhile, the real blame seemed to lie with the companies who were too short-sighted to realize that putting money into safe practices up front would save them more in the long run.

Time after time, the people in control have ignored blatant safety and health warnings in Montana only to be hit hard with lawsuits and shutdowns when the problem could no longer be ignored. These entities are the ones who often decided to shut down rather than put the money into doing what was best for the people in the region. And of course it has always been the taxpayers who pay for their decision to *not* do the right thing. Libby became one of the largest Superfund sites in the country in 1999, and the EPA has spent over $50 million to clean it up. That money did not come from the mine that caused the problem. It filed for bankruptcy and fled without paying for any of it. It was the taxpayers who suffered. It's a sad but common story in Montana.

Just as one other example, in the late 1980s, a Canadian company called Pegasus Gold hired an Anaconda native to sell the public on an open-pit gold mine on Forest Service property on the upper reaches of the Clark Fork River. This spokesman promised the public that they had developed a state-of-the-art method of extracting this gold that would not harm the environment.

This local pitchman made a very convincing case, and the Forest Service as well as the state-approved operations. Almost twenty years later, we taxpayers are still paying for efforts to clean up the waste at Beal Mountain Mine caused by this operation, which closed down in 1998. Their $6 million bond has long since been exhausted, and as of 2014, close to $20 million had been devoted to trying to pump clean water into the Clark Fork to prevent the fish from dying. So two-thirds of that money came from the public, and the job is still underway. A permanent solution has been estimated at $40 million. Pegasus also gifted Montanans with another mess in the form of another open pit mine in the Little Rockies, and another $65 million has been devoted to trying to clean up the pollution caused there. One-third of that came from our pockets.

There had been rumors for years that the water in Libby was causing health problems for its residents. In the 1980s, a geologist friend of mine, Kirk Miller, was working in Libby, investigating groundwater contamination resulting from an old wood treatment plant at the St. Regis sawmill. After some homeowners suspected that they smelled creosote in the groundwater when they dug their wells, they reported the issue to authorities. The EPA investigated the problem and declared Libby a Superfund site. They sent people like Kirk in to test the water and, if necessary, to offer the opportunity to switch to city water. Most of the residents took him up on the offer, of course. But one gentleman refused because he claimed the creosote made his vegetables taste better.

Things heated up in Libby when it became clear that the cancer level was way higher than it should be. The EPA came in and did tests, and the asbestos levels in the local water and soil were found to be astronomical. In 1999, the EPA verified what many people already knew, that a vermiculite mine just a few miles out of town was poisoning Libby's population, killing them by the dozens. The mine had been pulling vermiculite from the hills around Libby since 1919, exposing generations of Libby residents to asbestos dust. The rate of death from lung-related illnesses in the area was far higher than the national average. In 1963, a company called W. R. Grace acquired the mine and claimed later that it had no knowledge of the dangers of the operation. But documents proved this claim to be false, and once again, we have an example of a corporation that put its own profit margin ahead of the safety and health of the people it employed, not to mention the families of these workers.

According to recent EPA reports, the results of this cleanup effort have been extremely successful, and there's little reason to question their claim. They have found the current levels of asbestos in the area to be below those of most towns in Montana, but they plan to continue to run tests in the region to make sure this trend continues.

That said, the damage done to this region in terms of morale and image is impossible to overstate, impossible to measure. Half of the downtown buildings are empty. As with almost every small town I visit, the people of Libby somehow manage to sustain an almost painful devotion to the place where they live. Even though there appears to be very little evidence for their optimism, the desire to see what is best about their town, the desire to believe that it's going to recover, or that it's not as bad as people say, is akin to the worst kind of denial. But it feels like a necessary denial. It's that kind of denial that prevents people from being overwhelmed by hopelessness. Like someone in a miserable marriage clinging to small signs of change in their spouse. A few days without a fight. A brief tender touch to the arm.

DAVID HARMAN IS THE brother of Steve Harman, one of my best friends in Billings. David is a lawyer in Libby, and he agreed to host me on my stay there. He has lived there since the 1970s when he took a job working on the dam. At that time, Libby was a AA school and competitive against the biggest cities in Montana in all sports. They won the AA basketball tournament in 1966, and they were among the top teams in the state when I was in high school. David raised three kids in Libby and developed a solid practice. An avid tennis player, David spends a couple of months in San Diego every year just playing tennis, partly because there's nobody from his age group in Libby that's good enough to give him solid competition. But it's clear that David loves Libby.

David's devotion to fitness showed right away. Although he's in his late sixties, he is one of those guys who seems to be most comfortable when he's in motion. When I first arrived, he took me on a power walk around his neighborhood and peppered me with information about Libby. I could feel the pain in his voice when he talked about the strain the asbestos issue has been on Libby's residents.

"One winter when I was in San Diego, I introduced myself to the guy I was playing against, and when he asked where I'm from, I told him Libby. 'Oh, the asbestos capital of the world!' he said." David looked down, shaking his head. Eventually he would tell me that his wife left in large part because of the stress of the situation.

But he poured out positive information about Libby with the same enthusiasm one might expect from a native of one of the most amazing cities in the world. He told me about their new hospital, where he later took me for lunch. He took me on a tour of the new fitness center, a state-of-the-art facility that had attracted a large membership. When I asked about the biggest draw to Libby, he said, without hesitation, "quality of life." It is indeed a beautiful area, surrounded by pine-covered mountains. We later visited the Libby Dam, the surrounding area of which had been developed into a campground. There were play structures for the kids, multiple picnic tables, boat launches, and platforms a hundred yards out in the lake for swimmers. The area was stunning, serene. I asked whether this was an area that attracted people who liked to hide from the world.

"Oh yeah," David laughed, "criminals used to come up here all the time in the old days."

For my entire visit, David listed the positive things that were happening in his town. But when I drove down the main streets of Libby, nothing I saw indicated an upswing. Nothing even indicated a reason to be optimistic. The lumber mills that once dominated the economy in Libby were all gone. And of course the mines were also gone.

David told me about a federal law, the Equal Access to Justice Act, which required that the government cover the attorney fees for anyone who filed suit against the government, provided the plaintiffs won the case.

"The regulations for logging and mining are so complicated," David explained, "that if someone wants to find a way to challenge any proposed operation, it's almost guaranteed that they'll find something." David said lawyers are taking advantage of this legislation to file suits by the score, which has clogged the courts with lawsuits and brought the logging and mining industries to a standstill. I later heard this same claim from a sheep rancher. It's no wonder, I thought, that when you asked someone from Northwestern Montana what's wrong with the logging industry, the first thing they said was "environmentalists." From their perspective, the evidence is overwhelming.

But of course the real story is way more complicated. After all, there is no other town in Montana whose residents were more at threat than Libby. Problems with the environment are part of the history of nearly every industry in Montana, and finding a way to extract our resources in a way that doesn't damage the local ecology and its people needed to become a bigger priority. If it weren't for people bringing these issues to light, Libby's population would be dying at a higher rate than they already are. The trick to figuring out how to use our resources at the lowest possible risk has long been a challenge in Montana, as we'll see in several other chapters. It is, in part, for this very reason that Montana has one of the most environmentally aware constitutions in the country.

David took me to the Chamber of Commerce office, and
the director there shared David's enthusiasm for Libby. She
rattled off a list of events scheduled for every weekend until
the end of summer, including the Chamber Duck Race, the
Kootenai Highland Gathering, and the Kootenai River Quilt
Fest. Quilts! Ducks! Who wouldn't be excited? Her excitement
made me wish I was going to be in town. She was also clearly
convinced that Libby was on the rebound.

But as I left town, I stopped at a funky little coffee shop and
I asked the woman at the counter how long the business had
been there. "I opened the shop thirty-three years ago, when
I was forty." Other than her curly gray hair, she did not look
seventy-three, and I took special note of the fact that this place
offered a wide variety of products that promoted healthy food,
meditation, and so forth. She practiced what she preached, and
she was fit, with that healthy glow to her skin.

"From what I've gathered in my stay here, it looks like this
place is on the upswing," I said.

"Really?" She smiled, with a look that was kind but questioning. Perhaps I had been talking to the wrong people, I
thought.

"Well that's what most of the people I talked to seem to
think."

She shook her head. "I've always been a very optimistic person," she said. "But I don't see that."

She went on to tell a story about meeting with the director of the new hospital. She said they were planning to open a
coffee shop in the hospital, so she and the owners of the other
coffee shops in town arranged a meeting to try to talk him out
of it.

"He doesn't get it," she said. "We told him that any one of
us, or all of us, would be more than happy to deliver coffee,
and he nodded and said all the right things, but it was clear he
wasn't about to budge. So a few days later, he came in here, and
I walked right up next to him, and I nudged his pocket...I just
kept tapping my hand against his wallet, and I said, 'Unless it
gets you here, you don't understand how important this stuff

is.' And I think he finally started to get it, because his wife came in the other day and bought a few things."

She still didn't know whether they were going to open a coffee shop in the hospital, but she said it over and over again. "Some of the people here just don't get it that you need to support the local businesses or we'll never make it. This town will never survive."

THE NEXT TWO TOWNS I visited both claimed to have the lowest per capita income in the state. I would eventually encounter two other counties that made the same claim, which just goes to show how competitive people can be when it comes to having some mark of distinction. "We're the worst!" "*No, we are!*" People are funny.

But on the positive side, the drive from Libby to Thompson Falls was one of the most beautiful stretches of highway I'd ever seen. The land around Highway 56 seems to have fallen into place to accommodate this narrow road, with the Bull River running alongside, and the mountains stretching up on either side. It was a foggy the day I made this trip, and the fog seemed to somehow bring out the green in this incredibly lush valley, hovering just above the trees like a layer of cotton.

Like most towns in this part of the state, Thompson Falls came into being because of the railroad. But the original source of jobs in Thompson Falls was logging, with mining a close second. All three of these industries have pretty much come to a halt here, which explained the lack of income. There was one lumber mill, Thompson River Lumber, just outside of town, but according to the locals, there used to be eight within a forty-mile range. Like its neighbor, Libby, Thompson Falls was having a hard time providing jobs, especially for its younger people.

The town was named for David Thompson, a cartographer who charted much of western Canada and the northwest corner of the United States in the late 1700s. Some consider Thompson the greatest geographer who ever lived, and the fact that he mapped out 4.9 million square kilometers of land in North America seems to support that claim. Despite his accomplishments, which also included a successful career as a fur trader, Thompson was broke and living in obscurity when he died. He was buried in an unmarked grave. His stamp on Canadian and American history wasn't appreciated or acknowledged until decades after his death. Thompson's legacy somehow seemed to fit this little town, which also felt forgotten. But Thompson Falls had its own charm. It snuggled up against a beautiful stretch of the Clark Fork River, and the mountains surrounded it like protective big brothers. Because of its beauty, the town has attracted a large number of retirees in recent years. And like many small towns in Montana that attract tourists, it liked to show off its local artists.

DOUG IS A VISUAL ARTIST who volunteers at an artists' co-op on Main Street in Thompson Falls. He grew up on a sheep ranch just outside of town but left the area to pursue a career as a teacher. Although he left Thompson Falls, he never left Montana, moving around to several different school districts before retiring and—in what was to become an increasingly familiar story—decided to return to the town where he grew up. He now lived with his parents on the ranch where he was raised, although they no longer ran the place. They leased out the land to other local ranchers.

Doug's memories of the Thompson Falls of his youth were happy ones, much like those of many small-town boys, burning the point (driving up and down Main Street, looking for girls or someone to buy beer) in their parents' cars, or frequenting the local movie theater. He told me how exciting it was when they finally got a phone on the ranch. They were on a party line, and Doug said that one of their neighbors was notorious for listening in on others' conversations. She was also known to be fond of baking, so one day when Doug was on the phone with his cousin, he heard the familiar breathing. He made a sniffing noise and said, "Hey, do you smell cookies burning?" which was followed by a squeal, and the click of a receiver. Minutes later, as the boys were still laughing, she came back on the line just long enough to say "That wasn't very nice!"

"The biggest change here is all the retirees moving in," Doug told me. "This place seems to attract a lot of them. And the young people are moving away because there aren't any jobs. So it's become an older town. There aren't a lot of kids around." It wasn't hard to imagine why retirees would be attracted to a place like Thompson Falls. I found it quiet and peaceful, with the familiar, friendly atmosphere of most Montana towns. But just up the road in a small town called Trout Creek I got a taste of the cautious nature of small Montana towns. After arranging to meet a friend for lunch in a small local café, I entered and the place went completely silent. Heads turned. Eyes bugged out a little. I was a stranger.

And the mood never changed. It was the quietest café I've ever been in, with no background music and the conversation so muted that it felt as if saying something in full voice might get us kicked out of the joint. I wanted to ask my friend what it was like to live here, but private conversation was impossible. So we talked in hushed tones about things that wouldn't attract too much attention. But it never did get comfortable.

THE VOLUNTEER WORKING AT the Sanders County Museum in Thompson Falls was a delightful character, an older man who couldn't hear a word anyone said. I would find as I went further along that most of these small-town museums are all pretty quiet, with not a lot of visitors, but because I didn't know that yet, it didn't strike me as odd that this museum was busy that day. The old man tottered around asking each of the visitors where they were from, and you could just see from the look on his face that he was delighted to be there and couldn't wait to have someone ask him a question so he could be useful. He smiled at everyone through glasses so thick they looked like frosted glass, and he asked questions in a voice like Andy Devine, one of the character actors they used to trot out for every Western ever made. The buddy of the main character.

There was a young family there, and at one point a little blond girl came rushing down the stairs, trying to keep up with her sister, asking anyone who would listen where her daddy was. The old man somehow heard her, and it became his mission to find the answer to her question. He did not hear the mother tell the little girl that her father was in the restroom. So he started to climb the stairs, which was a task. He moved slowly, chuckling to himself, and making an occasional noise that indicated some physical ailment that made this climb painful.

The little girl raced up the stairs past him, clueless, and he chuckled again, following her, asking her whether she found her daddy. She didn't answer, and he continued to the top of the stairs, where I could hear his heavy footsteps, wandering, looking for the father, who by this time had emerged from the restroom and was looking at the displays downstairs. Everyone else in the museum was oblivious to the fact that the old man was still on a mission. And it warmed my heart to think that our state is still full of people like this. People who worry about things like a little girl being separated from her father.

ALTHOUGH I READ THAT Superior, Montana, had a population of more than eight hundred people, it seemed much smaller, tucked in at the base of the Bitterroot Mountains. What was *not* surprising was the fact that Superior was founded as a logging and mining community. One look at the surrounding area and you could almost see a trail of rugged prospectors leading their pack horses into these fertile hills to spend months sluicing the local rivers and streams. Or a line of wagons laden with thick logs winding their way down a narrow trail.

It had become part of my routine to drive around each town upon my arrival and look for buildings, businesses, or landmarks that might be of interest. In Superior, this drive took about ten minutes, but I did spot a fascinating building on one of the main streets. It looked like an old school converted for small businesses. I had already seen how many small Montana towns included such services as yoga studios and CrossFit gyms, and here in this beautiful old building, I was surprised to find a massage therapist and a coffee shop. There couldn't have been more than twenty businesses in the whole town, and they had a massage therapist!

But it was the coffee shop that called to me, as I am addicted to lattés.

The owner of the shop was not a native of the area and in fact had moved here from California. She told me that with a hint of embarrassment, as if she had become accustomed to a negative response. But she didn't look like someone who had made much of an effort to hide her roots, given her heavy makeup, studded belt, and manicured nails. She seemed relieved when I told her that I had lived in San Francisco for twelve years. When I asked her why she liked Superior, she stated an oft-repeated litany about quality of life. She seemed genuinely happy, although the more questions I asked, the more she also seemed blissfully unfamiliar with the area.

Finally, I asked where the local museum was.

She blinked a couple of times, her eyes lifting to the sky. "I don't think there is a museum here."

I found the museum two blocks from the coffee shop.

More accurately, I found the library, which also housed the museum. The museum was closed, but a sign announced that special tours could be arranged. So I asked the librarian, and she eagerly made a phone call. I started to protest, but it was clear that she wanted so badly to be helpful that I didn't want to insult her. And I was very happy that I trusted my instincts.

Ten minutes later I met Kay Strombo, who turned out to be one of the most enthusiastic tour guides ever. Kay is the kind of person I'd love to introduce to people who have stereotypical ideas of what Montanans are like. Smart, and not just about her area, Kay was a slim older woman, with bright eyes and a ready smile. She spoke with a low, steady voice and made references to other parts of the world, showing great sophistication in her description of how Superior had changed. I have known way more people like Kay in my time in Montana than my friends back East would ever imagine.

It turned out that the building holding the museum and library used to be the local hospital. It was small for a library…

and even smaller for a hospital, it seemed. But Kay had an en-
cyclopedic knowledge of the building. So much so that I had
a hard time keeping up. The building was first built at a cost
of only $27,000. It closed as a hospital in 1974 and became the
library/museum two years later.

Then she started in about Superior.

Gold was first discovered in the area in 1869, near Cedar
Creek. And of course this brought many ambitious prospectors to the area. But unlike many Montana towns that sprung
up because of mining, Superior was already a thriving community before its local gold strike, due to the construction of the
Mullan Road. The government had long been planning some
kind of passage to accommodate the influx of people flocking
to the West, and an engineer named John Mullan was finally
hired to take on the task. Mullan began planning construction
in 1854, but his plans were interrupted by the Yakima War, a
conflict between the US government and the Yakima tribe of
southern Washington. So his crew of about two hundred men
had to wait to begin construction until 1859. The road—and
in a minute I'll explain exactly what we mean by a road—led
from Fort Walla Walla in Washington and eventually trailed
through the mountains to Fort Benton, right along the Missouri River where the steamships docked. The "road" was
twenty-five feet wide, narrower than the width of a single lane
street by today's standards. And of course they didn't have the
resources for gravel. So it was really just a trail for horses and
wagons that would have previously been forced to wend their
way through whatever halfway flat stretch of land they could
find in this rugged country. The effect of carving this narrow
trail (now long gone) out of the wilderness was immense, leading to increased travel and ease in shipping supplies. Looking
at the mountains and heavy timber around Superior, I found
it hard to imagine how anyone traveled anywhere back then,
much less managed to haul lumber and brick and stone in to
build their houses and businesses.

Because travel was so slow, there tended to be a new town
every twenty or thirty miles, and Superior was one of those

towns. One of my favorite facts that Kay shared about this period is that, in the early years, camels were frequently used to haul supplies along the Mullan Road.

"So they were planning their big party for the Fourth of July in 1865," Kay began, "and a huge herd of camels was hauling all of the booze from somewhere. But there was another group going the opposite direction, led by a pack of mules." Kay started laughing. "Well, mules and camels apparently do not get along very well, so before they knew it, these animals starting going after each other, and that ended up being one of the driest summers in the history of Superior." She ended the story with laughter before moving on to the next topic.

Ultimately, the rocky ground in the area proved to be too hard on the softer hooves of camels, and they were replaced by sturdier animals.

In 1895 the Northern Pacific made its way to Superior, and the town's growth continued, with active mining, logging, and all the services necessary for the growing population. The construction of the railroad also led to the growth of some rougher towns in the county, most notably a town called Taft, which housed many of the men who helped build a nearby tunnel. Taft at one time boasted a population of close to three thousand people, mostly men, as well as another three thousand in surrounding tent camps. At its height, the town featured twenty-seven saloons, and an estimated two to five hundred canaries, the local term for prostitutes. There was also a murder every week. So Taft would certainly give McCarthyville a run for its money as the worst town in Montana to raise a family.

"Maybe the best story we have about Superior," Kay said, "is about a Bible salesman named Archie Bailey. He came here and booked a room at the Superior Hotel in 1908. He convinced the manager to put a Bible in every room in the hotel, and so the Superior Hotel was the first hotel in America to have a Gideon Bible in every room."

Kay told me much the same story that I had heard in Libby and in Thompson Falls, about how the death of the logging and mining had caused the population here to consistently decline.

The last mill in the area closed in 1994. The Amador Mine, which once produced silver, gold, and copper, along with several other minerals, had been closed for many years. The main source of income here, Kay said, is the county, and she estimated that 30 to 40 percent of the population received some kind of government assistance. Of course that included Social Security for the high percentage of senior citizens.

I said farewell to Kay Strombo feeling as if my life had been enriched by spending time with someone who cared so deeply about our history and its people. The museum in Superior wasn't big—not big at all—but she kept me engaged for more than two hours, and finally took me into a room where they were gathering and organizing their archives, a task that probably would not get done if it wasn't for Kay. It's not too much to say that we owe our collective history to people like Kay.

As I left Superior, I stopped by the coffee shop and told the barista where the museum was.

So what happened to these towns? One look around and you could see that there was still plenty of timber in the area. Even an untrained eye like my own could see that some of it was even overgrown, probably in need of harvesting to lower the risk of fires. But the lumber industry had come to a virtual standstill around Superior and, indeed, most of Montana.

The answer to how communities like Superior got to this place depends on who you talk to. For many, the dreaded E word was the immediate response. When I asked that group of businessmen in Kalispell why the lumber industry wasn't as strong there as it once was, one of them chuckled and said that there were a lot of people "who'd like to see a few environmentalists tied to those trees when they cut them down."

That might sound a little shocking, but after seeing how depressed the economy was in some parts, I could understand their desire to find someone to blame.

But the subject needs a deeper look to really capture why the economy left these towns behind. Of course the environmental movement has had a tremendous impact on how business is done. But that's just one piece in the puzzle. And of course, it has to be pointed out that their actions were usually inspired by very real problems, like the sawdust "teepee" burners that plagued Missoula for decades. A group of women finally rose up to protest these large metal teepees, where lumber companies burned their refuse and threw clouds of toxic gases into the air. Because Missoula is located where three valleys converge, this pollution had no escape route. Pollution was literally smothering the city until this group, called GASP (Gals Against Smog Pollution), helped raise awareness and put the pressure on the companies to do away with the teepees.

But there were other issues that weren't quite so cut and dried. The theory of how a forest should be harvested still draws varying opinions, with strong debate between "clear cutting" and "selective cutting." Clear cutting, which is pretty much just as it sounds, involves cutting an entire area at once, then allowing it to grow back as a new forest. The most obvious advantage to this method is cost. It is much cheaper and so much easier than cutting the more mature trees individually (selective cutting), then allowing the forest to grow back naturally.

Unlike many environmental issues, this one doesn't have much middle ground. So the conflict between environmentalists and people in the industry (including the US Forest Service) has been drawn along a pretty definite line.

There are quite a few drawbacks to clear cutting, including the fact that because they generally grow one species in these new growth areas, they are susceptible to disease, where a single disease or insect can wipe out an entire forest. Of course this can happen with either method, but clear cutting makes a forest more susceptible. There is also the increased erosion of clearing away such a large area, impacting stream and river health, and the increased risk of flooding because of the lack of deep roots. Add to this the argument that clear cutting creates fewer jobs because it is done almost entirely by machine, while selective cutting needs to be done by small groups of loggers.

This last notion has its faults, though, especially considering that the ban on clear cutting has led so many of these companies to shut down. Plus the more logs that are cut, the more jobs are created within the pulp and paper industry.

It has been a contentious, ugly fight at times, especially when the environmentalists took their protests so far as to drive spikes into trees, leading to damaged machinery, not to mention the increased risk of serious injury in an industry that is already extremely dangerous.

Unfortunately, this is an issue in which the two sides have been unable to reach a compromise. Like so many of the industries in our state, this one has become a power struggle, and although the environmentalists may consider themselves the winners in this fight, it's hard to agree when so many jobs have been lost. It's one of those situations where I can appreciate both sides of the argument but I can't fully agree with either of them.

Logging used to be among the leading sources of income in Montana, although we have never produced more than 1 percent of the nation's lumber. In 1909 there were 30 sawmills in or around Kalispell alone, with an annual cut of 150 million board feet of lumber. At that time the lumber mills were shipping about 3,500 railroad cars of lumber per year. These mills provided much of the lumber for the Anaconda Copper Company, not to mention the railroads that were being built here.

But the height of the logging industry in Montana actually came during the 1940s, and because of the need during the war and the advent of improved machinery, production during that period was more than double what it had been in the early part of the century. In 1948, there were 434 mills in Montana, producing nearly 600 million board feet of lumber a year.

Today in Montana, 12.9 million acres of forestland are considered "suitable for harvesting," according to the Montana Wood Products Association. But the industry reached a post–World War II low of less than 400 million board feet of production in 2009, after peaking at about 1.5 billion board feet in

1990. And although those numbers may seem high compared to the 1940s, with increased technology, it doesn't translate to a high number of jobs. As of March of 2015, there were only seven major saw mills (those that produce more than 2 million board feet per year) operating in Montana, and only about seven thousand employees in the industry statewide.

Unlike mining, logging relies on a renewable resource, so when you look at a place like Libby or Superior, with the trees thick as hair, you have to think that it's a shame they haven't been able to keep this industry going. Between the environmental issues and conflicts over access to forested land, timber production often gets tangled up in the courts.

WHICH BRINGS US TO Missoula. No other town in Montana brings up such a combination of mixed feelings for me than Missoula. Also known as Zootown, or Berkeley, Montana, Missoula has a very complex and interesting history. Because it started as a logging town, for many years there wasn't much to distinguish it from other towns in this part of the state. Missoula actually started out as a small trading post called Hellgate but moved a few miles from its original location and was renamed Missoula Mills, which was later shortened.

Four significant developments in the late nineteenth century altered the dynamics of Missoula in ways that were significant and completely different from each other. The first was the building of Fort Missoula. The second was the arrival of the railroad. The third was its designation as the site for the first college in the state. The fourth was a huge fire.

Missoula is known today for being the most diverse city in the state, due mostly to the fact that the University of Montana focuses more on the arts, giving the town a more liberal bent. But this is also fascinating because of the fact that this town was the site of some of the worst racial prejudice in our state's history. This wasn't the fault of the townspeople, though. During World War II, from 1941 to 1944, Fort Missoula imprisoned over one thousand Italians, more than one thousand Japanese, and twenty-two German nationals. None of these people were ever charged with an actual crime. So to give the story a little Missoulian twist, maybe there's a little bit of karma going on here that this town now treats its minorities, for the most part, with the kind of respect the rest of the state should envy.

What I find most amusing about Missoula, though, is that there is a sort of competition between this place and Bozeman for the hippest place in Montana. They are both very snippy about each other, and it runs much deeper than the rivalry between the colleges and their sports teams. It's almost like a sibling rivalry.

The snobbery in Missoula is much different than the snobbery in Bozeman. While Bozeman snobbery conveys the attitude that they really don't care whether you think they're the best town in Montana, Missoula works a little harder at it. I lived in San Francisco for twelve years, and Missoula reminds me very much of that city in that people put a lot of effort into appearing to be spiritually grounded and open-minded. And many of them are. But there's an interesting phenomenon that takes place when you have an entire city that is obsessed with this image.

When I lived in San Francisco, it became easy to assume that most of the people I met shared the same beliefs I did. And of course you hear over and over again when you live in San Francisco that it's such an amazing place, and you must feel so lucky to live there. It becomes impossible after a few years to not believe your own press. And in many ways, it's not such a bad thing. San Francisco is an amazing place. Missoula is also an amazing place.

But after a while, you start to notice that most folks in San Francisco, which has such a strong reputation for being open-minded, are actually very narrow in their views. The underlying message is basically, "We are very open-minded as long as you agree with us."

This is my impression of Missoula. And I say this with great fondness, because I've lived it. And I'm still—eight years after leaving San Francisco—trying to figure out how to incorporate conflicting ideas. Because it has become way more important to me as I get older. I don't find the same degree of comfort that I once did in writing people off just because I jump to certain conclusions about them from a few statements or a few actions.

So yes, I love Missoula. Some of my favorite Montanans live here.

But I also find it very hard to visit Missoula, mostly because I never feel like I'm in the club. You especially feel it as a writer. Which is ironic, because Missoula writers seem to complain more than any others in the West about being snubbed by the literary elite in the East. But if you are a Montana writer who didn't study at U of M or don't live in Missoula now, forget it. They don't show up at your readings. They don't invite you to their gatherings when you're at the book festival. It would be amusing if it didn't hurt so much.

I eventually realized that these gatherings of book people in Missoula remind me a little of being invited to the home of a family that is made up of remarkable people who know how remarkable they are. In families like this, their entire focus when they're together is to prove to themselves and to the others that they are remarkable enough to be part of the family. They are so intent on impressing and outsmarting and loving and killing each other that it takes up all of their energy. If you take this personally, you are missing the fact that they're so obsessed with each other that they don't have a clue you're in the room.

Once you realize this about Missoula, it's much easier to accept. And you are left with the realization that there are a lot of amazing things about Missoula.

There are many towns in Montana that have a farmer's market, but Missoula's is the best. There are many towns in Montana that have food co-ops, but Missoula's is the best. There are many towns in Montana that have a merry-go-round, but... wait, that's not true.

MISSOULA WAS MY FIRST stop on my tour of the state, and although I met and interviewed several people while I was there,

I would later look back at my notes and realize that I didn't
have a clue what I was looking for yet. I didn't know what
shape this book would take. Plus I've never been a big taker
of notes to begin with, so most of my notes had little bearing
on what I eventually wanted to address—which was a shame
because a friend of mine had arranged a meeting with a fascinating couple, Dale and Coby Johnson.

When we sat down at the Liquid Planet Coffee Shop, Coby
looked upset, and she quickly revealed why. They had just left
their house where a baby deer was nesting in their back yard.
The fawn's mother had been hit by a car and killed, and after calling the city authorities, they had been informed that
they weren't able to do anything until they could verify that
the mother was dead, which they hadn't been able to do. Coby
and Dale knew enough about wildlife to realize that the fawn
was probably going to die without proper care, and they were
upset about it. I felt as if I was interrupting something that was
way more important than my interview, but they also seemed
more than happy to talk.

Dale, a tall, slender, and distinguished-looking fellow in his
seventies, had a fascinating history. He came to Missoula in
the 1950s to teach at the university and eventually went on to
work for Senator Lee Metcalf. After Metcalf's retirement, Dale
worked with K. Ross Toole, one of the preeminent historians
of Montana, to compile the Mansfield Room at the University's
Maureen and Mike Mansfield Library.

"So was Missoula kind of conservative when you moved
here?" I asked. "Or was it already pretty progressive?"

Both of them jumped at that question. "Oh no, we were way
ahead of our time even then," Coby said, and she went on to
tell about her involvement in GASP, the women's group that
shut down the burn teepees. Dale talked about Metcalf being
a strong supporter of conservation way before it was fashionable, even though he came from Stevensville, which is a much
more conservative town in Ravalli County.

I left Coby and Dale feeling as if I had missed a big opportunity to mine a rich resource of material, and I was too em-

barrassed to contact them later. As we said goodbye, I could almost feel that they knew as well as I did that they were dealing with someone who hadn't quite figured out what he was doing.

It is one of the more humbling aspects of writing that you have to show how ignorant you are to begin the learning process. I would certainly prefer to start the process as an expert, but of course that's not how learning works.

Over the next couple of days, I went to hear a reading at Fact & Fiction, one of the best bookstores in Montana, from Colorado writer Laura Pritchett, who had just come out with an excellent novel called *Stars Go Blue*. This book, about a young woman dealing with her father's dementia, would later win the High Plains Book Award at a ceremony I attended in Billings.

I also met Katie Kane, a literature and cultural studies professor at the university who comes from an Irish family in North Dakota. Kane's interest in her heritage ties her closely with the Native American community and, in fact, she wrote an excellent article about how the Irish and Native Americans have become kindred spirits through history because of their shared experience of persecution. Kane draws a strong parallel between events in Ireland and the Sand Creek massacre, in which Colonel John Chivington led a raid that killed and mutilated close to two hundred men, women, and children. It was at this event that Chivington was said to have uttered the famous line, "Kill them all; nits make lice." But Kane's research led her to discover that the origin of this horrible phrase was actually an anonymous poet who was writing about a very similar, and even more brutal, massacre by Oliver Cromwell that took place in 1649 at the end of eight years of warfare. In Drogheda, Ireland, Cromwell and his troops breached the defenses of the Irish army and, between September 9 and 11, slaughtered 3,552 people.

The anonymous poet obviously applauded this action, writing:

> for then, brave Sir Charles Coote
> …I honour, who in's fathers stepps so trod

As to the Rebels, as the Scourge, or Rod
Of the Almight: He (by good advise)
Did kill the Nitts, that they might not growe lice

Since the 2010 earthquake in Haiti, Kane has traveled there twice to help out with victims of that catastrophe. People in Missoula do not do activism halfway.

Later I met up for coffee with Barb Schwartz Karst, who was in my class at Billings West High in 1976. After starting out as a high school art teacher, Barb has gone on to become a well-respected painter in Missoula. She has lived here for almost thirty years and has her own studio, where she produces abstracts that are often painted on old pieces of machinery or weathered wood rummaged from old buildings.

All of these people I met love Missoula, and I certainly understand why. It is a place that supports artists and people who think outside the box, people who challenge the status quo. It's not unusual to see colored hair or even dreadlocks in Missoula, whereas in my hometown dramatic fashion statements are rare, despite a population of over 100,000 people.

FOR MOST OF ITS FIRST 100 years, Missoula relied primarily on lumber as its main source of revenue. But in 1910 a massive forest fire broke out along the border between Idaho and Montana. Over the course of a couple of weeks—mostly two days—three million acres of timber burned. The fire could reportedly be seen from as far away as Denver. One-third of the town of Wallace, Idaho, went up in flames. Just before this fire, there was a plan in the works to do away with the Forest Service. Instead, this fire brought about legislation for a *larger* Forest Service, with more watchtowers, better training for firefighters, and the development of smoke jumpers. And the Montana headquarters was in Missoula. So even though timber production is no longer the force it once was in Missoula, the Forest Service is still a strong presence. In fact, one of the largest Forest Service experimental stations in the country is in Missoula.

But the presence of logging created a study in contrast in Missoula that is typical of many towns in Montana. For the next several decades, the timber industry provided an abundance of jobs for the working class in Missoula. But while the mills flourished, the by-product of their operations slowly wore down Missoula's natural resistance, and it became one of the most polluted cities in America. Because of the convergence of valleys I mentioned earlier, the air can still get so bad that the city passed an ordinance in 2009 that outlaws the use of woodstoves. But for decades, that was not an issue that people were willing to face. The impact on the job market would have been too profound.

Missoula County is also the site of one of the first as well as one of the largest EPA Superfund sites in the state. If you're counting, that makes Montana the home of three of the largest Superfund sites in the country.

In 1981, during a standard test for water quality, four wells near Bonner, just ten miles east of Missoula, showed traces of heavy metals. The EPA was called in, and it soon became evident that this was not a minor issue. After a two-year study, the EPA determined that the Milltown Dam, which was built in 1908 by William Clark to supply hydroelectricity for his local sawmills, had been collecting toxic materials for decades. After years of mining along the Clark Fork River by the Anaconda Copper Company, sediment that was thick with heavy metals had been building up from the dam all the way back to the Warm Springs Ponds, about 100 miles upstream.

Not surprisingly, this was one more case in which the residents of that area had been complaining for years about the quality of their water. It was clear to them way before this study was ever considered that something was wrong. The dam was finally designated as a Superfund site in 1992, and after several more years of study, the EPA established a plan that included removal of about three million tons of sediment, as well as destruction of the Milltown Dam. They also planned to build a bypass channel to route the river around the dam.

The dam was breached in May 2006, at which point about

300,000 cubic yards of sediment was removed. The breach was small in order to reduce the level of contaminants released into the river. According to a *New York Times* article from 2006, if they had released the water quickly, the rush of water would have scoured the bottom of the reservoir and brought the buildup of metals into the fresh water on the other side, probably choking the river, not to mention killing untold numbers of fish. According to the EPA website, this project is still ongoing, at a cost to taxpayers estimated at $120 million.

Ironically, one of the dump sites for all of this contaminated sediment is near a town called Opportunity. And as you can probably imagine, they are not happy about it.

So MISSOULA HAS OFTEN faced a dilemma familiar to many towns in Montana. Did the price of production balance out the benefits? And concern for health usually wins out in Missoula. For example, they recently procured a $30 million grant to redo all of the stoplights in Missoula in order to cut down on the use of fossil fuels by keeping traffic flowing rather than idling.

The downside of all this, as mentioned before, is that the lumber industry has all but disappeared in this part of the state. But Missoula has transformed instead into a town that relies on the university and its two hospitals to provide many of the local jobs. Although so many towns have been hit hard by the decline in jobs from the industry that first put them on the map, in Missoula these new job sources have proven to be more than enough. Missoula has grown faster than almost any other town in the state, passing Great Falls several years ago to become the second-largest city in Montana, with just over seventy thousand people.

The biggest influence in Missoula, without question, is the university. Along with a strong program in biology and ecology, the University of Montana has one of the highest-rated creative writing programs in the country. Founded in 1920, it was shaped by the likes of poet Richard Hugo and critic Leslie Fiedler and has produced many accomplished writers.

When William Kittredge took over the program after Hugo's untimely death in 1982, the program didn't miss a beat. Graduates continue to produce highly regarded novels and works of non-fiction. It also became known as a great place for aspiring writers to hang out and drink with such well-known Montana writers as A. B. Guthrie, James Crumley, and others who had reputations as big drinkers. When you get a chance to talk with Kittredge and other long-time members of the writing community about the old days, alcohol is always part of the discussion.

In 2010 Missoula became the first city in the state to pass a non-discrimination ordinance, which prevents discrimination based on sexual orientation. The city has a strong record of supporting the rights of minorities and women. This made it all the more surprising a few years ago when Missoula suddenly had to contend with a rash of sexual assaults. Or, more accurately, Missoula had to contend with a scandal about the way these cases were handled.

Part of the reason these cases drew national attention was because they involved players on the University of Montana football team, but this was just one alarming aspect of the situation. It drew so much attention that when noted journalist and author Jon Krakauer (who also wrote *Into the Wild* and *Into Thin Air*) decided to write about what has become known as the "rape culture" in America, he used Missoula as his example, and even titled the book *Missoula: Rape and the Justice System in a College Town.*

Although he went out of his way to emphasize the fact that he did not choose Missoula because it is any worse than the average college town in America, Krakauer's account, which details several cases over the period of a few years, reveals some disturbing facts about Missoula. From this outsider's perspective, perhaps the most unexpected thing about it was that it exposed many of the same old stereotypical issues that the American public is struggling with in terms of dealing with sexual assault. So in some ways, Missoula isn't special at all.

With so much national attention on athletes and domestic

violence and sexual assault, the fact that, in a very short time, several cases involved players on the team, was troubling. But in the bigger picture, the *more* troubling part was, and still is, the way these cases were handled, first by the police and then by the Missoula County Attorney's Office. Krakauer's account of what each of these women had to go through just to report the incidents was sadly not all that surprising. It has become such a common story that a victim of rape is first treated as if they are lying and then often encouraged (even by other victims) to not press charges given the brutal scrutiny they will have to endure.

I talked to Virginia Bryan, a lawyer in Billings who was part of Montana's first Rape Task Force, which she and other concerned citizens started in the late 1970s. They started the task force because it was almost impossible at the time to get a rape conviction in Yellowstone County. After a young woman was allegedly kidnapped and raped by three men in retaliation for a fight they had with her boyfriend, and her assailants were acquitted, Virginia and her friends had seen enough.

Virginia said reading Krakauer's account of the events in Missoula took her right back to those early days of the task force. "Not much has changed," she said.

It didn't help that the chief of police in Missoula liked to cite a pair of decades-old articles that claimed that almost 50 percent of women who claim they'd been raped were lying. These two articles were both discredited many years ago, and most experts now contend that the percentage is less than 10.

As is often the case, one of the young women who reported being raped by a player on the Griz football team was harassed incessantly from the time the story came out, even though the player had confessed to the crime. In a state where most rural towns plan their school year around the high school football and basketball games, it's not surprising that the University of Montana football program is considered a vital part of the community. They also happen to have been very good in recent years, winning the national championship for their small-college division a couple of times and nearly always finishing near the top of their division. To the most rabid fans, reporting one of their players for a crime is akin to taking a hammer to the Pietà. It's an attack on their religion. And of course many of them resort to the old "boys will be boys" mentality that has become a national scourge when it comes to holding young men responsible for their actions.

When a second woman came forward and accused the starting quarterback of sexual assault, the town didn't know what to think. Again, Krakauer's account shows a pattern in the reactions from both the police department and the county DA's office.

The reason this is worth mentioning here is because it came on the heels of another troubling event, one that took place in Yellowstone County (Billings), where a high school teacher, Stacy Rambold, was convicted of raping one of his students over a period of time. The girl, who was fifteen when these assaults started, committed suicide. When it came time for sentencing, Judge Todd Baugh came to the shocking decision to sentence Rambold to thirty days. Not only that, but Baugh took the opportunity to share some of his thoughts about the young girl in question, calling her "older than her chronological age" and suggesting that she was just as responsible for what happened as Rambold. The fact that Baugh ignored the basic letter of the law for statutory rape, which indicates that the very reason it's a crime is because these children are too young to make these kinds of decisions, was only one of many issues that came up when this case made the national news. It also indicated a long-standing underlying attitude that it's acceptable to place as much or more blame on the victims in rape cases as on the rapist.

To me, one of the things that's important about all of these events is that we have an opportunity here in Montana to serve as an example with regard to gender parity. Montana is a state with a very inconsistent track record in terms of how women have been treated. On the one hand, we were progressive enough to elect the very first woman to Congress. Missoula native Jeanette Rankin was elected to the House of Representatives in

1916, four years before Congress voted to give women the right
to vote. She was fond of saying that she was the only woman
who ever had the chance to vote for a woman's right to vote.
Rankin's terms in Congress—she was elected again more than
twenty years later, in 1940—were mostly quiet, probably due
in large part to the fact that she was the only woman. But she
did cast the only vote against US involvement in World War I,
and she did it again regarding World War II. We also elected a
woman governor, Judy Martz, although most would argue that
this wasn't one of our better choices.

But for a very long time now, we have fallen short of our
responsibility to make sure the women in our state have the
resources and support they need if they find themselves vic-
timized by domestic violence or sexual assault. Following the
events of the past few years in Missoula, a study was done of
Missoula County's track record for investigating and trying
sexual assault cases, and the results were more than troubling.
In Montana, each county attorney's office makes the determination, after reviewing the evidence, about whether to pursue
criminal charges in a reported rape case. And for years, the
Missoula County Attorney's Office actually chose not to press
charges in cases that included signed confessions and eyewit-
nesses. After the recent, University of Montana-related investigation, the Department of Justice decided to monitor the
County Attorney's office for the next two years. And I would
hope that, rather than see this as a reason to dig in our heels
and show how stubborn Montanans can be when the government tells us what to do, it will instead give us an opportunity
to be pioneers.

Women have played a vital role in the history of our state,
developing a sense of community in towns that were cobbled
together with twine and baling wire. They endured years of
solitude in drafty cabins, cooking and chopping wood and
hauling water until their shoulders slouched and their spirits
were beaten down by the relentless wind, snow, and loneliness.
We owe the women of our state the right to be treated with the
respect they deserve.

GWEN FLORIO HAS LIVED in Missoula since 2007, when she got a job as a reporter for the *Missoulian*. If you were to draw up a profile of the ideal Missoulian, someone who would love it there, Gwen would come pretty damn close. She was raised on a wildlife refuge in Delaware, where her father was the manager, so she grew up surrounded by nature, not to mention the mentality of those who value and work to preserve it. Her partner, Scott Crichton, is the recently retired and highly respected director of Montana's American Civil Liberties Union, a job for which he received great acclaim. I met with Gwen and Scott in Billings the day after an impressive retirement ceremony for Scott at The Yellowstone Art Museum, and then interviewed Gwen further on the phone a few months later.

"We have had no problem finding a sense of community in Missoula," Gwen said. "I think a lot of that had to do with the neighborhood where we ended up. We just made fast friends here, and developed strong friendships right away."

Gwen has since left the paper and gone on to publish a series of mystery novels featuring a delightful and strong character named Lola Wicks, who happens to be a journalist. The first two in the series, *Montana*, and *Dakota*, both sold well and won awards. With a new publisher, Gwen has recently released the third in the series, *Disgraced*, which takes place in Wyoming. She has just finished the fourth in the series, which is set on the Navajo reservation in Arizona. Because Gwen is fortunate enough to have developed her own circle of friends in Missoula, her interactions with the local writing community have developed naturally since her books started to do well. She is the first to admit that she doesn't even know most of the local writers that well, but that her experience with them has been mostly positive.

But before she became a successful novelist, Gwen covered the cases that Krakauer discusses in his book, as well as the aftermath of the book's release. I asked for her take on the accuracy of the book, both about the situation with sexual assaults and its depiction of Missoula in general.

"Oh, I thought his book was a very accurate account of the events here," she said. "One thing he really captured was how differently the cases involving members of the football team were handled. Even before all this started, I was amazed at how often we would get incredible backlash from the university whenever we did a story on a crime committed by a member of the football team. I came here from Denver, and of course they have the Broncos there, but I had never lived in a place that was so defensive about its athletes getting charged with a crime."

When asked about her experience with the DA's office, and whether her take on their handling of the matter was similar to Krakauer's, she also answered in the affirmative. "They were very defensive, even though the evidence that they fell down on the job was often very clear, even depressing. I just kept thinking, through the whole process, why don't they just own up to it? It didn't make sense that they couldn't just admit that they could have done a better job."

I asked about her dealings with Kristen Pabst, who was the DA that received the heaviest criticism from Krakauer. I had just read an article—not one of Gwen's—in which many people expressed their support and praise for the way Pabst had handled their cases.

"Didn't I read somewhere that Krakauer never interviewed her?" I asked.

"I think that's right," Gwen confirmed. "But I know he tried, several times. I always found her to be very defensive. She doesn't like criticism. But again, reading through the caseload…the evidence is depressing."

I trust Gwen's perspective on these matters, in particular because I've seldom met anyone who's so perpetually cheerful and generous in her attitude toward others—another reason she seems suited to Missoula. I don't know her well, but every time I've spent time around her, she exudes that kind of positive, calm energy that you can almost feel invading your psyche.

I FIND MISSOULA TO be a fascinating study. While it presents an erudite, sophisticated front, the working class still has a strong presence, rallying around their beloved Griz and buying into that strange notion that has become so prevalent in professional athletics as well, that anything that distracts "the team" is a threat to the very core of their existence.

The larger dilemma is perhaps best represented by a conversation I had with someone on the board for the museum at the University of Montana. "They just built a multi-million-dollar stadium a few years ago, and now they're putting millions of dollars into a study center, just for the athletes at the school," she explained. "Meanwhile, we have a basement full of amazing art by artists from all over Montana, and we don't have room to display it. But we can't even generate a discussion about building a new museum." And as further evidence of this alarming shift in priorities, the university also recently announced that it would be laying off more than 200 university employees due in part to declining enrollment. But after so much has been invested in the athletic program, this turn of events is troubling, especially considering that some of the departments who expect to be hardest hit are among the most respected of the university, including the journalism department.

CHAPTER SIX
Tracks

"The United States as we know it today is
largely the result of mechanical inventions, and in
particular of agricultural machinery and the railroad."
—John Moody

A drive across the Hi-Line of Montana serves as a particularly stark reminder of how much hope the arrival of the railroad must have brought to the people who lived there at the turn of the twentieth century. From Cut Bank, near the entrance to Glacier Park, all the way across the state to Sidney, a distance of 424 miles, you pass through nine counties, in a country that is mostly as flat and treeless as a table.

When I was a kid, I remember being so proud when I noticed that the chase scenes in my favorite Saturday morning cartoons featured the same backdrop repeated over and over again. The creators of these cartoons were obviously more concerned about budget than about realism. But driving across the Hi-Line reminds me of those cartoons. It sometimes feels as if I have passed the same pasture, the same farm, the same buildings, over and over again. Each town along this stretch of highway shares three features: a grain elevator, a railroad station, and a sign pointing north that says "Canada." Not any specific part of Canada. Just "Canada." And many of these towns look very much like the one before in other respects as well. There are too many empty buildings along the main streets, too many houses with boarded-up windows, abandoned cars—too much poverty.

Although some towns along the Hi-Line still rely a great deal on the railroad, the glory days of the railway are long gone. And when you delve deeply into the history, it becomes evident that those days didn't last very long and actually weren't all that glorious. Especially when you consider what the men who created these railways did to achieve their objectives.

In his book *Railroaded: The Transcontinentals and the Making of Modern America*, Richard White outlines the complicated relationship between politics, business, and commerce that made the building of the railroads possible. In fact, it's so complicated that after reading the passage describing their schemes several times, I still don't feel qualified to explain it. Which is part of what made it work. Many of the people who should have monitored the maze of paperwork and trail of money these men created were just as confused. Tax auditors and anti-trust regulators never could untangle the maze enough to determine how corrupt it had become.

The men who masterminded this massive endeavor created fake construction companies, convinced the government to give them land and also approve hundreds of millions of dollars' worth of subsidies, sold stocks and bonds without any intention of paying dividends, and borrowed indiscriminately from whomever was willing to believe in their dreams. And it's not hard to see how people would have bought into those dreams. What could possibly go wrong when you have thousands of people looking for a way to move or travel to this new frontier? But as it turned out, there were many things that can go wrong when companies build a business entirely on speculation.

One of the most interesting aspects of White's account is the fact that this was one of the first examples of American business in which the demand for something was created before it existed. Although there were certainly people who wanted to move west, and many people living in the West who pined for the kind of service a railway could provide, the demand was not strong enough to justify building these railroads, especially in such great numbers. But a few incredibly ambitious men simply decided they would get them built, and then create the demand with a brilliant (and dishonest) campaign of what the West had to offer. And they had plenty of cooperation.

The first town in Montana to hear the click and clack of a train was in Beaverhead County. But the first *effort* to reach Montana came from the Northern Pacific Railroad. Once the first transcontinental railroad was established from Omaha to Sacramento, the Northern Pacific convinced Congress that there was also a need up north. So in 1864, Congress gifted the Northern Pacific with a generous subsidy. But instead of providing all of their support in the form of money, they granted the Northern Pacific a massive swath of land, including seventeen million acres within the Montana Territory. Yes, seventeen *million*. This automatically made the Northern Pacific Railroad the second largest landowner in the territory, behind the US government.

But they faced a huge challenge from the start. Because this was so soon after the Civil War, money for construction was hard to come by. After several false starts, banker Jay Cooke from Pennsylvania stepped forward, providing $100 million to fund the construction. Another of the early obstacles was the fact that the area they were building on was pretty much uninhabited, providing almost no opportunity for immediate profit. So although the construction of the railroad moved quickly, reaching Bismarck, North Dakota (just a little over 100 miles from the Montana border) in 1873, Cooke had overextended himself to the point that his bank went under. The Northern Pacific went into bankruptcy, an event so significant that the entire country went into a financial crisis known as the Panic of 1873. You would think that these men would learn a lesson from this sequence of events, and consider the possibility that this region

simply wasn't ready for such an ambitious venture, but despite
the lack of potential customers, the race to reach Montana had
become an obsession among a group of powerful, ambitious
men. These moguls included Brigham Young's son John W.
Young, and Samuel Hauser, the banker from Virginia City and
later Helena, who tried to persuade the Montana legislature
to provide subsidies for Young's Utah Northern Railroad to
complete a line north from Utah. For once, the legislature said
no to the railroad, rightfully predicting that the competition
between the various companies was strong enough that *someone* would come up with the money. Eventually Jay Gould and
Sidney Dillon of the Union Pacific Railroad bought into the
Utah Northern to form the Utah and Northern Railroad, and
in 1880, the first train reached Dillon, named after Mr. Dillon.

A few months later, in December of 1881, the first train
pulled into their ultimate destination—Butte—and Montana
was never the same.

It had to have been an incredible experience for the people in these small towns in Montana, after years of rumors
and speculation and anticipation, to finally have a locomotive
steam into their midst. Picture the approach of this massive
iron machine, with its tooting whistles, and the chugging engine, the clatter of wheels. The smells and sounds and motion
of the whole thing must have been so foreign to these people,
in a place where the quiet is sometimes as pure as it can get.

Imagine the sense of hope that these machines must have
brought to these dusty, isolated places—the promise of travel,
of supplies, of delivery of their loved ones from distant places.
They must have felt as if their lives had been transformed overnight. And for a time, they were.

In a matter of months, the whole concept of time and space
changed in the West. A town that was one hundred miles away
was suddenly within a few hours' travel time—closer in terms
of time than a town thirty miles away when traveling by horse
or wagon. Towns sprang up based on the simple fact that they
were the perfect distance from a major hub. And other towns
died because they were a few miles too far south or west or

north of the railroad. Towns that felt as if they were perfectly situated because of their access to water were suddenly irrelevant. Politics and money had a whole new vehicle.

Soon after the Utah and Northern reached Butte, the Northern Pacific recovered and renewed its goal of reaching the West Coast. A new group of investors stepped in, led at first by Frederick Billings, a lawyer from Vermont who had become president of the company. But the politics of location soon kicked in, and some powerful men led by Henry Villard—who preferred Portland, Oregon, to Tacoma, Washington, as the final destination of the Northern Pacific Line—orchestrated a takeover by buying up a majority of the stock. Villard, who was already president of the Oregon Railway and Navigation Association, managed to raise $8 million. He not only took over as president of the Northern Pacific but he pushed production at a frenzied pace, leading to a ceremony in 1883 in Gold Creek, Montana, just outside of Helena, where the two converging lines met.

Unfortunately, the romance between the public and the railroad soon wore thin. The Northern Pacific and the Utah and Northern had forged an agreement not to tread on each other's territory so that they could both keep their prices high. And for the most part, their prices were not affordable to a growing number of people who were barely surviving in this new country.

But soon another player came into the picture. And a familiar story emerged. Aside from William Clark, James Hill was perhaps the most unpleasant of a series of entrepreneurs that sank their teeth into the flesh of Montana's resources. Hill was president of the Great Northern Railroad, and it was Hill who decided that another line could be built even farther north of the Northern Pacific, along what would eventually become known as the Hi-Line. Perhaps more than any of the other ambitious men, Hill was driven by hatred toward his competitors. White's book cites several examples, including Thomas Oakes, the president of the Northern Pacific, who said Hill was "out of his mind." William Mellen, Northern Pacific's general manager, told friends that Hill's inability to keep his promises had given him the nickname of "Ananias Hill," after a figure in the Bible whom God struck dead for lying.

Hill had been a major investor in the Canadian Pacific Railway, and was instrumental in building a line from his home state of Minnesota up into Canada. But Hill's ultimate ambition was to build a route from Minneapolis across to the Pacific Northwest. His first move was to establish a partnership with old Minnesota friend Paris Gibson to build a line from Butte, through Helena, to a new town site they planned near the Great Falls on the Missouri River. While they were laying these lines, and building the town of Great Falls, Hill next tried to find a way to access the lands north of the Missouri, through the Hi-Line. But these lands were still considered Indian lands, and President Grover Cleveland, a man who was known for his high sense of morality, was hesitant to grant permission that would likely anger the already wounded Native American population.

But Hill was relentless, and he eventually convinced Cleveland along with Congress to grant him an easement through northern Montana, land that was once again taken away from the Native Americans. Hill pushed his workers forward, beyond reasonable expectations, and within a short time, they had a line from Minnesota to Havre, Montana. But there was still one major impediment in his ultimate goal to reach the Pacific Northwest. As far as anyone knew, there was no easy passage through the Rocky Mountains north of Butte, near what is now Glacier Park. For Hill, insurmountable obstacles were nothing more than challenges.

There had been rumors for years about a forgotten pass in that area. This mystery pass had originally been reported by the brilliant cartographer David Thompson, whom I mentioned earlier as the namesake for Thompson Falls.

Just after Hill and his associates formed the Great Northern Railway, which included the route from Butte to Great Falls, as well as the line from Minneapolis to Havre, Hill asked a man named Elbridge H. Beckler to investigate whether there was any truth to the rumor. Beckler decided to send his location engineer, a man named John Stevens, to search for this mythical pass. Stevens had looked for Marias Pass before without success, but he headed north to try again, hiring a Flathead Indian to serve as his guide. Knowing Hill was not a patient man, Stevens set out immediately, in a blizzard so severe that his Indian guide turned back. But Stevens sensed that he was close, and he pushed on, finding the pass in a moment that must have felt fairly anticlimactic in the freezing cold, all alone. Stevens assessed the situation and decided he had no choice but to keep going or he was going to freeze to death. Stevens barely survived the journey, but he emerged a hero, providing what became the last crucial piece to Hill's dream, which was realized soon after.

I WAS ABOUT A THIRD of the way through my journey by the time I got to the Hi-Line. I had done the entire Western part of the state in one big loop, then returned to Billings to rest up for a week or two. I then worked my way up through the middle of the state, stopping in Helena, on my way to make a big circle up around the Hi-Line. By the time I got a chance to talk to people along the Hi-Line, I thought I spoke fluent Eastern Montanan. It's a language I know well, being from a ranch family from Carter County. But the more people I talked to, and the more time passed, the more I came to recognize certain nuances of this language that I hadn't noticed before.

Among them was the way the people in Eastern Montana build their optimism in small increments.

"We got new desks at the school."

"It looks like we might have a real good basketball team this year."

"They finally paved that street that runs out by the Walmart."

There is no gentle way of saying this, but Eastern Montana has been hard hit, a victim of the dying middle class, the slow decline of small farms and ranches, and the growing reliance on huge operations. People are fighting for a reason to feel relevant, and you can sense it.

THE TOWN OF CUT BANK in Glacier County is known as one of the coldest towns in Montana, which makes it one of the coldest towns in America. We've all heard that saying about waiting five minutes and the weather will change. It's a claim you hear all over the country, but in Montana, you can point to very specific evidence. There are conflicting reports about the biggest drop and the biggest rise in temperature in the country, but one claim about the biggest drop comes in Glacier County, in Browning, where the temperature dropped from forty-four degrees to minus fifty-six degrees (exactly 100 degrees if you'd rather not do the math) in a twenty-four-hour period. This happened in January of 1916.

The largest rise in temperature is also claimed by a town in Montana—Loma, which is in Chouteau County—where the temperature rose from fifty-four degrees below zero to forty-nine degrees (103 degrees!) in a twenty-four-hour period on January 15, 1972.

Cut Bank still has passenger trains that run daily, one in each direction, keeping alive the industry that brought the town to life in 1891. A huge steel bridge was built in 1900, bringing in 250 workers, which helped to grow the town. At that time, the railroads needed a train station every six miles to provide water for the steam engines. Later engines were able to go slightly further, about fifteen miles. Each of these stations required a water tank, a station agent, and section workers. So the railroad provided many jobs. Towns grew up around many of these stations, but as trains became more sophisticated, most of those towns faded away.

Today, a train that stops twice a day is hardly enough to keep the town itself alive. Cut Bank has gone through a lot since then. Like its close neighbor Shelby, the greatest period for Cut Bank may have been the early thirties when a nearby oil boom brought jobs and money into the area at a time when jobs and money were scarce. But in typical boom/bust fashion, that oil boom lasted a short time. Carter Oil, an oil company that was founded in Cut Bank, was bought out by Standard Oil in 1944. There were several oil refineries in the area, but those are all gone now.

Now Cut Bank relies on county jobs, or jobs with the Border Patrol and the Highway Patrol. There are a few jobs for people maintaining the tracks. The population that once peaked at 5,000 people is now about 3,100. And I also found one telling (albeit unofficial and very personal) indicator that things weren't going well for the town. I ordered a prime rib dinner at the Village Dining and Lounge Restaurant, including salad, baked potato, and a huge piece of pie, and it cost me less than fifteen dollars. It was a welcome change from road food, although I must admit that when I'm traveling, I have a strange magnetic attraction to McDonald's, which I never eat when I'm home.

The back seat of my 2006 Subaru Outback, which I dubbed the Fifty-Six Mobile, was piling up with McDonald's wrappers and plastic cups from iced lattés, my morning drink of choice. I would soon learn that these are hard to find on the Hi-Line.

On reflection, Cut Bank was the first of many towns in Central and Eastern Montana that left me feeling sad in the same way that you feel when you visit the family of someone who is dying. There is that period of time before they fully realize that it's almost over, where they are still trying to rally, still hoping that the next meal, the next medicine, the next surgery is going to turn things around. I visited the museum there, where I talked with Director Dennis Seglem, a long-time resident of Cut Bank, and I left with that feeling that I wished I could offer something. I wanted to be one of those people with money to burn who could just write a $2,000 check to help with what appeared to be a never-ending effort to remodel.

But it also brought up the much more difficult and painful question of what makes these places worth saving. It's not a fair question to ask the people who live here, of course. Their emotional investment makes it impossible for them to be objective. And when it comes down to it, I'm not ever sure whether there's an answer to the question. Or whether the answer matters as much as the discussion. Because many of these places feel stuck, trying to cling to an identity that has long ago withered away, and too afraid to let go of that identity to discuss finding a new one. That's what I kept wondering—whether they are having these discussions.

MEANWHILE, SHELBY WAS one of the few towns along the Hi-Line that seemed to resonate with a feeling of optimism. I just happened to arrive in Shelby on the day of their annual fair and parade—also known as the Marias Four County Fair. After living in Montana for most of my life, I have been to more than my share of these small-town fairs. So I knew what to expect. And over the past twenty years, what I've come to expect is a pale imitation of what these fairs and parades *used* to be. Small-town Montana, especially in the eastern half of the state, has become increasingly infused with a feeling of melancholy, a sad reminder of what used to be the highlight of the year, especially for the local kids.

Not so in Shelby. The Shelby parade brought a thick crowd of people to the main street. And the spirit of the event was joyful, optimistic, exciting, although there was nothing particularly unique about the parade itself. It featured the usual array of fire trucks, men driving tiny little cars, members of the local service clubs riding horses, restored old cars, and cute kids on floats. Candy flew from the cabs of vehicles and scattered along the pavement, where children scrambled to fill their plastic bags. Almost as good as Halloween. I was particularly amused by one small boy who wasn't getting his way somehow and had buried himself in the bushes along the main street.

I approached an older couple and told them why I was there. "Well you came to the right people," the woman said. "We're both former county commissioners."

It turned out they were not a couple. Her name was Geneva Sisk, and she married into a longtime ranch family in the area. The man was John Nesbitt. Both of these people thought that Shelby is on the upswing, despite the fact that farming, the main source of income, is on the decline. But unlike many of the Hi-Line towns, Shelby has other options. For one thing, Shelby houses much of the border patrol for northern Montana, as well as the Homeland Security contingent in Montana. I realized that it never occurred to me that we would need a border patrol on the northern border, but of course we do. The realization conjured up the image of a man stealthily opening the back door of a semi, with a passel of pasty people in hockey jerseys tumbling out into an isolated pasture. It's amazing how different our country is depending on where you are. Imagine anyone suggesting a wall on the Canadian border.

Shelby, of course, was one of many towns that was started as a stop for the Great Northern, and it was dubbed Shelby by the general manager, Allen Manvel, who named many of the towns along that route. P. P. Shelby was one of Manvel's associates, a man who would eventually succeed him as general manager, and he was apparently not thrilled with having a "mudhole" serve as his namesake.

It was indeed a place that was isolated from much of the basic essentials needed to make a living, prompting one departing soul to post a sign on his wagon stating: "Twenty miles from water, forty miles from wood. We're leaving old Montana, and we're leaving her for good."

But the town slowly gained some footing, attracting a few small businesses, a hotel. Eventually a man named H. F. Guth, who had inherited a small fortune from a relative just before he moved to Shelby, decided to use his money to build a general store, and his commitment to Shelby had a tremendous impact. Unlike the town's indifferent namesake, Guth eventually became known as its founding father.

But the most fascinating story to ever come out of Shelby is the fiasco that was the Jack Dempsey-Tommy Gibbons fight in 1923. The Dempsey fight was the harebrained idea of a realtor in town who thought it would be an interesting, but completely unlikely, way to promote the town. He didn't really expect the fight to happen.

Somehow, in a series of unexpected developments, Jack Dempsey agreed to come to Shelby and fight for the sum of three payments of $100,000. A representative of Shelby agreed to the sum at a contract meeting in Chicago, despite the fact that he had no authority to approve such a promise. He signed the contract out of fear of being ridiculed. But once the townspeople found out that Dempsey was in, the excitement grew quickly, and the first $100,000 was raised in short order. Dempsey's manager insisted on the second payment before the fight, but that proved difficult to raise until a local business-man stepped forward to provide most of the money. Although Dempsey's manager initially insisted on the third payment as well, he eventually agreed to accept this payment, as well as the purse for his opponent, Tommy Gibbons, from the ticket sales.

At the time, the population of Shelby was only 600 people, but they optimistically built a 40,000-seat arena. Dempsey had earned a $1 million dollar purse for his previous fight, so orga-nizers were optimistic that they would make enough to cover the costs. The Great Northern made arrangements for extra passenger trains to bring spectators to Shelby. The organizers must have imagined a windfall. People were expected to travel from all over the country to see the fight, despite the fact that Gibbons was a relative unknown. Boxing matches in those days were guaranteed draws. But the fact that Gibbons was not considered a strong contender, combined with the distance, proved to be bigger obstacles than they anticipated.

The turnout was a disaster, with only about 8,000 people buying tickets. An estimated 14,000 people protested the ticket prices, and stormed the gates, and tiny Shelby was ill-equipped to handle a crowd of that size. The final take was so low that by the time they paid Dempsey his third installment, there was no money left for Gibbons. Fortunately, the fight led to a career in Hollywood for Gibbons, so he did benefit in the long run.

Shelby managed to recover from this financial hit, most-ly due to oil that had been discovered in the nearby fields in the twenties. This was one of the first oil booms in the state, and it continued to provide steady jobs and income during the Depression. So while the rest of the state limped through the thirties, Shelby was one of the few Montana towns that main-tained a steady economy.

Kelly Addy, a former state legislator who also worked as a city attorney in Billings as well as a Methodist minister, tells a wonderful story about his grandfather, Earl Addy. Grandpa Addy came to Montana in the 1930s with no money but a natural talent for working with engines. Earl was living in Great Falls, and he applied for a job that he saw in the local paper for a mechanic. The man who ran the ad told him that another man had expressed an interest…he also informed Earl that the job was in Shelby. Earl said that was fine, so the man told him that if the other guy didn't show up that evening as he said he would, Earl would get the job. Addy came back, the other guy didn't show, and the employer bought him and his new bride train tickets to Shelby along with two box lunches. They had almost no money.

Grandpa Addy eventually went to work for a man who owned several businesses in Shelby, including an appliance company. Addy was assigned the task of selling propane refrigerators. On one of his deliveries to a local farmer, the customer wasn't home, so Earl took the fridge on to the next farmhouse, where he offered to allow the man to use it overnight if he let him leave it there. The next day, when he came to retrieve it, the man refused to give it back. Earl worked out a payment plan for that man to buy that fridge, and he came back the next day with two more—one for his original customer and another that he delivered to someone else, telling them the same story, that it was intended for a neighbor who wasn't home. Before long he was the top salesman in the whole country.

Earl was successful enough that his boss owed him more money than he could afford to pay. So instead of paying him, he signed over his car dealership to Addy.

Earl Addy's story provides a nice parallel to Shelby's development as a town. Much of the reason that Shelby is doing better than most of the towns along the Hi-Line is due to simple luck of the draw—location, mostly. For one thing, the freight trains that come east through the Marias Pass most often turn south at Shelby toward Great Falls or Billings rather than continuing along the Hi-Line. Shelby also served as headquarters for much of the construction done during the 1960s for the missile silos in much of Western and middle Montana. The population of Shelby reached its height during that decade. And the Addy car dealership was thriving.

At that time, there were several car dealerships, but they are all gone now. It is a common story in the small towns in Central and Eastern Montana, where business has become more and more concentrated in a few urban areas, particularly Billings, Helena, and Great Falls.

Earlier in the day, I went to the fairgrounds to see the usual exhibits, but found that there wasn't much going on. But I did get a chance to observe the judging of a few young kids showing their dogs doing a few basic drills. I struck up a conversation with a young man who was watching his daughter wrestle with her German Shepherd. It turned out that he lived in Conrad, but that he was originally from Billings, my hometown.

"My folks used to own Buck's Bar," he told me.

When he told me their name (Enebo), I realized that my parents were friends with his parents. So I asked my mother about it later, and she told me that Mrs. Enebo taught my father how to do stained glass, one of his favorite pastimes in his later years. This is one of many instances during my journey that remind me of the old saying that Montana is just one big town with a main street running down the middle.

Shelby still serves as one of the few stops for the Amtrak route in Montana, which is called "The Empire Builder," a nickname for James Hill.

Perhaps one of the most fascinating facts about this town of just over 3,000 people is that it serves as the hometown of two of the most famous scientists to come out of Montana. The first is Jack Horner, one of most well-known paleontologists in the United States. Kelly Addy describes Horner in his school days as a kid who couldn't pass any subject except science because he was so obsessed with dinosaurs. Horner is also dyslexic. He discovered his first bone when he was seven, and went on to write several books about dinosaurs, and also to serve as advisor for the *Jurassic Park* movies.

The second scientist, Leroy Hood, who was born in Missoula but grew up in Shelby, has become one of the most renowned specialists in DNA in the country. Hood has received numerous awards and been granted honorary degrees by several reputable institutions. I love the story Kelly Addy tells in which there were three featured speakers at a big international science conference, and two of them were from Shelby, Montana. The third was Stephen Hawking.

THIS LANDSCAPE ALONG THE Hi-Line, with its repetition and its wide openness, can have a hypnotic effect on a person, whether you're driving the straight-as-a-string stretch of Highway 2 or simply staring out across one of the kelly green wheat fields that stretch out for miles on either side.

While Montana is mostly known for its mountains, this landscape makes up at least half of the state, and it has also been known to inspire. Perhaps this is in part because surviving in the vast openness of this part of the state requires a special kind of personality. I'm reminded of a story I recently heard about a family who decided to drive from their home back East to visit Montana. They got to the Dakotas, and they actually got so freaked out by the amount of wide-open space that they turned around and went home.

Empty space, and the lack of people, can create a sense of loneliness that can challenge the mental state of someone who isn't comfortable with their own company. In the homestead days, the combination of isolation, lack of company, and wind often drove people completely insane. The condition was even referred to as "the loneliness" in some parts of the state. But for those who are strong enough to adapt, this kind of quiet serenity often produces people capable of amazing things.

Montana has long been known for its writers. Wallace Stegner, Ivan Doig, Norman MacLean, Richard Hugo, and A.B. Guthrie all either grew up in Montana or spent part of their childhoods here. Many other well-known writers developed a career after moving here later in life, and still others adopted the state after building a successful career. But it may surprise some people to know that Montana also boasts the highest ratio of people per capita who classify themselves as artists.

While Toole County is known for its scientific minds, the next county over, Liberty County, has produced an inordinate number of highly respected artists, in various mediums. Clyde Aspevig, born in the small town of Rudyard, is considered one of the best landscape artists in Montana. And Tami Haaland, who claims Inverness, seven miles from Rudyard, as her hometown, served for two years as poet laureate of Montana. Tami also happens to be Clyde's first cousin. But perhaps the most well-known artist from Liberty County comes from a medium for which Montana is not as well known.

Chester, Montana, in Liberty County, is another small town fighting to stay alive. Just forty miles from Shelby, Chester was one of so many towns situated fifteen miles from the previous one in order to accommodate the railroad. And although passenger and freight trains still make their way through this tiny little town, the railroad has lost most of its impact here. Chester now has a population of a little more than 800 people.

According to musician Philip Aaberg, the most famous citizen of Chester, Liberty County has the smallest decline in the area in terms of income. Which is a bit of a backhanded compliment. It is still declining, and Phil repeats the oft-stated theory that a big part of that decline can be attributed to the fact that small family farms are no longer as viable as they once were.

"Larger farms with less people running them," Phil said.

But Aaberg has that familiar Montana optimism, and much of that seems to be built around the fact that his own businesses are doing well. I would imagine if you talk to all 800 people in Chester, at least fifty percent of them would mention Aaberg as one of the bright spots of Liberty County. Perhaps the most appealing thing about Aaberg is that he was very reluctant to be interviewed for that very reason. "I get too much of the press up here." It's a very Montana thing to say. But he was a perfect choice to talk about the Hi-Line, because after being away from Montana for many years, he has thought a lot about

what this place means to him, and to his work. This is something I have noticed about many other artists in Montana. The
ones who have left and spent time elsewhere often have a deeper appreciation for what Montana has to offer. Although I have
yet to meet Phil in person, photos show a big man, with dis-
tinctly Scandinavian features—ruddy complexion, round face,
accentuated by a full beard.

"I was born in Havre to a long-time Montana farming family that immigrated to Montana in the early twentieth century.
My grandparents first moved to Great Falls, but my grandfather was working for a lumber company there and the company moved him to Chester. My grandfather started a small
farm, and like most people during that period, they struggled
to get by, even spending a few years in the poorhouse."

This term brought me up short. It hardly seems possible
that just a couple of generations ago people were relegated to
poorhouses.

Aaberg showed musical talent from an early age, and when
he graduated from high school, he was accepted to study music at Harvard. After finishing his degree, Phil moved to Iowa,
where he studied the Beethoven sonatas at Drake University.

"Eventually I moved to San Francisco where I had the good
fortune of meeting Elvin Bishop. We got along really well, and
he liked my playing, so I started playing with the Elvin Bishop
Group, and soon after that he hit it big with "Fooled Around
and Fell in Love." For the next several years, I got to live the
life of a rock star. We opened for a bunch of the biggest acts of
the 1970s. But it got to the point where we were often the main
act."

"Was that fun?" I asked.

"Oh, it was a blast. It's everything you can imagine. And
for a guy from Montana, from Chester, where it's one hundred
miles between traffic lights, are you kidding? I got to see so
much of the world."

The gig also catapulted Aaberg's reputation so that he was
in great demand as a studio musician, and with his classical
training, he proved to be adept at playing just about any style

of music, although he always preferred jazz. Aaberg recorded seven albums with Bishop before he decided it was time to stay home, and stick to studio music. "I was really lucky. I got to record with Peter Gabriel, John Hiatt, Roy Rogers and Tom Johnston, the founder of the Doobie Brothers."

But Aaberg eventually tired of playing other peoples' music, as well as the long hours in the studio.

"I got a chance to record a few of my own songs at a studio at Cal State Hayword, and from there I was able to get a recording deal with Windham Hill."

Windham Hill is a label that was developing a solid reputation for solo artists playing what came to be known as "New Age" music. But anyone who has listened to these artists knows that this term gives the wrong impression of the music this label produced. Although it was primarily instrumental, and leaned heavily toward a mellow jazz sound, Windham Hill's music had more depth than the average Yanni or Vangelis record. Artists like John Gorka and fellow Montanan George Winston were also featured on the label, and Aaberg was happy for the opportunity to produce his own music with the label for several years.

"During that time, my wife and I decided it was time to come back, and we moved into the house where I grew up. We converted the house into a bed and breakfast, and then I decided to turn the old grain elevator into my own recording studio."

With his own studio built, Aaberg was able to leave Windham Hill and form his own label, Sweetgrass Music, which features more than his own music although he is clearly the main act.

"My music reflects not only the landscape here but also the lifestyle, where there are long stretches where nothing happens. Some would call it monotony; I call it calm. And then that's followed by a small moment of strong, raw emotion. I depend a lot on emotional triggers in my compositions."

I listened to Aaberg's music a lot while writing this part of the book, because it does capture that very quality of Eastern

Montana, the long periods of quiet, interrupted by an occasional flurry of beauty or fright, or immense sadness. It's all there in pieces like "High Plains," which opens with a simple, quiet melody, builds to a full thunderstorm of heavy syncopation, and then slides into a slow trickle before ending on one single-line repetition of the simple melody. There are also songs that represent specific aspects of life in Eastern Montana, like "Westbound," which replicates the sound of a train. Other songs feature the many influences Aaberg has had in his musical career, from ragtime to his beloved jazz, to classical. His versatility is really astonishing. But the thing I love most about Aaberg's music is the way it conveys the vast loneliness that defines this part of the state. It's difficult to capture that kind of space with photographs or paintings. Even the best writers struggle to describe this place in a way that truly captures the distance, the quiet. So in a way, music is the perfect vehicle.

ASIDE FROM HIS MUSIC, Aaberg also said his bed and breakfast is always busy, serving as a stopping point for people on their way to Glacier National Park. And he says they are surprisingly busy during more than just the summer months.

I came away from my conversation with Philip thinking that he had every right to believe that Liberty County was a strong, growing community. He cited the fact that the schools had not lost nearly as many students as some of the neighboring counties.

Because Aaberg had been gone for so long and came back, I suspected he would have some interesting thoughts about some of the issues I wanted to explore in my journey. And he did. When I brought up the issue of Montana myths, he said, "Well one of the biggest myths to me is that Montanans are independent. The truth is we are very interdependent. As much as people like to think they don't need other people, everyone needs other people to survive. This idea that people up here are completely self-sufficient is ridiculous." He also rejected the notion that Montana men are tougher and more able to handle their own problems. "That whole scene of a guy with a gun, confronting his enemies, has nothing to do with most of the people who've ever lived here. The only rugged individualists in Montana are probably hanging from a rope somewhere," and by that he meant by their own hand.

The thing about Phillip Aaberg's story is that it can't really serve as a model for most Eastern Montanans. He has been able to build a good life around an exceptional gift, something most of us will never have, with hard work and a lot of years living someplace where that gift proved to be more profitable than it would have been if he stayed in Montana. But he can serve as an example of an age-old theme of Montana, which is ingenuity. Of course not every town in Montana is going to need a recording studio, but I kept thinking that as long as one person in these small towns is figuring out a way to contribute and bring the community together, there is that chance of piling up those small increments of hope, brick by brick.

SIXTY MILES FURTHER ALONG Highway 2 is another town that originally came into being because of the railroad. Havre is the county seat of Hill County, named for railroad bully James J. Hill. In fact there is a statue of Hill in front of the railway station in Havre. But it's very oddly located. The railway station is off the beaten path, one street over from the main drag, so this statue is tucked away from where most people would see it.

For obvious reasons, the people of Havre did not stick with the first name given to their town, which was Bullhook Bottoms. When a change was called for, the residents settled on Havre after a town in France called Le Havre, thanks in large part to a strong European influence.

Havre came about much like many of the towns along the railways: An astute businessman approached James J. Hill with the right pitch. Hill was famously cantankerous about such approaches, and often decided on a different town because he didn't like someone who was trying to profit from his venture (Columbia Falls is a classic example, where a businessman bought up huge tracts of land in anticipation of the arrival of the railroad, only to have Hill decide to circumvent the town just to spite this man).

But Hill apparently approved of Simon Pepin, a Canadian businessman who became known as the "Father of Havre." Pepin had made his fortune as a contractor, specifically providing the supplies and workforce for many of the forts built in the area. It helped that Havre was strategically located halfway between Minneapolis and Seattle.

Havre is still the largest town along the Hi-Line, and the eighth largest city in Montana. But it is yet another of the many towns along this desolate stretch of highway that does not inspire great promise for the future. On the day I visited Havre, a strong wind blew dust and stray litter along the streets. It brought to mind the many clichés from old Westerns, with the people cowering in their homes to avoid being spotted by a cold-blooded gunslinger. Except the only thing evil happening here was the quiet relentlessness of economic decline.

The indications are all here. People hesitate to look you in the eye, and there aren't that many people on the streets to begin with. A look at the local paper also gives a few hints. Houses in Havre are cheap...you can get a nice three-bedroom home for less than $200,000, some even listing around $120,000. And the news is filled with stories about meth, especially on the Rocky Boy Reservation just thirty miles south of Havre. Since I was there, the Fort Belknap Indian Community Council declared a state of emergency from meth addiction on the reservation after ten meth-related deaths in just a few months' time. They allocated $150,000 from the reservation's profit-sharing arrangement with the Island Mountain Development Group to fund a pilot program. The new Aaniiih Nakoda Anti-Drug Program will focus its effort on treatment, law enforcement, and prevention.

I try to picture what it must have been like for a family to step off a train in one of these towns along the Hi-Line. Between the railroad and the local government, the propaganda created around this region was legendary for its complete lack of truth: the promise of as many as fifty bushels of produce, thick waves of grain, knee-high grass for their livestock. It was all exaggerated to draw people to this new world. A Northern

Pacific Promotional Brochure from 1892 lists Montana, Dakota, Idaho, and Washington and announces in bold letters: "MAKE MONEY. VAST GOLD AND SILVER REGIONS." It adds, "THE GREAT WHEAT BELT!" The railroads also produced slick, magazine-style brochures with pages of beautifully produced photography and descriptions of what they would find here. It's hard to imagine how even the most hearty and optimistic must have felt when they saw what this land really looked like. What did they think when they looked down at this dry ground, kicked it with their already dusty boots, and raised more dust?

They came for the promise of free land, and they got that all right. But what nobody told them was that they had come to a place where 160 acres wasn't even close to being enough to support a family. It must have sounded like a gold mine to these people, coming from places where land was in incredibly short supply. Imagine, 160 acres! Free! And later, twice that amount! And then four times that amount! And all they had to do was build a small house, and stay on that land for at least five years. Five years must have seemed like such a small price to pay for their own tract of land. Their own piece of America. Their own American Dream.

What they also were not told was that much of the prime land had already been given to the railroads. When the government passed the Pacific Railway Act of 1862, it agreed to provide 12,800 acres of land to the railroads for each mile of track they built. That included mineral rights. According to Richard White, the amount of land eventually given to the railroads by the government amounted to the size of New Jersey and New Hampshire combined. The land was divided like a checkerboard, with every other section going to the railroad, up to ten miles out from the railway. So half of the prime land was in the hands of the railroad.

The original idea of the Homestead Act was to provide a chance for new folks to make a go of it. But like so many other well-intentioned plans, once it became evident that the small operator could not make a living on such a tiny piece of land, the ones who benefited were usually those who already had an abundance of land. The land did not go back to the Homestead Act for someone else to claim. It went to a bank, which sold it. Some landowners coveted the land of the small operators, waiting for the little farms to fail because they bordered their own property and would give them another pasture where they could graze their cattle, or raise another field of hay. In some ways, this proved to benefit the more successful operators, who were able to grow their ranches and farms, operations that were well run. So their expansion was well earned.

In a way, it's easy to say that the decline along the Hi-Line has been happening from the time those tracks were first laid. There were people who knew from the very beginning that this part of the state did not have the resources necessary to support the kind of lifestyle that was promised them. Those who bought into this pipe dream were duped from the beginning, and when it comes right down to it, it's a miracle that any of them survived.

IF YOU WALK ALONG certain downtown streets in Havre, you'll notice some odd little purple squares embedded in the sidewalk. These squares are made of glass, and they serve as a source of light for a fascinating little underground maze of rooms that have been around for over a hundred years. When a fire ravaged the businesses in Havre in 1904, a few businesses opened up in this underground tunnel while they completed the new buildings above ground.

When I started the tour of these underground businesses, the tour guide, a retired teacher who had the demeanor of a teacher—friendly, but someone I didn't want to annoy— turned to one of the people in the tour and said, "Pat, you probably don't remember me, but we bought your old place." Another Montana moment, as the person she was talking to didn't even live in Havre.

I expected this underground bunker to be a quaint little getaway, with a few tiny rooms. I was surprised to find that it's actually quite extensive. The tour took a couple of hours, and our guide led about twenty of us, all tourists, through several tunnels, business to business, all of them decorated with items from an earlier time. There was a bordello, with thin, sheer curtains separating beds no bigger than cots (privacy was apparently not a big priority in those days, or perhaps it just wasn't possible); there was a pharmacy, and a saloon, of course, a barber shop, and even a doctor's office, where I would imagine a few of the bordello's customers came for whatever ailments they got down the hall. And finally, there was a home, as it were. It turns out that a single man controlled many of these enterprises; a short little fellow from Brooklyn named Christopher "Shorty" Young. A former boxer and jockey, Young had good business sense, and didn't hesitate to dabble in the activities that were a little more nefarious. And it apparently made him a wealthy man.

Emerging from this underground world, I looked around to see little chance of anyone becoming wealthy in Havre, although I have learned never to make these kinds of assumptions in Montana. This is about the time that I began to develop a deeper understanding of why so many middle class people are so angry these days. I think if I lived in a place like this, the sense of purpose, of hope, would be hard to muster day after day. I feel for these people.

IT MAKES ME SAD to say that the next three counties inspired very much the same quiet despair that I experienced in Havre. These three counties, Blaine, Phillips, and Valley, make up a huge part of the Hi-Line, covering a combined, astonishing 14,513 square miles. Chinook, Malta, and Glasgow all look very much like most small towns in Eastern Montana. A few businesses open their doors each morning, showing the same smiling, friendly face that Montanans have shown for decades. But each of these three counties, while sharing a depressed economy, also had their own unique features.

It was about this time in my travels that I started to question my own judgment, my perspective. Had I come into this project with higher expectations than I realized? Or was I actually looking for reasons to believe that this part of the state is depressed? Of course the statistics support what I was seeing, but there was a part of me that still wanted to find some sense of hope and promise here, and wondered whether I just wasn't looking hard enough.

But one thing did occur to me, and it resonated throughout the rest of my trip because it seems so uniquely relevant to this part of the state. For decades, the people in Eastern Montana have worked very very hard. And the quality of their lives depended a great deal on the level of work they did, although there were certainly outside factors. But when you produce food, when you see your crops grow, see your cattle get fat, there is a sense of purpose that comes with this work that is very hard to replicate. I worked on my grandparents' ranch the summer I was sixteen—my very first job—and it remains to this day the most viscerally satisfying work I have ever done, because the results were tangible. You could taste them, feel them in your hands, and measure them from one day to the next.

To have that sense of purpose taken away from family after family has to have a tremendous impact on a town that is as small as these towns along the Hi-Line. There's no way it couldn't. Young people are flocking away from these towns, and it was at this point in the trip that I began to really grasp why that is true. These towns have nothing to give them right now. And it's nobody's fault; nobody here, anyway. But where are they supposed to go with that anger? It's a strong, powerful poison, this kind of anger. And I don't envy them having to figure out a way to live with it.

PERHAPS BECAUSE I HAD come to expect so little, the Blaine County Wildlife Museum in Chinook was one of the most pleasant surprises I encountered on my travels. The museum was first conceived in 1991 when a local group of business owners were able to acquire the local Blaine County Theater for a dollar from the Blaine Bank of Montana. Dave Taylor is on the board of directors for the museum, and the story of how this museum went from an empty building to the really impressive facility it is today is another great example of how small communities in Montana sometimes come together and accomplish amazing things when they're determined enough.

After acquiring the theater, the museum board planned an annual fundraising dinner (Taylor said that this dinner now raises about $20,000 annually), and solicited private donations so that they were able to slowly act on a plan to create a unique place for people to come and see all the various forms of wildlife from Montana in their natural settings. They were fortunate to be able to acquire many of the animals, which are stuffed, from a wildlife museum in Livingston that closed down just about the time they were getting started.

From there, they went searching for the right artists to build the dioramas around these animals, a search that led them to a couple from Minnesota. Kurt Wohnsen and Elizabeth Marshall are the founders and artistic genius behind a company called Acorn Exhibits. They have designed and created the exhibits in such museums as the Charles M. Russell Museum of Western Art in Great Falls, the International Wildlife Museum in Tucson, Arizona, the Science Museum of Minnesota, and the New Mexico Museum of Natural History and Science. So they came to Blaine County with an impressive body of work behind them.

Wohnsen and Marshall took the animals that the museum had acquired and designed and built six exhibits around them—Peaks to Plains, Wetlands, Buffalo Jump, Moose/Grizzly Encounter, Swift Fox, and Nocturnal. And each of them is impressive.

According to Taylor, the board decided from the beginning that they wanted to do this museum right. So they waited until they had enough money to pay Wohnsen and Marshall for the previous section of the exhibit before bringing them in to do the next section. Meanwhile, local businesses did most of the work of remodeling the building. And other local citizens pitched in when needed. Taylor said it was a genuine community effort, but because of their insistence on getting it right they did not finally open their doors until 2010, about twenty years after they started the process.

Of course their biggest hope from the time they opened the museum was to draw more tourists to the area. When I asked Taylor whether that had been the case, he answered with an enthusiastic yes. School buses come from all over the state, he said, bringing students to the exhibit. And their guest book revealed visitors from all over the world. Taylor was proud to mention that the town of Big Sandy brought its entire student body last year.

The museum's ambiance is complemented by a music soundtrack along with the sounds of the various animals, which makes it that much more unique compared to many similar facilities. After paying the entrace fee, you walk down a small corridor leading to the displays, and you can actually hear the animals before you see them, which seemed corny at first but once you round that corner and see the quality of the displays, it's very impressive. And I'm sure it makes a big impression on kids.

I experienced another amazing small world moment after writing about this museum. I received an email from my editor when he was reading this chapter for the first time, and he informed me that the wildlife museum in Livingston where the display animals came from had been started by his father, and that many of these animals were the product of his father's own hunting trips. Allen, his brother, and father had mounted some of these animals themselves. They had sold the wildlife museum to a local businessman, only to see the mounts later sold piecemeal. They never knew what happened to them. So Allen was thrilled to find out that they have been put to good use.

For this agricultural community along the Hi-Line, I find it admirable that they would make such a concerted effort to draw people to their town. Taylor told me that the businesses that still exist in Chinook—and there weren't very many—were doing well. He said that his own business, a trailer company called Triple T Sales, was the biggest hydra bed trailer dealership in the country. Hydra beds are the most common method of moving round bales, and consist of a large flatbed mounted with hydraulic arms that lift the bales onto the bed.

But again, my admittedly unscientific eye test indicated that Chinook, a town of just over 1,000 people, was on the decline. There was only one restaurant left in town, and it was in a casino.

ANOTHER SEVENTY MILES along the highway, Malta also boasts a beautiful new museum, this one featuring a full dinosaur skeleton named Leonardo, which was found in the area in 2000. Leonardo is considered one of the best-preserved dinosaur skeletons ever found, and is only one of four found in the world that is mummified.

This museum was also where I met another of my favorite people on my tour, a woman named Dollyann Willcutt. Dollyann was one of those people who inspires you to want to give them a big hug. She was short and soft, with strawberry blond hair and a wayward eye, and she exuded an infectious kind of enthusiasm. I wasn't surprised to learn that Dollyann had been a superintendent of schools, now retired. I pictured young children and teachers alike flocking to her with their troubles, and her patting them on the arm, assuring them that everything would be okay. For some reason, I also came away from talking to Dollyann with a strong image of her as a young girl, determined and smart, hunching over her homework and wiping away tears when she couldn't quite word something exactly as she wanted. I was so taken by Dollyann that I was too absorbed to take notes, which I kicked myself over later. She talked as if she had a personal relationship with Leonardo... as if they hung out together, and I could just imagine she has this same effect wherever she goes. I didn't buy many souvenirs on my travels, but I felt compelled to buy something from Dollyann, and I ended up with a purple coffee mug, shaped and speckled like one of those old tin mugs from cowboy days, although it is ceramic, with a nice dinosaur like Leonardo etched deep into its body. I use this mug every day.

JUST TWENTY MILES OUTSIDE of Malta is the tiny town of Dodson, which claims just over 100 residents now. My good friend Lenore Pomeroy grew up on a farm near Dodson, where her parents homesteaded and raised ten children. Lenore has lived in Billings for decades, and that's where I talked to her, but her memories of Phillips County still resonate. A tiny woman with eyes as blue and bright as the sky, Lenore laughs a lot, even when talking about some of the most heartbreaking of events from her childhood.

Hers is a classic tale from that time, one that is filled with fond and funny memories, but mostly genuine hardship. Lenore described her father as a man who always managed to turn a solemn moment around by pulling out his fiddle, which she loved to hear him play. But when she was about ten, she and two of her sisters came up over the hill after school one day to find that their house was gone. A fire had destroyed everything her family had built over the previous fifteen years.

"He never played the fiddle again," Lenore said, and her eyes went moist.

Being the seventh of those ten children, Lenore became accustomed to burying whatever injuries or hurts she endured. She told me a story about finding a board that she thought would make an excellent slide and propping it up against the house before climbing on and sliding down. Predictably, a massive sliver buried itself in her bottom. Lenore was horrified that she would get in big trouble, so she tried to keep it from the rest of the family. But that night, when she climbed in bed with her sisters, and one of them tried to snuggle up to her, as was the norm, the pain was too much and the truth came out.

"My dad pulled that thing out and never said a word," she said. "To this day I'm not sure why I was always so afraid of telling someone I was hurt."

It is not hard to imagine the reason, when her parents were dealing with the challenges of a homestead farm in the hardest years of our history, with no phone, no electricity, and no water. Plus ten children.

GLASGOW WAS ONCE A very active community thanks to the air force base, which used to be just outside of town. But the population was cut in half when the government closed that base in the late sixties. The real heyday of this town was the 1930s during the building of the Fort Peck Dam, still the largest hydraulically filled dam in the United States. The New Deal construction of this dam, at its height, brought jobs to over ten thousand people.

One of the largest cattle ranches in the state was located near Glasgow in the late nineteenth century. The N Bar N ranch once employed fifteen wagon crews during the open range days, and ran about one hundred thousand head of cattle. They eventually sold out to what would become *the* largest ranch in Montana, owned by Conrad Kohrs.

I spent the better part of a half hour trying to find a place to eat breakfast in Glasgow. It brought to mind one of the saddest parts, for me, of what has changed in small town Montana. There is no longer a café in every town, no longer a place where you can go to get a cup of coffee and see the local ranchers gather to hear the latest news and gossip. The only place I could find to eat breakfast was a casino, although they did have a Pizza Hut and a McDonald's.

Just twenty miles from Glasgow is the structure that dominated the news in Montana during the 1930s, when there wasn't a lot of good news going on around here. When President Roosevelt announced his intentions to invest over $3 billion in public works programs, Senator Burton K. Wheeler lobbied hard to get the Fort Peck Dam on the list of projects, and he succeeded. On the day that I visited Valley County, I started my drive down to visit the dam, which I have never seen, only to have my engine light come on. So I had to turn around, and I didn't have time to go back. So I am sorry to say that I still haven't seen this structure.

The dam went under construction in 1934, and of course with it being the Depression, people flocked from all over the country, in a scene reminiscent of the current-day Bakken oil boom, for much-needed jobs. The project employed about

10,500 workers at the peak of its construction. At the time, it was the largest construction project in America.

Fort Peck Lake is the fifth-largest man-made lake in the United States. The uncompleted spillway for the dam was famously featured on the cover of the very first issue of *Life* magazine in September of 1936 in a photo by Margaret Bourke-White. Bourke-White also drew some ire from the locals when her photo essay inside focused mostly on the nightlife at the dam. Like many projects that were thrown together in Montana's history, the towns that grew up around the dam were slapdash, with plenty of bars, and Bourke-White was apparently as fascinated by the people as she was with the construction.

At the time it was built, the Fort Peck Dam was five times bigger than any other dam built to that date. This job was so important to Roosevelt's New Deal that he made two visits to the site, in 1934 and in 1937. Because a presidential visit to our state was very rare in those days, this made Roosevelt immensely popular in Montana.

But like most such projects, there was also a dark side. Sixty men lost their lives in the construction of the dam, and six of them were forever entombed in the dam. But perhaps most importantly, a vast number of homesteaders were forced to sell their farms because they were located in the area to be flooded once the dam was complete. Because they had to sell at market value, at a time when the market was at its worst, they often came away with practically nothing for their many years of effort trying to put together their own little American dream.

In the long run, though, most people were happy to take the money, and to then have the opportunity to work. The dam opened in 1940, providing many Montanans with a working wage through the most difficult decade of our state's history.

MY FIRST IMPRESSION OF current-day Glasgow was that there is not much going on there, but that idea was put to rest by one conversation.

Tess Fahlgren teaches art and creative writing at the high school in Nashua, just fifteen miles due east of Glasgow, where her grandmother grew up on a farm. Tess grew up in Glasgow, and went to the University of Montana to study creative writing. She came back in large part because she was able to get this teaching job, but she was also compelled to come back home after spending a few years on the other side of the mountains.

I found Tess by way of an editorial she wrote for the *Glasgow Courier*. She had some interesting things to say about the issue of land management, so I contacted her and she agreed to an interview. She is twenty-five years old, and her father's family has been in Montana for several generations. Her mother is from Texas. Tess's father raises bulls, but he also spent several years working for the Bureau of Land Management, and he now works for the Sage Grouse Initiative, an organization whose goal is stated as "a partnership of ranchers, agencies, universities, non-profit groups, and businesses that embrace a common vision: wildlife conservation through sustainable ranching."

I was happy to have Tess shatter some of my misconceptions about Glasgow when I asked whether there has been an exodus of young people from their county.

"Our ranches have done well, so people have the money to send their kids to college. The average age of a rancher here is around sixty years old. I don't see this is as necessarily bad or good; it's just the natural ebb and flow of economy. However, since the railroad began hiring a lot more people since the Bakken blew up, I've seen an influx of young people coming back to the area. Kids I graduated with who didn't go to college are married and own homes in the area. It's been good for our economy, I think, but it's different. Now that the oil has slowed down people are getting furloughed and laid off from the railroad, but I haven't felt a sense of panic from that."

Glasgow is nearly two hundred miles from Sidney, and even farther from Williston, North Dakota, the heart of the oil boom, which gives an indication of how far the reach of this oil boom has extended.

Tess thinks her time in Missoula, as well as stints in Arizona and Washington State, have made her appreciate where she lives even more than she once did. "I was exposed to political beliefs different from the ones I grew up with, because I was able to meet people and make connections in the art world that don't exist in Northeastern Montana. That being said, I believe both areas have shaped my work in very important ways, and I'm glad I was able to experience life in Glasgow before moving to Missoula. Creative stuff aside, I made great friends in Missoula. People from home talk about Missoula with low tones. They don't like 'the weirdos,' which I think is hilarious, because I know those weirdos, and they're my friends. I might even be one!"

Her experience also seems to have given Tess a great appreciation for how complicated some of the issues can be when you're dealing with farming and ranching and the environment.

"Most people love the land and want to see it healthy. It's easy for people who don't live here to think they have the solution. In Missoula I saw people forgetting that there are whole generational families working their hardest to make ends meet out here. These people actually have good ideas on how to conserve the environment, too, and they seem to be more reasonable and achievable. The conversations are difficult because there are extremists on both sides, but what my dad does with the Sage Grouse Initiative is a step in the right direction, because it works with ranchers toward a solution instead of against them."

Tess also cites the presence of the Fort Peck Theater, and a very active arts community, as positive influences on the county. Fort Peck, the town, is about twenty miles directly south of Glasgow, and the theater there puts on several musical productions during the summer months. The theater was built in 1934 by the Army Corps of Engineers as a movie theater for the thousands of workers building the dam. It was only meant to be temporary, but in those early days it was open 24 hours a day, seven days a week, and was often filled to capacity for all of those hours as there was little else to do in the area at the time.

The building, which was built in a style reminiscent of a Swiss chalet, with beautiful handcrafted wood fixtures throughout, is very striking and was so structurally sound that it has stood the test of time ever since. Through local fundraising efforts and donations from supporters, the theater is able to get by while only being open for about three months out of the year.

I didn't realize it until long after our conversation was over, but Tess Fahlgren brought a much-needed sense of perspective to my view of the Hi-Line. For someone so young, she gave me some of the most valuable insights into what it means to live in this part of the state, in a place so small and seemingly modest.

"One of the things that people don't realize about a place like this is how important it is that we all have a common enemy, but that it's not other people. It's the economy, or the weather, or the government," she explained. "It really tends to bring people together in a way that is much different than if you're banding together to fight against other people. It's somehow a more humane fight."

Tess also talked about how frustrating it can be knowing that people assume that the ranchers in places like Glasgow are too stupid or too invested in their own interests to be able to form intelligent opinions about what should be done with the land and with the environment. "There are really two definitions of sustainability in a place like this," she explained. "Most people only think of it in terms of the land, or the water, or the wildlife. But when you ask my dad what sustainability means to him, he will talk about sustaining an ability for the members of his family to take care of themselves in the future. It's all tied together with the environment, of course, but the lines are much more blurry than most people realize."

I love that! Tess made me think back to the very beginning of my journey, to the group of men I met in a Kalispell coffee shop—men who had much more in their favor than most people on the Hi-Line can even imagine. And I began to appreciate the fact that no matter where you go in Montana, there is this need to find your tribe, to find the people who think like you, even if there are just a handful of them. And how important it is for those people you surround yourself with to support whatever thoughts and opinions you have that keep you going.

I think it's an important part of our fabric as Americans, and especially as small-town Americans.

Again, Tess put it beautifully: "The biggest threat to our community is the attitude that a community has to be proven valuable to be valued."

I believe I'm going to adopt this as my motto.

ALTHOUGH EVERY OTHER town on the Hi-Line, as well as half of the other towns in Eastern Montana, could fit into a chapter about the railroad, just as most of them could fall under the chapters about farming and ranching, I covered Roosevelt County in an earlier chapter, and Sidney, Scobey, and Plentywood are coming along in the next chapter. Instead, I want to take you down through some of the other counties whose identities were stitched together around the solid foundation of parallel iron tracks.

PERHAPS ONE OF THE most significant towns that originally came about because of the railroad is Great Falls, although Great Falls developed a strong foundation around many other industries after its founding. When I was in high school, Great Falls and Billings were always neck-and-neck for the claim as the largest city in Montana, lingering close to 90,000 apiece during the 1970s. Today, Great Falls is the third largest city in Montana, having been surpassed by Missoula. Great Falls' population has dropped below sixty thousand people, while Billings' has continued to grow well past a hundred thousand.

The town was founded by Paris Gibson, who saw the great potential for growth thanks to the hydroelectric possibilities of the falls. He enlisted the help of Helena businessman Charles Broadwater to build the basic businesses to get the town going, starting with a store and a flour mill. The town grew fairly quickly, with the ultimate goal being to provide a solid town before the arrival of the railroad, which happened in 1887. By that time, Great Falls had a planing mill, a lumber yard, a school, a bank, and a newspaper.

When the Anaconda Copper Company decided to open a

second smelter in Great Falls, the city really took off.

Like many Montana cities, most of the character and tone of Great Falls was determined by the industries that formed its core. So with the railroad and the smelter, and other industrial enterprises, Great Falls already had a strong blue-collar population before it became the site of the largest military base in Montana. The base that would eventually be known as Malmstrom Air Force Base was first conceived in the late thirties and finally opened in 1942 as Great Falls Army Air Base. It was renamed Malmstrom in 1955 to honor a decorated colonel who died in a crash while stationed at the base. Malmstrom is the only military base left in Montana, and today one of their main functions is to maintain and operate the Minuteman II missile operations.

Having a military presence in Great Falls led to some interesting cultural influences that were not all that common for Montana, the most striking being one of the most active jazz scenes in the state. This scene was led by a club called the Ozark, which was a very popular venue for great jazz musicians until it burned down in 1962. The club was founded by a former boxer named Leo LeMar who moved to Great Falls in 1916. LeMar, who was African American, developed his boxing skills while supporting himself by waiting tables in the dining cars on the railroad. He opened the jazz club in 1933, and built a strong following as there was already a surprising number of African Americans living in Great Falls due to the presence of the railroad. As the military presence grew in Great Falls, so did LeMar's business. The club was known to host a few tables in the back for gamblers as well.

Perhaps the most surprising thing about Great Falls, despite it being one of the largest cities in the state, is that it seems to have very little presence, at least compared to places like Missoula, Bozeman, Butte, and Helena. You rarely hear anything about Great Falls, good or bad. For decades Great Falls has seemingly provided a steady supply of good solid workers and services to a large part of Montana's population without drawing much attention to itself. Great Falls lies solidly in the middle of the state, both geographically and in per capita income, although it is the only one of the major cities in Montana to show a decline in economic growth since 1970. There is no doubt, whether you go by every measure of economic growth or by the eye test, that Great Falls has seen better days.

But if you say this to someone from Great Falls, be prepared.

"You must be living in the eighties," Ken Robison told me when I said Great Falls seemed to be on the decline. Robison is an historian, specializing in the Mullan Road, a subject that he is passionate about after growing up in Chouteau County. But he now lives in Great Falls.

"Great Falls suffered two severe economic blows in the 1970s and early 1980s with the closure of the Anaconda Smelting and Refining Company and the Great Northern Railroad repair yards. Thousands of jobs were lost, and Great Falls declined economically," he said. "It took about two decades until the early 2000s to begin to rebound significantly. It has rebounded, fueled by a combination of factors, until today it is growing and prospering."

Robison says that the continuing growth of agriculture in the area, along with the strength of the air force base, has kept the economy strong in Great Falls. He goes on to list a string of businesses that have opened in the area, along with several new facilities, including the largest soccer complex in Montana.

There are some wonderful tourist attractions in Great Falls, including the Lewis and Clark Interpretive Center, with Giant Springs State Park just up the road. And finally there is the museum inspired by perhaps the most well known Montanan of all time.

It might be fitting that the most famous man to be associated with Great Falls started as a ranch hand. Charles Russell was one of the most prolific Western artists in history. After something of a misspent youth, he became famous for his vivid depictions of life on the range. He captured motion, especially when painting livestock; he also captured many of the more striking colors of the Western plains with his sunsets and paintings of the men at work. The thing that is most evident when you study his paintings is that each of them implies a story.

Although there's no questioning his talent, a lot of Russell's success was also a product of excellent timing. His first bit of exposure to the world came when he was working as a hand for a cattle ranch in the Judith Basin, and he painted a small, postcard-sized watercolor of a gaunt steer being stalked by some hungry wolves. He painted this sketch during the harshest winter in Montana history, 1886–1887, and the foreman of the ranch included the painting in a letter to explain how badly things were going. The tiny painting found its way to a store window in Helena, which led to Russell's eventual "discovery." He became famous in a fairly short period of time due in large part to the world's fascination with the West. There were few artists actually living and producing their work in the Northern Rockies, and Russell stood out among those who were. He was soon able to devote most of his time to his art. Another aspect that added to Russell's success was his down-home charm. By most accounts, he was an affable fellow who made friends easily, whether it was with his fellow ranch hands and hunting buddies, or the cultured crowds of Great Falls, or the various Native American tribes he visited in his travels. He had a Will Rogers kind of folk wisdom, and it served him well in his efforts to market himself. His ability to spin a good yarn no doubt also contributed to the fact that his paintings always seemed to be snapshots into a much longer story.

He was also one of those fortunate artistic types who managed to marry someone who was much better at marketing than he would have ever been on his own. His wife, Nancy, whom he married when he was thirty-two and she was eighteen, was known to be an astute businesswoman, as well as someone who was very protective of her husband's time.

So it was a combination of much good fortune, a strong sense of telling a good story, and the fact that Russell lived in Montana that made him one of the most famous Western artists ever.

AMONG OTHERS WHO HAVE a history in Great Falls are two of my literary heroes. Wallace Stegner lived in Great Falls as a boy, and for a time his father made a living running bootleg liquor from Canada. Stegner wrote *A Big Rock Candy Mountain,* one of my personal favorite Montana novels, based on this time in his life. I was fortunate to meet Mr. Stegner's daughter-in-law at a book festival in 2008, and I was pleased to learn from Lynn that Wallace Stegner's reputation as a good and generous person was well earned. She adored her father-in-law, and although he was not the type of person to throw his weight around to open doors for her as a writer, he was always ready to provide her with advice and encouragement.

Joseph Kinsey Howard also spent a good portion of his childhood in Great Falls, graduating from high school there. After starting out as a journalist, Howard eventually wrote several non-fiction books about Montana, with his first, *Montana: High, Wide and Handsome,* being one of the best historical accounts of Montana. Howard had a knack for writing lovingly about Montana while also addressing issues that needed attention, particularly the undue influence of corporations on Montana's economy. He was one of the more outspoken opponents of the influence of the Anaconda Copper Company at a time when few were speaking out about it. Howard became the preeminent Montana historian of his time before he died of a heart attack at the age of forty-five. At the time of his death, he was working on a massive history of Louis Reil, the leader of the Métis, a group of people who grew out of the unions between indigenous women and French trappers in Canada. The book, *Strange Empire: Narrative of the Northwest,* was published posthumously.

Great Falls can also boast one of the best newspapers in the state. For decades, the *Great Falls Tribune* was the only major newspaper in the state that wasn't controlled by "The Company," which also made it the only newspaper that had the courage to write honestly about what was going on in Butte and Anaconda.

I really want to believe Ken Robison in the worst way. Robison is a likeable guy, with a round face and twinkling blue eyes that exude kindness. I don't want any town in Montana to suffer. I want them all to thrive and grow. But Great Falls doesn't seem to have the signs I've seen in other places. The downtown looks as if it is about thirty years behind the times. In the middle of the day, it is surprisingly quiet. And again, I tend to go by the body language of the people in each of these towns. The people of Great Falls are friendly, as friendly as anyone else in the state. But there simply isn't that sense of hope and optimism that I see in places like Bozeman or Helena. I believe that Ken is probably right about this town being on the rebound. But I think perhaps it will take longer than he realizes.

TOWNSEND, IN BROADWATER County, is a quaint town, with one of the best bakeries in the state. The Mountie Moose Bakery features fabulous donuts and pastries, especially their apple fritters. Townsend was planned by the railroad, The Northern Pacific specifically, and named for Alma Townsend, the wife of Northern Pacific president Charles B. Wright. Aside from the railroad, farming, ranching, and the lumber industry provided most of the jobs for this area, and now that the railroad is gone, this is still true. But there is one little gem in this town—in addition to the fritters—that makes it unique: a place called Goose Bay Handblown Glass.

Goose Bay was started by Jim and Terry Gunderson, a local couple who sort of stumbled into the craft of blowing glass. Jim worked as a blacksmith for thirty years, and Terry was an RN in Helena, which is just thirty-five miles up Highway 287 from Townsend. But Jim's body was starting to complain about the physical aspects of his job. Jim had been fascinated with glassblowing since he was a child, and he searched out a class, which he found in Washington state. He persuaded Terry to join him, and they signed up for the class and found an immediate affinity to the craft.

In an interview I found online, Jim compared glassblowing to his old blacksmithing job: "I would categorize horseshoeing and blacksmithing more as craft with a bit of art, and glass is more art with a bit of craft."

Jim was able to build the equipment for their operation himself, some of it by simply converting some of what he used for his old profession. In 2002 they started making blown glass objects in their home in Goose Bay, which is tucked away along Canyon Ferry Lake about twenty-five miles from Townsend. One thing they noticed right away was that a lot of people wanted to watch them do their work, so they started to entertain the idea of opening a shop in a more convenient location. Thankfully, a small building right on the main highway through town came up for sale, and with a lot of work, they were able to convert it for their purposes.

I stopped into their shop twice, and the Gundersons were out each time, but fortunately, the man who works with them, Paul Hamilton, showed me the process. I found it fascinating, not to mention a little frightening. The ovens used to heat the glass are set at around 2000 degrees, and Paul explained that having this glass touch your skin would take it right off. He's seen it happen. It was clear from watching him do his thing that the possibility was in the back of his mind all the time. It was a craft that is carried out with slow, deliberate motion, with a steady eye on that molten glob.

Hamilton started by rolling a hollow tube in various colors of ground up glass, then holding the tube inside the inferno. In just a matter of minutes, the particles morphed into a glowing orange form in the shape of a pod. And of course then comes the part of the process that has defined it—Hamilton presses his lips to the opposite end of the tube and blows, expanding it into more of a bulb. Shaping and manipulating that bulb into the desired shape is the tricky part, and it was fascinating to watch Hamilton use various tools as he rolled the tube along a bench and pressed against the glass, forming grooves, or indentations.

Hamilton was an engaging fellow who liked to talk, and although he didn't lose his focus while he worked, he continued telling stories the whole time I was there. He found his way into this profession after suffering a serious back injury working on a pipeline. Hamilton's back still gave him constant pain, which made the continuous motion but low physical effort of this job a good fit for him. One of Hamilton's specialties is a sort of globe that features a tree rising up inside. I watched him make one of these, completely baffled by how he'd managed it. But it was beautiful.

And I appreciated the contrast between the delicate, almost feminine pieces of work he was creating and his heavy metal appearance. Hamilton wore jeans with a studded black belt, a T-shirt featuring a metal band, and a bandana. He looked like every guy you might see at a Metallica concert, and in fact there was heavy metal playing in the background.

"This is a great gig," he told me. "But I don't live here. There's nothing to do here." The first time I visited him, Paul was living in Bozeman, but by the time I paid a second visit, he and his girlfriend had moved to Helena because it was cheaper.

I left Townsend feeling as if I'd somehow seen the best it had to offer, although I'm sure the farmers and ranchers nearby all had their own interesting and unique stories to tell. To me it seemed almost miraculous that a place like Goose Bay Glass could be found in a place like Townsend, much less that it could survive. It was a testament to the quality of the work that a bouquet of glass flowers could flourish in such a dusty corner of the world. And it made me appreciate the passion and dedication of people who take risks, people who follow their dreams. It's nice to see that some of the myths about Montana are true—that you really can re-invent yourself here and sometimes it can work out very, very well.

GLENDIVE IS A TOWN worthy of its own book, with a history that's rich with scandal and intrigue. Thankfully, a man named H. Norman Hyatt became enamored with Dawson County when he found out that his grandmother was buried there and he couldn't find her gravestone. Hyatt came into possession of two of his great uncle's unpublished memoirs about Dawson County, and he turned one of them into a fascinating book about the area, called *An Uncommon Journey: The History of Old Dawson County, Montana Territory.*

Hyatt concentrated on one of the memoirs, written by Stephen Norton Van Blaricom. He produced a thoughtful account of that part of Montana in the late nineteenth century that expresses some surprising opinions. It might help that Van Blaricom left the area later in life, and was living in Ohio when he wrote his memoirs, because his take on the events that took place in Glendive while he was there would have undoubtedly been unpopular, and possibly even dangerous.

Here's Van Blaricom's summarized opinion of that period of time:

> This is my personal memoir, and I reserve the right to express my opinion on anything that comes to my mind as I have understood or appreciate it. I do know that if some of these old-timers from Dawson County should see or hear what I have to say in these next few paragraphs, they would come here to Ohio, or telegraph, to have me shot.
>
> First, the government and the army corralled the Indians so the Northern Pacific Railroad could pass through. The government and the railroad then took title to all the land so they could sell it for profit to settlers who believed their wild claims of it being the Land of Milk and Honey. At the same time the hunters, with the silent approval of the US Government, were slaughtering the buffalo to extinction for their hides, humps, and tongues. A few people (like my Uncle Jay Orr Woods) even polished their horns and made furniture of them: chairs, beds, and divans...
>
> With the buffalo gone, the Indians had to become entirely dependent on the government for their food resource. They couldn't leave their shrinking reservations and return to the land. The native peoples were...assigned agents early on who were nefarious, parsimonious with the food rations and with other supplies, and who were responsible, along with the

government, for unconscionable misery and suffering and many deaths on the reservation. I never blamed Gall or Sitting Bull or Joseph or their people one whit for not wanting to be pulled into the reservation system....

After the winter of 1886–1887, the cattlemen saw they couldn't survive winter on an open range basis without stored supplies or feed. Even without overgrazing—even if the winter grass had been there—the cattle wouldn't paw through the snow cover to get to the feed like the bison or horses would.

Within two decades, the big open range outfits followed the trail of the Indians and the buffalo. The land surveys were complete and deeds or leases were then required to control the grazing areas. There were exceptions, men with vision like Pierre Wibaux of the W (W Bar) and Henry Boice at the 777 (Three Sevens) who understood the value of both assemblage and conservation. And there were a few ranches like the W and the XIT that lasted longer than twenty years. Even before the big cattle outfits pulled out, however, the farm-settlers (the "honyockers") came in and started fencing it all and, where they could, they plowed up the native grass and replaced it with tilled crops.

And now you old sourdoughs can get ready to shoot, for I'm about to do my stuff. In my opinion, it is an absolute tragedy that the white people ever invaded Eastern Montana. Eastern Montana and the Western Dakota territories should have all been left to the Indians and the buffalo and the elk, the grizzly and the wolf, the coyote and the antelope, the beaver and the curlew—and the rattlesnakes. It was a land of deer and jackrabbits and birds by the thousands. These creatures and Indians were the natural inhabitants of Eastern Montana and Western Dakota. All of that country west of the Missouri and north of the Platte clear up to Canada and then to the eastern foothills of the Rockies should have been left

to them. I have always understood the necessity for
the railroad to connect the rest of the country to the
east. Transcontinental transportation was a necessary thing. I also understand the necessity of having to build a centrally located roundhouse in such
a place as Glendive or Forsyth or Billings so that
the long-distance trains might have some point of
repair. Beyond that we should have built those rails
straight through from Bismarck and kept right on
going until they got to Bozeman and Helena.

Up to the time I left Glendive in 1900, Dawson
and Custer counties were nothing more than grave-
yards for the burial of lost hopes and failed dreams.
It may be more inhabitable than the steppes of Russia—but not much.

Then Van Blaricom ended with typical Montana humor:

(To my Dear Wife: In the event of my sudden demise
you will find my last will and testament in the upper
right-hand drawer of my desk.)

Whether you agree with Van Blaricom's assessment of the
situation or not, his opinions come as a shock from someone
who lived during the time that Montana was settled. It's easy
to assume that most of the people who were there for this period fell in line and swallowed the accepted version of what
was happening. And it's impossible to know whether Van Blaricom actually had more foresight than his contemporaries,
or whether he was simply more courageous about expressing
these views, but he proved to be fairly prophetic about what
was happening around him.

Van Blaricom's book also gives an interesting account of
Montana's second-most famous vigilante group. And perhaps
our most notorious.

Unlike the Virginia City Vigilance Committee, the members of the Stranglers never did come forward, although a
man named "Floppin' Bill" Cantrell was acknowledged as

the leader, and there was plenty of speculation about who the others were. The group was supposedly organized in 1884 by Granville Stuart, who was also present during the events of the first vigilante movement in Bannack/Virginia City. At a time when horses were the most valuable commodity a man could own, a complete necessity for most jobs, a sudden rash of horse thieves and cattle rustlers inspired some of the locals in Glendive and the surrounding area to take action.

Over the next several months, these men hung or shot somewhere between sixty and a hundred men whom they suspected of rustling. According to Hyatt, who did extensive research on the activities of these men, many of their victims were not guilty and were in fact considered to be reputable men.

Floppin' Bill, whose nickname came from his unusual method of handling an axe, was himself a victim of horse thieves, having his team of horses stolen twice. The second time Cantrell went out on foot to find his horses, without success, and returned home to find his wife kidnapped. He never saw her again, and it doesn't take a professional psychologist to guess what motivated Cantrell to say yes when Granville Stuart approached him about organizing a vigilante group. One of the most famous stories about the Stranglers was the rumor that Teddy Roosevelt and his friend the Marquis de Mores approached Stuart and offered to join the cause. Stuart purportedly advised them against it for the good of their own reputations, but others have suggested that he was worried about Roosevelt being too much of a loose cannon. Not a stretch from what we know about Roosevelt. Especially considering his mental state at that time, just a few years after losing his wife and his mother.

But perhaps the most interesting part of the story of the Stranglers is the opinion of many that they killed several innocent men. Most accounts agree that the first action taken by the Stranglers was to go after a notorious band of rustlers led by a man named John Stringer, known as "Stringer Jack." Stringer's band of outlaws was known to be camped out in the Missouri Breaks, and the Stranglers went after the group and killed eleven of them in an ambush, taking the rest into custody, where they were soon hanged.

From there, the story starts to sound a lot like the Virginia City vigilantes, where their early success went to their heads and they went on a murderous binge. There has been much speculation about whether the actions of this group were carried out by a single large group, or several smaller ones. But either way, it's generally accepted that they took care of their business in a fairly short period of time, and that results were immediate. For the next several years, rustling was at a minimum.

But Vic Smith, a highly respected buffalo hunter in the region, wrote of several innocent men who were killed by the Stranglers, and listed them by name. Because so much of this activity was never investigated, and never tried, we will never know whether Smith was right. But of course the point is clear. If these men had followed the letter of the law and brought the suspects in for questioning and trial, there would be far fewer questions about whether their work was legitimate.

The significance of all this? Well, it's one more example of events that have attained legendary status over the years, sketchy behavior that's been glorified in the name of the same old Montana myth of independence and take-charge attitudes. Today our highway patrol has badges that feature the motto 3-7-77, a code, from the original vigilante committee, that is still somewhat mysterious with regard to its origin and meaning (though it might refer to the ideal dimensions of a hand-dug grave: 3 feet wide, 7 feet long, 77 inches deep). But the point is, the behavior of these people is considered honorable enough to be included on the uniforms of today's law enforcement officers.

Today's Glendive is probably not a whole lot different from the old Glendive in many respects. Although the passenger trains are long gone, and the number of railway employees has greatly decreased, Glendive is still very much a working-class town. The recent oil boom to the north has had a dramatic impact on Glendive. Because of the high cost of living in the

Williston and Sidney areas, many people commute from Glendive. And several brand new hotels have suddenly risen from the ground in a town that showed little growth for decades. The night I spent in Glendive, I heard the clerk at my hotel tell one of her co-workers that she hadn't had a day off in two weeks. So in a place where people can earn six figures working as a roughneck, there's *also* a growing need for good workers in service jobs.

For my money, one of the most interesting people in Glendive is Dr. Joan "Mutt" Dickson. For anyone who wonders what people are talking about when they complain that Montana is deficient in the necessary care for people who have mental issues, what would you say to the fact that Dr. Dickson is the only Montana psychiatrist who lives and works east of Billings? That is roughly 50,000 square miles of territory, although there are a few psychologists in Glendive. I heard about Dr. Dickson after my visit to the area, and interviewed her by phone a few weeks later.

Dr. Dickson is a straight shooter, something you would almost have to be in her position. She grew up on a farm near Scobey, and she and her sister still own the farm, which they now lease to another local farmer.

I found her to be a wonderful combination of throwback and progressive. She charges cash, refuses to rush her appointments with her patients, and always books each patient for at least a half hour so she can visit with them rather than push them through like cattle. She even does house calls, which is virtually unheard of now.

On the progressive side, "I believe in the 'ideal medical practice' model, which basically means that giving my patients the time they deserve serves both of us better in the long run. This not only gives my patients better service, but it also allows me the balance I need to avoid getting burnt out on this job."

She knows the perils of this possibility first-hand as she had a brother who was also a successful doctor who got caught up in the "hamster wheel" of making as much money as possible. After going through a painful divorce, her brother moved back to Montana but never seemed to be able to get back to the old fun-loving person she remembered. He eventually turned to pills, which he started prescribing for himself, and then he took his own life.

Dr. Dickson went through her own period of feeling overwhelmed just a few years after she started practicing. She came to the profession fairly late in life, taking her first job as a doctor in 2002 at the Glendive Medical Center. Because she was working as both a family physician and a psychiatrist, she was very much in demand. On top of her job at the medical center, she served as medical director of the Eastern Montana Community Mental Health Center as well as director of the Eastern Montana Sexual Assault Forensic Examiner Program. "I was on call twenty-four hours a day, seven days a week, and after four years, I knew I couldn't do it anymore."

After unsuccessfully trying to renegotiate a part-time contract with the medical center, she knew it was time to open her own practice, which she did in 2007.

When I interviewed her, Dr. Dickson didn't pull any punches about the current state of mental health care in Eastern Montana.

"It's medication management," she admitted. And she even said that she had become part of this system, in large part because she didn't have the time or the resources to provide for the needs of so many people. On top of her practice, which she calls Plains Synergy Healthcare (with a caseload of over 1,400 patients), she also provides mental health services to the VA hospital, but most of that work has to be done by video. She ends up prescribing a lot of medication. She doesn't like it, but for the time being it's the best she can do.

But she also has very little patience with the self-sufficient mentality of many Montanans. "I tell people who talk about killing themselves, 'I will work with you if you want help, but if you are determined to kill yourself, there's nothing I can do to help you.'" This may seem contradictory to what you'd expect from the doctor whose patients universally say, "We know she cares." But in a place where so many people stubbornly refuse to get the help they need, and perhaps in some sense in response to her own brother's experience, Mutt knows that she can't afford to get emotionally invested in people who aren't interested in getting better. She can only do so much.

And it is perhaps a typical reaction from a good many Montanans to a problem that is becoming increasingly worse as the resources continue to dwindle.

"ROCKS AND WINDMILLS." THAT's how I heard someone describe the foundation of Harlowton in Wheatland County. "Who knew that the two things people complain about the most would end up being what saved the county?" is another common refrain.

Just up Highway 191 from Harlowton is the Judith Gap Wind Farm and Energy Center, which is the biggest wind energy source in the state. It is also an awesome sight. Ninety huge white four-bladed windmills tower 262 feet above the prairie, each providing 1,500 kilowatts of power. Invenergy is the company that built this windfarm, which recently celebrated its tenth anniversary, and it's hard to imagine anyone having a negative thing to say about their presence in Wheatland County. But the truth is, aside from the obvious presence of wind, this was not one of the more likely places for such a business to find such solid support.

Wheatland County is not one of the more progressive counties in the state. The idea of a wind farm received plenty of skepticism when it was first suggested. In the end, however, it wasn't much of a decision when people started to hear the numbers. When the company first came into the county, they paid $65,000 a month for three years as an impact fee. That money is still sitting in a fund, some of which has been used to finance various community projects. The incentive for the company to pay this was an initial tax break. For the first year, they received a 50 percent tax break, with their taxes gradually increasing until they now pay full taxes. The wind farm now brings more than $3 million a year in taxes to the county, not to mention jobs and business. Although according to John

Bacon, who manages one of the smaller wind farms in the county, it's not always easy to find people to climb these huge towers at seventeen dollars an hour. But it also has the benefit of cheaper energy and lower property taxes for the residents. It is yet another example of a small community slowly opening its fist from around the idea that they have to rely on the old ways to keep their county alive.

Harlowton was born because of the railroad, and it contains one of the better railroad museums in the state. But not a single rail car has passed through this town since 1979. And the tracks were torn up the following year. So for many years after that, Harlowton was struggling. "One of the worst five counties in the state," according to one local bar owner.

So the wind farm has provided a huge boost, not only to the economy but also to the morale in Wheatland County.

And the rocks? Well, there are several companies in Harlowton that provide rocks. Yeah, rocks. And it's hard to imagine how important a rock company is unless you've lived somewhere that doesn't have rocks. When I lived in Savannah, Georgia for a short time, I was surprised to find that there were no rocks there. When my wife at the time first stated this fact, I couldn't understand what she even meant. No rocks? None at all?

But it was true. The land around that area was all broken down so much by wind and water that it was all sand. If anyone got it into their heads that they wanted something built out of stone, they had to order it. E S Stone & Structure is one of the largest stone suppliers in Montana, and they are based in Harlowton, where they specialize in massive slabs of stone used for landscaping or, of course, headstones.

Harlowton is also the center for a few other unique small businesses, including Bear Love-Un Honey, one of the bigger honey providers in the state. Steve Park Apiaries, a company out of California, utilizes many of the local farms and ranches to provide housing for their bees, and they then ship millions of bees to the West Coast each winter to prevent them from freezing to death. Steve Park Aviaries produces the honey for

Bear Love-Un Honey, which is packaged and shipped from a small facility in Harlowton.

There is also Elk River Systems, a company that prints tickets for major events and employs about thirty people. And last but not least, Harlowton is home to one of the most beloved breakfast cereals in the West, a more substantive version of Cream of Wheat called Cream of the West, which is made from seven different variations of Montana grains. Although the origin of company has three different versions, all in different places and taking place in different years, the company has decided to adopt the year 1914 as the year of their founding.

Alicia Moe is one of the owners of Cream of the West, and she gave me a tour of their facilities, which were surprisingly simple. Alicia and her husband, Richard, live on a ranch that has been in Richard's family for generations, between Harlowton and Two Dot. But they jumped on the opportunity to buy Cream of the West when they saw it was up for sale in 2002. The small building that houses the Cream of the West operations consists of several big vats where they mix the product, and a conveyor machine that allows them to package it.

Harlowton does not appear at first glance to be a town that would be home to so many interesting little ventures. I became friends with one of the locals in Harlowton, Wendy Elwood, who took the excellent cover photo for this book, and had the opportunity to get to know the charm of this little town and what it has to offer. Among other things, they have a nice nine-hole golf course called the Jawbone, after one of the old railway lines, and a café called Jailhouse Pizza, which makes some excellent desserts. Some of the local businessmen also remodeled the restaurant in one of the town's most treasured businesses, the Graves Hotel, which recently reopened for lunch and dinner. I spent a delightful Saturday afternoon at the local community center where one of Harlowton's churches held a fundraising event called The Stick Horse Rodeo. For a couple of hours, kids of every shape and size galloped around "barrels," weaved between poles, and tried not to get bucked off by their ferocious stick horses, or giraffes, or elephants. It was pretty adorable, especially when one little girl who was about two insisted on following her older brother each time he performed. She even stopped to pick up his hat for him when it fell off during the pole-bending event.

Harlowton is deceptively alive, and I attribute this to their willingness to entertain the idea of non-traditional forms of business. Farming and ranching still maintain a healthy presence in Wheatland County as well, and the county also houses two of the larger Hutterite colonies in the state, with Duncan Ranch Colony and Springwater Colony.

The Hutterites have been a presence in North America since a group of them decided to send some of their members from Russia in the 1860s to find suitable land in this area. The reason for this move was that the Russian government at that time had decided to make it compulsory that all males serve in the military, which went against their pacifist beliefs. Although the Hutterites originally settled in Nebraska and the Dakotas, many of them moved to Canada during World War I after the Hutterite men decided they had no choice but to report for military duty. Because of their beliefs, they refused to wear uniforms or perform any of their duties, so they were beaten and tortured.

They suffered much the same prejudice during the Second World War, and even Canada passed a law during World War II making it illegal to sell land to Hutterites. But since then, they have been able to settle peacefully wherever they choose. According to a website called Hutterian Brotherhood, there are now about 45,000 Hutterites throughout North America, on approximately 450 colonies. According to their map, there are at least 25 of these colonies in Montana, where they raise a wide variety of crops and livestock. Their methods are unapologetically traditional, with the men making all the decisions and controlling the money, while the women are relegated to kitchen and housekeeping duties. But there's no denying that they have a system that works, as most of these colonies and their communal approach to farming have proven to be successful for decades now.

I HAVE YET TO VISIT a town in Montana where I felt unwelcome. Oh, some of the small towns, just like small towns everywhere, have that vibe. Where you get a few looks from people that say, "Marge, I don't know who that is…do you know who that is?" But it is inevitably followed by a wave. Since I was a kid visiting my grandparent's ranch in Carter County, I always loved how everyone waved in Montana's rural communities, and I'm happy to see this tradition is alive and well all over Montana.

But there is one town where I would pack my things and move tomorrow. People in Fort Benton wave with an expression that says, "Hey, we thought you were going to get here yesterday!" It is a town filled with people who are so clearly in love with the place they live, people who think they have been touched by the golden rod of residential destiny, and it shows in their businesses and museums and every goddam thing about it.

And on top of that, it's beautiful, planted within cherry-pit-spitting distance of the Missouri River. The buildings are incredibly interesting, including the fabulous Grand Union Hotel, and they even have one of the best coffee shops I've seen, although the name could use some work: Wake Cup.

At first it might seem odd to place Fort Benton in the chapter on railroads, but I made that decision because there are few towns that were more deeply affected by the arrival of the railroad than Fort Benton. Before the railroads, everything went through Fort Benton. Fort Benton was the original shipping point, the end of the line for the barges and steamboats coming up the Missouri River. It was also where the famous Mullan Road reached its final destination, or its starting point, depending on which direction you were going.

Fort Benton was first constructed in 1846 by a man named Alexander Culbertson, who had been given charge of Fort Union, a fur trading post. Culbertson was married to a Blackfeet woman, so he was able to establish a strong relationship with the Blackfeet, with whom the fur companies did a lot of trade. Culbertson first built a post upstream in 1845, called Fort Lewis, but when he learned that the Blackfeet didn't like the location of this post, he built a new post farther downstream, with better access to the Missouri. The fort was also originally called Fort Lewis, but they eventually decided to change the name to honor the company's biggest supporter in Congress, Senator Thomas Hart Benton from Missouri.

When the fur trade became less significant, Fort Benton became a quiet little trading post. Then the Mullan Road was built in 1859 and 1860, leading from Fort Walla Walla to Fort Benton. As stated in an earlier chapter, this road was the only real thoroughfare through the state, even though it was barely navigable. But when the gold rush started, it provided access for prospectors to get from Fort Benton to the source of their dreams.

The gold rush turned Fort Benton into a busy river port, with the number of boats docking there increasing every year except 1862, when the water was too low. According to K. Ross Toole in *Montana: An Uncommon Land,* at its peak in 1867, Fort Benton served as port to thirty-nine boats. This amounted to over eight thousand tons of freight and about ten thousand passengers. At $150 a passenger, that accounted for $1.5 million in passenger fare alone.

With most of the people coming into Fort Benton being fur traders, prospectors, cowboys, or Native Americans hoping to trade their wares, it's not surprising that it was a rough town in those early days. Perhaps the most notorious story was about a drunk cowboy who insisted on riding his horse up to his second story room in the Grand Union Hotel. The hotel clerk tried to stop him, and the confrontation that followed eventually led to gunfire, which left the cowboy dead.

Accounts from Fort Benton during this period are filled with fights, talk about filthy conditions all over town, rotting garbage, and an abundance of booze and bordellos. According to Teddy "Blue" Abbott, there were towns in Montana at that time where you could spend a week with a prostitute, walking all over town, without getting a second look from the townsfolk. And there were other towns where this kind of behavior was frowned upon. Fort Benton definitely fit into the first category.

One of the better stories from those early days serves as something of an echo of Bannack and Henry Plummer. In 1868, Fort Benton hired a new marshal by the name of Bill Hensel. Soon after his arrival, a rash of robberies hit Fort Benton, and after some sleuthing around, the citizens were able to determine that Hensel was the culprit. They went to Hensel and told him that they had captured the robber and were going to hang him, but they needed his noose. So he went to retrieve it and when he returned, of course they informed him that the noose was meant for him.

In later years, Fort Benton had some important distinctions, such as being the first town in Montana to elect a woman mayor when voters chose Marion Smith in 1961. It was also the very first town in America to accept a woman as a member of the local Kiwanis Club, in 1994. On the other hand, a doctor named Peter Burnett moved to Fort Benton back in the early twentieth century, and he was not allowed to practice because he was married to a black woman. She eventually won the hearts of the locals with her singing talents, although I'm not sure whether that made them change their mind about him practicing medicine.

With the birth of the railroad, Fort Benton eventually became more of what it is today, described this way by Fort Benton native Ken Robison:

> Fort Benton...in the past has been too modest and laid back in its promotion and advertising. For instance, Fort Benton has a strong case as "The Birthplace of Montana," yet it has allowed Stevensville's claims to go largely unchallenged...Proud of their history, but concerned that it might attract too much attention. Perhaps 90 percent of the town has traditionally had that attitude, but times are changing.
>
> Fort Benton is the heart of the Golden Triangle

with Chouteau County among the top grain growing counties in the nation...Several new value-added ag businesses have moved in as have three high-speed grain loading elevators—ag business is booming in general.

Finally, the fact that almost 100 percent of Fort Benton's presentation of history and tourist promotion has been done without government money is most remarkable...We'd love to have the federal millions that have been poured into the Silver Bow-Butte Archives, but as a research center for scholars and families, as a source for information and photos for historical publications, our Overholser Historical Research Center, staffed by volunteers and operating on a shoestring, holds its own.

From my experience, Robison's assessment is right on the money. The people of Fort Benton were fabulous examples of the old "attraction rather than promotion" method of drawing fans. River Break Bookstore introduced me to one of the more interesting booksellers I've ever met, a man named Tom Carrels. His bookstore was crammed with piles of books.—and hats. Tom intends to combine books with outdoor gear in the long run, and he has apparently started with hats. Although I didn't intend to buy any souvenirs on my journey, I couldn't stop myself from buying a hat from Mr. Carrels.

To me, Fort Benton is exactly what Virginia City could be if it didn't take itself so seriously. It has the charm, the incredible buildings, the history, and the vista to become a huge tourist attraction, and with even some small effort, it hopefully will draw enough travelers to bring some more money into the area. But they seem so content here that they might not be interested in achieving that end. And ironically, that might be exactly what makes it such a wonderful place to visit.

THERE ARE SEVERAL OTHER small towns that exist today almost entirely because the railroad decided they would. A map of the railroad towns in the early twentieth century shows the names of town after town, stacked like firewood, a stop every fifteen miles to refuel the steam engines. Names like Hoyt, Weeksville, Bearmouth, Elbow, Portage, and Bernice have long disappeared. And it's hard not to assume that many of these other towns would be well on their way to extinction if it weren't for the fact that they still served as county seats.

Perhaps the most interesting thing to consider when it comes to the impact of the railroad on Montana is whether we would have ever grown to the extent that we did without it. Between the Homestead Act and the easy access to the area that the railroad provided, the population of the Great Plains grew by leaps and bounds in the late nineteenth century, and it's hard to imagine that so many people would have found it an attractive destination without these factors.

Such speculation is a pointless exercise, of course. But every story has a shape, and it's interesting to explore how that shape came about and how different it might have been if the factors had been scrambled, or changed. The influx of people who came out because of the Homestead Act had a dramatic impact on our region, and some would say we are still fighting to recover from much of what happened because of that flood of wannabe farmers. And the railroad played a significant role in that chapter of our history.

CHAPTER SEVEN
Plants

"What we do to the land, we do to ourselves."
—Wendell Berry

There is no line marking the change from Western Montana to Eastern Montana. Whether you're driving along Highway 2 from Kalispell to Cut Bank, or traveling east along Highway 90 from Bozeman, you won't see a sign that says "Welcome to Eastern Montana." But you *will* notice the difference.

I used to say that Eastern Montana was flat until I married a woman from Savannah, Georgia. When I brought her to Montana and we drove across the eastern part of the state, she said with some degree of disbelief, "This isn't flat! This isn't flat at all!"

I didn't quite grasp how she could say that until we did a similar road trip through Georgia. Of course she was right. Although there are definitely long stretches, especially on the Hi-Line, where you can see for miles, the terrain in Eastern Montana is almost never flat. There are subtle changes everywhere. A big reason for its reputation for being flat is the lack of trees. You can drive for hours without seeing as much as a handful of trees, and those are generally shelter belts that were planted to give someone's ranch house a little relief from the persistent winds.

But a closer look at this half of the state reveals a land that is rich with texture. Whether it's a long, delicate slope or a hidden coulee, there are indications everywhere that the elements have been hard at work. There are also moments of absolute magnificence, like the badlands of Makoshika State Park in Glendive, which resemble the Southwest more than Montana, and the Absaroka or Crazy Mountains, which give almost every other range in the state a decent run for most scenic mountain range. There are the sandstone cliffs along Ryegate and Billings, and Medicine Rocks State Park near Ekalaka. I can't forget the sheer beauty of the lakes in the Beartooth Mountains—East and West Rosebud. This variety of geological formations and makeup is part of what makes this state unique.

But much of Eastern Montana is an acquired taste, especially if you expect or are accustomed to something like the majesty of the mountains. That said, they call this "Big Sky Country" for a very good reason. When you stand in the middle of a pasture in Eastern Montana, the sky really does look absolutely huge. I have heard this over and over again from people who've never been here before. It makes no sense that the sky actually looks bigger, but it does. Although it's interesting to note that the reason we became known as the "Big Sky State" was an advertising campaign concocted by the Montana Highway Department in the early sixties. They utilized the title of A. B. Guthrie's famous novel, as well as the persistent observations among visitors that the sky looks bigger here. But in the end, it's all about advertising. But still, the sky.

This kind of open country seems to attract two very different types of people and create two kinds of towns. First there's a town like Fort Benton, where everyplace you go, people greet you like a long-lost relative. There are many small towns like this in Eastern Montana, where the people appear to be living rich, happy lives.

The other extreme is a little harder to grasp, and to the

outsider I'm sure it can be intimidating. But in most of the smaller towns in Eastern Montana, what you're going to encounter when you first walk into the local café is "the stare."

Those who encounter "the stare" should not panic. Although at first glance, the stare suggests that you might want to turn around and go back to your car, the explanation is pretty simple. The stare comes from seeing the same twenty-five or thirty people day after day for the past five or ten years. And then suddenly being presented with someone they've never seen before. You're a specimen that needs to be studied and analyzed. The stare may seem rude at first, but it's really a compliment. You are exotic, worthy of examination. You are something they can spend a good hour talking about later.

But there's another factor that contributes to the stare. Economics. A few years ago, I read that every county east of Billings except Custer (Miles City) had decreased in population since the 1950s. I'm sure with the oil boom this is no longer true, but that trend is still very much alive for almost all of Eastern Montana. According to *Business Insider,* the average wage among Montana residents is the fourth lowest in the nation, and Eastern Montana's average is lower than the western half of the state. The natural result is a large number of people that are struggling and unhappy. Maybe depressed. Some are drinking too much. And many are angry—at the government, at each other, at themselves. It is part of the cycle of economic struggle, and most of Eastern Montana has been fighting this battle for a long time now.

So don't take it personally if they don't meet you with a smile and a cheery greeting.

THE THING I HAVE always loved most about Eastern Montana is that this land *is* so open. There is nowhere to hide. This vast openness is also the greatest challenge about Eastern Montana. When the wind or the snow or the simple need for some privacy hits a person, the options are few or none.

One of my grandmother's brothers was a heavy drinker, and he and his wife, who also liked her whiskey, were infamous for their brawls. One night they got into it again, and she stormed out of the house, not for the first time. Unfortunately, she made the decision to leave in the middle of one of Montana's notorious blizzards. With the snow swirling around her, by the time she regained her wits and realized she should find her way back to the house, she was lost.

My uncle tried to find her, but the chances of that were just as slim as the odds of her finding her way back to the house. She froze to death about one hundred yards from her home.

There are countless stories like this among long-time Montana residents: Ancestors who drowned, were struck by lightning, or died from exposure. This doesn't even account for the occupational hazards, like tipping over on a tractor (my grandfather's brother), or getting your arm ripped from its socket in a thresher, suffocating in a grain bin, or being dragged behind a horse, or trampled by a stampeding herd of cattle. Many young mothers were left widowed in Montana's pioneering days. And of course many others simply lost their minds from the constant challenge of isolation along with the relentless wind or snow, not to mention the constant financial strain.

Most people don't think of farming or ranching as boom and bust industries, but the truth is that the people who farm or ranch experience a boom and bust cycle pretty much every single year. The only question, year after year, is whether the boom is going to be big enough to compensate for the bust.

ODDLY ENOUGH, TWO OF the men who may have had the biggest impact on the early days of farming in Montana never lived here.

John Wesley Powell was a powerful combination of tenacious personality, gifted fundraiser, and someone with an insatiable thirst to explore as much of the West as possible. On top of that, he was an eternal optimist. As the head of the American Geological Survey, part of his duties were to explore and analyze what had become known as "The Great American Desert." After he and his team did a thorough study of the area between the Missouri River and the Rocky Mountains, Powell submitted his recommendations to Congress about how this area should be developed. And his timing could not have been worse.

Much to the dismay of people who were touting the West as a land of opportunity, Powell determined that only two percent of the land in the West was suitable for agricultural production. He knew that the notion that a family could make a living on 160 acres in this part of the West was absurd, and in fact he proposed two other options. According to Powell's bill, a homestead claim could be made for eighty acres of land that was irrigable. But for un-irrigable land, Powell was emphatic that a family would need at least 2,560 acres of land, twenty of which would have to have access to water that was irrigable. Also, in an effort to prevent an ever-increasing problem of people setting up irrigation systems upstream that left little or nothing for their neighbors downstream, Powell recommended a co-op system that teamed homesteaders into groups of eight, wherein they worked out a system of shared responsibility for the use of water.

Powell's suggestions were so far ahead of their time (although the cooperative system had proven to be very beneficial to many Mormon farmers) that his bill was practically laughed out of Congress. But the negative response, and it was brutal, could actually be attributed more to the fact that Powell had proposed a system that completely undermined a business plan—funded and devised by the railroads and other strong business entities—that was already well underway.

Another part of the unfortunate timing for Powell lay in the fact that the West had just gone through an uncharacteristic wet period—several years with way higher moisture levels than normal. So it was easy for Powell's detractors to point to these figures and say he was crazy. They dismissed Powell's assertion that there is a natural cycle in the West, where an inevitable drought would no doubt follow. Of course he was right about that as well.

The railroads, busy campaigning to encourage prospective landowners to move West and start a new life, found Powell's recommendations to be very inconvenient. They hired experts to dispute his claims, and eventually convinced Congress that Powell was misguided. Congress passed the Homestead Act and other legislation to encourage people to migrate West, and when Powell protested these decisions, he was branded a crackpot and an alarmist, and went from being the most highly regarded man in his field to a laughingstock.

But to Powell's credit, his story was not destined to end like so many people who suffer this kind of public humiliation. Powell seemed to have an inherent, unshakable knowledge that he would someday be proven right, so at a time when many would have slinked away from the public spotlight and either drank themselves into obscurity or lived a quiet life of solitude, Powell remained a faithful public servant, and a decade later he got an opportunity to redeem himself by convincing Congress to give him the responsibility to do a massive survey of the West.

This second chance was due in large part to Powell's predicted drought, followed by one of the worst winters in the history of the West. The winter of 1886–1887, which has been mentioned before and will come up again, saw the demise of over half the livestock in the West, and left people with a lot of questions about the promise of this place. Homesteads failed twice as often as they succeeded, and people began to notice that perhaps this place wasn't quite as advertised. In a move fueled by complete desperation, Congress was forced to turn to the man they had ridiculed just a decade before.

On October 8, 1888, they passed the Sundry Civil Bill, issuing an initial $100,000 to the National Geological Survey in order, under Powell's direction, to survey all irrigable lands west of the Mississippi. Powell knew this was an enormous task, and that it would eventually require a topographic, a hydrographic, and an engineering survey of millions of square miles of land. He initially estimated that it would take six or seven years at a cost of $5.5 million, but he knew Congress would not approve this sum. He also knew the urgency of getting this bill passed and starting what he considered the most important work he could possibly do in the West.

Sadly, this part of Powell's story also ended badly. For one thing, people started to wise up to the fact that many of the survey crews assigned out West had come to survey areas that were designated for irrigation projects. So speculators started staking claims in the areas where they spotted surveyors. When they realized this was happening, Congress voted to discontinue *all* claims until the survey was completed. But the project was so massive that even the most optimistic estimates came out to several long years. There was no way they could discontinue claims for that long. The blame for the inability to stake claims fell on Powell, who had nothing to do with the fact that people were smart enough to follow his crews.

After completing only a small portion of the proposed survey, and with his political rivals pumping up the charges against Powell for both overestimating and misappropriating funds (never proven), Congress decided to discontinue the project. Powell resigned from his post soon after. But again, he continued to express an optimism that one has to admire. Sadly, he didn't live much longer, due in large part to injuries suffered fighting in the Civil War (Powell had lost his right arm). For many years afterward, Powell's work was largely forgotten. But thanks to Wallace Stegner's outstanding book, *Beyond the 100th Meridian; John Wesley Powell and the Second Opening of the West,* published in 1953, Powell's foresight eventually became known. Most experts now think that if people had listened to Powell from the beginning, the West would have had a much better chance of getting through those tough early years with a stronger infrastructure of water and land use.

And Powell's long-term influence went far beyond the issues of water and soil conservation and use. It's clear when you read his writings and speeches that Powell shared the views of Adam Smith (author of *The Wealth of Nations*) that a nation that utilizes the strengths of each of its citizens, rather than trying to survive as an individual entity, has a much better chance of thriving. Unlike Thomas Jefferson, who created what he believed to be a self-sustaining entity at Monticello, only to die in debt, Smith predicted (way before Henry Ford proved it) that if you train one person to do one thing well and create a system in which everyone contributes to the overall productivity, the system has a much better chance of succeeding for everyone. Everything about Powell's proposals echoes this same philosophy, that the greater good will always create an atmosphere in which each individual also benefits. In other words, the opposite of the trickle-down theory.

It's difficult to imagine what it must have been like for Powell, after devoting his life to his field and viewing the assignment of exploring the West as the most important task of his life, to have his findings discredited by a marketing scheme. It must have broken his heart.

One of the most damaging byproducts of Powell's theories being dismissed was that it opened the door for many opposing theories, especially about farming, that were sadly misguided. Among them was the idea formulated by Cyrus Thomas, an ethnologist and entomologist who was part of an 1869 scientific expedition in the West headed by Ferdinand Vandeveer Hayden, that stated, "Rain follows the plow." This would become a rallying cry for many other "experts" in the field of dryland farming, particularly a man named Hardy Webster Campbell. Campbell was the second man who had a heavy influence on early farming practices in the West, and as I suggested, he could attribute much of his success to Powell's failure.

CAMPBELL WAS BORN ON a farm in Vermont, and came to the Dakota Territory in 1879 when he was twenty-nine years old. Like most early farmers, Campbell went through some ups and downs, but one day he noticed that grass grew in horse tracks or wheel ruts more than in the open fields around them, and from that single observation he built an entire career around a theory about the effects of packing the earth. Campbell theorized that if farmers packed the earth below the surface as much as possible, while at the same time loosening the topsoil, it would provide a better foundation for crops. He went so far as to develop and build his own machine, which consisted of a huge metal wheel to pack the earth, mounted with a series of rotating wedges that loosened the topsoil.

Campbell apparently got very little support for this theory among his fellow local farmers, but he did manage to sell his ideas to a group who had way more influence than his neighbors; namely, the railroads. Campbell formed a corporation, the Western Agricultural Improvement Society, and soon the railroad hired him to operate farms in five different states. He also taught classes for farmers who were interested in learning his techniques. By 1906, Campbell had developed several model farms that demonstrated his methods, and had also developed a national reputation. Campbell started his own science journal, *Campbell's Scientific Farmer,* and by 1914, it had a circulation of over thirty thousand.

Campbell's influence extended to every significant farming organization. By the time the Dry Farming Congress was formed in 1907, Campbell's methods were widely supported as the standard for dryland farming. Cities began to fight to host the annual meeting of the Dry Farming Congress and, in 1909, it was held in Billings. But there were signs from the beginning that not everyone was on Campbell's side.

Eventually, the inevitable happened, and it happened for one simple reason. Aside from the packing machine, the other aspects of Campbell's methods involved deep plowing, summer fallow, and frequent surface cultivation. Ideally, Campbell encouraged farmers to harrow their fields every time a crust formed. They were to disk the fields before and after planting, and deep plow after harvesting. The number of times they were supposed to plow or disk their fields was essentially limitless according to the conditions outlined by Campbell. He made almost no adjustments based on the type of crops, and had very little interest in the idea of rotating crops. His theory was based almost entirely on the idea that if you keep the soil cultivated, it will hold more moisture.

Clearly, Campbell was not a man whose intentions should be questioned. He wasn't evil or greedy so much as someone who drew his conclusions based on a very narrow sample size.

Although his technique sometimes led to immediate results, it also had the inevitable effect of loosening the topsoil to the point that it would slowly blow away. Can you see where this is going?

But it took time. The teens proved to work in Campbell's favor. Moisture in the Great Northern Plains from 1910 to 1919 was much higher than normal. Homesteaders rejoiced in the results, and the population in Montana grew in steady increments. Banks opened on every other corner. It was during this time that the county splitters came sweeping through the state and convinced town after town to apply to become a new county. The number of counties in Montana doubled between 1910 and 1925.

But Campbell's methods continued to draw criticism, especially among his fellow members of the Dry Farming Congress. Although some of that may have come from professional jealousy, there were also those among this group who had begun to question the wisdom of his system. Campbell still had plenty of supporters, though, including many in the field of farm research. Among them were several scientists involved in the experiment stations in Montana.

It would be impossible to measure, of course, the extent of his influence. And absurd to put the blame for what was to come on his shoulders. But there's no question that, between the practice of his methods and the ignorant policy of many early ranchers to graze the hell out of whatever source of grass they could find, the ground in Montana took a beating before the Depression rolled into town. And as many Montanans are aware, the Depression hit our state ten years earlier than it did the rest of the country. The dry years started in the early twenties, with very little relief all the way through the thirties. Half of the banks in Montana closed during the twenties. The number of families who lost everything is impossible to even estimate. But it was a devastating time in our history.

So LET'S REVIEW. FIRST, the government and the railroads decided to ignore decades' worth of evidence and scientific theory that the Northern Plains were almost uninhabitable, especially for people who planned to make a living raising crops or livestock. According to Stegner's *Beyond the Hundredth Meridian,* from as far back as 1810, when Zebulon Pike reported that he had discovered a desert between the Missouri River and the Rocky Mountains, other experts, such as Dr. Edward James, who took part in an expedition led by Stephen Long in 1820, had declared that this land was "wholly unfit for cultivation, and of course uninhabitable by a people depending on agriculture for their subsistence."

They also chose to ignore John Wesley Powell's assertion that people would need at least 2,560 acres to survive here, and instead offered less than ten percent of that amount to anyone willing to make the trek out this way and establish a homestead.

So people came out by the thousands. And it's not hard to imagine that most of them had no idea how much money they would need just to establish themselves in this desolate place. First they needed enough to build a home, because that was part of the bargain for a homestead. You had to have a house that was at least 12 feet by 16 feet. Then they needed seed in order to plant crops. They needed the machinery to cultivate the land. They needed a good team to pull that machinery. They needed machinery to harvest those crops. And finally, they needed at least two years' worth of capital on which to survive before they started to benefit from their labors. I would love to see a study of how many of these poor, idealistic thrill-seekers came close to having that kind of capital when they arrived. The percentage had to have been infinitesimal. It's no wonder that, before 1900, no more than forty thousand families had homesteaded and retained their land by the Homestead Act. According to Stegner, during that same time, from 1862 to 1900, the population of the United States grew by 45 million. So the success of this venture was not good, although you would never guess that by the government's reports.

And yet…somehow, all these decades later, we have a strong legacy in Montana of amazing success in the field of agriculture. It's a fascinating testament that, despite unbelievable odds, there were people who managed to build a life for themselves here, and eventually establish Montana as a leader in production of many of our most important crops.

My theory on this is kind of complicated. I think our success can be attributed to two very opposite forces. The first is a sort of Darwinian desperation. The people who came here were risk takers to begin with or they never would have come. So there was a certain personality type who was willing to sacrifice everything they had to try something new, something that most of them probably had very little knowledge about. The people who came here thinking it would be easy probably didn't last long. But this risk-taking attitude often carries with it a certain competitive spirit, and I think it's fair to say that many of those early pioneers had that spark in them. They wanted to prove they could do it.

But there's no question that there was another contributing factor to all but the most ruthless people who made their way West in those early days, and it was a spirit of cooperation and teamwork in times of need, or when a task required more than the average farm crew. You hear the stories over and over again from farm or ranch families in Montana, of how their neighbors would gather when it was time to harvest, or brand, or dock their lambs. Or especially if there was a tragedy. I told the story earlier of my friend Lenore Pomeroy, whose family lost their home to a fire. The neighbors stepped forward, first offering them a house where they could stay and then working together to build them a new home. This is not an uncommon story in Montana.

The people who came out of this period alive were hearty, resilient, adaptable, and hardworking. And of course, they had to have some luck as well. Because there were others who were just as hearty, resilient, adaptable, and hardworking who did not make it. Perhaps one of the hardest lessons people must have learned from this period was that hard work guarantees nothing. God-fearing, good-hearted people had to have suffered from horrible crises of faith when their lives completely fell apart no matter how hard they prayed or how many hours they bent their backs over a plow.

But those who survived came out of it with a strong resolve and a stubborn determination. Most of us who are the offspring of those people know these qualities well. And we also know that there is a flip side to this coin, and that is where we find the dark side of the Montana personality.

I think it is especially true in Eastern Montana that people struggle with asking for help. It has been deeply ingrained that this is not the way things are done. When the area was settled, everyone was struggling to survive. It was almost unusual for a family to have *not* lost a child. And the problems that faced each family were very much the same: Lack of moisture, the battle to put enough money together to get through the winter or buy a much-needed piece of machinery. There was a commonality to everyone's experience that created an immediate alliance, but it also created an atmosphere wherein people did not discuss any of this stuff directly. Because of their shared problems, the person who talked about it was considered a complainer. And they risked finding themselves on the outside if they brought that kind of negative energy into a world where people were doing all they could to hang on.

I hear it all the time from people who grew up in Eastern Montana—that their grandparents' generation never talked about their aches and pains, or their money problems. Nothing. As one person said it, "Everyone knew everyone's business, but you damn well better not *talk* about your business." You didn't expose your dirty laundry.

IN THE SUMMER OF 1939, when a woman I will call Mary was about four years old, she and her sister were playing in the yard of their home near a small Montana town when a blue 1936 Ford coupe pulled into the yard. A young couple emerged from the car, accompanied by a girl younger than they were. The two girls raced to the house in anticipation of what brought these strangers to their home.

The couple entered the house "without knocking, through the kitchen and into the dining room," where the girls had joined their mother and father.

Moments later, these two young girls were shocked to find out that these people they had known as their parents were not their parents, as the woman declared "abruptly and unceremoniously" that the girls would from this day forward refer to her as "Mother" and to the man with her as "Daddy," and that they were to refer to the woman they had thought was their mother as "Gram." They then left without fanfare, leaving the girls behind with this revelation.

Mary was to learn much later, after several years of "a living hell" with this couple, that she and her sister were not the only two people in the room who were stunned by these revelations. The man with her mother had no idea that his wife had two other children who were obviously not his, nor did her parents have any idea their daughter had a third child.

Mary would also eventually find out that her real father, whom she never met, died several months after completing the Bataan Death March in the Philippines.

A few months later, Mary's mother and her stepfather, whom I will call Eddie, came and retrieved the girls to live with them so that they would be closer to a public school. But that was about the only positive; over the next few years of their lives they were shuttled from one tar paper shack to another while Eddie worked as a ranch hand or in mining camps.

"My mother treated our younger sister as if she could do no wrong, but we ran the constant risk of a beating with a razor strap for dropping one of the eggs gathered from the chicken coop or stepping in excrement when we went to relieve ourselves behind the barn since we didn't have an outhouse. None of the shacks we lived in had electricity or running water."

Often, when her younger sister went down for her afternoon nap and while Eddie was at work, Mary's mother would doll herself up and instruct the girls not to wake up their sister as she would sneak off for trysts. Mary would later learn that her mother had spent several years as a prostitute in Butte.

There are several things about Mary's story that are pertinent to the history of Montana. The most obvious is the fact that, in a place where the Depression lasted ten years longer than it did in much of the rest of the country, people often had to resort to the most desperate measures to survive. History often presents this period as a time that brought out the best in people, as they had to help each other out and do whatever it took to get through. But not everyone fit the mold, and for people like Mary's mother, the desperation to survive led to a kind of self-preservation that precluded all others. It sometimes brought out the worst.

I picture what must have led to the mother's decision to storm into her parents' house that day. She must have thought that she was only going to be able to keep the secret of these two little girls from her second husband for so long, and that she likewise could only avoid her parents for so long. And rather than leave these revelations to chance, she decided to do a preemptive strike and put it all out there at once, with no thought whatsoever to the pain it caused all the others involved.

At nearly eighty years old, Mary is a tiny little thing, but not in personality or drive. Her sterling silver hair is cut in a stylish bob, and she dresses fashionably in jeans and a black leather coat. Mary married a rancher, had several children, and endured years of isolation combined with verbal and psychological abuse from her husband before she left him and went on to become a nurse, working for several years at a leading medical facility before moving back to Montana and working in a hospital here.

In a funny way, Mary inherited her mother's instincts to do whatever it took to survive—with one crucial difference. which showed when I asked whatever happened to that younger sister who was treated like such a princess.

"She had the saddest life of almost anyone I've ever known," Mary told me. "This little girl never heard the word 'no' in her life, so she grew up with no sense of accountability for her behavior at all. My sister and I always felt kind of sorry for her, and she ended up moving to a larger town in Montana where she also became a prostitute, and died in her middle sixties of third-stage syphilis."

Mary's story symbolizes this time and place as well as any

I've ever heard, and the fact it took her decades to feel comfortable sharing it tells you all you need to know about the way people in Montana were conditioned to behave during those early years. Suffering was pretty much universal and "the common people" were expected to endure their circumstances quietly. The price many people paid for keeping their suffering to themselves is really impossible to measure.

DANIELS COUNTY IS ONE of the most successful farming communities in Montana. At first glance, the county seat, Scobey, appears to be just another small Montana town, perhaps a little more prosperous than most of those along the Hi-Line but otherwise unremarkable. But a closer look reveals more. There are more neat houses, with more finely tended lawns. There is less chipping paint and fewer dilapidated old cars parked in front of the houses. It's a tidy little town, with clean streets and well-maintained sidewalks.

When I arrived at the Daniels County Museum, there was a note taped to the door, "Be back in 30 minutes—giving a tour."

Looking around at the near-empty streets, I thought, "A tour of what?" But further exploration indicated several rows of restored old buildings in a fenced area just down the way from the main museum building. I wandered through a gate to a dirt path that led me back in time. These buildings weren't anything out of the ordinary for a museum: An old pharmacy. A bank. A church. Another church! Like many other museums I saw along the way, they were stocked with furniture and knick-knacks from a bygone era. But again, there was something different about this little place.

I finally caught up with the tour as they were nearly finished. The tour guide was a young woman, still in college. She was giving a tour to two other men. But like so many of the amazing volunteers I encountered on my journey, she did not recite her speech with the monotone of someone who had dutifully memorized a script. She knew her stuff and delivered the information with pride and delight. And although I wondered, bemused, when she would experience enough of the world to realize that the history she was sharing wasn't really all that unique, I ended up chiding myself for being so cynical. Let her believe that this place is that much different, for God's sake.

And then I found out that, at least in one respect, it is. The final stop on our little journey through the weather-beaten businesses took us to a fabulous old theater. Our tour guide went on to explain that for one week out of every summer, the theater comes to life with a nightly performance called the Dirty Shame Show. For that one week, locals present sketches, dance routines, and songs.

"My father has been part of the show for years. My sister was part of the show. I've been part of the show. It's a long family tradition. My father is such a great comedian. He was usually a big hit." She also passed along the surprising information that the building that housed the theater used to be a granary, not a natural transition and not one I would have guessed looking around at the structure.

As we walked back to the main building, we spotted a car parked out front with a very small old man standing next to it.

"Oh good, Edgar is here," my guide announced. "He's the guy you're going to want to talk to." She leaned close and confided, "He's really old, but he's super nice."

I bit my tongue. Ah, youth.

Edgar Richardson turned out to be the perfect person to interview about Daniels County, as well as one of the biggest gems I came across on my trip.

"Edgar, this guy is traveling to every county and then he's going to write a book about his travels," my guide announced. I shook Edgar's hand, a little worried about gripping too hard. He was stooped in a way that indicated some kind of degeneration in his spine. But he held my hand firmly, in both of his, and looked me directly in the eye with a wonderful smile.

"Oh, I read about you!" he said, referring to an article in my hometown paper. "I was hoping I would catch you when you came here."

This was one of only two times that this happened on my trip, and it happened in a place over 350 miles from my home.

First Edgar took me on a tour of the museum. Scobey had been a farm town from the beginning, although there has always been plenty of cattle in the county. But at the height of the homestead boom, around 1910, the town served, for a time, as the largest shipping point for grain in the world.

The population of the county is only about two thousand people, and about half of them live in Scobey. But according to Edgar, who later took me on a driving tour, whenever Scobey has needed something, whether it was a baseball field or a gym, all they had to do was spread the word and the money appeared. This past year, they decided their swimming pool was finally at the end of its run, so they put the word out that they needed to build a new pool. In no time at all, they had raised almost a million dollars. The community also has a long history of pitching in with sweat and labor, as evidenced by a town hall that they built for $40,000 rather than the $150,000 it would have cost if they'd hired it out.

Edgar himself built a movie theater in Scobey and donated it to the town.

Although Edgar was tiny, made smaller still by this congenital issue, pictures in the museum of a young Edgar showed a dapper, handsome young man standing tall and proud beside a gorgeous wife. When I asked what he did for a living, Edgar told me that he had been a farmer and also owned a bar. Neither of which I would have guessed. I admit these were my own biases, but Edgar seemed too small for the kind of physical labor you need for agriculture, especially in the time he would have been working, and he seemed too sophisticated to be a bar owner. But those are the kinds of surprises you encounter in Montana.

Edgar told me that the area had been rich with buffalo back in the nineteenth century. The grass was once thick, ideal for livestock. But then the government allowed the slaughter of the area's buffalo to starve out the Native Americans.

A carpenter named Daniels founded the town in 1901, building a twenty-three-room mansion at the outrageous cost of $2,000. He named the town after the local Native American agent. When the railroad came to town in 1913, they had to move all the buildings because the town lay in a river bottom where the railroad wasn't comfortable laying track. Edgar's grandfather moved to Scobey that same year, and went on to produce thirteen children.

At its peak, the town claimed five thousand residents and had seven hotels, five restaurants, and a livery stable. It also had a very fancy brothel, which now serves as the county courthouse, the only town in Montana that can make that claim. The madam was named One-Eyed Molly.

But maybe my favorite thing about Scobey is the fact that it's home to a local celebrity named Alvin Straight. Like me, you might not think you know who Alvin Straight is. But Alvin Straight was the man who decided he needed to visit his dying brother, despite no longer being allowed to drive a car. So Straight drove his lawn mower from Laurens, Iowa, to Blue River, Wisconsin. Although the trip was only 240 miles, it took Straight six weeks to make the journey. David Lynch, another Montana native, turned the trip into a movie, *The Straight Story*, starring Sissy Spacek and Richard Farnsworth, who was nominated for an Oscar for his performance as Alvin.

ONE OF THE FUNNIEST incidents on my trip happened in Plentywood (Sheridan County), another strong farming community. Just a couple of nights before my arrival, I had watched an old Spencer Tracy movie called *Bad Day at Black Rock*. Being a huge Spencer Tracy fan, I had seen this movie before, but this time around, it didn't escape my notice that the storyline had a little more relevance to my current situation.

The story is about a one-armed man named John McCreedy who shows up in the small town of Black Rock for purposes that he doesn't divulge at first. The townspeople indicate from the time he steps off the train that they're not a real welcoming bunch. The hotel refuses to rent him a room, the local garage won't rent him a car, and all in all, people are just not very goddamn friendly. Their mood turns even nastier when they find out that McCreedy is there in search of an old army buddy named Kamoko. It is the classic story of the worst of small-town America. Despite my best efforts, after watching this movie, I had been unable to shake the paranoia each time I pulled into another small Montana town and encountered "the stare."

When I arrived in Plentywood and began to drive around, looking for something interesting to explore, I couldn't help but notice that a big, ominous black pickup fell in behind me. At first, I thought it was just coincidence, but after I took several completely random turns, it become clear that I was not being paranoid. This guy was tailing me.

I finally decided it was best to just confront the situation directly. I pulled into a parking lot and turned around, waiting for my new friend to join me there. Which he did. He pulled in, rolled down his window and waved, so I rolled down my window as well.

The truck pulled up beside me, and a man about my age, wearing a soiled ball cap and a big ol' smile, said, "Your right rear tire is low. You better get that thing pumped up or you're going to find yourself with a flat out there on the highway."

I laughed, a small outburst of relief, and thanked him before he pulled out and moved along.

PLENTYWOOD HAS ONE OF the more interesting histories in Montana, starting with its name, which makes absolutely no sense in an area where there are almost no trees. According to local legend, Plentywood Creek and the town of Plentywood derive their name from a search for firewood. One day, cowboys from the Diamond Ranch watched in exasperation as the chuck wagon cook attempted to start a fire with damp buffalo chips. Finally, a notorious local named Dutch Henry said, "If you'll go two miles up this creek, you'll find plenty wood."

Like most towns along the Hi-Line, Plentywood originally came into being because of the railroad, although before 1910, there was no station in Plentywood itself. The closest was in Culbertson, about forty-five miles south. A spur to Plentywood was built and, by 1910, it was being touted by the Great

Northern Railroad as "a new metropolis in the Northwest." By that time, it had two general stores, four lumber yards, two hotels, a newspaper, two banks, a millinery store, a law firm, and a doctor's office.

In her excellent book, *Red Corner: The Rise and Fall of Communism in Northeastern Montana*, Verlaine McDonald lays out the events that led to some very interesting developments over the next few years. In 1907, about twenty-five miles southeast of Plentywood, a Danish pastor named Madsen founded a new community and invited his Danish friends back East to "put sixty or seventy dollars in your pocket, go to the nearest railroad station, and get out here." Madsen named his new community after the Danish queen of that time, Dagmar. A Norwegian community, Antelope, sprung up between Plentywood and Dagmar. "Locators" helped the farmers find the best piece of land available, with the results depending a great deal on the honesty of the locator. The heavy Scandinavian influence in the county would eventually come into play as events unfolded, as many of the Scandinavian countries had adopted very progressive political ideas during this period.

Many of these immigrants would build a house and then return home for six months to save money, as they weren't legally required to live on their claim for the first six months. But if they left, they ran the risk of a claim jumper coming onto their land and declaring it his own. With a government infrastructure that was still finding its feet, there was often little recourse. A man named William Hass came back to find a claim jumper on his claim, so he simply walked another twenty miles and made another claim, eventually realizing that he had stumbled onto one of the best pieces of ground in the county.

Between 1900 and 1910, the population of Valley County grew from fewer than five thousand to almost fourteen thousand people. By 1920, Valley County had been split into three counties, and Sheridan County itself consisted of almost fourteen thousand people. By contrast, Sheridan County's population today numbers fewer than four thousand. One of the other early challenges for these new Montanans was the falling price of wheat. In the 1870s, wheat was running around a dollar a bushel, but by 1910 the price had dropped closer to 60 cents. The homesteaders also had to live with the very real threat of hailstorms, common in this part of the state. At a time when there was no insurance for hail damage, a farmer could lose an entire years' worth of labor in a matter of minutes. At least today there is some compensation through insurance. In those days, it was not unusual for people to lose farms due to a single storm.

This part of the state was also notoriously dangerous in the early years, especially when railroads brought in crews to build new lines. These crews took advantage of the Plentywood saloons as well as several brothels, and as is often the case when you mix young men and booze, crime became a problem. A sheriff and his deputy were murdered in 1913 by a bridge construction worker who had been reported for causing a disturbance. The perpetrator was hanged and mutilated by an angry crowd soon after he surrendered.

There is an inclination, not entirely accurate, to think that Eastern Montana has always been a bastion of politically conservative thought. But there has also been a strong resistance among industrial labor and agriculturalists to the undue influence of both the government and major corporations over the working class. Although they seldom formed a majority, groups like the Nonpartisan League and the People's Party found a following in rural communities. Although Montanans have proven to be unpredictable when it comes to political choices, there are two things that seem to sway our decisions. The first is the economic condition of whatever region is at stake, and the second is someone presenting a convincing idea of how to improve those conditions. And there's no better example of this than Sheridan County in the late 1910s and early 1920s.

Because of the convergence of several factors—low grain prices, the influx of "honyockers" (as the new homesteaders came to be called), and yet another drought—the people of Sheridan County found themselves fighting that familiar, infernal battle of how to make a go of it. They were ripe for a strong voice, someone who would stand up and take their cause into account. They found it in Charles Taylor, a newspaper editor who was assigned by the Nonpartisan League to launch a radical newspaper in Sheridan County called *The Producer's News.*

Taylor was a massive man with a massive personality. He wrote with a flair for the dramatic, giving his opponents and friends alike colorful nicknames, and cultivating an antagonistic tension between farmers and big business. Taylor was apparently charming and even more convincing in person, and he soon developed a strong following not only among the farmers of Sheridan County but among many of its more influential leaders as well. He welcomed attacks and responded with counterattacks that kept people buying the paper to see what he would say next. He created drama and thrived on it.

But more than anything, he helped to develop a strong sense of community in a county that was sorely looking for this kind of leadership. Even his chief rival, the editor of the newspaper in neighboring Daniels County—a man with the most excellent name of Burley Bower—showed a certain admiration for Taylor even as they battled for years over many local issues.

Taylor's main focus was always on the farmers, and in a county where the farmers were fighting to survive, his strong support soon led him and some of his friends to run for public office, under the banner of a new party called the Farmer-Labor Party. The rise of his support was so meteoric that he was elected to the state senate after living in Plentywood for only a few years. Fellow party member Clair Stoner was elected as a state representative that same year, and another party member named Rodney Salisbury won the race for county sheriff.

These men and others who shared their views came to wield great power in Sheridan County throughout the 1920s, and Taylor's influence spread so that he was eventually elected as president of the national Farmer-Labor Party in 1924, an event that made the front page of *The New York Times.*

Although Taylor and his cohorts brought a positive shift to the county and to the surrounding communities, it slowly became evident, especially to those who opposed him, that Taylor was a Socialist, perhaps even a Communist. This didn't deter his followers from supporting him. For a time, at least. It was impossible to deny that Taylor's influence on the county had been positive. But unlike Western Montana, which had witnessed a similar rise of unions, this area consisted primarily of independent farmers. So while it was easy to rally workers in mines and smelters around specific issues, Taylor was dealing with a group of individuals with less cohesion. Without a specific cause to focus on, the movement became more and more dependent on Taylor's simple declarations about supporting the farmers.

By the sheer force of Taylor's personality, he had caused a radical shift in the political focus of his community. But in 1925, Taylor got roped into a business deal in Minnesota that required his presence in his home state. For the next few years, he tried to sustain his influence on Sheridan County, continuing to provide articles for *The Producer's News*. He even managed to hold on to his senate seat for the next term, despite protests (probably valid) that he was no longer a Montana citizen.

But when *The Producer's News* hired a new editor, P. J. Wallace, Wallace ran a few articles that were overtly in support of communism. People had known about the implicit leanings of the paper, of course, so although the backlash was immediate, it wasn't all that forceful. Wallace took this as a sign to continue, which he did. The grumblings became louder, and people had finally seen enough when the aforementioned Farmer-Labor Party Sheriff Rodney Salisbury, who had developed a shady reputation for giving special treatment to bootleggers and brothels, conducted a "Bolshevik" funeral for his teenage daughter, Janis, who had died from appendicitis.

Without Taylor there to hold back the tide, the sentiment against the movement he had created couldn't be contained. The cult of personality had lost its power. Taylor eventually lost his seat in the legislature, Salisbury lost the next election, and *The Producer's News* folded soon after.

The socialist/communist movement in Northeastern Montana slowly faded into a foggy past, leaving behind only a colorful name for this part of the state—the Red Corner.

I find this brief period in a small town to be a fascinating look at how Montanans can be open-minded toward any politics or ideology, as long as it shows some promise of making their lives better. The residents of Sheridan County were willing to entertain the possibility that Taylor's radical ideas might improve their situation. These people were ready for that kind of leadership, and they got it, and it actually helped their community until those in power lost their focus.

"WE MOVED TO HARDIN when I was four, in 1916."

This sounds like a line out of a memoir, right? Or maybe an interview published decades ago. But it's actually something I heard from the mouth of Margaret Ping as I drove her to visit the Big Horn County Historical Museum in Hardin on a fall day in 2015.

Margaret's mother had two sisters who started a women's clothing store in Sheridan, Wyoming, and they spent years trying to convince Margaret's parents to come out West and do something similar. The two sisters finally scouted out the area and decided that Hardin would be a good choice for a new store, and Margaret's parents agreed to give it a try.

Margaret remembered the first Ping's Ladies' Ready-to-Wear store being very small, taking up part of a lean-to structure that jutted out from one of the hotels in town. In an account that her father James Ping wrote about his own life, a woman came into their store and admired a fur coat. She asked Mrs. Ping the price of the coat, and when Mrs. Ping quoted $24.50, the woman told her that she would not buy a coat for less than $50. She came back and ogled the coat several more times, trying to convince Mrs. Ping to raise the price. But Margaret's mother wasn't about to compromise their prices just to make the sale.

Margaret also remembered her parents being indignant about the custom of some of the local businesses who were charging a different price for Native American customers. At that time, the Native Americans were not included in the public school system. It was the time that many Native American children were shuttled off to private schools that beat their cultural beliefs out of them.

"They were not treated well in Hardin," Margaret said, just one small indication of the compassion that has inspired her decisions.

Margaret—who if you did the math, was 103 years old at the time of our interview—wasn't eager to talk about herself, but reluctantly answered my questions. She is adorable, with a pageboy haircut and a round face and glasses. She uses a walker to get around nowadays, but that does *not* slow her down.

Margaret has led a remarkable life. She has carried on the generous, progressive spirit of her parents, who encouraged her to go to college, in the thirties, when it was unusual for women. She went to Oberlin, the first college in the United States to welcome African American students as well as the first to go co-ed. After completing a degree in religious studies, Margaret went on to graduate school at Columbia where she heard about an opportunity that seemed like a good fit for her training and interests. For the next four decades, Margaret worked for the YWCA; her specialties were working with troubled teens and creating support groups for women who were victims of domestic violence. Her work took her to Detroit, Mexico, Chile, Boston, and finally back to Montana, where she retired.

But "retired" is a relative term for many people, and Margaret has been extremely active since then, starting the Billings branch of Habitat for Humanity and taking an active role in supporting causes that are important to her. But her proudest achievement was in providing the land and much of the motivation for the Big Horn County Historical Museum.

"When I was a girl, my father bought a small farm just outside of Hardin, where he planted a huge garden, something he loved to do. My father was known for his gladiolas—he planted more than a thousand each year. But his main passion was vegetables, which he raised by the bushel. I remember him coming home every night and telling my mother who to prepare baskets for."

I had a feeling I knew the answer to my next question, but I asked anyway. "So did he charge people for those baskets?"

Margaret seemed slightly offended. "Nope. Not a thing. He gave them away."

I think it's safe to say that Margaret Ping came by her predilection toward philanthropy honestly. The ground where Mr. Ping's farm once stood is now the home of the Big Horn County Historical Museum, which houses twenty-six buildings from the homestead years, including a church, a filling station, the old Ping farmhouse, and the dining hall and barracks from the Campbell Farming Corporation, once one of the biggest wheat farms in the world. It is a beautiful facility, with a recently completed main structure featuring many interesting exhibits, including one of Will James, and another for the old missionary schools that were started for the Native American population before they were allowed to attend public schools. Margaret said that her father would have been astonished to see such an elegant facility on his property, and that the staff and the board have "worked like beavers" to turn it into the impressive facility it has become.

ONE OF THE BUILDINGS at Hardin's museum is the chow hall from the Campbell Farming Corporation. The Campbell Farming Corporation came about because of the vision of one man. Thomas Campbell, Jr. (no relation to Hardy) was born in North Dakota, where his parents homesteaded in the late nineteenth century. His father, Thomas Sr., was a very successful farmer, but he became ill when Thomas Jr. was a teenager. Thomas, Jr. took over management of the farm, learning the basics before he decided to move to California to work as an engineer and invest in real estate.

When World War I broke out, he came up with the idea of leasing land in Montana to raise wheat for the troops, and approached Secretary of the Interior Franklin Lane, who approved of the idea, and contacted J. P. Morgan about providing the capital to finance it. Campbell initially started his farm on the Fort Peck Reservation, but decided to move it to the Crow Reservation where he leased ninety-five thousand acres of land and hired Native Americans and other locals to farm and harvest his wheat crop.

When the war was over and the Depression hit, Morgan and Campbell's other New York investors withdrew their support, but by then he had a strong enough operation to keep it going on his own. He bought up land from the reservation, and continued to lease whatever else he could.

In light of the desperation of some of the people Campbell leased and bought from, it's easy to assume that he was simply another rich guy who figured out a way to exploit those who were in need. But from all indications, Campbell seems like one of the good guys. Not only did he hire Native Americans to work his farms, but also he hoped to someday sell the land back to the reservation. But for reasons I couldn't determine, he eventually sold out to his partner, Floyd Slattery, and a 1959 *Life* magazine article identifies Slattery as the manager of the nation's largest wheat farm.

Today Hardin still relies primarily on agriculture, although tourism is big in this county, with the Little Big Horn Battlefield just fifteen miles up the road and plenty of good fishing in the area.

But perhaps the weirdest story to come out of Big Horn County is that of a private prison that was built in Hardin. In 2004, a Texas company convinced the members of Hardin's financial authority to float bonds to finance a $27 million jail to house 464 prisoners. The Two Rivers Detention Facility was supposed to open in 2007, but the State of Montana refused to approve it, based in large part on the fact that the facility was not considered adequate for housing prisoners. One sheriff described it as "a warehouse."

Over the next few years, the fate of the facility became something of a comedy of errors. First the Hardin City Council unanimously voted to approve bringing prisoners from

Guantanamo Bay to Two Rivers, but that idea was shot down by Montana's congressional caucus, with Senator Max Baucus famously saying, "We're not bringing al-Qaeda to Montana—not on my watch."

Next, a mysterious fellow named Michael Hilton showed up with a story that he was part of a US police force that was supposed to be a test case for President Obama's plan to establish government-funded private police forces across the country. Hilton had the residents of Hardin excited for a while that they might finally be able to make some money off this whole fiasco, but he turned out to be a an ex-convict Serbian immigrant with more than a dozen aliases and criminal convictions, not to mention many fraud, rescission and unlawful detainer cases with over $1 million in adverse judgments against him.

Finally, after almost seven years of sitting empty, Two Rivers Detention Facility felt the first footsteps of prisoners in 2014 when a man named Kenneth Keller was brought in as warden. He was contacted by a company called Emerald Correctional Management who expressed their interest in taking charge of the facility. This company was supposed to manage the jail in the first place, back when it was built, and the reason they chose not to then, as well as the reason they changed their minds, are a complete mystery. Journalist Ed Kemmick, who wrote extensively about this project, made several attempts to get in touch with them, but they never responded. There's no way of knowing what the motivation was, but they were able to secure a contract with the Bureau of Indian Affairs (BIA) to house prisoners from the Blackfeet, Northern Cheyenne, and Crow tribes in Montana; the Mandan, Hidatsa, and Arikara Nation in North Dakota; and two tribes in Wyoming.

At its peak, in 2014, the Two Rivers Detention Facility housed about 250 prisoners and employed a workforce of about the same size. But there was still one more twist in store for this beleaguered project. In early 2016, the tribes all withdrew their contracts with the jail, and as of January 7, the jail was again completely empty. Although they are waiting to hear whether the BIA will entertain a new contract, they have sent all of their employees home.

"DEAD DEAD DEAD DEAD dead dead dead." Fallon County farmer Jerry Sikorski pointed toward a cement-colored field that belonged to one of his neighbors. "You see the color of that ground? You see how dull it is? That's because all the nutrients are gone…it has no *soil health!*" Jerry shook his head. "I know, I know, I'm obsessed with this stuff."

Like Gil Mengels from the Museum of America, Jerry's hands were massive—huge, but not swollen. They looked like the hands of a man six inches taller, thanks to years of physical labor.

"Okay, now look at this." He bent down and dug into the soil at our feet, scooping a handful from the hole. He held it to his own nose, the hands looking cartoon-like next to his normal-sized head, and then poured some into my hand. "Smell that," he said.

The soil looked like chocolate cake, almost black, with a firm but tender texture. It smelled alive, as fresh as a prairie rainstorm. "See what I'm saying?" Jerry said. Then he broke the soil apart, revealing an intricate network of tiny roots. "And if you put that under a microscope," he said, "you'd find thousands of tiny little bugs and organisms of all kinds. Because that's what gives it that kind of life…that kind of *health.*"

It was striking, driving across one of the Sikorski farm's fields, how the ground felt more like a golf course than most farm or ranch land. Normally, driving over a pasture or a field, especially in Eastern Montana, is a bit like riding a roller coaster, with bumps and dips that you often don't see coming, and sometimes send you careening against the door. "I like to plant crossways every year too," Jerry explained. "One year I'll go north and south, and the next year I'll go east and west. It levels out the land."

Over the course of many years, Jerry has devised a unique strategy for farming that involves no cultivation at all, constant experimentation with crop rotation, planting cover crops, and even planting small sections of pollination crops, designed for the sole purpose of attracting more bugs. Jerry is a big believer in generating the whole process of interaction between insects, animals, and crops. He even leaves a wide swath of wheat un-mown every time he harvests so that the insects and critters have something to feed upon.

So what's this guy's story? Is he some hippy from Califor-nia who moved to Montana with a trunkful of loopy ideas he picked up from some commune? Or is he one of these trust fund babies who had the money to get a graduate degree in agriculture and decided to buck decades' worth of solid expe-rience?

Actually, neither of those is remotely close. Jerry was born and raised on this very farm, about fifteen miles south of Bak-er, the county seat. He's a Vietnam vet, a man who served in the National Guard for over twenty years as a helicopter pilot, and who moved back to the farm as a young man and has nev-er left. He's completely self-taught, although if you suggest that to him, he'll dismiss it out of hand. "I've been to a lot of talks and conferences through the years." Jerry, it seems, has had many mentors.

Jerry's grandfather homesteaded this piece of land in 1911. He came to Montana from Minnesota after immigrating first from Poland. Jerry's dad was one of seven kids—five boys and two girls—and as with most families in those days, he went through a complicated and sometimes contentious competi-tion with his siblings before he emerged with the farm.

One of my few questions that brought Jerry to a silent halt was, "How did they get through the Depression?"

Jerry has an amusing habit of chewing his tongue, and this question really got his jaw going. He apparently doesn't chew very hard, as there's never any sign of blood, but he gnawed on it constantly. "You know, I really should know more about that," he said. "I know they did pretty well, because they came out of the Depression with more land than when they went in. But I have no idea how they got through it."

Eventually, his father married and had five boys, of which Jerry was the youngest. Although there was nothing remark-able about the farm when he was a kid, they managed to survive, and his father showed some flashes of innovation, including being one of the first in that era to incorporate, which they did in 1956. Ironically, this decision ended up turning on Jerry's father when he got involved with a younger woman and Jerry's mom along with the rest of the family voted Dad out of the corporation.

Jerry's oldest brother took over, and when Jerry moved back to the farm, he worked for his brother while at the same time serving his time in the Guard.

"My back is a mess after flying helicopters for twenty-six years," he said. "All that bouncing around."

Jerry was refreshingly honest about the dynamics in his family, a rarity among rural Montanans, and he admitted that his brother had been very difficult to work for. But eventually his brother became too old to run the place, and Jerry was the natural choice to take over. As is often the case, this was because he was the only one who was interested. By that time he had been thinking a great deal about what he would do if he ever got that chance.

Before we left the house for a tour of the farm, Jerry handed me a copy of the book, *Dirt*, by David R. Montgomery. "This is what it's all about," he said. He went on to explain how the book documented the decline of farming among several civilizations, some of which I'd never heard of, because the farmers turned the farmland into deserts by overusing it, by plowing it up, or leaving it fallow so that the topsoil blew away, and with it all the crucial nutrients and organisms that keep soil healthy and productive. Basically, the Campbell Method.

Hearing it described this way, soil conservation seemed like such simple common sense that it's hard to imagine how anyone could believe that plowing up the earth over and over again could possibly be a good idea. But ever since people have broken ground, or gathered livestock in a bunch and tried to raise them as their own, theories of every stripe have gained traction and found a following. When I read this book later, I was struck by the many examples from around the world where thriving civilizations collapsed in large part because they didn't manage their soil properly, including Jordan, Iran, and Mesopotamia. And the pattern was essentially the same every time. But in the days of the homesteaders, the research was not extensive or readily available. Today we know better. But that doesn't necessarily make a difference.

Jerry is always experimenting, so it's hard to pin down his method to a simple routine. But there are a few consistent truths. The most important is the commitment to never cultivating. Instead of plowing before he plants, Jerry uses a drill that buries the seed just a little deeper, below the surface of the cover crops, which he makes no effort to clear. The depth is different depending on the crop. The cover crop then provides both warmth and a natural mulch fertilizer. Plus it holds all the nutrients below the surface that would otherwise be exposed, and perhaps blown away by the wind if you turn the earth.

He also sometimes plants an entire field with a blend of seeds designed to form this cover crop. For example, this year's cover crop consists of buckwheat, chicory, flax, safflower, and sunflowers. To many, spending the money to plant a field that he will not harvest would seem like a waste, but it is this long-term vision that has enabled Jerry to develop such healthy soil. And it has ended up saving him money in other areas, primarily in fuel and equipment costs. A few minutes later, we passed the neighbor whose field Jerry ridiculed, and Jerry pointed at the neighbor's tractor, a monstrosity that had tracks like an army tank. "Six hundred-and-fifty horsepower!" he shouted. "Imagine how much dirt that thing is throwing up into the air, and how much fuel he uses just to run that thing for a day!"

I asked whether any of his neighbors have come around to his way of thinking.

"Oh yeah," he said. "This guy over here." His big thick finger punched the air. "He won't admit that he's following my lead, but he never plows anymore, and he started planting crossways a few years ago. Also, I started planting corn in 2008, and nobody around here was planting corn then. Now everybody does."

The crops that Jerry was planning for that season's rotation were spring wheat, corn, canola, lentils, alfalfa, safflower, and mustard. But he was always trying new things. "I grew sunflowers a few years ago. I hate sunflowers," he said. Lentils are one of his staples, and for good reason. Not only have lentils become very popular in the organic food industry, but the lentil plant is also one of the few crops that generates its own natural fertilizer.

Technically, the Sikorski farm doesn't qualify as organic, which sort of makes a mockery of the whole concept of organic. They occasionally use pesticides and fertilizer, so they don't meet the standards of organic crops. This doesn't matter to Jerry. He is much more interested in creating soil that will continue to become more healthy with each passing year. In *Dirt*, Montgomery contends that an inch of topsoil takes about a century to restore. When I asked Jerry how long it takes to restore a field to healthy soil, he said, "Ten years." No matter what your objective is, the more important figure is how much topsoil is being lost each year, and that figure is frightening. According to estimates, twenty-four billion tons of soil are lost around the globe each year. In the United States alone, enough soil is lost to fill a pickup for every family in the country. Much of this is preventable by applying a different approach. And not very many people are concerned about it.

So what happens with this place when Jerry can no longer do the work? He has been diagnosed with rheumatoid arthritis, although his wife, Kathy, doesn't agree with the diagnosis. But there are days when he can't get out of bed because of his back. He's seventy-one years old, and he attributes many of his health issues to Agent Orange.

"Our grandson could run this place," he said, and Kathy quickly agreed.

"He came home from high school one day after he took one of those tests that show what you're most suited for," Kathy said. "He threw this piece of paper on the table, and said, 'What the hell is this all about?' And every single category on that thing showed that his biggest strength would be agriculture. It was the last thing in the world he wanted to hear."

"But he loves it out here now," Jerry said. "And he has the right personality for it."

The only problem is he lives in L.A. And, according to his grandmother, "Oh, he loves the night life. I think he's going to be there for a while."

And then I heard a sentence I never thought I'd hear in a farmhouse in Montana. "Plus he's gay…I'm not sure how comfortable he'd be living out here."

To my surprise, the Sikorskis informed me a few months later that their grandson was indeed moving back to the farm, in preparation for taking over from Jerry. I think it's a wonderful sign of change.

JERRY WAS ONE OF many small farmers I visited with who seemed to be doing just fine, challenging the common theory that bigger farms are the way to go. There's no question that overall, Montana is moving in the same direction as the rest of the country, with large corporations swallowing up the family farms one after the other. And of course the machinery has become much more sophisticated, and huge, as evidenced by Jerry Sikorski's neighbor. These tractors now cost several hundred thousand dollars.

There's no reason to think that these larger farms are a bad idea, or that people should go back to small family farms, but I did find it interesting that many small farms are thriving, which throws the conventional wisdom under the bus.

AMONG MY FAVORITE PEOPLE that I met on this trip were the Paulus family, Ralph and Myrna, who own a farm near Choteau, in Teton County. Ralph Paulus had one of the most infectious smiles I've ever seen. He was also disarmingly unconcerned about his appearance. When he greeted me on his front porch, the first thing I noticed was that the collar of his T-shirt had completely separated from the bodice. So there was a gap that ran all the way from one shoulder to the other. Ralph's hair flew up from his head like a salt and pepper feather duster, and best of all, his smile made you forget every other detail about him. His wife, Myrna, was a typical farm wife—sturdy, both in form and in personality—with a firm handshake and a ready smile. Ralph and Myrna welcomed me eagerly into their warm, well-lived-in home. There were books and magazines piled everywhere, and the space smelled of happiness. Spices, wood, bread, bacon.

Ralph and Myrna inherited two family farms, which are thirteen miles apart. They raise mostly barley, but not malt barley: They raise barley for hay. And they are among the few farmers left who bale their hay in the small, rectangular bales as opposed to big round bales. And although the reason is that they've simply never been able to upgrade to the bigger baler, this has actually worked to their advantage as they've developed a clientele of customers who prefer the smaller bales because they're easier to transfer and manage.

My favorite fact about the Pauluses is that they read to each other every morning.

Myrna explained how this came about. "Quite a few years ago, we decided to start reading classic books, and rather than read them separately, we thought it would be fun to read them out loud. So every morning we sit down with Shakespeare or Hemingway, and we take turns reading a section out loud. We started with the Bible."

My second favorite thing about the Pauluses is that, for several years, they were part of a theater group that compiled the histories from several of the families in their community and combined them into a play, called *The Coming Home: An Anniversary,* complete with music. They performed this play for several communities as part of The Prairie Mountain Players and Roadside Theater, eventually traveling all the way to Kentucky to perform it for a similar community theater there.

I asked how they got along with their neighbors. Turns out, they really only have one, a Hutterite colony whose property surrounds their farm.

"Our relationship with them depends a lot on who is leading

their group," Myrna said. "I'll give you a good example…A few years ago, I was elected chairman of the school board, and the leader of their colony stopped by one day and decided to let us know that he didn't approve of having women as the chairman of anything. He even turned to Ralph and said, 'You shouldn't allow your wife to take a position like that.'" Myrna shook her head and Ralph just laughed. Myrna lowered her chin and looked me straight in the eye. "I'm sure you can imagine how well that would go over if Ralph were to tell me that."

Again, Ralph laughed.

I found a lot of laughter in the Paulus household, especially when Ralph told me one of his favorite stories about the Hutterites. Their relationship with the colony became strained after the school board incident, to the point where Ralph informed them that they would no longer be allowed to use the Paulus road, even though it led to one of the Hutterite fields. They had another way to get there, but it was through other fields, so it was very inconvenient for them not to have access to the road.

One day, when Ralph and Myrna were working on their other farm, thirteen miles down the road, some of the younger members of the colony decided they would take advantage of the Paulus's absence and use the Paulus road. Little did they know that Ralph's ninety-year-old mother was taking her daily walk along that very road. When she saw their truck approaching, and realized who it was, Ralph's mother stood in the middle of the road and wouldn't let them pass. "She's about this high!" Ralph said, his laughter ringing throughout the house. He held his hand about four feet above the floor. "But by god, they turned around. Things got a little smoother after that. They had a change of heart about the way they treated Myrna."

NOT TOO FAR DOWN THE highway from the Paulus family is another family farm, one with a very different history. Jacob and Courtney Cowgill own about thirty acres near Power, Montana. They call their operation Prairie Heritage Farm, and it's certified organic by the Montana Department of Agriculture. This certification requires a yearly audit and extensive paperwork. They are not allowed to use any synthetic fertilizers or any herbicides or pesticides at all. According to Courtney, keeping the pests away requires a lot of manual labor, which may explain in part why their farm is thirty acres rather than several hundred.

Jacob and Courtney are in their thirties, so they are bucking the current trend among farming communities wherein a vast majority of the younger generation are doing anything they can to avoid going back to the family farm. Courtney grew up on a farm in Dutton, Montana, not far from where they are now, and when her parents sold the farm while Courtney was in college, she thought that chapter of her life was behind her, and she was fine with that.

Jacob came to farming from a different direction, although he was also raised in the country, just south of Great Falls. But his family did not farm, and he didn't become interested in farming until he was in graduate school. Jacob was studying environmental studies in Missoula, and he started farming at the PEAS Farm (Program in Ecological Agriculture and Society), and according to Courtney, "it was all downhill (or uphill!) from there." The PEAS Farm is a collaboration between Garden City Harvest and the University of Montana's Environmental Studies Program, and it apparently fit his personality. After he graduated, Jacob went to work for Kamut International, an organic wheat farm near Big Sandy, and he and Courtney eventually realized that this was an interest they shared.

"We both saw local food as an opportunity to come home to Central Montana and buck the trend of rural flight," Courtney said. "In 2009, we found a place to lease near Conrad and we farmed there for four years before we bought this place."

I asked her what reasons she heard from younger people as to why they weren't interested in farming. I loved Courtney's response: "This is hard complex work and more often than not, I hear reasons from *myself* on why this isn't the best life. But then I wake up in this beautiful prairie, watch the sunrise, and listen to my kids running wild outside, and those thoughts quiet a bit. That's what drew me back— the wind, the dirt, the food, the open space, the community, the freedom. It's how I grew up, and whether I wanted to believe it or not in my twenties, that was all part of me. When I got closer to having kids, I realized I wanted it to be a part of them too. Logistically, it was the whole local food thing that inspired me to believe that we could farm on a small scale and make a living, but it was the life I missed that really brought me back."

Courtney's description of what she and Jacob are doing sounded so much like the ideal that people have in their heads when they think about moving to Montana and living off the land. But like most people who farm, Courtney emphasized how hard the work is. Plus, also like many other farmers, they do not rely entirely on farming to make a living. Courtney studied journalism at the University of Montana, and she has a part-time job as managing editor for PBS MediaShift, an online site that documents trends in online media. As managing editor, Courtney is responsible for sorting through unsolicited articles as well as writing an article of her own now and then. She devotes "about twenty-five hours a week" to this job. Does she sometimes fantasize about doing this kind of work full time?

"I still wonder about my alternative life—the one where I'm an editor in a big city, eating food I didn't have to grow and cook myself (ordering pizzas to my door!) and taking my kids to plays and concerts and museums and libraries and parks. It could have gone either way and either way, we would have been happy, and neither path is better than the other. But this is the life we chose and I love it.

"Most of the time," she added.

Oh, and she teaches at the University of Montana. *And* she's on the board for the Red Ants Pants Foundation, a non-profit organization started by Sarah Calhoun, owner of Red Ants Pants, which I mentioned in an earlier chapter. The foundation offers grants to women who are involved in leadership roles, and also to small agricultural operations.

And Courtney has two kids.

"Did you leave anything out?" I asked.

"Well, the one thing most people don't know about me is that I used to sing the national anthem for the Lady Griz," she said.

NOT FAR UP THE ROAD in the other direction from Choteau, near Conrad (in Pondera County), is another farm that breaks many of the old rules. This farm is owned by a man named David Oien. As with so many who farm these fields in the middle of the state, Oien is the product of grandparents who homesteaded here in the early 1900s. His grandmother's family originally homesteaded on a farm just three miles from a town called Brady. His grandfather ran a dairy farm, also near Brady. Although they lived so close to each other, and were only ten days apart in age, they did not go to school together until high school, where his grandfather was the only boy.

David's father bought a different farm in 1939, and he discouraged David from picking up the family business. David took this advice to heart and started college at the University of Chicago, where he studied religious studies and philosophy. He finished school at Missoula, and told me that what he learned in various philosophy and religion classes had a great influence on his life. He spent a couple of years in Europe, where he became interested in renewable energy. As with many of the people who ended up taking a slightly different approach to their family business, it is worth noting that David spent time in other places, exploring other pursuits. He was exposed to alternative ideas, which have served him well.

By the time he moved back to the farm in 1976, he was committed to converting the farm to a more organic model. Much like Jerry Sikorski, who has become a friend of David's, much of his approach involved rotating crops in order to develop the soil in a healthy way.

David freely admitted that it was a struggle making a living in those early days, when people looked askance at those who wanted to do things differently. When I asked whether people in his small rural community treated him badly during that time, he said, "No, I don't recall animosity as much as indifference. Alternative agriculture (the more common term in those days) was likely seen more as misguided than threatening." Unlike Jerry, David does till the land, because "nobody has figured out how to farm organically without tilling." But the biggest obstacle from the beginning was trying to figure out a way to distinguish his products from those of the thousands of other organic farms that came about in the late seventies and early eighties.

His solution to that problem was to form a company, with three of his high school friends, to market their wares. The company, called Timeless Seeds, Inc., was formed in 1987, and again, results were meager at first. But patience and time have been good to David. Today he has contracts with a dozen organic farms, and business is going very well. Well enough that David has hired someone to run the farm because he's too busy running the company. For those who think that organic farming makes no sense financially, Jerry and David are fabulous examples of the fact that although it can take time, the financial rewards can be significant, while also honoring a strong belief system. It also helps that these two businesses were highlighted in a recent, well-regarded book, *The Lentil Underground*.

David Oien told me that Pondera County has suffered from many of the same maladies that plague so many rural communities nowadays. The farms are becoming bigger and the town is becoming smaller. There are almost no businesses left in Conrad. "They once had two or three grocery stores, a creamery, a bakery, at least two clothing stores, two or three hardware stores, and four farm equipment dealers. We now have one grocery store, one stand-alone bakery, one women's clothing store, a farm store that sells hardware, and two farm equipment dealers. Today, you can't buy a pair of shoes (that are not work boots), underwear, or a men's shirt in town. On Saturday, Main Street in Conrad has only a car or two in the business district, and dozens of 26 license plates would be in parking lots in Great Falls. Basically, forty years ago or longer, Conrad was the trade center. Now it is not. Not an atypical story, of course. Good roads, fast cars, cheap gas, and big box stores."

THERE ARE MANY FACTORS that contribute to the flight of young people from rural Montana. Although livestock prices are high at this particular moment, this certainly hasn't been the norm. It has become much more difficult than it used to be for a small farm or ranch to produce enough to cover operating expenses. Especially when they're competing with bigger and bigger operations, with bigger and more sophisticated machinery.

At the very peak of the homestead boom, the percentage of Americans who were farmers was close to 50 percent. People often forget that many of our founding fathers, including our first president, were farmers of a sort. But coinciding with the decades following the homestead boom was a dramatic increase in efficiency. It started, of course, with the tractor. Suddenly what took a man weeks to accomplish could be done in a matter of days. Or even hours.

But it actually goes back even further than that. It came as a surprise to me that John Deere did not start out as a tractor company. John Deere actually created the first plow, back in the 1820s. Before Mr. Deere came along, the Great Plains was covered with a thick coat of grass with a tangle of roots just below the surface that a man couldn't cut through with the crude tools of the time. But with the help of an ox or a good horse, John Deere's plow cut through those root structures easily, and the face of the plains was transformed forever.

Today, despite solid evidence to support the theory that bigger farms are no more efficient or profitable than the small family farm, the trend continues toward big, corporate farms. According to David Montgomery in his book *Dirt*, there were fewer than two million families living on farms as of 2009. That compares to six million in 1920.

Since the Depression, when soil conservation practices were

promoted to prevent the same thing from happening again, it is estimated that two hundred million acres of US farmland was either marginalized or lost to crop production by the 1970s. Montgomery's research shows that this is almost a third of what was available before the Depression. And for the most part, plans by the government to prevent this kind of erosion have proven to be ineffective, or downright wrong.

But there have been exceptions. In the early 1930s, Coon Creek, Wisconsin, had suffered an enormous amount of erosion. Somehow it was chosen as the very first conservation demonstration area in 1933, and for the next four decades, the Soil Conservation Service helped farmers adopt contour plowing, using cover crops in crop rotation, using manure as fertilizer, and plowing crop residue back into the soil. By 1975, the erosion rate in the area had been reduced to one quarter what it had been.

MEANWHILE, UP ALONG the Hi-Line, an organization in Montana is working to preserve the land and restore it to its original condition. The nonprofit American Prairie Reserve (APR) has been buying land along the Missouri River since 2001. They now control over three hundred thousand acres, mostly in Phillips and Valley Counties. This is about one tenth of their ultimate goal of acquiring three and a half million acres and turning them into a wildlife reserve. Their objective for this land, in their own words, is "to create and manage a prairie-based wildlife reserve that, when combined with public lands already devoted to wildlife, will protect a unique natural habitat, provide lasting economic benefits, and improve public access to and enjoyment of the prairie landscape."

The basic premise is to continue to accumulate this land and allow it to return to its natural state, which also encourages the wildlife in the area to live and breed without the interruptions of modern industry. The preserve is open to campers, hunters, and has recently added biking and hiking trails, and they plan to continue to find ways to provide public access. But there is something unique about the way the APR is approaching this project, in that they are working with the local ranchers in an effort to find a balance between preservation and maintaining the way of life the local people have been accustomed to for decades.

And how did they decide on this area? The Temperate Grasslands Conservation Initiative (TGCI) did a study in the late twentieth century to determine which parts of the world are viable options for landscape-scale grasslands conservation. They came up with only *four* areas on the globe, four areas that still had the capacity to be restored to something close to their original state, and this part of Montana was one of them.

Sean Gerrity organized the American Prairie Reserve, which also enlists a Scientific Advisory Council consisting of professors from Stanford (including the president), Duke, Princeton, and Harvard, among others. With the help of these advisors, this is one of the few regions in the country where organizations like the World Wildlife Fund (WWF), US Fish and Wildlife Service, Montana Fish, Wildlife and Parks, and the Bureau of Land Management are able to conduct experiments in such a large area.

Hilary Parker is the communications and outreach manager for the APR, and much of her job involves creating a working relationship with the neighbors. The development of this reserve has been very controversial in Northern Montana, and much of that controversy has to do with the simple matter of change. To rural Montanans, change is synonymous with a threat to their way of life, and it often creates a divide. There is a natural tendency among Montanans to think that outsiders have no business coming into our territory and telling us what's best for us. We've been here for so many years, after all, and we've done just fine without you.

Much of the resistance also came about because of a previous effort to do something similar called the Buffalo Commons. Buffalo Commons was a theory developed by a couple from back East named Frank and Deborah Popper. In an essay published in 1987, the Poppers declared that much of the region known as the Great Plains was not sustainable under the current patterns of use, and that the best approach to making use of this land was to create a nature reserve and populate it with bison.

Although the Poppers may have had some sound research to back up their theories, including those old studies done decades ago by John Wesley Powell, their approach to this subject matter was extremely clumsy, and basically insulted a whole swath of people who have lived on this land for decades. They also underestimated two things: the intelligence of the people who have managed to make a living on this land, and their devotion to it. Farmers in Montana do not like to be told by people from back East how they should run their lives. When the American Prairie Reserve came along with a somewhat similar theory for this region, they had to overcome a lot of damage done by the Poppers.

The staff at APR is very aware of this dynamic, and they are also aware that one of the best ways to work with people who are resistant is to provide incentives. People are much more likely to listen if there is some benefit for them, of course. And they are even more likely to come around to your way of thinking if there's money involved. So the APR has worked out arrangements with several local ranchers to lease their land back to them for however many years they want to continue ranching, in exchange for buying their land. The APR land currently holds seven thousand head of cattle, and much of it belongs to those who sold them this land.

Another program they have recently initiated is offered through a company called Wild Sky Beef, which will offer a portion of their profits to ranchers who produce organic, wildlife-friendly beef grown near the APR. The reserve will pay ranchers a premium in order to raise beef under the guidelines required for it to qualify as organic and wildlife friendly. So that prohibits the ranchers from shooting prairie dogs, it requires them to install fences that allow pronghorn to slide underneath, and allows the APR staff onto participating ranchers' land once a year to inspect and make sure ranchers comply with these guidelines. To date, Wild Sky Beef has found customers in many parts of the country, and is working to make similar deals with other ranchers in Montana.

The APR has raised $80 million out of the $500 million they estimate they'll need in order to acquire the 3.5 million acres to complete their goal. They are raising six hundred head of bison on the reserve, confined to a grazing area of about thirty-one thousand acres. Their ultimate goal is to see ten thousand head of bison in the region.

Most of the local resistance involves the bison. Local ranchers are worried that the bison will bring disease into their region—disease that will spread to their cattle. To this, Hilary responded, "Our ranching neighbors' fear of disease is concentrated on brucellosis. Some of the bison in Yellowstone National Park, for instance, are infected with brucellosis, and there's concern that the cows just outside the border might contract it from bison. Our bison are brucellosis-free, so once we proved that, their concern went away pretty quickly.

"The other concern—bison damaging property—we handled directly by giving our neighbors permission to shoot any bison that were wrecking their property (should they get outside the fence). We also gave ourselves twenty-four hours to get an escaped bison back inside our fence (whereas the standard around here for cows is at least forty-eight hours). That has engendered a good amount of trust. Well, that and the fact that our fences are incredible...we've only had two instances of bison outside the fence in ten years. The first one was when a really snowy winter allowed them (and neighboring cows) to walk right over the top of fences (but we got them back shortly afterwards). The second was just a few months ago, when a gate was left open (we think possibly by hunters) and a few wandered out. This time, even though it took us a while to round up the last bison, our neighbors were patient, tolerant, and even kindly toward the animals. So that makes us feel good."

With all of the effort that the APR is putting into creating a sense of goodwill, and even giving the locals an opportunity to make some money off of their venture, it might seem odd to the outsider that they are still meeting such resistance. But in order to understand the reactions of the people along the Hi-Line, you have to delve deeper into their history.

This is the part of the state where the railroad dumped a lot of people fresh from the East, or from Europe, with the promise of great things. It is also one of the areas of Montana where the ranchers suffered the greatest losses early on, and then had to contend with the influx of "honyockers." There was a period where the relationship between farmers and ranchers was extremely contentious, and the end of glory days of the open range just happened to coincide with the heyday of the Homestead Act. Just after the ranchers had lost half their stock in the blizzard of 1886, the farmers started showing up in droves, propping their tiny shacks in places where cattlemen were used to grazing their livestock.

The point is, these are Montanans who don't have a high level of trust for outsiders. And they don't embrace change with open arms, for reasons that are easy to understand. But the situation has reached a point where the stubborn determination to cling to the old ways *should* be challenged. The younger people are leaving in waves, and the cost of running a family farm has become prohibitive to many of the people who have been here for decades. It is in their best interest to entertain new ideas, and with the American Prairie Reserve putting as much effort into helping the people of this region find new ways to improve their quality of life, it seems reasonable that they be given a chance.

But these ranchers also have some concerns, as voiced by Tess Fahlgren, my Glasgow friend from the chapter about the railroad. Tess still believes that the APR has not addressed, to the satisfaction of many local ranchers, the brucellosis question. "They have said that there's no scientific evidence to support the theory that buffalo can pass brucellosis on to cattle, but we have veterinarians who have come forward and said otherwise." So even though there are no documented cases of this happening, the fear is still out there.

But from what I can tell, if the APR continues to approach the local ranchers with the kind of respect they've shown so far, they have a much better chance of achieving their goals in a way that can benefit both groups.

WHAT THE AMERICAN PRAIRIE Reserve is trying to accomplish is especially significant in today's West because of the growing controversy surrounding access to public and private lands. At this writing, this issue has drawn a lot of unwanted attention because of the occupation of a wildlife refuge in Oregon by some militant ranchers who think the government has been wielding too much power over access to public lands. The world watched a bizarre drama play out there over this group occupying the refuge, under the banner of patriotism, claiming that some friends of theirs were treated unfairly because they got fined and jailed for setting illegal fires on their ranch. These men were inspired by a mentor who was recently quoted in a *New York Times* editorial by Bozeman writer Betsy Gaines Quammen, as believing that the US Constitution was written by Jesus.

Many people in Montana agree with the goal of these men, which is taking control of federal land, whether they support the methods or not. There has been a contentious relationship between the BLM and ranchers, farmers, hunters, and fishermen for decades. It is yet another topic that requires a book of its own. But in a place where land is the most important of many important resources, it is naturally a significant issue here. It's interesting to note that polls show that a wide majority of Montanans do not support giving control over public lands to the state. So the issues are more about how the feds have managed this delicate balance than who controls it.

I'M NOT SURE WHETHER most of us have noticed that among all these amazing resources we've been blessed with in Montana, the most important is the soil. It often seems that soil is the last asset we consider in our decisions about what to do next. In Butte, we tore away half a town—and then just left the hole in the ground. In the Northwest, we stripped away the forests, leaving whole mountainsides to be washed away with the rains. But perhaps worst of all, in the name of quick returns and high yields, we have peeled away the very skin that covers our earth. And there's no simple or quick way of grafting that skin back. There's no way of guaranteeing it will ever *come* back, especially in our lifetime, or the lifetime of anyone we will ever know. I think it is a metaphor for how we treat each other, but more importantly, how we treat ourselves. Because when we ignore the warnings, which came loud and clear from the people who were here before us, we are hurting ourselves more than anyone else. We are putting instant gratification ahead of good long healthy lives for ourselves and those who come after. And I hope it's something we as a people, as a region, will take the time to study and ponder.

CHAPTER EIGHT
Animals

"I know a rancher like you down below Hell's Canyon.
He runs about six cows and five thousand sheep.
But he calls himself a cattleman."
—Loren C. Estleman

For a long time, there was a stigma in Montana about sheep. Sheep were considered dirty and stupid, and for years people denied their significance to our agricultural development. Even the term used for those who raise sheep—"sheep farmer" (heard just as often, or perhaps more often, than "sheep rancher" or "wool grower")—would seem to infer that raising sheep is somehow less prestigious than raising cattle. I've never in my life heard someone referred to as a "cattle farmer."

The truth, of course, is that sheep made their way into this country just about the same time cattle did, and may have been even more significant in terms of allowing people to break into the business in the early days of ranching. For newcomers who were short on cash flow, sheep provided an avenue to get into the business with less capital than it took for cattle. It was also much more common for a rancher to raise both cattle and sheep than we have been led to believe. Raising both often created a nice balance because of the variation in their grazing habits.

The myths about sheep being stupid and dirty were mostly created by cattlemen to support their opposition to sheep ranchers. The fact that sheep gather together so closely and don't seem to act independently is due to their natural survival instinct. Because they have no real fighting ability, their best chance for surviving an attack from a predator is to stick with the flock. And the idea that they are especially dirty and prone to contaminate watering holes is simply false. Cattle are much more likely to wade into a water source and drink, while sheep tend to stand at the edge.

But sheep are slowly becoming less common, mainly because of the problems of working with the BLM (Bureau of Land Management) to arrange grazing leases, according to a wool buyer in Billings. He claims that the government is working harder than ever to push sheep men off the land.

JIM HAGENBARTH COMES from a long line of sheep men. I heard an interview with Jim on National Public Radio's (NPR's) *Home Ground*, and was able to contact him for a phone interview thanks to Brian Kahn, the host of that show. Jim proved to be a valuable source of information, eager to talk, and very knowledgeable about the history of all aspects of agriculture in the West. Plus he had a great, gravelly voice, the kind I can listen to all day.

In the late nineteenth century, Jim's great-grandmother and her second husband, who was a freighter, drove a herd of twelve thousand sheep from Washington to Idaho, where Jim's grandfather Frank was the first white child born in Lemhi County. Frank started an operation called Wood Livestock and at one time had one hundred fifty thousand head of sheep and another fifty thousand head of cattle on two million acres. But Frank eventually lost the place, and Jim thinks it was because Frank became too involved in other business ventures and didn't pay close enough attention to the operations at home. It's hard to imagine how one could ignore an operation involving that much livestock, but whatever the case, Jim's father Dave was determined to continue the family business, and he borrowed money from a friend to start his own sheep ranch about five years after his own father lost Wood Livestock.

Jim and his brother now run Hagenbarth Livestock, and oddly enough, much of the land they own is the same land that their grandfather acquired back in the late nineteenth century. But the amount of livestock they run now is much smaller than their grandfather ran then. And despite the fact that Jim is a huge proponent of sheep, Hagenbarth Livestock's focus now lies on cattle. It has become a common theme in Montana, due to the many obstacles for sheep ranchers, most notably limitations as to where they can graze. Having the Wool Act repealed in 1993 also had a dramatic impact on wool growers in the United States, as the secretary of agriculture no longer had the authority to determine wool prices based on production and demand. But according to Jim, the biggest issue is that the BLM and some environmental groups have been incredibly shortsighted when it comes to their policies on sheep grazing.

For example, the Gallatin Wildlife Association and the Cottonwood Environmental Law Center recently filed a suit to try to prevent sheep ranchers in Beaverhead County from utilizing grazing land in the Gravelly Range, an area that has been used for decades by such people as the Helle family, who run one of the most successful sheep ranches in the state. The environmental groups claim that grazing this land endangers grizzly bears and bighorn sheep, because a couple of grizzlies have been killed after encounters with local sheep, and bighorn sheep have been known to contract diseases from domestic sheep.

The Helles have cooperated in the past in similar circumstances, reaching a compromise with the BLM after initially protesting the reintroduction of the bighorn sheep into the area. In that instance, they agreed to the move as long as nobody tried to challenge their longstanding grazing agreements with the Forest Service. But now, the potential outcome of the

Gravelly lawsuit puts their whole operation in a holding pattern. As Jim Helle pointed out in an interview with KULR-8 TV, "This affects a lot more people other than just our family. There are distributors and buyers who rely on our production, and those entities are also left to worry about the future of their businesses."

It's another classic example of the awkward relationship between commerce and conservation here in Montana, and although I'm able to see both sides of the issue, I have a harder time sympathizing with those who would protect a handful of wild animals (with no real guarantee that they're even protecting them) at the expense of a neighbor's livelihood. Jim finds the grazing issue especially problematic in areas that carry an abundance of weeds like larkspur, which sheep love and which is completely toxic to cattle and other animals. To keep the sheep out of those areas means allowing a different kind of threat to the animals that remain. Jim is a big believer in variation. Because sheep and cattle affect the land in different ways, he finds it only natural that finding a balance is the best way to avoid the problems that come from running the same species on the same ground over and over again. But it has become increasingly difficult to manage that kind of balance.

Another misconception about sheep, according to Jim, is that they are bad for grazing land. He says that if you leave sheep in a certain area for too long, naturally they can do damage to that ground, just like any other grazing animal. But if they are allowed to graze for a short period of time, he believes they provide one of the better ways of disrupting that land in the way that is most natural and productive for the environment.

Thinking back on this conversation with Mr. Hagenbarth, I was struck by how often I have thought that the conflicts between ranchers and environmentalists often imply that ranchers are not concerned about the environment. But it's clear from his views that the differences between these two groups are much more likely to be defined by the fact that they view abuse of the land very differently. I'm reminded of my conversation with Tess Fahlgren. It is in the best interest of farmers and ranchers to see themselves as stewards of the land, and it became clear to me that the best of them approach it just that way. And nobody knows the land and the patterns of animals and crops better than the people who work that land and raise those livestock.

People like Jim Hagenbarth, or the Helles, are always thinking long term in the way they approach their operations. As Jim describes it, they are always going to recognize that dealing with disease and predators "is part of doing business." The idea that ranchers always want to do away with predators is not accurate. Since poisons were outlawed in 1970, the ways of dealing with predators have been limited to shooting them, relocating them, or using some kind of diversionary tactic, like dogs. When dogs mark the territory, they tend to keep coyotes away, and they also deter bears by providing an obstruction.

In other words, most of the best farmers and ranchers I talked to understood the value of conserving all aspects of the environment, not just for the world but also for their own operations. It seems counterintuitive, but it really isn't. And in the long run, it also serves them well financially, which is what matters to most of us. In the end, it seems to me that environmentalists and farmers/ranchers are much more aligned than they often realize...they just have different ways of approaching a given problem. It's another classic example of two groups who could, and do, find a lot more common ground than they anticipate, if and when they sit down to talk.

FROM THE BEGINNING, despite the fact that ranchers have raised everything from pigs to bison to goats to ostriches, cattle have dominated the world of livestock in Montana. My friend Toni Pullum Quinn and her husband, Chris, even raised llamas for a time. From what I can tell, Toni came to hate llamas with a healthy passion. They never sold a single one, which probably didn't help her attitude toward them. I just recently heard that llamas have become quite the delicacy in South America, which means they're probably about to become popular here too. So Toni and Chris may have been ahead of their time.

But that has been true of many of the pioneers in Montana's livestock industry.

As one might expect, the first appearance of livestock in Montana came about thanks to basic supply and demand. When young men traveled home to the West after the Civil War, particularly to Texas, they found the plains crowded with cattle—so many that there was not enough of a market in their own region. The price for cows fell as low as two or three dollars a head in Texas. Thus began the famous cattle drives north, first to the railheads of Nebraska and Kansas, but eventually turning north toward the plains.

Like so many industries in Montana, cattle ranching in those early years was often financed by outside sources. During the late nineteenth century, investing in cattle became something of a fad for eastern bankers and financiers, with mixed results. But those who made smart investments and hired the right men to handle their stock could make a lot of money, and often did. Much of the early money as well as the early ranchers happened to come from Scotland.

Scotsman John Clay was an early pioneer in the ranching business, financing and managing ranches from California to Nebraska. He wrote a wonderful memoir, *My Life on the Range,* which is refreshingly frank. It reminds me of one of my favorite Montana memoirs, *We Pointed them North,* by Teddy "Blue" Abbott, who also tells his story without the usual romantic whitewash. And yet these men have very different stories to tell. Clay was a moneyman, one of the original members of the famous Cheyenne Social Club—a man familiar with a brandy snifter and cigars—while Abbott was a hard drinker and a frequent visitor to the bordellos of the day. But the one thing they shared was a love and respect for cattle, as well as for the men who loved and respected cattle. And you can sense this by the way they talk about the relationships that developed between the men who worked these cattle.

Abbott tells a moving story about sitting for a week with a young man who had tuberculosis, and had no one else willing to spend his final days with him. Abbott got almost no sleep during that week, and his friend was so afraid of dying alone that he didn't want him to leave the room, so Abbott had people bring food while he sat at this man's bedside until he died.

Clay tells a similar story about a group of men, himself included, searching in a snowstorm for an old sheep man who had gotten lost in the storm. When they found him frozen to death, these tough pioneer men stood in a semi-circle and wept. Both Abbott and Clay also make countless references to men breaking into song together. Not something you'd expect from modern-day cowboys, I would guess.

Clay and Abbott are also forthright about the fact that many of the men who got involved in the early days of ranching were less-than-stellar role models. This willingness to not romanticize their experiences is exactly what makes their stories believable. And informative. Because for years we have been led to believe that the people who came here and settled this place were almost superhuman. It is the kind of mythology that does the rest of us a disservice by implying that we are somehow flawed for feeling frightened or insecure at times.

BUT BACK TO THE cattle. The main thing that opened up millions of acres of thick grassland to the cattle ranchers was the slaughter of the buffalo. With all that grass left untouched, they came, literally in droves. A cattle drive usually traveled around ten miles on a good day. The crew consisted of a wagon boss, seven to nine cowpunchers, a cook, a wrangler, a mess wagon, a bed wagon, and usually around one hundred horses. The enormity of this endeavor is hard to even fathom in today's world, where shipping cattle is a simple matter of loading them onto trucks and sending them off to their destination where they arrive just a day or two later. These cattle drives took months, day after day of fighting the elements, trying to avoid a stampede, providing food and shelter not only for the animals but for the crew, and managing all those personalities. Just dealing with the dust proved to be a constant battle. The worst of the cowboys were assigned to the rear, where they had to bear the brunt of dust from thousands of hooves. It was a nasty, horrible job.

People tend to believe, even today, that raising animals is just a matter of providing land, feed, and shelter. But dealing with livestock has long been considered an art at which few really excel. My uncle likes to talk about a man named Charlie Osgood, a sheep man who worked on our family ranch on and off for many years. Uncle Lee describes how Charlie could walk through a sheep shed without making a single animal stir, his tread was so light. And the reason this is so important is that, over time, the less your animals move, the less excitable they are, the more weight they retain. And of course the easier they are to work with.

My uncle and I recently met with an old neighbor of his, Phyllis Oliver, who is now in her nineties and is still as sharp as hell. Her family also hired Charlie from time to time and she talked with great affection about how much he taught her as a young girl about working with stock. According to my uncle, Phyllis was much better with livestock than either her father or her brother, and she attributed this to Charlie. But according to my uncle, it has a lot more to do with a person's instincts than anything. In other words, in his view, it's not something that can be taught.

Phyllis told about how she used to ride out to Charlie's sheepwagon to get his food order, and when she brought the order back to her father, he would cross off the items that he didn't think were necessary. Phyllis would then go to town and buy Charlie's food, including the items that were crossed off. Her father never reprimanded her for it. He knew Charlie's value as well as she did.

Good sheep men were a rare commodity not only because they had to be good with the stock but also because they had to endure weeks or months of solitude when they took the sheep to the mountains for grazing. My uncle told a funny story, perhaps a tall tale, about a sheep rancher taking the month's supply of food to his sheepherder and telling him, "Hey, I thought you might want to know that the war is over."

"What war?" the sheep man asked.

The value of a good hand is hard to overstate when you think of how much the livestock industry came to rely on these men and women. The mention of ranch hands always conjures up a certain image for me, and I think it's probably a fairly common one. There was a man named Frank Wondercek who used to work for my grandfather. He was a hard worker—a good hand, as they say. Except for one thing, a recurring issue. Occasionally, he would disappear for a few days. Sometimes for good. And the reason was simple…he was on a bender.

It is a stereotype that has become common around the West, but it's one of those stereotypes that has come about honestly. Hired hands are often solitary men—men who have suffered some loss that pesters them like an open wound that won't heal. Frank Wondercek would sit at my grandparents' table each meal and rarely speak, and there were many who came to work for my grandfather who were just like him. They would do the hardest physical labor imaginable, collect their handful of ten-dollar bills at the end of the week, and slink off to some smoky bar to seek escape from whatever memories haunted them.

IT'S IMPOSSIBLE TO KNOW, of course, whether cows ever wonder about anything at all, but if they do, the cattle who were subjected to those long drives from Texas must have been very confused about being forced to walk for weeks through miles and miles of grass that looked perfectly fine.

Johnny Grant, mentioned early on, is usually credited as the first to start raising cattle for trade in Montana. Along with his father, Richard, and brother, James, Grant began acquiring cattle from weary travelers who were desperate for money or food. He developed a policy of trading one healthy cow for two that were worn out from months of travel, and in that way, he gathered a huge herd, which would eventually become known as the Grant-Kohrs Ranch near Deer Lodge. Conrad Kohrs would eventually buy Grant's ranch from him and build it into the biggest cattle operation in the state.

BUT IF THERE IS A town in Montana that is more associated with cattle than Miles City (in Custer County), I can't imagine what it would be. Aside from being the final destination for many of the early cattle drives from Texas (as well as playing a prominent role in Larry McMurtry's Pulitzer-prize winning novel, *Lonesome Dove*), Miles City was also a popular gathering place for some of the early cattle barons in the state. It is home to one of the more secretive clubs in the state, the Miles City Club, which is rumored to have had Teddy Roosevelt among its membership, along with most of the early big names in the cattle business.

Miles City started as a fort. Just after the Battle of the Little Big Horn, the US Army decided to beef up the military presence in Eastern Montana. So they built several forts, including one near the mouth of the Tongue River called Fort Keogh. The fort was named for Captain Myles Keogh, who was one of the officers killed in the battle. Keogh became famous for his horse, Comanche—mythically, the only survivor of the Little Big Horn (there were actually several horses that survived this battle from the cavalry side…the Comanche version just made for a great story). General Nelson Miles was in charge of this fort, much to his dismay, as it turned out to be manned by a group of hard-drinking soldiers who Miles would later claim to be worse than any Indians he'd ever dealt with. Probably a bunch of lonely kids dealing with PTSD. But at the time, he wasn't feeling very compassionate about what they'd been through.

In 1877, Miles got so fed up dealing with drunk soldiers that he evicted the suppliers of their booze, who packed their stock and headed a few miles downstream, where they set up shop in what would eventually become Miles City, named for the general.

Much like the fort, Miles City was known as a wild place in these early years. Teddy "Blue" Abbott spoke fondly of this town in *We Pointed Them North*, relating stories of the weeks he spent strolling the streets of Miles City with a rented companion or enjoying the camaraderie of men who liked whiskey and gambling as much as he did. But there was also a lot of business getting done in early Miles City.

Texas cattlemen drove thousands of cattle north to the

open range of Eastern Montana, and Miles City became a popular destination because of the thick grasses in the area. It was also a convenient place to gather the herds for shipment east to Chicago. With the prairies free of buffalo, the belief seemed to be that the range in the Northern Plains would support an endless supply of livestock. And based on the millions of buffalo that had previously roamed the range, it's easy to see how they drew that conclusion.

But one thing they couldn't have possibly foreseen was the blizzard of 1886–1887. The events leading up to that storm, which is still considered the worst in our history, added to the disastrous outcome. The spring of 1885 was drier than usual, and beef prices dropped lower than they had been for quite some time, convincing many cattlemen to hang onto the calves they would have normally shipped. So the range was as crowded with cattle and sheep as it had ever been.

As mentioned earlier, the effect of that storm on the cattle business was devastating, and because it was quickly followed by a huge influx of homesteaders, many cattlemen left the area. So those who stayed were among the best at what they did, not to mention the most resilient. And it is those people who are the ancestors of so many of the people who are still there. We came by our tough, stoic attitudes honestly.

There is a lot of pride in Miles City about their history, as is evidenced by the Range Rider's Museum, a sprawling structure that features artifacts and photos from the early ranching days, guns (of course), as well as memorabilia from the Miles City Bucking Horse Sale. This event was officially established in 1951, although it was preceded by the Miles City Roundup, which started in 1914. The Bucking Horse Sale has become one of the biggest stock sales events in the country. But the most impressive feature at the museum is a huge Cowboy Hall of Fame, where the walls are covered with pictures of men and women who have passed along to the big corral in the sky. There are hundreds of photos, and most of the subjects are wearing cowboy hats.

Sylvia Danforth moved to Miles City in the 1970s when she married Duane Danforth. Duane was a descendent of homesteaders, although his family had sold the ranch by the time Sylvia married Duane. She was working in the area as a speech pathologist when they met, and would find Miles City to be a wonderful place to raise a family. "We could let the kids leave the house anytime they wanted and we knew we never had to worry."

Sylvia was something of a pioneer in the field of child development services in the area, and she is still very active in that field. Today she is the director of the Development Educational Assistance Program (DEAP), a not-for-profit organization started in 1976 to help families with children who have special needs. Over the years, DEAP has expanded its services to offer counseling and assistance for all kinds of family issues, and their services are available in seventeen counties in Eastern Montana. They have recently devoted much of their time to working on early intervention programs for autistic children, so that they can get the help they need to get an education.

Sylvia grew up in Billings, where her father worked for the city water company and her mother ran the Billings Receiving Home, a home for kids who were being abused or neglected. Sylvia's parents also took in foster children throughout her childhood, and they even lived in the receiving home for a time. Her mother was also active in the Friendship House, another facility that provided help for people in trouble or in need. Sylvia's mother just recently died a few months short of her hundredth birthday, and the family celebrated that day just as planned, as a celebration of a life well lived.

Sylvia and Duane had three children, two of whom they adopted. Their youngest, Emily, has gone on to become a highly respected writer, author of the acclaimed young adult novel, *The Miseducation of Cameron Post.* And it says a lot about Miles City that this novel, which is a coming-of-age story about a young lesbian girl in Miles City, is a source of great pride among many of the locals. Although it has been included on many banned book lists around the country, the people of Miles City clearly respect the Danforths enough that even those who may have issues with the subject matter still admire Emily's accomplishment.

But Emily is quick to point out that this does not necessarily reflect the attitudes of the Miles City where she grew up. "High school was hard."

Emily realized that she was gay at a young age, although she wouldn't have used that label then. She remembers feeling much more comfortable with short hair and pants. She was never at home in girly clothes or activities. It was the kind of behavior that could easily be explained away as "tomboy" until she reached puberty, which is when the discomfort really started to kick in, especially when she'd hear the stereotypical slurs about gays. She remembers one incident in particular where a boy was allowed to perform a song *in class* that talked about gays going back into the closet. "I was struggling so hard not to blush or break into tears."

Emily figures that it might have been easier, and her appearance and mannerisms might have been more acceptable, if she'd been more athletically inclined. "But my only interest athletically was swimming, and that wasn't a huge draw in Miles City. Plus it only lasted a couple of months of the year." So she hid her insecurities with humor, being named class clown in her yearbook. Although she was active in high school, she always felt as if she was on the fringe, and to some extent she was. "I had many pals and acquaintances, but I didn't have any real friends because I couldn't be honest with anyone about who I was or how I felt."

So Emily was kind of shocked when she got such positive responses to her book. She relates one of her favorites, from a former classmate. "She told me that she knew the general plot of the novel before reading it and, in her words, 'opened the book bracing herself for the scathing takedown of Miles City,' and then was so pleased and surprised not to find that, and instead, to find aspects of it rendered lovingly on the page."

This is a great testament to Emily's ability to look at her childhood and sort through the worst of it to focus on what was good. The narrative voice of Cameron Post reminded me very much of Scout Finch in *To Kill a Mockingbird,* with its wonderfully nostalgic tone, but with the underlying tension— in *Mockingbird's* case the tension came from racism, and in Cameron's case, from the danger of having her sexuality revealed.

Emily attributes much of the fact that she has been embraced by Miles City as pride in their own, despite the subject matter of her book. But she also thinks it is a reflection of our time, with marriage equality becoming more accepted (ten years ago, Emily married her long-time partner, Erica Edsell), and a stronger presence of the LGBT community. Montana's own recent legislation would certainly support her theory, as all of the major cities in Montana (except Billings) have adopted a Non-Discrimination Ordnance, preventing employers, landlords, and business owners from discriminating against people because of their sexual orientation. The Billings ordnance missed passing by one vote.

When I moved back to Montana in 2007, I had just left San Francisco, so I was shocked how homophobic our state still is. I had become used to giving hugs to men, and even telling some of my male friends I loved them. To their faces! I quickly realized that I was not in California any more, and although I have never had any homosexual tendencies, I suddenly wondered whether I was giving off some kind of vibe when men seemed to pull away from me when I complimented them, or had the audacity to touch them.

I can attribute some of this to my upbringing as well. Although both of my parents grew up in families where physical affection, and phrases like "I love you," were rare, they each approached parenthood very differently, showing us great affection, both physically and verbally, from the beginning. Their approach was unusual for that time, but not completely unique.

When I returned to Montana, I also noticed signs that times had changed. I was surprised to learn that there are LGBT clubs in the high schools, something that would have been unheard of when I was in high school. Emily Danforth says there are now a handful of people who are "out" in Miles City, and that one young man came up after one of her readings and proudly told her that he was the first to ever come out in the high school. She is hopeful that the recent Supreme Court decision allowing gay marriage will give gays and lesbians even more reason to feel comfortable being themselves.

I can't help but relate this to another of the overriding themes of this book, and hope that the more accepting we become as a state, the more effect this will have on the suicide rate as well. It will be interesting to see whether this is true.

I ASKED SYLVIA DANFORTH whether Miles City is experiencing a lot of the same exodus of young people that other small towns in Eastern Montana have, and she said she didn't think so. I had read something a few years ago about Custer County being the only county east of Yellowstone County that hasn't had a decline in population, a statistic that has probably changed since the advent of the Bakken. So I wasn't entirely surprised.

Sylvia also presented an explanation. She told me about a group of young men who all went to high school together and have moved back to Miles City over the course of the past few years. After acquiring advanced degrees and establishing themselves in the business community, these men returned home and formed an organization called Milestown Community Improvement, devoted to helping to spruce up their town. The group started out by focusing on things that were important to them as children. So for instance they built new dugouts at the Little League field.

The next step was to sell beer at local events like the Bucking Horse Sale to raise money for their next project, a folf course. Folf, of course, is the sport of golf using disks similar to Frisbees. They have also organized projects to clean up various areas of their town. Sylvia Danforth said she asked one of the organizers of the group why it was all guys, and he told her that they've been open to including women since they started, but it just hasn't happened.

Milestown Community Improvement's most recent project was to design and sell a custom license plate. They hired
someone to design the plate, and their optimistic hope
was to make $10,000 if the plate sold well. To their sur-
prise, they ended up pulling in $70,000, and they now plan
to use this money to provide grants for good causes. So
Miles City seems to be defying the odds somehow, finding ways to revitalize the community from within while
still relying on much of the old methods of making a living.

ONE THING YOU NOTICE driving along the highways of Montana is that there are very few stretches of road that don't have
a few houses or farms along the way. But the ribbon of asphalt
from Miles City to Jordan may be one of the loneliest highways in the United States. It is an eighty-five-mile drive, and
I counted fewer than twenty houses along the way. I actually
felt lonely by the time I got to Jordan. And it's no wonder this
place feels so isolated. At 175 miles from the nearest airport, 85
miles from the nearest bus line, and 115 miles from the nearest
train, Jordan, Montana, is the most isolated county seat in the
United States, and the farthest from any public transportation.
So I was happy that the Garfield County Fair was happening
that day, and that I had arranged to meet my friend Karla
Christiansen at the fair.

Karla is a rail of a woman, built like a teenage boy, with a
similar haircut. I met her when she took a writing workshop
I taught at Miles Community College. Behind wire-rimmed
glasses are blue eyes that reflect a hint of anxiety but also ready
humor. She laughs easily but not without a bit of embarrassment. Karla is warm and incredibly friendly, and has led a fascinating life. As a young woman, in the 1960s, she and one of
her best friends crossed the country on horseback, from Maine
to Montana. She and her husband have also rafted all but an
eight-mile stretch of the Missouri River. And she recently met
up in real life with a woman in Sweden with whom she has
been pen pals for over fifty years, after she drew her name out
of a machine at the World's Fair in New York City in 1964. But

today she is not interested in talking about herself. She wants me to meet her friends.

Karla set me up at a table and introduced me to Mareta Brusett, whose husband owns the Brusett Angus Ranch. A 2012 poster for Brusett Angus tells us "Our Cattle Just Do It!"— a claim that leaves much to the imagination. But whatever it is they do, they've been doing it for over a hundred years, a fact that Mareta delivered with a typical Montana combination of pride and understatement. In fact, I discovered later that there is actually a town called Brusett, about twenty miles west of Jordan, and a search on Google Earth reveals that it now consists of a post office, the Brusett Community Church, and the Brusett Ranch.

"Jordan still had board sidewalks when I moved here," Mareta said.

"Which was…?"

"1952."

"And how big was it?"

"I'm not sure how big it was then, but the biggest it ever got was about five hundred. It's about three hundred people now."

Among other interesting facts I learned from Mareta is that because of the isolation of this community, the high school in Jordan used to have a dorm for the ranch kids. With Garfield County being close to five thousand square miles (nearly the size of Connecticut), and with all but the main highway being gravel roads, it's easy to understand the need for that. But the dorm closed down about twenty-five years ago, and they tore it down last year. Today the high school, which celebrated its centennial in 2015, only graduates about ten or twelve seniors each year. Mareta told me there used to be close to one hundred country schools in Garfield County, but now there are only five.

The isolation of Jordan, which finally has its first form of public transportation now that one of the senior centers provides bus service to a hospital in Miles City, has drawn some interesting characters to the region. One of them was a man named Benny Binion. Benny was a native of Texas and son of a hard-drinking father who lost the family ranch when Benny was a kid. Benny always had romantic notions of owning a ranch of his own, but he started out by making money as a gambler. Benny was so successful that he became one of the founding fathers of Las Vegas, where he opened the Horseshoe Casino and came up with the idea for the World Series of Poker.

But Benny was not satisfied to hang out in Vegas, and his success allowed him to pursue his old boyhood dream. He began by buying land near Hardin in the 1940s, where he started a small cattle ranch. He eventually acquired more land around Jordan, and moved his cattle the two hundred miles, Texas style, to his Jordan ranch, which would eventually grow to about eighty-five thousand acres.

Although Benny was not known to be showy, he was hard to miss in Jordan, with his big black Cadillac with longhorns mounted on the hood, and a huge bodyguard, the first black resident anyone can remember in Jordan. He was also the only cowboy in the area who broke an unspoken rule by wearing his pants tucked into his boots. Benny Binion raised cattle and thoroughbred horses. He wasn't particularly popular with the people of Jordan and mostly kept to himself, although he was known to hand out free advice, particularly about paying your taxes, which he encouraged.

Apparently he didn't always follow his own advice, and after a few bouts with the IRS, he lost his ranch in 1989 for failure to pay his own taxes.

BUT I IMAGINE THE people of Jordan would prefer not to be reminded of the event for which they are best known. It's a classic Montana tale, with the central characters embracing the long-held belief that the best government is the one that leaves its people alone.

In the mid-nineties, a group called the Montana Freemen, led by a Montana pilot named LeRoy Schweitzer (a cousin of former governor Brian Schweitzer), formed its own community, which they named Justus Township. Schweitzer was a failed businessman from Washington state who moved to Jordan, where he found enough like-minded folks to declare themselves no longer under the jurisdiction of the US government. According to people who knew the men, they were incredibly intelligent. Ralph Clark, on whose ranch (under foreclosure at the time) the township was located, was even known to have built his own tractor, which was way more advanced than anything on the market.

But those close to them agree that they had lost their way, eventually devising a plan to fund their operations by filing liens against public officials, and creating bogus checks and money orders. They also held mock trials for local officials, including one in which they declared a death sentence on a county attorney.

It took two years of such nonsense, with the FBI investigating them for most of that time, before the feds finally decided to take action. They surrounded the compound, which led to a standoff in 1996 that lasted for eighty-one days. There were moments where the confrontation threatened to become violent, but this was not long after the Branch Davidian disaster in Texas, as well as the showdown in Ruby Ridge, Idaho, so the feds were more cautious than ever about doing anything to indicate fault. The Montana Freemen finally surrendered, and were tried and convicted of several federal crimes.

The arrests were made in June 1996, just two months after Ted Kaczynski was arrested in Lincoln, Montana, for the series of mail bombings he had carried out under the name of the Unabomber. And it makes me proud of Garfield County that they are embarrassed about these events, which threatened peoples' lives and, along with the Unabomber story, created a completely unrealistic image of the average Montanan. I was living out of the state at the time, and I had to endure endless jokes about our state. I could see the humor, but it also troubled me greatly because I knew better. I think it's worth noting that neither of the men responsible for these events, Schweitzer nor Kaczynski, were native Montanans. They came here because they assumed, like many people do, that Montana is a good place to hide.

Although we tend to be leery of outsiders in Montana, we are also prone to welcome them once they prove their worth to the community, and by all accounts, people accepted Kaczynski because he minded his own business and seemed like a nice enough fellow. In the case of the Montana Freemen, their actions were more blatant and obnoxious, and although they may have had their supporters while they were making their big stand, it's safe to say that most Montanans would rather people outside of Montana not measure our standard of behavior by people like this.

The people of Jordan, Montana, may be intensely private, and they may even have some strong feelings against the government, but sitting among them, enjoying a state fair dinner of ham sandwiches and potato salad, I had many pleasant conversations, and felt as welcome as I have anywhere else in the state. So although the actions of a few may have affected the views of other people about Jordan, they certainly haven't colored mine. It's clear that these men did not represent the norm in Garfield County.

What does represent them is the story of Owen Murnion, a young rancher who was killed while unloading a piece of machinery from a flatbed truck. A hydraulic arm from the machine suddenly dropped while they were unloading, and instantly killed Murnion, who was thirty-eight. A friend of mine from Miles City had a relative who was there when it happened, and said he was worried about the arm doing just what it did, and almost said something but didn't, a simple human decision that he will have to live with.

Murnion had seven children, all girls, and when the news got out about his death, one of the locals decided to set up a GoFundMe account to raise money for the family. They set the goal at $15,000 and hoped to make a little more. Three days later, the total had reached $54,000. Not only that, but when the community heard that Murnion had just started calving on the day of his death, they set up a schedule and worked shifts to get his calving done. The GoFundMe campaign lasted a month, eventually reaching a total of $113,820. That's the real Garfield County.

DIRECTLY SOUTH OF GARFIELD County, Rosebud is one of the
biggest counties in Montana (county seat, Forsyth), and another county whose primary source of income has traditional-
ly been agriculture. But there are currently five coal mines in
Rosebud County, so mining has become the primary source of
jobs and tax money. Forsyth is no longer the largest town in
Rosebud County, thanks to the coal mines and power plants
in Colstrip.

Forsyth was actually the first settlement established along
the Yellowstone River, in 1876, and it served as a stopping
point for steamboats in the late nineteenth century. In 1882,
a man named Thomas Alexander exchanged some of his land
with the railroad, and the town was officially established. The
railroad arrived that same year, as did the first post office.

The town grew quickly, and soon something of a rivalry
began to develop between Alexander and another local businessman, Hiram Marcey. The two men could not have been
more different. Marcey was a teetotaling Southern Methodist
and Alexander a hard-drinking Catholic. But they shared a
good nose for business, and eventually they built competing
hotels: The Alexander, obviously owned by Alexander, and
the Commercial Hotel, by Marcey. It was Clark vs. Daly on a
smaller scale. But unlike the most famous rivalry in Montana,
this one was mostly clean, and according to Gordon Dean,
great-grandson of Marcey, his great-grandfather was one of
the few state congressmen who returned the bribe that Clark
offered legislators to vote him into the Senate.

Gordon is the unofficial historian of Rosebud County, particularly of Forsyth, and his grandfather was the first white
child born in the county. Gordon's grandfather also became
an excellent photographer, and when I met with Gordon and
several other residents of Forsyth at the Speedway Café, a local
café that has been open twenty-four hours a day for almost
one hundred years, the walls were lined with Gordon's grandfather's photographs.

Gordon Dean is a thoughtful man with a trim grey mustache, and I could have based an entire book on his musings

about the county alone. His passion for our history was infectious, and I wished I could include more of his stories. But space only allows so much.

TODAY PERHAPS THE MOST intense competition that takes place in Rosebud County happens just a few miles outside of Forsyth at the Lee Ranch. Every year on Father's Day, hundreds of people from all over the world gather to take eight shots from six different stations with a traditional, single-shot or lever-action .375 caliber or larger rifle, or buffalo gun, with cast bullets. The event has become known as the Matthew Quigley Buffalo Rifle Match, or the Quigley Shoot, named after Tom Selleck's character in the 1990 film *Quigley Down Under*. After seeing the movie together, Al Lee, whose ranch hosts the event, and his buddy Earnie Cornett got the idea for the competition, and in 1991, they attracted twenty-nine contestants to the first annual shoot.

In 2015, over six hundred people came to Forsyth for the two-day event, which has become known as the biggest single-shot shooting competition of its kind, although most of those involved admit that the focus of this gathering is more on the guns than on the competition. It's an opportunity to talk about a passion all of them share for these old weapons. Targets are set up 350 to 805 yards away, with the largest shaped like buffalo. Shooters are allowed to use cross sticks to prop up their rifles, but they are not allowed to shoot from a prone position. They can sit, though, and that is the preferred position. The event also has a hilariously twisted slogan, "The biggest rifle shooting event in Eastern Montana since the Custer massacre."

MY FAVORITE STORY ABOUT the history of Rosebud County comes from Cathy Byron, who has many amazing stories from her family history, which goes back to the homestead days. In 1883, a cousin of Marcus Daly's named Patrick Lynch, Cathy Byron's great-great-grandfather, came to the United States at Daly's urging to help take care of a cattle ranch Daly had started near Lame Deer. Lynch had loaned a small amount of money to Daly when he was still in Ireland, and Daly made this offer as a way of repaying his cousin.

Like most homesteaders of the time, the Lynches struggled during those early years, but they were generous people and invited many of their other relatives to come to Montana. One of those visitors was a nephew named Hugh Boyle, who came from Chicago in 1890 to spend a summer with Patrick Lynch's sister, Ellen, and her husband.

Boyle earned his keep by helping out around the ranch, with one of his duties being to bring in the milk cows every day. On a September day when he went out to do this task, he came upon two young Cheyenne men who had killed a cow and were in the process of butchering it. The boys panicked, and ended up killing Boyle, then panicked again and decided they needed to hide the body, which was not found for several days.

What happened next serves as a wonderful example that not everyone during this time was caught up in the idea that whites and Native Americans were natural enemies. Remember this would have been toward the end of the Indian Wars, just a few months before the massacre at Wounded Knee, which was in December 1890.

Patrick Lynch had become very fond of the Cheyenne people during his stay in Montana, and the feeling was mutual. He had developed an especially close friendship with Chief Two Moon. When Boyle's body was discovered, it became clear to Chief Two Moon what had happened, as the boys had been unable to keep their secret to themselves. Two Moon contacted Lynch and told him that he knew who had committed the crime. The boys were ready to pay for their actions, but Two Moon did not want the boys to hang for the crime, as hanging would prevent their souls from entering the great beyond, according to Cheyenne custom. So Two Moon offered a proposal.

There was a specific day of the week when the Cheyenne came to town to collect their government allotment of meat, and Two Moon suggested that the boys would come with the rest of the warriors, riding in the front of the group. They would thus provide easy targets for a firing squad.

Lynch sympathized with the boys, knowing that many of the Native Americans were starving to death out in the prairie now that the buffalo were gone. So he agreed, and that is how Head Chief and Johnny Young Mule met their ends, with the dignity of two young warriors on their horses.

To me, the mutual respect that is evident in this story says so much about how wrongly history has portrayed the relationship between the settlers and Native Americans. Of course there were examples of extreme animosity on both sides. But even at the end of this sixty-year period of horrible bloodshed, there were still people who were trying to find a way to get along.

MUSSELSHELL COUNTY, LOCATED just off the northwest tip of Rosebud County, has been through a lot lately, including a serious flood in 2011. Dozens of homes in the county seat of Roundup were evacuated when a May rainstorm brought the Musselshell River to almost six feet above its normal level.

Roundup was established along the Musselshell as a convenient place for cattlemen in the open range days to gather their cattle for the annual roundup, thus the name. Although agriculture still plays a major role in Roundup's economy, the biggest employer in the county is the only underground coal mine in the state, Signal Peak Energy, which employs 330 people and produces about seven trainloads of 120 cars of coal every day.

But that's not the most interesting part of Roundup today. At first glance, you wouldn't expect Roundup to have much of a cultural life. It's another one-big-street town with two gas stations and only a couple of restaurants. But in the middle of town is a quaint little jewel, recently created by an enterprising young couple named Troy and Coila (pronounced like the bear) Evans. Troy is an accomplished artist, known especially for his exquisite woodwork, which adorns many of the nicer restaurants in Billings. His tables are individual sculptures, the kind of pieces that you would never look at and think, "I believe I'll set my drink on there."

Troy specializes in taking a smooth, finished tabletop and somehow combining it with a rougher cut of log to create a resting piece of contradiction. He also paints, and does other types of furniture, as well as small interior design jobs, like the inside of a surprising new restaurant fifteen miles outside of Roundup called Dirty Oscar's Annex. Dirty Oscar's is a branch of a restaurant based in Tacoma, Washington. They serve specialty dishes like the Dead Elvis Burger (topped with peanut butter and candied bacon), elk sliders, and Parmesan tots, which are tater tots stuffed with cheese. This is not a place to eat if you're on a diet. But the food is incredible.

But I need to finish telling you about the Evanses. A few years ago, friends of Troy's in Billings introduced him to a relative of theirs who was a Florida hairdresser. Coila was smitten with this Montana ranch kid who had become an artist, as she was something of an aspiring artist herself. She ended up moving to Montana and now, almost ten years later, Coila—who, like Troy, is completely self-taught—has developed a solid reputation as a painter, and recently opened an art gallery right on Main Street in Roundup. Coila has managed to attract works from some of the more talented artists in Montana, including Michael and Meagan Blessing and Kathy Burk.

The appeal is easy to understand once you spend time around the Evanses. Their enthusiasm for art, for Roundup, and for people, is infectious. And it's nice to see such a beacon of optimism in a place that hasn't seen much of that lately. It is particularly encouraging when you compare it to a shadow that lingers in Roundup's past.

In 1923, on July 4, one of the largest KKK rallies ever held in Montana took place on a ranch just outside of Roundup. Ninety-four men were initiated into the Klan on that day, cheered on by several hundred more like-minded followers. It may be surprising to some to hear that the Ku Klux Klan had a presence in Montana, but at its height, the Klan in Montana had over five thousand members. And in most of the state, they were not particularly secretive about it. They held rallies, burned a huge cross on the rims in Billings at a rally in September of 1923, and regularly scheduled public parades and picnics.

It's easier to understand when you consider the circumstances of the time. As I mentioned earlier, the twenties were a very difficult period for Montana's working class. Half of the banks in Montana closed during that decade, and farms and ranches were repossessed left and right. While much of the country was enjoying the Roaring Twenties, Montana already showed signs of what was coming. People needed somewhere to point a finger. Despite the fact that there were so few minorities in Montana (except Native Americans, of course, who were surprisingly ignored by the Klan…apparently they didn't even rate enough of a presence to inspire their hatred), much of what the Klan was espousing at the time appealed to angry and disgruntled farmers and ranchers.

The Montana Klan was headed by a former mayor of Livingston named Lewis Terwilliger. At one time there were forty chapters listed in the state, with most of them concentrated in the middle of Montana, in counties like Wheatland, Sweetgrass, Golden Valley, Park, Yellowstone, and Musselshell. They drew up a list of tenets, and at first glance, it's easy to see how they appealed to some people:

> The Tenets of the Christian Religion
> Upholding the Constitution of the United States
> The Sovereignty of our States Rights
> The Separation of Church and State
> Religious Liberty
> Freedom of Speech and Press
> Compulsory Education in Free Public Schools
> Protection of our Pure Womanhood
> White Supremacy
> Limitation of Foreign Immigration
> Closer Relationship between Capital and American Labor
> Just Laws and Liberty

Of course it's number nine that always ended up getting these guys into trouble. The funny thing about the Montana Klan of the twenties was that they had to find someone to become the focus of their prejudice. That turned out to be Catholics. Hard to imagine Catholics would have ever been a source of so much disdain, but again, considering the time, there was a lot of animosity toward certain groups of immigrants, particularly Irish, and there happened to be a large contingent of Irish who had come over to work in the mines. They tended to be progressive, union folks, with just the kind of political views that the KKK would find troubling. Because Butte was predominantly Irish and Catholic, the Klan met in a much more clandestine manner there, but in Roundup, Livingston, Billings, and many other communities, they made very little effort to hide.

The ugliest incident to come out of this period was when the Klan decided to try to scare away a black man named James Belden who made his home in Crow Agency, where he repaired shoes. Belden had been wrongly accused of petty theft, and a few of the locals paid him a visit and told him to "leave town or suffer the consequences." Belden refused. Hardin Sheriff Robert Gilmore, who was known as an official in that town's Klan, brought one of his deputies to Crow Agency for a "campaign trip." When the two men approached Belden's house, Belden opened fire, killing Gilmore instantly. Word quickly spread, and a mob gathered. What followed was a two-hour standoff in which Belden's house was first riddled with bullets and then set on fire. Belden fled the blaze, but the mob threw him back inside after shooting him several dozen times. Belden also killed one other man, John McLeod, in the gun battle. The news stories that reported the incident in the *Billings Gazette* and the Hardin paper glorified the actions of the mob, and no charges were ever filed.

The Klan eventually died out in the early thirties, and the anti-immigrant sentiment slowly withered away, perhaps in part because everyone was just as desperate as the next person.

A few years ago, a man in Great Falls, who I will not bother to name, tried to start a new KKK chapter, and he claimed that this one was going to include more minorities. Despite the fact that this man had been involved in several other white supremacist groups in the past, he claimed to be a changed man who only wanted to start a group that focused on making "a stronger America." The group didn't gain much traction, but it highlights a sad truth about Montana: Although our state has not been rated as one of the top states in the nation for hate groups per capita, they continue to make their presence known from time to time.

IT WOULDN'T BE RIGHT to talk about cattle without mentioning Libby Smith Collins, affectionately known as The Cattle Queen of Montana. I shared some of Libby's story before, as she was one of the early arrivals in Bannack, where she had traveled with her brother as the cook for a wagon train. Over the course of her life, Libby lost her home to a fire and survived several Native American attacks, including a short period when she was captured. When Libby became a nurse and took a job working as the cook for a silver camp near Helena, she fell in love with the owner of the mine, Nathanial Collins. Nathaniel sold his mine, and once he and Libby were married, they started a ranch near Prickly Pear Creek. That particular venture didn't fare well, so Nathaniel decided to explore another area.

They ended up starting a ranch near Choteau in 1877, where Libby was the first white woman. She also gave birth to the first white baby in Choteau. After years of growing their herd, the Collinses went against the standard procedure of their day, which was to sell their cattle to cattle buyers who traveled from ranch to ranch, and instead shipped their cattle to Chicago. It went so well the first time they did it that it became their routine, as well as the eventual routine of many other ranchers. But one year, Nathaniel was too sick to accompany the cattle. Libby decided she would do it.

The only problem was that a woman shipping cattle was unheard of at the time. Not only that, it was against the rules of the railroad for a woman to accompany livestock on the train. After a ten-day delay, during which she petitioned the representative of the Chicago commission firm (with headquarters in Great Falls) for permission to accompany her cattle, not only did he approve the request, but he sent instructions that the employees along her route should "provide for the comfort of Mrs. Nat Collins." Thus was born the legend, and the fabulous nickname, of The Cattle Queen of Montana. There is even a movie starring Barbara Stanwyck based on Libby's life.

Libby Smith Collins went on to become more than just a figurehead, as she was known as a tough negotiator and an expert on cattle—a woman way ahead of her time. Oddly enough, there are still very few women who run cattle ranches, although you occasionally hear about them.

TERRY, MONTANA, IN PRAIRIE County, has one very famous former resident, although she did not become famous until well after her death. Evelyn Jephson Flower was born near London in 1868, to a family of privilege. Evelyn could have easily drifted along in that life of comfort, but she had a sense of adventure, and so did the man she eventually married, an aspiring ornithologist and horse trainer named Ewen Cameron. The Camerons decided to spend their honeymoon on the Great Plains, where they hunted and immediately fell in love with the region. They decided to stay, with the plan that Ewen would raise polo ponies.

They bought land near Terry and began their life together in a land that was very different from that to which they were accustomed. Ewen proved to be a horrible businessman (polo ponies?! In Montana?!). But one of his other interests, which was writing about birds, led Evelyn to try her hand at taking some photos to go along with his writings. They had become so impoverished from Ewen's failed business dealings that they had to take on lodgers, and one of them had introduced Evelyn to photography.

As is usually the case with the very gifted, this hobby soon proved to be more of an obsession. Despite their financial difficulties, Evelyn did whatever she had to do to acquire the equipment and supplies necessary to photograph everything around her.

The thing I love most about Evelyn's work is the innovative approach she took toward her subjects. Because the equipment of the day was so cumbersome—the plates required such lengthy exposures—most subjects had to be carefully posed, which is why so many of the portraits show people wearing such stiff, unsmiling faces. Any motion would blur the photo so people often had to hold still for a matter of many seconds.

But Evelyn's photos show her subjects smiling, playful, standing on horses, even laughing. But it is her nature photographs that are absolutely stunning. There was also no such thing as a telephoto lens in those days, so Evelyn would sit for hours in a strategic position to capture a bird in its nest, or a critter on the hunt.

Evelyn ultimately developed enough of a reputation during her lifetime to earn a living, mostly taking photographs for the railroads; photos that helped them romanticize the plains in order to attract tourists and homesteaders. But after she died in 1928, she faded into obscurity for many decades.

It wasn't until a *Time-Life* editor named Donna Lucey began working on a book about women in the West that Evelyn's resurgence began. Lucey had heard rumors about a woman, Janet Williams, who kept a cache of photo plates in her basement. Evelyn Cameron had entrusted all of her life's work to Williams. Lucey worked hard to gain Williams's trust, and the work paid off when Lucey discovered thirty-five leather-bound volumes of Cameron diaries, and 1,400 glass plate and nitrate negatives.

Cameron was soon a national celebrity, and today her work is considered the best to come out of that time period in Montana. Terry itself now features the Evelyn Cameron Museum, which displays a select handful of those 1,400 masterpieces.

Cattle ranching is still the most significant source of income for most of the residents of Prairie County. As with so many rural towns in the eastern part of the state, there are few businesses here. With the transition from rural to urban life in full swing, this is clearly one more county seat that relies as much on county money as anything else to keep its inhabitants employed. It is also one of the counties that could probably be eliminated if that kind of movement was ever employed. But with the Evelyn Cameron Museum, at least it can say that it will not easily be forgotten.

McCone County's Circle, Montana—with just over 600 residents—is another small town struggling with a changing economy. McCone was born during that early period of explosive growth in Montana, coming into being in 1919. Not quite a century later, Circle's Chamber of Commerce website boasts how close they are to Miles City and Glendive, which should tell you something. The town is still deeply embedded in the world of cattle ranching. Even the name was derived from one of the largest ranches in the area, the Mabry Ranch, started in 1884. Their brand was a simple circle. When the first post office in the area was opened in the ranch house, they adopted the name for the post office.

Circle has an excellent museum, a sprawling, barn-like 6,200-square-foot structure that is very nicely arranged, filled with machinery and amazing artifacts from families and events in McCone County. The curator of the museum, Wendell Pawlowski, was proud to show me a row of photographs of him and his brothers, Larry, Wayne, and Howard, when they were young, all decked out in their military uniforms. Wendell, the last surviving brother, had a scratchy, seldom-used quality in his voice, and he seemed to barely contain a desire to laugh. He never stopped smiling the whole time I was there.

The museum was founded by his father, Leonard, who began collecting items in the 1950s with the idea that they would someday form the foundation of a local history. By the time Leonard convinced the county to construct the building that houses the museum in 1982, he had accumulated over three thousand items, and he donated the entire collection. He never stopped looking for more, a pursuit that Wendell has inherited. He frequents the local estate and yard sales in search of treasures to add to an already outstanding collection.

The Pawlowskis came to Circle in 1936, when Wendell was three. Wendell ran the family ranch until he was in his early seventies in 2005. Like most of the landowners in Eastern Montana, the Pawlowskis did not limit the output of their ranch to either livestock or crops but combined both in order to make a living.

After a few hours with Wendell and his museum, I left another tiny Montana town feeling the familiar heartache that comes from seeing the inevitability of its decline. Meeting someone like Wendell Pawlowski, a man who clearly loves his town and his state and his people as much as anyone could possibly love anything, makes me ache on his behalf.

It feels very much like meeting up with an old friend and the new love of their life and coming away with that sinking feeling that they see something in this person that is not there. You hope with all your heart to be mistaken, and you celebrate if you are, because you also know that there is not a single thing you can say or do to change this person's mind. Or more importantly, their heart.

SPEAKING OF WHICH, IT is impossible for me to be even slightly objective about Carter County, Montana. This is where my grandparents' ranch is located. It's where my mother grew up, and where we spent almost every single Christmas of my childhood. It is where I spent the summer of my sixteenth year working fourteen-hour days, six days a week—an experience that transformed my life. To me, the Arbuckle Ranch was the biggest playground in the world, a place full of wonder and mystery, completely different from my dead-end street in Sheridan, Wyoming.

One day, when I was about eight, my grandparents took me to spend the day at the neighbors, who had a boy the same age. Kelly Kornemann was a typical ranch kid. He was quiet but friendly, with a dry wit and a great sense of adventure. When I went to visit Kelly, I knew it was going to be a good day. On this particular day, Kelly asked me whether I'd ever ridden a calf.

"Of course!" I said. This was a bold-faced lie.

But I was a Montana kid, and my dad had been on the rodeo team at Montana State University in Bozeman, where I was born. He was even a rodeo clown for several years, before he got stepped on by a bull when I was a baby, and my mother insisted that he give it up. So I just knew, in that way that kids know things without any evidence whatsoever, that I would be able to ride that calf like a real goddamn cowboy.

Kelly took me to the barn, and he fixed me up with chaps, gloves, and even spurs. He fastened a rigging around the calf's torso, and showed me how to tuck my hand tight around that rope. We guided the calf into the chute, where I lowered myself from the rails onto his back.

Kelly whipped that gate open just like they did at the Days of '85 Rodeo, and for about five seconds, I rode that calf like a champion. But suddenly, the calf stopped dead in its tracks, and I went flying. The way I remember it, I looked sort of like Superman. But I think there's a very good chance I looked a lot more like someone falling off a calf.

I landed flat on my stomach, and my legs kicked up, so my spurs popped me right in the back. For the next ten minutes, I was pretty sure I was going to die.

Kelly must have thought the same thing, because he rolled me onto my back, and he was crying like a baby.

And then Kelly did something that I didn't understand at all. He crawled down to my feet and started to pull my boots off.

What Kelly and I didn't know was that his father, Donny, was watching this whole scene play out from the barn, laughing his ass off. And for years afterwards, both of our families had a good laugh over the fact that Kelly Kornemann wasn't about to let his friend die with his boots on.

THIS MEMORY HAS BECOME more than just a funny story to me. It is an indication of one of the great gifts of growing up in a place like Montana, where we learn valuable life lessons from direct contact with the earth, and with the animals that share this marvelous place with us. Or do we share it with them? Either way, I have always cherished the fact that because of where I live, I have experiences that end up serving as metaphors for much bigger issues.

I have also found it a little maddening that because writers and artists from the West often focus on the connection between the people and the land, or the dynamic between people and animals, they are not taken as seriously by the literary elite. Some of the farmers and ranchers I've met in Montana are among the smartest people I know, and I've lived in Boston, San Francisco, Washington, DC, and Seattle, where I met plenty of smart people. For some reason, any association with agriculture conjures up an image of ignorance in the minds of many people. But the fact is, working and writing about this part of our culture provides some of the most beautiful and natural symbols for our relationships with each other.

When you live on a ranch, you are exposed to the cycle of life in visceral ways that most people never experience. You see live birth, you see dead carcasses and watch them transform into decay, then bones, and finally just another part of the earth. These experiences change your perspective. They change your life.

You also experience the realities of raising food for a living. My uncle instructed me to hold a sheep's head while he slit her throat when I was a teenager, and it made me sick to my stomach. It also left me with a personal experience that I can apply to every piece of meat I eat for the rest of my life. I choose whether to be affected by how cruel some of these practices seem, or I can accept that this is part of the cycle of life. Many people would come away from that experience with a strong aversion to eating meat, and I can understand why. It was life changing for me. I also shot a deer when I was sixteen, and watching that graceful animal tumble to the ground in a heap left me shaken to my core. I never hunted again. But so far it hasn't stopped me from enjoying a good venison sausage.

Rural Montana has a reputation for people who are stoic, and who have a difficult time expressing their feelings. This reputation is well earned, and it happens for a reason. When you are presented with these choices day after day, and when you watch the people around you make the choice to suppress whatever emotional response they may have to dealing with livestock, you learn to follow the crowd or suffer the consequences.

When I worked on my grandparents' ranch that summer, and before I became a writer, it was the most satisfying work I had ever done. It was also the hardest by a long ways. My uncle roused me before dawn every morning and we worked until the sun was just above the horizon. I never even thought about grumbling about being shaken awake at 5:00 in the morning, as I had been conditioned in earlier years by my grandfather to know that when you are at the ranch, you do not sleep in.

I have never felt so exhausted from work, but in the best possible way, and this isn't some kind of romanticized euphoric recall either. I loved it while it was happening. We stacked hay, in the days when it was still the square bales and the hay stacker picked up about seven bales at a time. I learned to drive this machine as well as a baler and a swather, before I even had my driver's license. And we moved cattle, docked lambs, branded, fixed fence.

I remember one day I was sent out to retrieve two bulls that had broken through a fence into the neighbor's pasture. After fixing the fence where they broke through, I found the bulls and tried to maneuver these stubborn, mean animals toward the gate, a task that took what seemed like hours. It may have *been* hours. Finally, I got them through the gate, closed it, and headed back for the house. And as I was riding away, I looked back only to see them break right through the fence again.

That proved to be a crucial point of that summer, because a part of me wanted to go home and pretend it hadn't happened. The petulant teenager in me didn't want to have to spend another couple of hours trying to deal with these stubborn animals. But I knew exactly what would happen if I did that. I would be right out there, either that evening or the next morning, doing the same thing. There was no way in hell they were going to send someone else to do it.

So I took a deep breath and went through the same routine again. And this time they stayed.

One of the most valuable lessons I took away from that summer was the fact that when you're doing work that involves animals and crops that depend on you to survive, there is no choice. You don't call in sick; you don't just decide to take a day off. These are not even options. The work ethic that came out of that summer served me well. And it gave me profound respect for the people who have done this work for their entire lives. It made me realize how completely wedded they are to their work. It is their life, whether they like it or not.

My uncle Lee now owns the Arbuckle Ranch, and as with many ranch families, there were some contentious years leading up to him taking over. Because it is a common practice among rural families to never discuss who is going to take over the ranch or the farm. The idea of putting this stuff down on paper is not even a consideration in many cases, even today. So there is generally much maneuvering and manipulation.

In my family's case, the ranch belonged to my grandfather, but he was actually not my mother's birth father. When my grandmother married him, she had four children, the youngest of which was my mother. Lee was born a few years later, so he was the youngest, but the only one with Arbuckle blood. So when my grandfather died, Lee inherited a much larger share of the ranch than the other four children. Which was actually generous of my grandfather. He could have done what many ranchers do and simply turned the whole thing over to Lee.

But it wasn't enough to satisfy my other uncles, who had hoped for a more even split. A corporation was formed, and the meetings were not pleasant for anyone. But aside from being the only blood relative, Lee was always the one who was most interested and dedicated to the ranch, so it made way more sense no matter how you looked at it that he would take over. I'm sure it was a relief to everyone when he was able to buy the others out, and since then he has leased the place out, first to one family for twenty-five years, and now to another family for the past three years. But despite living with multiple sclerosis since 1974, Lee is still very active in the operations of the ranch. Much like my grandfather, and his father before him (the original homesteader), Lee is always looking for ways to make better use of the scant supply of moisture in Carter County.

They built a series of dikes in the thirties that hold the water in certain pastures and meadows, and one year they dug some deep burrows into another large pasture to give it a scalloped surface. This pasture was used for grazing for years, and those scallops gathered water each year, so that grass has slowly become more and more abundant there. Any little thing they can do to retain a tiny bit more of those ten-plus inches of rainfall they get each year is invaluable to the operations of the ranch.

Lee is also constantly experimenting with different types of grasses, and a couple of years ago he tried a type of grass he heard about through a grass-seed expert. The grass is called Bozoisky, and it has proven to be a favorite among his lessee's cattle. The thing about farming and ranching that the average non-rural person doesn't realize is that it requires constant innovation. If you keep doing the same thing over and over again, year after year, it will eventually stop working, and those practices will have a negative impact on your land.

Recently Lee took me out in one of their meadows and pointed out how they had bladed the surface of the meadow so that it had a slope that was exactly three degrees, which would allow just enough runoff toward a pasture where he wanted more water without taking too much topsoil off the surface. And it is a thrill to people like Lee that this kind of precision is now possible with modern survey and cultivating equipment. When he talks about these innovations, his eyes get big and his whole body comes to life. He loves the ranch in a way that I'm not sure most people can possibly understand.

My uncle Lee has also recently made plans for two new reservoirs, both intended to bring water to very specific corners of very specific pastures, to provide for better grazing opportunities in those pastures. This kind of attention to detail blows my mind, and it makes me realize how the practice of farming and ranching has always been a very delicate combination of instinct and scientific study. It's one of those subjects that you can never possibly know everything there is to know about. Not even close.

CARTER COUNTY IS COW country, although ranchers have always raised plenty of sheep and crops there as well. But cattle are the foundation. Carter County has some of the best grazing land in the state, even though it's so dry that it requires a massive amount of land to support livestock. It is not unusual to see a ranch with over twenty thousand acres.

It is striking to me how much Carter County has changed since I was a child, in many of the same ways that most farming and ranching communities have changed. In the sixties, every town in Carter County had a town hall. There were country dances at one or the other of these town halls almost every weekend. My grandmother played the piano for these dances, and it was not unusual for us to fall asleep on one of the benches while my parents and grandparents danced the night away. As a kid, my favorite part of the night was the midnight lunch, when they would bring out plates of sandwiches and cookies. Cake. It was so exotic to have something to eat that time of day. It was the only time we ever did such a thing.

But it was also these country dances where I learned to appreciate the best of country music. Because it was the sixties, they were still playing the stuff that had come from bluegrass and honky tonks, the kind of country music that came up through the soles of the boots of those who wrote it. Even at that young age, the songs of Hank Williams moved me to the core. The way he expressed heartache still cuts deep into me in ways that modern music never will, no matter what genre. Even if it was just a few scratchy amateurs, the power of those songs still resonates.

If they did not have a dance some weekend, you could always count on something else, a card party or a basketball game at that same town hall. For decades, these people made the effort to gather. I don't know whether they were conscious of why this was important, but I suspect it grew out of those early years when no one had telephones or television, so the need to have some kind of connection to other people was intense. My grandparents' ranch was two miles from the nearest neighbor, and fifteen miles from the nearest town. So the isolation was built into the region. It was physical, and when you are that isolated from others, the fight to avoid emotional isolation becomes a constant. But it's more than the isolation. It was also a necessary chance to connect with someone besides your family. As romantic as it may sound to some people, spending every hour of every day with no one but members of your family can create stress that needs some kind of release.

Today the Internet and satellite television have completely eroded that sense of community. I asked people in county after county when the last country dance was, and most of them couldn't even remember. Card parties are also a thing of the past. People still make the effort to get together from time to time, but the main reason the people in these small towns gather now is for high school sports. In almost every one of these rural communities, the local sports teams are the primary source of social interaction, which puts a premium on athletes, and creates the kind of dynamic in the schools that perpetuates the idea that those who are most physically gifted are the most vital to the community.

I still frequently visit Carter County, sometimes accompanying my mother to her class reunions, which take place during the Days of '85, the annual rodeo and fair. My mother graduated from high school in Ekalaka in 1953, and from a class of twenty-seven, eleven people made the trip to her last reunion, in 2013. At that time, only five had died since 1953, so half of the surviving members were there.

One of the best things about places like Ekalaka is the fact that they seldom change. One can find comfort in knowing that the Wagon Wheel Café will always open at 5:30 a.m. on Main Street, and that the Old Stand Bar next door will always host the street dance on Saturday night of the Days of '85. It seems unlikely that the *Ekalaka Eagle* office will ever move from the stone building a block away from the Wagon Wheel, considering that they've been in that same tiny building for decades. But that year, there was a change, and it was not a small one. That year, the citizens of Ekalaka tore down several buildings along Main Street, just across the street from the Wagon Wheel and the Old Stand. One entire block on that side of Main Street is now an empty lot. A block that used to be lined with businesses and houses.

On Friday afternoon, I was sitting on a bench across the street from these ghosts, along with several of the members of Mom's class. They were lamenting the fact that the town didn't look the same. It didn't matter that most of these buildings hadn't served any real purpose for many years.

"It just doesn't look like Ekalaka anymore," one of the class of '53 complained. The others nodded, staring quietly at the empty space across from us, like missing teeth in a big smile. Pickups traveled back and forth in front of us, kicking up dust. Although Main Street in Ekalaka is paved, it is the only street that is. So it almost looks as if it's not paved, as the dust from the cross streets forms a perpetual blanket.

"Remember when they opened the pool hall right there on the corner?" One of my mother's classmates pointed across the street.

"Oh, that was so exciting," someone added.

Finally, Jim Tom Padden took a deep breath and said, "Well, you have to admit it does look better."

This was symbolic of so many things that happen when I am in Ekalaka. There is a sense of acceptance that you can expect from people in small towns. It may come slow, and it may first require some discussion. But it will most likely come. It's an attitude borne of experience. This is a country where disappointment comes in bunches. This is a country where the people rely on water for their livelihood, and it is a rare thing.

The ancestors of today's people of Ekalaka survived the influx of amateurs, the farmers and ranchers who had no sense of the long-term effects of grazing the grass to nubs, or digging too deep with their plows. Once the topsoil blew away with the winds of the Depression, a few hearty souls stayed. They learned to live with disappointment, and debt. They adopted the typically Montana attitude that there will always be people who don't appreciate what we have here enough to preserve it. There will always be people who take without giving back.

"We have each worked second jobs for the past twenty years," one ranching couple told me. "And we still run the ranch ourselves."

"What keeps you here?" I asked.

"We love this land. We love working the land, and seeing the results of our efforts."

This part is easy to understand. Carter County, especially that year, was gorgeous. Thanks to one of the biggest snowstorms this country had seen in years, the grass of Carter County was thick and green. But even that storm had its price. Some of the locals were without electricity for three weeks because the wind knocked down thousands of power poles. Usually in late August the dark gumbo shows between the sparse clumps of browning grass. But that year hearkened back to the nineteenth century teens, when the land played a cruel joke on those early settlers, giving them the brief illusion that the railroad was telling them the truth.

Is it possible that almost one hundred years later, this fertile but fragile soil has finally recovered? Can the residents of Ekalaka get used to the idea of having plenty of good thick grass, and enough water to keep their country green? Or is this too much of a change from that to which they are accustomed?

The answer to that question will only come with time. Meanwhile, Ekalaka will quietly survive. Good citizens will do their part. Until a couple of years ago, Brice Lambert and his wife Lois continued to put out the weekly edition of the *Ekalaka Eagle,* despite Lois' crippling multiple sclerosis, which reduced her ability to write by freezing her right arm, and draining all but a few hours of energy per day. Lois now writes with a voice-generated computer program, which requires "a hell of a lot of editing," she says. "I just try to stay one step ahead of the disease," she adds. "I won't allow it to rule me. I want to rule it."

The Carter County Museum, the first county-owned museum in Montana, will continue to surprise visitors with its full dinosaur skeleton. And good solid natives like Fulton Castleberry and Lloyd Carroll will continue to organize the reunions for the handful of classmates who are still alive.

CHAPTER NINE
Different Shades of Purple

"The one thing our Founding Fathers could not foresee—
they were farmers, professional men, businessmen giving of
their time and effort to an idea that became a country—was
a nation governed by professional politicians who had an
interest in getting re-elected. They probably envisioned a
fellow serving a couple of hitches and then eagerly looking
forward to getting back to the farm."
— Ronald Reagan

Anyone who thinks they can easily categorize Montana politics just hasn't been paying attention. There isn't now and never has been anything predictable about the political game in our state, except, perhaps, that it's completely unpredictable. The line between conservative and progressive is blurred, often invisible, and depends entirely on the subject matter.

How many people in the United States, if asked which state elected the first woman to Congress, would guess Montana? And even within Montana, how many would know what year Jeanette Rankin was elected? (It was 1916, four years before women were nationally given the right to vote.) And how many Montanans would know who succeeded Jeanette Rankin in the House of Representatives when she decided not to seek re-election after her second term, in 1942? That would be Mike Mansfield, an unassuming young lawyer who had spent part of his childhood in an orphanage and would go on to be the longest-running Senate Majority Leader in American history.

Montana politics got off to a rocky start with Sidney Edgerton, the federal judge who was apparently not that interested in working as a judge. He was much more interested in promoting himself for governor, a tactic that initially worked but finally led to his downfall in Montana. To be fair, Edgerton was given an almost impossible task when he was appointed, as the war had just ended and the federal government was in turmoil. For almost a year and a half after he was appointed, Edgerton had no secretary, and was the only officer who could sign federal warrants. For those first sixteen months, Edgerton had no federal funds to cover the costs of running the territory. When they finally sent a secretary, Edgerton appointed him temporary governor, in part so he could go to Washington to try to sort out the financial situation for his territory. But he had neglected the formality of applying for a leave of absence, an act that might not have been a big deal if not for the fact that Andrew Johnson had it in for radical Republicans, and decided to fire him as governor.

But there has been no more colorful figure in our political history than Thomas Meagher, the namesake of Meagher County and the man who succeeded Edgerton. Our second governor was from Ireland, a war hero who had led a group called the Young Irelanders in the Rebellion of 1848. The rebellion took place in large part because of the Great Famine, and although it failed, Meagher became a hero, especially when he escaped from his imprisonment in Tasmania. Meagher made his way to the United States and quickly threw himself into the war here, eventually rising to the rank of brigadier general for the Union Army. He was especially effective at recruiting Irishmen to join the cause.

After the war, Meagher was appointed the secretary of the territory of Montana, and it wasn't long after he arrived that

Edgerton's run as governor was terminated, and Meagher was chosen to succeed him.

Meagher soon proved himself to be a controversial figure, first by deciding to switch party affiliations almost immediately after his appointment. Although Meagher had been appointed as a Union Democrat—part of the reason Johnson had chosen him—most of the Democrats in Montana at the time were strong Confederate supporters. Meagher found himself conflicted about whom to trust. So his first instinct was to throw in with the Republicans. But it didn't take long for Meagher to notice that a good many of the Democrats in this new territory were Irish, and that they had a majority in the state. So he changed his mind once again, a decision that earned him many enemies among the Republicans. They responded by sending reports to Washington that Meagher was a drunk and that he frequently entertained prostitutes at the executive office. It didn't help that the claims happened to be true.

Meagher was only in Montana for a little over two years, but it was without a doubt the most turbulent two years of any Montana official. But to Meagher's credit, he did try to get things done. Upon his appointment, Meagher decided two things—to form a new legislature and to apply for statehood, despite the fact that the population didn't yet meet the requirements. Meagher's new friends, the Montana Democratic Party, had a strong majority, and were determined to apply for statehood, knowing that they would easily gain control of the legislature if they got it. Meagher called for a legislative session, and he also called for a constitutional convention. After several years without any legislative actions, this new legislature passed many much-needed laws while the convention went to work drafting a constitution. In the meantime, the Montana Territorial Supreme Court, run by two strong Republican foes of Meagher, declared the legislative actions "null and void."

Meagher and his legislature simply ignored the ruling, and even rearranged the districts to send one of the justices to the most isolated part of the territory. By then the Republicans were angry enough to bring in the big guns, and they went to Washington, asking for intervention. In a move that was "highly unusual," Congress agreed with the Supreme Court's ruling that the legislature's actions be declared null and void, eliminating many laws that Montana badly needed at the time.

Despite this blow, Meagher's convention continued their work, and a constitution was drawn up. But in a story that sounds as if it must be made up, the constitution got lost before it made it to the printers. Nobody knows what happened to it. And nobody but those who drafted it ever saw it again. It was perhaps a fitting metaphor for Meagher's reign in office.

Over the next several months, Meagher's life became more and more complicated. The Lakota launched several attacks along the Bozeman Trail, and when people started to panic, Meagher became obsessed with taking action against the Lakota. He sent message after message to Washington, requesting permission to form a special militia. His actions were so over the top that none other than William Tecumseh Sherman advised the president that Meagher was obsessed with starting some kind of war.

But when John Bozeman was killed, Meagher finally got the okay to start his militia, although there was no specific indication of how much money he would get. He organized an army of six hundred men who camped along the Bozeman Trail and along the Yellowstone River for months, to no avail as the attacks had already stopped. When Congress decided to disband the militia, Meagher sent a bill to the government for over $1 million. After an investigation, the government discovered that the local merchants had vastly overcharged them, and it paid only about half of what Meagher and his crew had spent.

Meagher was getting it from all sides by this time, and there was more and more evidence to support the rumors about his drinking and temperamental ways. In what turned out to be a perfectly timed twist of fate, Meagher's term came to a sudden end near Fort Benton when, late one night, he was wandering around drunk on the deck of a steamboat and either fell off, was pushed, or jumped. Although several people heard the splash, his body was never found, leading some to believe that he had been murdered.

I'm not sure what it says about Montana that Meagher's statue is firmly planted in front of our state capitol. That we're proud of our crackpots? He may be crazy, but he's *our* crazy! Still, in many ways, Meagher does serve as an interesting symbol of our past, given his strong will and determination. But more than anything, his story probably serves as a cautionary tale.

HELENA IS ONE OF my favorite Montana towns. The downtown in Helena has the feel of an old friend's living room. It's comfortable. It's cozy. It feels welcoming. There is a trolley tour you can catch at the Montana Historical Society that takes you through the downtown and around some of the more interesting neighborhoods in Helena. The day I decided to take this tour, it started pouring rain about five minutes after the tour started. I was not properly dressed for an hour of sitting in the rain. I was wearing shorts and a T-shirt, and my seat was right in the front row corner of this open-air trolley. So by the time we reached the downtown, I was sopping wet and shivering, feeling miserable about paying $3.50 for a drive through the rain. When I suddenly heard someone call my name.

When I saw my high school friend, Dave Dalthorp, walking along the sidewalk, I could have hugged him. I had planned to stay with Dave that evening, and he just happened to be headed to his office. I've never been so happy to see an old friend as I climbed out of that tinny car and followed Dave to his warm, dry car.

For the next couple of days, as I explored Helena, I thought about the election back in the late nineteenth century, when Anaconda and Helena battled it out to become the state capital. William Clark, just to spite his nemesis, Marcus Daly, poured hundreds of thousands of dollars into buying the votes for Helena. Maybe this was one of the things he managed to get right. Helena *is* stately. It has some of the most amazing homes in the state, due in large part to the fact that Helena once had more millionaires per capita than any town in the United States.

But more importantly, Helena has a certain soul. There is a rich abundance of art in this community, especially with the incredible Archie Bray Foundation just outside of town. This facility provides some of the best ceramic artists in the world a place to improve their craft. It was founded in 1951 by a philanthropist named, of course, Archie Bray. Bray was a brickmaker rather than an artist, but he had a dream to "make available for all who are seriously interested in the ceramic arts, a fine place to work." Such a simple concept, but he apparently knew the importance of simplicity. He knew that by providing a place for people to create their art he was doing something magnificent. It helped that the first managers he hired were also incredible talents. Rudy Autio and Peter Voulkos, very different in style, would both achieve international renown for their work.

Autio was more of an impressionistic sculptor, who incorporated Picasso-like figures into his pieces, while Voulkos's style was more classical, using simple shapes and forms with his own unique touch. The Bray, as it is affectionately known, started offering workshops and classes from its early inception, and the quality of teachers it attracted soon established its credibility as a world-class facility.

I met Josh DeWeese, one of the former directors of the Bray, when we both took part in an event in Bozeman called "Pecha Kucha" a few months after my visit to Helena. The idea behind Pecha Kucha is to give people from all walks of life an opportunity to give a presentation about something important to them, complete with a slideshow. The twist is that you have exactly twenty seconds for each slide, and you present exactly twenty slides during your presentation. So each presentation is the same length—six minutes and forty seconds. I took an immediately liking to Josh, with his big ol' walrus mustache and his firm handshake. So I contacted him later and asked him about the history of the Bray.

"There was a time around 1960 when it almost went under, when the Western Clay Manufacturing Company, commonly known as "the brickyard," went bankrupt. For the next several years, the Bray—or, as it was referred to by those in the know, 'the Pottery"—consisted of a few artists who were essentially squatting on the property. The property was auctioned off in 1966, at which point the potters were able to buy the pottery building as well as some of the acreage surrounding it. The rest of the property was bought up and mothballed for the next couple of decades, which created something of a bad image for the Bray in Helena because it was considered a failed business." DeWeese went on to say, "It didn't help that they started holding pottery workshops at the Bray that gave Helena the false impression that they had become a drug rehab, a concept that was apparently offensive to certain segments of Helena society.

"While the artists managed to maintain the Pottery, the production of clay and bricks was shut down for twenty-five years, until the Pottery was finally able to purchase the remaining property in 1984. The directors at that time put a lot of energy into establishing the Bray's international reputation but without making much of an effort to connect with the local community. But when I took over in 1992, I recognized the importance of creating more of a relationship with both Helena and the Montana cultural community, and the Bray continues to nurture those relationships."

Over the last several decades, the Bray has provided a place to live and work for more than six hundred artists, supporting itself through the workshops and classes and an in-house gallery, which sells works by the various guest artists. The ceramics in the gift shop display the wonderful variety of styles that find their way to this place. Everything from pottery-based Japanese anime figures to the most simple white ceramic vases, to explosions of glass that seem to be held together by magic. Visitors also have the opportunity to wander through the grounds and watch the resident artists work. The Bray also sells ceramic supplies and clay.

In so many ways, the Bray exemplifies what's best about Montana enterprise. For one thing, it feels like a local secret; it is not nearly as well-known as perhaps it should be. From the outside, you would never guess that it's a world-renowned facility. It is, after all, just an old brick factory. But a closer look reveals something unusual about this place. There are pieces of artwork planted in the yard, along the paths, in the most unlikely places. What appears to be a nondescript little cluster of brick buildings turns out to be a piece of art itself. And this is what makes the Bray so thoroughly Montanan in my eyes. It requires a closer look to appreciate how beautiful and special it is. This is true of so many inspiring places in our state. Glacier Park, Flathead Lake, the Beartooth Pass. Those are easy. Those are magnificent in a way that you can't help but notice. But it is the subtleties that bring Montana to a whole 'nother level. The quiet beauty of the plains. And the very, very quiet wisdom of our people.

ONCE A WEEK, THE Montana Club hosts what's called Hometown Helena. At 7:00 a.m. every Thursday, about seventy-five people, including city officials and business leaders, meet to discuss what's happening around Helena, and to hear a presentation. The event is casual, with the chairman making constant jokes at the expense of the attendees, and them firing back in kind. I attended the week before Thanksgiving, invited by my friend Bruce Wittenberg, the director of the Montana Historical Society, and one after another, people got up and announced another charitable activity that was going on in the city. I was impressed with the compassion. And the laughter. These people showed genuine affection toward each other, and were gracious toward their guests. Although many public figures and political leaders were there, I didn't get that vibe you sometimes get around successful people, the one where you need to earn a spot at their table. The people of Helena showed a love for their town that felt completely genuine.

It made me think of an incident that occurred during a year that I lived in Washington, D.C. I was invited to a party one evening by a guy who was in his twenties. I figured it would be a typical party for people that age, so I showed up in jeans and a T-shirt. My hair was a little bit longer then. When I walked in, I immediately realized that I was out of my element. Almost every young man there was wearing a suit and tie. The women were in power suits or very conservative dresses. I tried to make conversation with a few people, but the topics of conversation—as always, in DC—revolved around where you went to school, whom you were working for, and who you knew. I didn't stay long. And I couldn't get out of that city fast enough.

That experience made me appreciate my time in Helena that much more. Although I'm sure I would find the distasteful side of politics in Helena if I stuck around long enough, it wasn't predominant. Instead, I was struck by the number of art galleries, numerous coffee shops, and locally owned specialty shops and restaurants. Unlike some of the other mid-sized towns in Montana, Helena is not dominated by franchises.

Maybe this is why the Montana legislature has been refreshingly free of rumors of corruption, although Montana politics has its own dark side, which I'll get to. Of course it would be naive to believe that our legislature has been untouched by bribery, and of course there were the many years of influence by the Anaconda Copper Company, especially when the company controlled so many of the newspapers. But for the most part, there have been few scandals, and when you look at the voting record, it's easy to make the argument that, for most of our history, Montana legislators have been fairly consistent about hammering out compromises in the interest of the people of Montana. They do it like it was intended to be done.

I would submit, without any scientific evidence whatsoever, that the very ambience of Helena has an effect on how the legislature operates. This town has one of the highest-rated bicycle trails in the country. It is a town filled with people who *look* healthy. Nestled at the foot of the Elkhorn Mountains, Helena seems more like a resort town than a state capital. Hiking trails snake their way into the hills behind town, and provide an incredible view not just of Helena but of the mountains as well. Whether or not people appreciate this aspect of Helena when they're here to sit in dull meetings and hammer out bills, it's hard to imagine how an entire body, or even half of that body, could fall victim to greed in a place like this. Maybe it's my idealistic naiveté coming through, but I'd like to believe that Helena serves as a reminder of the best of what this state has to offer, and that this is something that these people think about when they're passing laws for its people.

It could certainly explain, at least in part, why the Montana Constitution, which was revised in 1972, has one of the strongest environmental clauses in the country. That version of the Montana Constitution actually states that "the right to a clean and healthful environment" has priority over even the basic rights of religion, assembly, and speech. The constitution then goes on to devote an entire article—Article IX—to the environment. Although that article has been amended and now consists of seven sections, the original four sections read as follows:

Section 1 - Protection and Improvement

(1) The state and each person shall maintain and improve a clean and healthful environment in Montana for present and future generations.
(2) The legislature shall provide for the administration and enforcement of this duty.
(3) The legislature shall provide adequate remedies for the protection of the environmental life support system from degradation and provide adequate remedies to prevent unreasonable depletion and degradation of natural resources.

Section 2 - Reclamation

(1) All lands disturbed by the taking of natural resources shall be reclaimed. The legislature shall provide effective requirements and standards for the reclamation of lands disturbed.
(2) The legislature shall provide for a fund, to be known as the resource indemnity trust of the state of Montana, to be funded by such taxes on the extraction of natural resources as the legislature may from time to time impose for that purpose.

(3) The principal of the resource indemnity trust shall forever remain inviolate in an amount of one hundred million dollars ($100,000,000), guaranteed by the state against loss or diversion.

Section 3 - Water Rights

(1) All existing rights to the use of any waters for any useful or beneficial purpose are hereby recognized and confirmed.
(2) The use of all water that is now or may hereafter be appropriated for sale, rent, distribution, or other beneficial use, the right of way over the lands of others for all ditches, drains, flumes, canals, and aqueducts necessarily used in connection therewith, and the sites for reservoirs necessary for collecting and storing water shall be held to be a public use.
(3) All surface, underground, flood, and atmospheric waters within the boundaries of the state are the property of the state for the use of its people and are subject to appropriation for beneficial uses as provided by law.
(4) The legislature shall provide for the administration, control, and regulation of water rights and shall establish a system of centralized records, in addition to the present system of local records.

Section 4 - Cultural Resources

The legislature shall provide for the identification, acquisition, restoration, enhancement, preservation, and administration of scenic, historic, archeologic, scientific, cultural, and recreational areas, sites, records, and objects, and for their use and enjoyment by the people.

The fact that this article exists is due in large part to the determination of one woman, C. Louise Cross, who was the chairperson for the Committee on Natural Resources and Agriculture at that Constitutional Convention. Cross stood up to opposition from several members of the committee to insist

that this article be included. Cross brought in heavy hitters
like Senator Lee Metcalf, a life-long proponent of conservation, to convince the committee to push this article through,
and I can't help but wonder whether the setting played some
small role in their willingness to be convinced.

I often tell people that Helena would be my first choice if I
were forced to decide where I wanted to live in Montana. But
the choices are so many that I seem to change my mind almost
every time someone asks. It's part of the beauty of this state.
So many options, and my taste is often affected by my mood.
But the things I love most about Helena—its people, its rich,
varied culture, the strong commitment to our history with the
Montana Historical Society, where Bruce Wittenberg gave me
a private tour of the hidden treasures that they don't even have
room to display, and the renovation of the Last Chance Gulch
section of town—all these things make this place feel special.

IF THERE IS SUCH a thing as royalty in the world of Montana
politics, I would have to nominate Pat and Carol Williams
for King and Queen, although they would reject these titles
out of hand, with all the associated sense of entitlement and
opulence. Plus there is the small fact that their commitment
to politics has always been driven by a sense of service rather
than a desire for status.

It's hard to imagine a couple that has played more of a role
in the political leadership in our state, especially in contemporary Montana. Although Pat was not the longest-serving
congressman from Montana, he did serve the most consecu-
tive terms, winning nine straight elections to the US Congress,
the next to last of which was the very hotly contested election
between the last two incumbent House members before they
reduced Montana's number of seats from two to one.

One of Pat's best stories came out of that election, when he
tells about running into his opponent Ron Marlenee in an elevator in Washington just after his victory. "So was there one big
surprise that came out of that election?" Pat asked Marlenee.

"Yeah, I thought I was going to win," Marlenee quipped.

But he went on to give a more serious answer, as a reflection of one of the hot-button topics of that election. There was a strong opposition that year to funding for the arts, particularly the NEA, after some controversial works, such as Robert Mapplethorpe's photo exhibit, drew heavy criticism from the public. Williams showed strong support for the NEA's right to fund artists based on their talent rather than their content, and Marlenee focused on this issue a lot during the campaign.

"I underestimated the dedication of people in Montana toward the arts, even in Eastern Montana," he told Williams. "They weren't happy that I spoke out against that. I heard that from a lot of people." Carol Williams has also been a force in the political arena, serving one term in the state House of Representatives before being elected to the state Senate in 2004, where she would eventually become the first woman Senate Majority Leader in Montana history.

Both the Williamses are retired from public office now, but that doesn't mean they are no longer active in politics. Carol started a group, originally called Williams Works, to raise money for women running for office in Montana. The group's name was eventually changed to Carol's List, and their focus is still on creating a better balance in the Montana legislature.

Pat told me, "Whenever anyone asks me what we can do to improve the state of politics in America, I always say, 'we need more women, and we need more people of color in Congress.'"

I was hoping Pat and Carol would confirm my opinions that you really can't categorize people in Montana as conservative or liberal, and that the legislature here has a strong history of working together because of the common goals most Montanans share. For the most part they did.

Pat was especially adamant that people in Montana don't fit the mold of straight conservative or liberal. "Most of the people in Montana, especially Eastern Montana, fit much better into the libertarian mold," he explained. "They want the government and probably other people, too, to leave them alone as long as they mind their own business."

But Carol was quick to correct me on the cooperative

nature of the Montana legislature. "It entirely depends on who the leaders are in each party," she said. "If you have the right mix, it can be very productive, that's true. But when I first joined the Senate, that wasn't the case at all. There were a few people in positions of power that really poisoned the process. They were poison."

Pat and Carol grew up in Butte, where Pat's parents owned a business called The American Candy Company, which was a restaurant that also made its own candy. Carol's father, Vern Griffith, was also in the food business, owning a grocery store. Carol came by her love of politics honestly, as her father became the mayor of Butte when she was in high school, and only gave up that position when Lyndon Johnson appointed him as Montana director of the EDA (Economic Development Association). He spent much of the next few years traveling to the Indian reservations, where he worked to develop the education programs.

Williams was an only child, and although his parents were not inclined to run for office, they instilled in him an interest in politics, and it was at a meeting of the Young Democrats at Montana Tech that Carol heard Pat give a speech that made a big impression on her. She was finishing her degree in Dillon at what was then Western Montana College, and she approached him about coming to speak for the Young Democrats Group that she was planning to start down there. He was the club's first speaker, "and things just went from there," Carol said. "We were married about a year and a half later."

I was hoping Pat would have an opinion on how the current Congress conducts business, and he certainly did. "Things really started to shift the last few years I was in Congress." (Pat left office in 1997). "Before that, one of the mainstays of the congressional process was the give and take between the two parties when it came to earmarking appropriations in bills. Members from both sides would make compromises to get a line item entered into another member's bill to help out their constituents. Then Newt Gingrich came along and started to create a real sense of animosity between the parties. The final straw was the disastrous Bridge to Nowhere." (Nearly $400 million was appropriated in several increments to build a bridge in Alaska between the city of Ketchikan and the airport that serves it.)

"The use of earmarks is pretty much non-existent now, and the two sides have gotten to the point where they honestly hate each other." Pat also cited the different roles that lobbyists play now. "They used to be incredibly valuable as a source of information. You could get a brief explanation on an issue that would take hours to research on your own. And then money came into the equation, and it's been a mess ever since."

So WHAT ABOUT THIS same dark side of Montana politics? Well for the most part, there has been less indication of this kind of nefarious behavior than you might find in many states. Of course that excludes the fact that the public seldom knows what's truly going on. But as far as scandals go, there have been refreshingly few since the days of the Copper Kings, or Thomas Meagher.

What you are more likely to hear about in Montana is a fight among the people against being influenced by outsiders, with an excellent example being an effort in 2015 by the Koch brothers to shoot down legislation to expand Medicaid in Montana. They formed a group called Americans for Prosperity, and sent in leaders who posed as locals to lead town hall meetings to persuade people to vote against this legislation. If there's one thing Montanans do not appreciate, it's someone posing as a Montanan. And it's even worse when they're really bad at it, which apparently many of these people were. The measure passed.

Similarly, just a month earlier, in a very strong bipartisan effort, the Montana state legislature passed the Montana Disclose Act, a bill that requires all candidates in Montana to disclose the source of their campaign contributions. This was in direct response to the 2010 Supreme Court Citizens United ruling that gave corporations the right to contribute to political campaigns. The Citizens United decision was coupled with an earlier ruling that allowed non-profits to run corporate-funded campaign ads close to an election, allowing an epidemic of so-called "dark money" to make its way into the American political arena over the next few years.

While many states have made an effort to pass legislation to stop this kind of behind-the-scenes activity, Montana was only the second state, behind California, to pass such a bill, and we did it despite a huge push by the National Rifle Association and Americans for Prosperity to finance opposition to the bill. To me, it's just one more indication of how often outsiders underestimate the ability of Montanans to think for themselves. We're good at that.

ON THE FLIP SIDE from Helena, one of the few towns where I received a very cool reception was Boulder (Jefferson County), home of several state institutions. When I entered the building that houses the Montana Developmental Center, a facility for the developmentally disabled, I approached the desk and told the woman about my project. And then I asked what I thought was a pretty benign question: "Do you think that the government is the largest employer in this county?"

She seemed offended somehow, and said she didn't know. So I asked a security guard who was standing nearby. "What?" he asked, and the look he gave me made me hesitant to repeat the question. My instincts were right. He showed no interest in even thinking about the answer.

Thankfully, I found someone else who was much more helpful, Jan Anderson, the editor of the *Boulder Monitor*. But even Jan seemed guarded. I learned later that Boulder had just gone through a horrible scandal where one of guards at the county jail was accused of sexually assaulting several inmates. I couldn't help but wonder whether this had an effect on the trust level for the people I spoke to.

But although we got off to an awkward start when Jan didn't recognize the name of the person who recommended that I talk to her, she was happy to answer my questions about Boulder. Boulder has a long history of institutions, starting with the Montana Deaf and Dumb Asylum in 1898. Despite the horrible name, this institution provided innovative training for handicapped children, expanding to include blind children in later years. Of course, this assessment is based on public relations reports from the facility itself, so we have no way of knowing what the true conditions of this school may have been. We all know by now that the standard methods during those years were often much different than what we would find acceptable today. But there's no denying that this facility provided a much-needed place for children with disabilities at a time when most families did not have the funds or the time to provide special needs to kids.

The Deaf and Dumb School is long closed, although the building still stands, and it's an anachronistic marvel. It really looks like an old institution—a red brick monstrosity that feels cold even from the outside. In addition to the Montana Developmental Center (MDC), there are several other state facilities in Boulder, although the numbers are way down from what they once were. The MDC once housed about one thousand people, but it now has about sixty. Riverside Youth Correctional Facility is a twenty-bed juvenile correction facility for girls. There is also the Elkhorn Treatment Center, which specializes specifically in women meth addicts.

Youth Dynamics is also very active in Boulder. It is not a state-run organization but rather a non-profit, which has been dealing with kids with behavioral issues for nearly thirty years all over the state of Montana.

Although these facilities provide the most jobs in Boulder, there is still a strong agricultural presence in an area that was once much more dependent on mining. The last big mine to close here was the Elkhorn Mine, which halted operations almost a decade ago, leaving about three hundred people unemployed, although there were rumors a few years ago that the mine might reopen. (Black Diamond Holdings, a private holding company from Denver, was supposedly going to invest over $7 million into getting the mine operating again, but this never came to fruition. But the possibility is not dead yet.)

Just north of Boulder in Jefferson City, a company called
Eastern Resources bought the Montana Tunnels, a mining
operation that produced gold, silver, copper, and lead until it
also closed down in the past decade. Eastern Resources announced the purchase of Montana Tunnels as well as Elkhorn
Goldfields in 2012 and is planning to resume operations. But
again, so far this is still very much in the planning stage. In the
meantime, Jefferson County continues to rely on the government jobs and agriculture.

Although she did not mention any of this herself, I learned
later that Jan Anderson is highly respected all over the state
as a journalist and editor, and was a recipient of the Montana
Newspaper Association's Master Editor & Publisher Award a
few years ago. Jan owns the *Monitor,* and merged it in 2011
with the *Jefferson County Courier,* which she started twelve
years ago. She is a strong advocate for local businesses and
resources, and has helped save such facilities as the County
Health Department, which was in danger of being discontin-
ued. And Jan displays much of the same forced optimism that I
love about almost everyone in Montana. In her newspaper, she
lists the upcoming community activities, including a citywide
garage sale right before Father's Day, Brother Van's Cowboy
Poetry and Music Festival, and of course high school sports
events, a staple for rural Montana.

But I felt an uncomfortable undercurrent in Boulder. Something disconcerting and awkward. I left this place feeling as
if I had trod on the feet of people who were either hurting or
perhaps distrustful, and it made me sad.

THE OTHER TOWN IN Montana that benefits most from government funding is Deer Lodge (Powell County), home of the
Montana State Prison. All across the state, "Deer Lodge" is an
eponym for state prison. You say so-and-so was sent to Deer
Lodge, everyone knows what you mean. But it's a shame that
the place has been distilled to this one fact, as it actually has a
rich history.

Deer Lodge, like so many municipalities in the western part

of the state, started as a mining town, when Granville Stuart and his brother, James, decided that the area provided a perfect access point to Clark Fork River and the Mullan Road. The Stuart brothers were entrepreneurs in the classic sense, dabbling in mining, cattle, and diplomacy. James died fairly young after trying to start a smelter near Philipsburg, but Granville remained active throughout his life in the development of Montana, serving as a librarian for the Butte Public Library as well as president of the Montana Stockgrowers Association. Sadly, although Stuart seemed to have the gift of starting businesses and organizations, he must not have handled his money all that well as he died with significant debt to his name.

It was the rich grass around Deer Lodge that first brought much of the business to the area, but everything changed when Deer Lodge won the contract for the state prison in 1867. It took several more years to construct the first building, due in large part to the cost of shipping and materials. But in 1871, the first nine prisoners were locked away inside the first fourteen cells. Within a month, the prison was overcrowded when six more prisoners arrived. Eventually two more tiers were completed, also with fourteen cells per tier. The newest version of the prison was built between 1974 and 1979, when the old one had degenerated beyond repair.

Perhaps one of the most influential people in the history of the prison was a man named Frank Conley, who took over as warden in 1890. Conley was one of the members of the (in)famous Vigilance Committee, and he was a big believer that idle prisoners were the most dangerous kind. He co-opted prison labor to continue expanding the facility, putting them to work on building after building as the population continued to grow. They also built the huge prison wall that surrounds the old facility, as well as a separate facility for the women once they complained about not feeling safe among the regular prison population.

Conley also utilized land owned by the state to raise cattle and crops, similarly forcing prisoners to do the work. Today the dairy farm at the prison is run by a man named Jerry

Roseliep, who moved to Deer Lodge about ten years ago for this job. The farm employs four hundred prisoners, and covers thirty-seven thousand acres. About nine hundred of those acres are used for farming while the rest serve as grazing land for fifteen hundred milk cows and fifteen hundred Angus beef cattle.

I became acquainted with Jerry when his wife, Billye, contacted me by email a few years ago. Billye is from Carter County, where my mom grew up, and when she read my first two novels, which are based there, she contacted me, and we have been in touch ever since, although we have never been able to coordinate a face-to-face meeting. Jerry is from St. Ignatius, one of my favorite parts of the state, where the Roselieps lived for a long time before Jerry got this job. "We'll move back to St. Ignatius when I retire, but for now, we really like it here. Deer Lodge has a great sense of community," Jerry told me over the phone. "Plus I love this job."

I'm surprised to hear this, drawing certain conclusions about working with prisoners, but Jerry goes on to explain. "These are the best jobs in the prison system. They get to work outside. They get to do actual physical labor. Plus they get better pay. On the inside, they can work in the sign shop, or they have a vehicle maintenance garage, and the license plate shop, and they all get paid around $2.35 to $4.00 a day. Out here, they get anywhere from $4.00 to $7.00 a day. So we get the best workers, plus they have a real motivation to do a good job, because there are a bunch of people waiting for them to fail. I've never had any problems with the prisoners."

The most frustrating part of Jerry's job is that they have to get approval from the legislature for every improvement they propose. "We really needed a new barn, and we couldn't build that barn until it was approved and financed through the legislature. When you're used to running your own place, it's really frustrating to have to wait for months. It just seems kind of ridiculous that the legislature has to approve every single thing, but that's the way it is."

DURING A HIGH SCHOOL choir tour, our director arranged for us to do a concert at Galen, the mental institution just down the road from the prison. Many of us had the attitude that you might expect from self-centered teenagers about this event. We thought it was stupid, which was mostly an indication that we were scared to death. As it turned out, the crowd was appreciative, although many seemed sadly unaware of what was happening. It turned out to be way more depressing than it was scary. What I didn't realize until later was that Galen also served as a treatment center for alcoholism, something I would struggle with just a few years later. And now that I think about it, I wonder whether there were any people in our choir who had experienced the pain of having someone from their family confined there. If so, that visit must have held a very different meaning for them.

As with most things, there is a plus side to having these facilities in Deer Lodge: jobs. Because of these two institutions, the prison and the state mental hospital, along with other county services, the government is the biggest employer in town by a long ways. And it's not hard to imagine that there must have been a great deal of conflicting opinions about having the prison built there. But one thing most people like is something that brings jobs to town.

Deer Lodge gets its unusual name from a geological foundation known as the Warm Springs Mound, the large saline content of which provides a natural salt lick for the local deer population. So it is where wildlife gathers once the winter weather pushes them out of the mountains.

One of the most surprising facts about Deer Lodge is that it is the home of the first college in Montana, then known as College of Montana, a school that was affiliated with the Presbyterian Church. It closed its doors in 1916 due to financial struggles.

The day I arrived in Deer Lodge the thermometer was pushing 95 degrees, which seemed to dull even further what was already a fairly colorless patch of land. The old prison is a museum, so I made a note to pay it a visit after I explored the rest of town. The main street wasn't especially long, and there wasn't much energy in town. Maybe it *was* the heat.

I circled back around and entered the museum, only to find out that there are actually several museums in town, and that a single fee would get me into all of them.

The prison part of the Old Montana Prison museum was a series of melancholy cubbyholes carved into a huge block of cement. The yard was surrounded by a stone wall at least 15 feet high, and who knows how thick. I tried to imagine living for any length of time inside these walls, and found it a difficult task.

After touring this huge block of concrete, reading about attempted escapes, the murder of a guard, and a few other uplifting stories, I made my way to the rest of the museum, which turned out to be a huge collection of old cars. It was, in fact, the Montana Auto Museum.

I wondered how on earth they decided that this would be a natural companion to the old prison. But then I considered that this was the beauty of small-town museums. A collection of stuff is considered worthy of attention, whether it makes any kind of logical statement or not. There were over 150 cars here, everything from old fire trucks to logging trucks to a whole flock of Corvettes. DeSotos, Model T's, even an electric car from 1913.

I have never given much of a damn about cars, partly because of my dad. Dad used to buy old cars and fix them up, and I don't think he did it for fun. He did it out of necessity, because it was cheap. And it did not bring him pleasure. I remember my mother "suggesting" that I go out and help him work on the car. And it would be absolutely miserable because he didn't want any help, and I wasn't the least bit interested. So I'd stand around with my hands in my pockets, and he would cuss and bang on engine parts, and finally I'd find an excuse or he'd just come out and tell me I could go on back inside.

But when I see a collection like this, I am always struck by the amount of money that must go into designing these machines. They are all so different from each other, each with their own unique feature. There is the elegant slope of the DeSoto Airflow, the distinctive fins of the Chevy Bel Air, and of course the cool simplicity of every single version of Porsche.

It wasn't until I left the car museum that I found out just how random the planning for the museums in Deer Lodge actually is. Right across the street was the doll museum! Which included an exclusive collection of Raggedy Ann and Andy dolls. And there were still two more museums to come. First, there was the inevitable pioneer museum (Frontier Montana Museum). And it was a good one, although I've seen enough rifles, old saddles, and buckskin outfits to dress out an entire year's worth of *Gunsmoke*. But I lost interest quickly mostly because I really wanted to see the last museum on the list.

In the 1850s, a Canadian fur trader named Johnny Grant could see that he wasn't going to be able to make a living much longer with the fur trade. As mentioned, he came up with the brilliant idea of trading one good healthy cow for two of the tired, worn-out cows the pioneers had just spent months pushing across the country. Grant quickly grew his herd, and eventually decided to build a place in what is now Deer Lodge.

Although Grant had established a solid operation within a few years, he sold his ranch to an enterprising young cattleman named Conrad Kohrs. Like the lives of so many of the people who came to the area at that time, Kohrs's life story reads like a Jack London story. Born in Denmark, Kohrs lost his father when he was only seven weeks old. After Grant had spent only a few years going to school off and on, his mother married a farmer, putting an end to his education. He did not like working for his stepfather and decided at the age of fifteen to go to sea, landing a job as a cabin boy. After traveling the world for the next several years, almost dying twice—once from yellow fever and once from typhoid—Kohrs caught "the California fever," as he called it, and made his way out West to hunt for gold.

After his efforts to find gold failed, Kohrs made a journey to Iowa to try to save a family business, traveled to Louisiana to sell some goods down there, traveled to New York for some business dealings there, and finally went back to San Francisco on a whim before hearing about the possibility of striking it rich in Montana.

Kohrs made his way to Beaverhead County around 1861. He didn't have much luck with his mining endeavors, but he did make a fortune selling beef to the miners. Kohrs was an innovator, experimenting with crossbreeding to determine which type of cattle suited the area best, and continuing to experiment with hybrids throughout his career. He would eventually own over ten million acres of land all over the West, and run more than fifty thousand head of cattle.

Kohrs maintained the home ranch that Grant had originally built in Deer Lodge. Like most ranchers of the era, Kohrs and his half-brother, John Bielenberg, took a big hit in the winter of 1886–1887, losing about half of their thousands of head of cattle. But they were able to survive that setback better than many by virtue of Kohrs's business sense. While others had sunk all of their money into their cattle operations, Kohrs had spent years letting Bielenberg run the cattle operation while he managed investments in mining and real estate. He ended up making a lot of money in mining, mostly using hydraulic methods, and put most of the money back into the cattle business.

When Kohrs became a state legislator, he also became known for introducing bills that went against the interests of the mining industry, particularly the Anaconda Copper Mining Company. He was one of the local ranchers who filed a suit complaining of the smoke affecting his grass and livestock, and while he won a few minor victories, for the most part even his wealth wasn't enough to battle "The Company."

Visiting the Kohrs Ranch and later reading about the family, I was struck by how their story lacked the drama of many of their more colorful Montana counterparts. Perhaps it was because Kohrs was a pretty straightforward, ethical human being; he did very little to bring attention to himself. Perhaps he'd had more than enough drama in his early life. God knows he went through his share of it. I suppose if a person dug deeply enough, you could find a few people with stories on the Kohrs family, a wayward relative, a conflict here and there. But on the surface, they seem to be a great example of a family who found success by hard work and good timing. Kohrs died in 1920 at the age of eighty-five, but the ranch stayed in his family until his grandson sold it to the National Park System in 1972. The ranch house has been preserved and the National Park Service still runs cattle and raises hay on the property.

To me the best part of the Kohrs Ranch was touring the house. In Montana, the houses that would have been considered mansions in their time, with the exception of the Daly Mansion, are pretty goddamn modest by today's standards, or by the standards of mansions in other parts of the country. The Kohrs house was certainly bigger than most homes of its time, with about six bedrooms, a dining room, a sitting room, and an office. Luxuries most people wouldn't have had at the time. But the rooms were small by today's standards. The dining room elegant but not overly gaudy. It was all, in a word, tasteful.

Along with the Conrad Mansion in Kalispell, the Bair Museum in Martinsdale, the Castle in White Sulphur Springs, and many of the beautiful homes in Helena, the Kohrs home showed a certain humility, which seemed consistent with the personality of even the most successful Montanans. Maybe it's because raising livestock or crops are humbling occupations. Nothing shows you how small you are in the overall scheme of things more than putting your heart and soul into your work only to see it fail after a hard winter or a hail storm, being shown time after time that you have no power whatsoever in the results.

THE HARDEST ASPECT OF my trip around Montana was visiting towns so clearly in decline that there seemed to be little or no hope of recovery. Many of the towns were almost completely reliant on the state and county for jobs, creating a strange combination of dependence and resentment. I can't help but wonder now how much the pressure of being self-reliant—a

pressure that people in the West get drummed into them from
the day they are born—weighs on these little communities. We
in the West do not like failure. We don't take kindly to having
to rely on others. And we don't appreciate being humbled in a
public way. But when you drive through Hysham, or Winnett,
or Circle, despite their best efforts to gussy their town up, it's
undeniable that these places have seen better days.

I love small towns and their small-town peculiarities. I love
the stories of the eccentrics who are completely accepted by
the locals. It's the whole "he may be a bit loony, but he's our
loony" attitude, which can be both charming and a bit stifling.
People in small towns take care of their own, especially when
tragedy strikes. There is a selflessness that brings out the best
in even the most unfortunate characters when tragedy hits a
small town.

But when it's the whole town that's suffering, when there
is no specific tragedy but a series of slow, steady setbacks that
persistently push the people further and further into the red,
you can see the spirit beaten out of these places in the chipping
paint, the shoddy streets, and most of all, in the empty store-
front windows.

Nearly one hundred years ago, a few enterprising souls, led
by a man named Dan McKay, made a sweep through Montana and convinced good, optimistic people that it was a damn
good idea to start their own county. It was just one more story
of men who had their own agenda taking advantage of people
who were trusting, people who wanted to believe that these
men had their interests at heart. McKay had a knack for rallying people to his way of thinking, to the point where they
didn't hesitate to raise the fee he requested to take care of the
paperwork and advertising required to further their agenda.

The movement was a huge success, and as I've mentioned
before, the number of counties in Montana doubled between
1910 and 1925. To be fair, there was a certain logic to it then,
especially considering the fact that most people didn't have
cars at the time. A trip to the county seat could take two
or three days in many cases, and now almost everyone in

Montana could make a needed trip to the courthouse in a day.

But it was soon apparent that the tax burden, which resulted from these splits, was more than many of the young families in these counties were able to pay. During the Depression, it was the tax bill that pushed many people over the line from just getting by to admitting that they couldn't hang on another day. Many deeds were handed over to the county treasurer to cover property taxes. Many a family's dream came to an end because the sheriff came to their door. I can't even imagine how humiliating that must have been. Especially for people who were as proud and hard-working as the average Montana farmer or rancher.

Several proposals have been put forward over the decades calling to combine some of the counties that are barely getting by. And of course people protest. The legislators from those regions protest, the people of those counties protest, and none of the proposals have come even close to coming to fruition, although there is currently a proposal in the works to do away with Petroleum County, the smallest county in the state in terms of population. What we're left with is a choice that is kind of like having a loved one on life support. We're left with the pressure of deciding whether it's more cruel to let the machine keep them alive or to let them die a natural death. It's easy to say from a distance that you should let nature take its course. But when it's a *loved* one, the question always becomes complicated by emotion. By history, by their story, by the importance they have in our lives.

Each of these towns has a history worthy of a book, and thankfully many of them have had books written about them. And each of them still has an abundance of character. And characters. They are part of who we are. Our children, our eccentric aunts and uncles, our grandmother who always made the best pies in the world. You don't just casually let these people go.

WHEN I ENTERED THE courthouse in Ryegate (seat of Golden Valley County), I was approached by a very friendly woman, probably about my age, who asked, "What can I do for you?" In the room behind her, a group of people were gathered around a table. I told her what I was doing, and said, "It looks like you're in the middle of a meeting, so maybe I can come back later."

"Oh no," she said. "We're just having our morning coffee. Come join us!"

So I entered the room. Six or seven people greeted me with hearty hellos, and introduced themselves. Among them was the local sheriff, a dark-haired man who looked as if he might still be in his twenties. He was wearing a bulletproof vest, although it was pushing ninety degrees outside, and it was... well, Ryegate, Montana.

"Aren't you hot?" I asked him.

"Oh, you get used to it," he replied with a laugh.

When I asked whether they all worked there, all but two said yes. The woman who greeted me pointed at the two who didn't work there, a couple in their late eighties. "They just come in here for coffee every day," she said, laughing.

They asked where I was from, and I told them, and added that my mother grew up on a ranch near Ekalaka. The old man at the end of the table piped up, "I'm from Ekalaka."

I asked his name, making a mental note to ask my mother whether she knew the family. Everyone in Carter County has heard of everyone else, whether they've met or not.

It was clear after just a few minutes of conversation that Ryegate wasn't doing well. The population was just over two hundred people, and the population of the county itself was well under one thousand. During those years when the number of counties in Montana doubled, many of the names chosen for these new counties were designed to inspire optimism. It was a time when that kind of forced positivity was easy to embrace, as banks were opening all over the state, the moisture levels were unnaturally high, and livestock and grain prices were rising steadily. But when the Depression kicked in a few years later, this restructuring of the counties caused way more problems than anticipated, and names like Golden Valley, and Treasure, must have felt wrong, almost taunting

"There used to be a grocery store here," someone said. "And the slaughterhouse closed a few years ago. They had about five employees there." There were five kids in the high school this past year, and only one in the graduating class.

But perhaps the most telling fact about Ryegate was that they no longer held their annual Testicle Festival. In Montana, there are few things more symbolic of things taking a turn for the worse than canceling the Testicle Festival.

HYSHAM, MONTANA, IN Treasure County, has one of the weirdest museums I've ever seen. Across from their regular museum, which is small and clearly underfunded, I found a Spanish-style building called the Yucca Theater. It looked a little bit like a whitewashed version of the Alamo, with what looked like guard towers on either side of the entrance. In front of the building, on the left side, were sculptures of Sacagawea, and Lewis and Clark. On the right side stood a white buffalo. Sacagawea and Lewis were pointing at the buffalo, which was unimpressed.

Walking through the door, I entered a movie theater, with a fairly decent capacity for such a small town. But behind the stage, there was a door that led to an apartment. It was like stepping back into the 1960s. The apartment belonged to a man named David Manning, one of the longest-running state senators in Montana history. In fact, when he retired from the Senate in 1985, he was the most senior state senator in the whole nation. He and his family lived in this place for many years, and its décor and layout suggest the best and worst of the 1960s and 1970s, with loud floral carpet and paneling on the walls. But it's a comfortable home, which was clearly well cared for.

Hysham was a thriving community in the early twentieth century, being one of the first towns in this part of the state to have electricity, sewer, and concrete sidewalks. Hysham is also one of the few towns that cites a woman as one of the founders. Ada Channel, who was the first teacher at the Hysham Public School, is listed along with James Lockard and F. L. Baker as the people who chose a site and started the process of building a town.

But now, the location of Hysham, whose population has dropped below three hundred, has worked against it. For one thing, it sits about two miles off the main highway, so it doesn't get the kind of spontaneous traffic that most small towns get along the main highways. It's also an hour from the biggest city in Montana. Anyone wanting to do any shopping is going to gladly drive another seventy-five miles to get to Billings rather than stop in Hysham.

THE TOWN OF WIBAUX, in Wibaux County, does not have a café that is open for breakfast. It's hard to think of any better indication that a town is losing its spirit than knowing that it doesn't have a place where people can gather for breakfast. There is hardly a more traditional morning activity in small Montana towns than having the locals flock to their favorite small-town café for a cup of coffee and a good dose of local gossip.

But for the past three years, Wibaux *has* had a microbrewery. Like many towns in Montana, Wibaux is counting on their local brewer—in this case, Beaver Creek Brewery—to bring more business into town.

Wibaux is named after one of the great cattlemen in Montana history. Pierre Wibaux came from a wealthy textile family, and moved to Montana with his friend the Marquis de Mores in order to get into the cattle business. The Marquis is best known as Teddy Roosevelt's trusted companion when Roosevelt moved to Medora and started the Elkhorn Ranch. The Marquis came up with the idea of starting a slaughterhouse and packing plant in the area, a plan that seemed innovative at the time. Everyone was spending a good deal of their earnings shipping their cattle back to Chicago, or down to Nebraska, and the Marquis figured on making a killing. But there were too many factors working against him, particularly the refusal of the Chicago beef trust to give him the same freight rates that they were giving his competitors.

So the Marquis didn't last long in the West, but Wibaux turned out to have a gift for working with cattle. He also had the benefit of a money supply, so that when the blizzard of 1886–1887 hit, he saw a prime opportunity to buy out many of the ranchers who were unable to continue. He expanded his herd until it was one of the largest in the country, at over sixty-five thousand head. Wibaux was business savvy enough to get into the banking business as well, starting banks in Miles City and Forsythe before he died at the age of sixty.

Pierre Wibaux was by all accounts one of the good guys, a man who donated much of his wealth to worthy causes like a hospital in his home country, as well as money to establish some model farms in France, which provided milk for those in need.

His memory is preserved not only with a huge statue outside the town that bears his name, but also with a museum of his home, and a church, which was built in his honor. It's one of the more unique buildings you'll ever see, formerly just a plain stucco building, but in the 1930s it was covered with varnished stones about the size of cantaloupe.

The best thing that happened to me in Wibaux? I found a Laundromat and asked the employee the closest place to get some breakfast. She told me that Beach, North Dakota, was just a few miles along the highway and then offered to do my laundry for me while I went to get some breakfast. This is why I love small towns.

IN PETROLEUM COUNTY, Winnett came into being because of a short-lived oil boom nearby. The need to get the oil from Petroleum County to one of the larger shipping areas led the Milwaukee Railroad to build a spur from Lewistown to Winnett. But eventually a pipeline was built to access that area, which eliminated the need for the railroad. Winnett is the smallest county seat in Montana, with just over one hundred eighty people. It is also one of the most desolate—a dusty little burg with just a handful of businesses.

Perhaps the most interesting thing about Winnett is the

story of its namesake, a man named Walter Winnett. Winnett was a Canadian who ran away from home as a boy in search of adventure in "Indian Country." And he certainly found it. Winnett was an excellent marksman, so he was able to make a living hunting for meat for various concerns until he was eventually captured by the Sioux and adopted into their tribe, who gave him the name Eagle Eye because of his marksmanship.

Winnett eventually established his own ranch and was successful enough that he was able to build a large house, which served as a gathering place for those who lived in the area. He hosted dances, school, and church services, and eventually filed for a post office for the area.

I stopped at the courthouse to ask if they could recommend someone to talk to about what's going on in Winnett, and there was a lot of hmm-ing. But someone eventually recommended Jack Barisich, who carries the mail.

So I went in search of Jack Barisich. I tried the post office first, and had to wait for a half hour until they were open, although the door was open and the clerk was behind the counter. When I was finally allowed to enter, the clerk there said that Jack had just been there but he thought he'd gone to lunch and then would probably be going home right afterward.

He gave me directions to Jack's house. I had some lunch, wondering whether Jack Barisich was one of the people staring at me, then followed the postmaster's directions, or so I thought, and found myself at the doorstep of someone who was most definitely not Jack Barisich. But she was kind enough to point me in the right direction. I found the Barisich house, only to discover that Jack was not there.

I know it's not right to jump to conclusions, but I got the distinct feeling that people in Winnett weren't particularly interested in having visitors. And yet I also know that if I had spent more time there, I would have found Mr. Barisich, and he would have been similar to Wendell Pawlowski, or Kay Strombo. He would have been like Edgar Danielsen. And I would have come away having been convinced that there isn't another place in the world quite like Winnett.

I felt guilty about it afterward, but the truth was, by the time I got to Winnett, I was struggling to feel optimistic about places like this. It was just a few months later that an article came out in the news stating that Winnett, or more accurately, Petroleum County, is going to put it up for a vote to the residents whether they will accept higher property taxes, or merge with neighboring Fergus County. The county raises only about $400,000 in property taxes at its current rate, and needs another $40,000-$60,000 to operate. So perhaps my instincts were right, but I still didn't feel good about giving up so easily. My apologies to Jack.

YOU KNOW IT IS a bad sign when you walk into a museum and tell the volunteer there that you are looking for interesting facts about the community, and the first words out of their mouth are "Nothing interesting has ever happened here!"

Welcome to Stanford, Montana, in Judith Gap County. Sadly, my afternoon spent in Stanford did little to prove that volunteer wrong, although they did have the most impressive stuffed white wolf I have ever seen. Well okay, it is also the only one.

This albino wolf terrorized the area for several years back in the twenties, killing local livestock until a price of $400 was put on its head. Eventually dubbed "Old Snowdrift," this wolf proved to be very adept at eluding capture as the best hunters in the area each took their crack at bringing him down.

I tried to picture what it must have been like during that time, with the locals gathering at the local café every morning, wondering whether there had been any more dead livestock or whether anyone had spotted Old Snowdrift and gotten a crack at him. For years, reports of sightings and close calls provided the community with an endless source of conversation. The legend was also boosted by the fact that this was considered the last wild free-ranging wolf in Montana.

A local named A. E. Close was finally able to bring Old Snowdrift down on May 8, 1930. Close and a friend lured the wolf out of hiding with dogs. When the wolf chased after the dogs, Close shot him. News of the death spread so quickly that by the time Close and his friend got back to town with the carcass, the streets were full of people. Their car was only able to move a few inches at a time. I love this account published in the *Democrat News,* the Lewistown paper, just a few days after the killing:

> Everyone was trembling including the hunters, but whether with cold or because of the excitement, it is difficult to say. Cameras clicked madly. Everyone wanted to see the man who did the shooting and personally ask him how it was done. Old stories of close calls and lucky escapes were brought out and refurbished, and the few persons who had been skeptical of the existence of such an animal, were either silent or unusually garrulous in an effort to cover up their confusion and discomfiture.

The wolf, which was estimated to be as old as eighteen years, is now immortalized in the Basin Trading Post, his fangs bared as if he is still trying to live up to the legend.

Of course, it's really not true that this is the only interesting thing that's ever happened here. At the Basin Trading Post, I met Don Dixon, a local artist who volunteers there, where the work of many of the local artists is on display.

Don was one of these genuinely nice people you often meet in Montana, someone who makes you immediately comfortable. He was eager to show me the art that he and his neighbors had produced, and I was reminded again of the fact that Montana has many people who designate themselves as artists. Of course the interesting thing about that is the wide variation in quality when you have that many self-proclaimed artists, and this was very much on display in Stanford. But there was some really nice work, and I particularly liked Don's paintings.

When Don started to plan his retirement, he began looking for land where he could build a home. The first place he looked was Bozeman, and the best price he could get there was around $30,000, just for the land. And this was in the 1970s. So Don asked a friend of his to look into lots about the same size in other parts of the state. And he ended up paying $1,000 for the lot where he eventually built his retirement home. Don Dixon loves Stanford, and it's clear that his reasons have become more than financial.

ON THE OFFICIAL WEB page for Big Timber, Montana, I clicked on the "Events" page, and got an image of the October calendar, which was completely blank, with this statement just above it:

PLEASE CHECK OUR HOME PAGE FOR SNOW PLOWING POLICY.

Big Timber is located in one of the more scenic settings in Montana, an area utilized for such films as *A River Runs Through It*, and *The Horse Whisperer*. But to my tastes, Big Timber itself has the feel of a postcard or a model. Pretty but somehow lacking in spirit. I really wanted to like Big Timber because it's such an amazing setting. I learned later that much of Big Timber is populated with people who work at Stillwater Mining Company's East Boulder Mine, so perhaps there are a lot of people who have only recently moved there, which maybe results in a less powerful sense of community. I stopped in at two art galleries, and the women working there were very nice, but again, I felt as if there was a serious lack of enthusiasm about their town and what it has to offer. It felt a little bit like talking to someone who can't stand their in-laws but has never quite allowed themselves to admit it.

I did find a fascinating little shop on Main Street—perhaps the only shop of its kind. It is cleverly called Little Timber Quilts and Candy. And yes, that's exactly what it is—a store that features quilting supplies as well as candy. There was a class taking place there, so I felt like a bit of an intruder, but the young woman who owns the place greeted me warmly and took a moment from her class to sell me a bag of candy.

Big Timber came about in large part because of the rail-road, when a smaller town named Dornix, Greek for "smooth stone," was moved to higher ground and renamed by the Great Northern executives. But it soon became known for its saw-mill, which is obviously how it got its name. The town is sur-rounded by cottonwood trees growing along the Yellowstone and Boulder Rivers, which converge just outside of town. There was also an early presence of sheep when two Irishmen, Charles McDonnell and Edward Veasey, drove three thousand head from California to Montana in 1880. For a brief period, in the mid-1890s, Big Timber shipped more wool, around five million pounds a year, than any town in the United States.

The sawmill is long gone, so agriculture forms the founda-tion of the region now, with some income coming into the re-gion from tourists looking for good fishing holes and hunting ground. The Grand Hotel serves as a cornerstone for Big Tim-ber's tourist trade, billing itself as "the finest bed and breakfast on the Yellowstone River."

The truth is, my time in Big Timber did not inspire me to learn more about Big Timber. At one point, I stopped to ask a couple walking along the street about a big building just out-side of town. The building was huge, and empty, and clearly only a few years old. It looked to me as if it was supposed to be a restaurant or something. So I asked this couple about it, and the man answered that it was a government warehouse. He said this with a challenging look, a look that told me he was testing me somehow, and it felt as if he had made some kind of judgment about me that was very unpleasant. I researched the building after I left, and discovered that it was the future home of a Cowboy Hall of Fame.

CHAPTER TEN
Fuel

> *"Not nature, but the 'genius of man' has
> knotted the hangman's noose with which
> it can execute itself at any moment."*
> — Carl Jung

K. Ross Toole, the acclaimed University of Montana historian, titled one of his books *Twentieth-Century Montana: A State of Extremes*. I find it poetic that in the early twenty-first century, people have been flocking to the extreme northeast corner of the state, the complete opposite corner from where the first economic boom took place. It says so much about how diverse this state is, especially considering that this current influx has been built around a completely different resource. We have been blessed with an abundance of nature, which has allowed us, as a state, to repeatedly turn to something new when one resource runs its course. Just look at the other two corners, with the thick forests in the northwest, and the rich grasses of Carter County, where some of the fattest cattle come from.

And yet, despite this abundance, we have somehow never been a wealthy state. One has to wonder how different our infrastructure might have been if the fair share of those billions of dollars that Misters Daly and Clark pulled from the hills of Silver Bow County would have been channeled properly, into the state treasury. And of course, we are now faced with a similar situation in many important ways, with the tax structure favoring the wealthy yet again, so that we have no idea how much of the millions that are being pumped from the ground in the Bakken are making their way into helping Montana's financial issues. One thing we do know—this boom has brought thousands of jobs to Montana, and not just in the oil fields. Fuel has become one of the main sources of income in our state, but even at this writing, there are reasons to wonder how long *that* will last.

In the late 1970s and early 1980s, four power plants were built in the small town of Colstrip, in Rosebud County. Colstrip already held a significant role in the state's energy production because of the coal mine that was opened there in the '20s. This open pit coal mine had provided coal for the Northern Pacific Railway, and was considered so vital during World War II that its employees were forbidden to quit their jobs. But the mine was shut down in 1958 when the railroad switched to diesel locomotives. After Montana Power Company purchased the mine in 1959, they re-opened it in conjunction with the power plants, and Colstrip grew both in size and in its rank among the highest per capita income in the state. Today, the average income per household in Colstrip is over $80,000, almost double the average income for the rest of Rosebud County, which includes the Crow Reservation. That is also about $30,000 above the national average.

But recent events have put the coal industry in a precarious position, and there are rumors that two of the four plants in Colstrip may be shut down in the near future. And although environmental concerns have become part of the discussion, the main reason that coal is in trouble is much more simple this time. It's the market. A decline in demand for coal, especially from foreign markets, as well as the concern about long-term effects of coal on global warming, have had a dramatic impact on the demand for coal, and have made the two oldest plants at Colstrip a natural target, because they are much less efficient than most plants of their kind.

However, there has also been heavy pressure from local groups, in an unlikely marriage between ranchers and members of the Blackfeet and Northern Cheyenne Tribes, who have been very vocal in their opposition to a proposed coal export terminal near Bellingham, Washington. They are upset about the environmental effects of transporting the coal to that region, which would interfere with the fishing for the Lummi Nation. There have also been active protests to a proposal by the Tongue River Railroad to ship the coal from local mines to the Pacific Northwest, where most of the coal is exported overseas. Assurances from the coal producers that their methods of shipping coal cut down dramatically on coal dust have not been convincing to most people.

Oddly enough, the Crow Tribe has a completely different agenda, as much of the coal that is being mined lies within the boundaries of their reservation, so it has become a significant source of income for the tribe. So once again, Montana faces another awkward dance between conservation and commerce, environment and jobs, and intertribal politics.

MEANWHILE, IT'S QUITE IMPOSSIBLE to tell the full story of what's happening in Richland County and Sidney, Montana, because the story is still unfolding. A few years ago, I went to Sidney for an annual event called the Sunrise Festival of the Arts. I went twice, but the first year was especially memorable because the man who invited me, Arch Elwine, told me that they had booked me a room at a certain hotel in town. I arrived late at night, and when I found the hotel, the office was closed. So I went ahead and checked into a different hotel.

The next day I told Arch what happened. "Oh no! They left the key out for you! It was taped to the door."

That would not happen today in Sidney, Montana. When I arrived in Sidney this time, I didn't even recognize it. I went in search of the park where the Sunrise Festival had taken place, and even when I found it I didn't realize that I'd found it. Not because the park itself looked so different but because the whole feel of the town had changed. Everything around the park was completely unrecognizable.

Sidney, of course, is caught up in one of the biggest oil booms in the history of the country. Although the actual center of the Bakken, as it has become known, is in North Dakota, it is only about ten miles from Sidney to the North Dakota border, and only forty-five miles to Williston, the hub of the activity. When oil was discovered there a few years ago, and reports indicated a supply that could provide millions of barrels for years to come, Montanans (as well as people from all over the country) responded as they have for decades.

"Jobs!" they cried.

And the rush began. The population of Williston in 2010 was a little over fourteen thousand. Three years later, it was well over twenty thousand, and that didn't include the transients, of which there are thousands more. Some estimates had it closer to fifty thousand. Similarly, Sidney's population in 2010 was just over five thousand, but in 2014, after many years without much growth, Sidney housed more than sixty-five hundred people. Again, not counting transients.

Stories came out of the area about families who had struggled for decades to make a living on the family farms, only to suddenly be cashing five-and-six figure checks every month from mineral rights. Young men could work on a rig at an annual salary of over $100,000. Truck drivers were in huge demand. Rumors circulated about people getting eighteen dollars an hour to work at McDonald's. But when people can make five or six figures working on a rig, eighteen dollars an hour is nothing. The service industries struggled to find employees. Keeping them was even harder as housing prices skyrocketed.

Sidney experienced a similar boom back in the late 1970s, although it was not of the same scale. And I've mentioned other booms throughout Montana, in Shelby back in the 1930s, and near Broadus in the 1960s. And just as with the gold rushes a hundred years before, the results were predictable. People flocked to the area. And the money poured in for a time. More taxes resulted in some nice buildings, like the courthouse and school in Broadus. And while only time will tell whether Sidney's story will play out as the others did, there are already indications that it could.

Just driving into present-day Sidney is a completely different experience from any other town in Montana. Every few miles, the road is lined with clusters of machines, or structures, or one of the standard hobbyhorse-style oil wells that used to fascinate me as a kid. This area has gone from a cozy agricultural community to one of the largest industrial complexes in the state in a matter of five years. And all around these indications of progress, the land looked tired and often dead, although it was the middle of summer. Trucks of every size rumbled by in an industrial parade, without fanfare or fun or any sign of beauty whatsoever. Of course progress has its price. We all know this. But knowing our history with this kind of thing, it certainly made me nervous, and skeptical of any assurances that this boom is not going to exact a much higher price than it's worth.

But what it really got me wondering about was how the locals are dealing with the change. Because it seems that whether a boom lasts or not, the survival of the community depends a great deal on how much effort they put into maintaining that sense of community. Butte is a classic example. The busts that have hit that town could not have been more devastating, from the closing of the mine, to the destruction of the Columbia Gardens, a huge amusement park that William Clark built for the town. It was purportedly burned down because it got in the way of the widening pit. The soul of Butte has been beaten and bloodied more times than most of us would ever survive, but the sense of community there is one of the strongest I encountered.

So how do they sustain this sense of community in a place like Sidney, with more and more people from different places coming to the area, people who have no ties here and have no reason to suspect that their time here will be more than temporary? Many of the people here have no emotional investment in this place.

A few years ago, Humanities Montana sponsored a roundtable in Miles City to discuss the effects of the Bakken boom on *that* town, which is about 125 miles from Sidney. I didn't do an actual head count, but I would guess there were close to one hundred people there. They had organized this event well ahead of time, so there were moderators ready to lead discussions on several topics related to how this phenomenon would affect their community. The topics ranged from how to deal with the influx of strangers, to safety, to rising prices. People were engaged and passionate about every aspect of the discussion, and I left there feeling as if Miles City was going to be just fine.

DAN FARR HAS BEEN the superintendent of schools in Sidney for the past seven years, and he was principal at the high school for eleven years before that. I went to high school with Dan, and even then he was a level-headed guy, someone who was most likely to respond to even the most unpleasant situations with a sideways grin and a dry remark. So I wasn't surprised when I asked him whether there's ever been a moment in the past ten years when he wondered what he'd gotten himself into.

"Not really," he said. "I've been able to look at the whole situation as a challenge." Dan was at his office when I spoke to him on the phone, even though it was a Saturday. "When I took over as superintendent, we had just a little over 700 kids in the schools here, and it's now 1,400. So it's been a *big* challenge, for sure. One of the hardest things about it is that so many of the people who came here for the oil boom were desperate for a job. So many of them are just trying to put their lives back together. And just because that was the dynamic, a lot of these kids that we got in the past few years had special needs. So it wasn't just a matter of adding more staff, but we had to train people or bring in people who had the kind of training to work with these kids."

Joy-Lyn MacDonald has been a science teacher in Sidney for more than thirty years, and she confirmed this. "I would guess that the percentage of special needs kids in our district has gone from about five to closer to twenty," she said.

"What about the salary situation, with the prices going up so dramatically?" I asked Dan.

"That's been a tricky situation all around Sidney. Part of the problem is that if we were to just increase salaries across the board, and then the economy suddenly went bust, which we know it could, we'd have a bunch of jobs that we can't pay with our county tax structure. So instead of increasing salaries, we've been able to use some of the money we get from oil and gas revenue to pay our teachers an impact stipend. This year we were able to pay most of our teachers about $3,000 extra, so we've been fortunate to not lose very many staff."

Dan has a strong connection to this area, as his wife grew up in Lambert, just a little less than thirty miles from Sidney. Dan went to Montana State University, where he got his degree in Secondary Education, then after teaching for five years in Culbertson, which is about forty miles north of Sidney, he decided to get his graduate degree so he could get into administration.

After that, he spent five years in Poplar, and eventually moved to Sidney in 1998. When I asked about whether the community has held meetings to discuss the various issues that have come up in relation to the boom, he said, "Oh yeah. People have been meeting ever since this thing started, talking about the schools, the crime rate, everything you can imagine. This was a very tight little community before all this happened, and that hasn't changed.

"On the other hand, at last count, we had new people in our school from twenty-six different states and two foreign countries, so it's bound to affect the dynamics around here."

THE POSITIVE SIDE OF the Bakken story is that some of the people who work at jobs that would normally provide just enough to get by—jobs like welders, builders, truck drivers,

and electricians—are becoming millionaires. But the demand
for workers has created a situation where quality and safety often take a back seat. According to the Center for Investigative
Reporting, there is an average of one death every six weeks
on oil rigs in the Bakken, a number they believe to be higher
because federal regulators don't have a systematic way of recording gas or oil-related deaths. The effort to keep up with
the demand leaves some workers pressed for the time to do the
quality of work they would normally do. There's a reality TV
series that takes place in the Bakken called "Boomtowners,"
and in one episode, a young man goes house hunting, only
to find that a house that has been slapped together is going to
cost well over $200,000. And as he's leaving the area, he stops
to visit with a neighbor, who warns him that the houses are in
horrible condition, some with floors that are still plywood. She
says that getting the builder to address problems with these
houses is next to impossible. But with so little competition,
and so much demand, there's no incentive. A later scene shows
the man still considering buying the house because it's the best
he can find in the market.

THERE ARE ALSO ECHOES of the early gold rush given the presence of "man camps," which are basically crudely constructed
dorms, some of which provide nothing more than a space big
enough for a bed. Some men even share these tiny spaces, an
arrangement that works as long as the two men are assigned
to different shifts. In Sidney, the rent on a one-bedroom house
has risen to nearly $2,000 a month, or about three times what
it would have been before the boom. Men have taken to cram-
ming several workers into these tiny homes, and it's almost
impossible for families to find affordable housing.

Doris Browning Cooper is another friend of mine from
high school. She and her husband Tom moved to Sidney thirteen years ago when Tom's company, Helena Chemicals, decided to open an office there. When they moved there, they
were able to buy a four-bedroom house for $45,000. "We could
sell it for four times that amount now," Doris told me. "And

when we bought it, it had two apartments in the basement. I'm not sorry we remodeled, but it would be worth even more if we'd kept those."

Just a couple of years ago, Doris underwent surgery that went horribly wrong, leaving her paralyzed from the waist down, and then about a year ago, she slipped off a shower bench and broke her leg, which because of the previous problems had to be amputated.

"The way people rally around each other in this town is just so inspiring sometimes," she told me. "I've seen it first-hand with my situation, but it shows in other ways too. The Elks Club came and built a ramp for me, and people have been incredibly supportive. You see it with the new people who come here, too. The ones that don't make it will have a yard sale to sell all their stuff, and people will pay way more than the stuff is worth just to help them get a new start wherever they go next. Or people will bring food to a family that just arrived. You see it a lot."

But safety is still a big issue, especially after the 2012 murder of Sherry Arnold, a beloved schoolteacher in Sidney who was abducted by two transients and raped and murdered while out for her morning run.

"My husband got me a gun," Doris told me. "Especially with my physical condition and him being off at work all day, we felt like it was necessary."

Joy-Lyn MacDonald knew Sherry Arnold well, and had just talked to her that day before she was killed. "That shook everyone up in this town. Especially before they figured out who did it. It has made people a lot more cautious here. I am much less likely to work late at night than I was before."

With the preponderance of workers, there also come the same kinds of legal problems that have always plagued boom economies. The workers are mostly young men with a lot of money, and the crime rate has gone through the roof. There are more drugs, fights, and excessive drinking, and in the case of the Bakken, a serious issue with sex trafficking. A recent article in *Marie Claire* reported a sting operation that led to the arrest of men trying to buy the services of girls as young as twelve. At this writing, a California man was sentenced to thirty-three years in prison for manipulating young women with drugs to work as prostitutes in the Bakken. The incidents of rape reported in Williston have reached four times the national average, with nearly one hundred rapes per one hundred thousand people, and of course those are only the ones on record. There have even been reports of rape among the men of these camps, although the shame and stigma attached to a crime of this nature keeps most of these crimes deep under wraps.

Four years ago in Sidney, the violent crime rate was one-quarter of the national average. Just two years later, it was higher than the national average. In Williston, calls to the police went from 4,163 in 2006 to 15,954 in 2011. Meanwhile, the police forces in the area are so understaffed that there is no possible way of addressing every crime. In 2010, there were ten police officers in Sidney, which at the time was still a fairly sleepy town of about twelve thousand people. In 2013, with the population nearly doubled, there were twelve police officers. The number of calls that came in during that year was over 4,800. And although the city has brought in outside help to try to address the problem, the math doesn't add up. The number of officers needed far exceeds the number at hand.

Meanwhile, there are already signs that the boom could shrink down to a firecracker. In 2012, oil prices hit one hundred dollars a barrel, and with the tax money rolling into the area, people were willing to put up with some of the inconveniences, which included roads that were taking a beating from all the new traffic and dust covering everything. (One woman complained that it didn't do her any good to cut her hay because the dust from all the trucks made it impossible to sell.) But the price of oil has dropped since then. And while production hasn't slowed all that much, the lower prices will have a profound effect on the area's tax revenue. The drop could mean as much as $600,000 less in tax revenue per year coming into Richland County. With a Sidney city budget of $11 million, that's a big chunk of change. Meanwhile, building continues. New hotels and restaurants are opening to try to meet the needs of the community, and all the elements are in place for yet another scenario that is all too common in Montana.

It is certainly human nature to respond to a booming economy by assuming, or at least hoping, that it is going to last forever. It is also human nature to take advantage of a sudden abundance of cash by buying as much as you can, and having as much fun as you can. It takes a special kind of discipline that is not generally associated with young men, especially young men in labor jobs, to think ahead and consider some kind of plan for this sudden windfall. When a boom happens, and when the inevitable bust comes along, many people are left with houses they can't make payments on, stuff they can no longer afford, and the emotional blast of suddenly losing everything they have in the blink of an eye. And this tends to happen in places where mental health services are meager at best.

Another common thread in these boom economies is the presence of outside money. Huge outside money, along with the power that accompanies such money, and often, the intimidation factor of men (because it usually is men) who have that kind of money. There are countless stories in the Bakken of farmers and ranchers who have been there for decades being scared into selling their property. Or the mineral rights to their property. Physical intimidation is not uncommon. Threats are not uncommon. And other, more subtle forms of intimidation are not uncommon.

These are scenarios wherein the price of success is extremely hard to measure. Where the cost to the community in terms of peace of mind and a feeling of being safe and happy is very, very high. In the Bakken, some women admit without hesitation that they live in constant fear, and will not go out in public by themselves, especially unarmed. Even if they are not physically threatened, the constant barrage of catcalls and suggestive comments can be exhausting. This is, for lack of a better term, the Wild West revisited. And how people feel about it depends very much on who you ask. If it's a local, they are most likely to be very unhappy about it. If it's someone who came here because they were desperate for a job, they got what they wanted, so they are more likely to see the bright side.

I feel especially bad for the natives of Sidney, because you just know that when this is over, they will likely be left holding the bag for any damage from these outside operations. Why would any of these companies care about how they leave this land without someone telling them they must? They have no incentive to treat this place and its people with any kind of respect other than basic human decency, and that's not something you can count on in a place where profit is the main motivation for just about everything.

I don't know enough about fracking to make any kind of prediction or present any kind of argument against it. I have talked to some geologist friends of mine—people who have no connection to the oil business, and people I expect to be honest—and they don't consider fracking dangerous if it's done right. But there is plenty of evidence to suggest otherwise. And plenty of scientists who think otherwise. There is also the matter of water, which is increasingly scarce. From what I've read, fracking takes far less water and is far less environmentally damaging than extracting oil by way of tar sands, a method which is more prevalent, especially in Canada. I have also never been convinced that building a new pipeline was a bad idea, especially after some of the spills that we've endured since the Bakken opened, most notably when 40,000 gallons of crude was spilled into the Yellowstone River in January of 2015. There has been convincing evidence that at least some of these spills are the result of old pipelines. The only thing that seems clear is that there hasn't been enough foresight, planning, or focus on the long-term effects of these people's actions. It is a familiar, frightening story, and I am troubled by the fact that it's happening again and that there's not much anyone can do about it.

I FOUND THIS ENTRY, referring to a writer named Louis Logan, from a 1968 anthology of stories written by Stegner fellows at Stanford University:

> Married, with two children, he is at present living in Broadus, Montana, where an oil boom is in progress. He says, "The streets are unpaved, and it rains all the time. Yesterday a cowboy went by our house with only his nose above the mud. I said, 'It's bad, ain't it?' He said it would be worse if he wasn't riding a tall horse."

I had not heard of Mr. Logan, nor of the novel cited in his biography, *Alligator Dreams of a Tadpole Town*. But the oil boom they refer to was a big deal in Broadus (Powder River County). In 1961, a Denver oilman named Sam Gary started drilling for oil just outside of Broadus. He called his operation the Bell Creek Oil Field. For the first few years, Gray had limited success with what he thought was a very promising source, but in 1967 they hit the big one. And for the next several years, this oil field produced almost 50 million barrels of oil a year, bringing a whole host of Louis Logans to the area to earn good livings as roughnecks.

Within a decade, however, all but a handful of the hundreds of oil rigs built around Broadus had come to a halt, and all Broadus had to show for this influx of money was a beautiful new courthouse and a few other new buildings.

In recent years, a company called Denbury Resources out of Texas saw what was happening in Northeastern Montana and decided to explore the possibility of reopening the Belle Creek oil fields. They decided to employ a method called tertiary recovery, which involves injecting carbon dioxide into the oil reservoir, to build up pressure in an oil field that is no longer producing by traditional means. Early reports showed production by this method to be only about one hundred barrels a day, but the CEO of the company, Phil Rykhoek, predicted production to reach five to ten thousand barrels a day by 2019.

Denbury invested $400 million into this project, which includes building a 230-mile carbon dioxide pipeline from the Lost Cabin natural gas processing plant in Central Wyoming to the Belle Creek oil fields. This is part of a much bigger project, in which Denbury plans to invest $2.5 billion into pumping carbon dioxide into a geologic formation one hundred miles long and four miles wide, stretching from Glendive, past Baker and into North Dakota.

So does this mean that Broadus will get a chance to live up to that bumper sticker up on the barroom wall—the one that says, "PLEASE GOD, BRING US ANOTHER OIL BOOM AND WE PROMISE WE WON'T PISS IT AWAY THIS TIME"?

Only time will tell, but it's clear from one look around Broadus that the people here would most likely welcome the opportunity to find out. Broadus is another town that looks to be dying a slow, quiet death. For a few years, there was an amazing little café in Broadus called The Judge's Chambers. This place served food that was on par with the best restaurants in Billings. But that restaurant went away, as did another wonderful little café called Hoofers, a takeoff on Hooters, except with a pig theme. This place was painted pink, with pigs everywhere, and it offered excellent sandwiches and some of the biggest cookies I've ever seen.

Broadus has generally relied on agriculture as its major source of income. As the livestock market goes, so goes Broadus—unless there's an oil boom. Because Broadus is on the way to my grandparents' ranch, I have seen it dwindle in size over the years, and watched business after business close down. It is one more example of a town that gives very little physical evidence of ever recovering again. But the same thing could have been said about Glendive and Sidney just a few short years ago. So much of the future of Broadus and Powder River County depends on what happens with Denbury Resources. And what happens with Denbury will also determine what kind of quality of life the people in Broadus have for years to come. I might recommend they take a drive up to Sidney and get a few pointers.

I HAVE LEFT BILLINGS and Yellowstone County last for several reasons. For one thing, Billings serves as a nice tidy conglomeration of everything that has come before. As the biggest city in the state, and with a fairly central geographical location, Billings is the center of finance, shipping, sales, service, and shopping for much of the state, especially Eastern Montana. In fact, Billings is the largest city between Minneapolis and Spokane, as well as the largest city between Denver and Alberta, Canada, making it a centralized location for trade and distribution. So almost everything that is produced in Montana finds its way either to or through Billings at some point in time.

Billings has two oil refineries, a sugar beet factory, and a stockyard, and it serves as the main office for many national and international businesses. Billings has also become the city of franchises. You can find almost any chain restaurant you've heard of and many you haven't in Billings. Not to mention the big box stores—Walmart (two!), Costco, Sam's Club, Home Depot, and Lowe's. Billings provides everything in terms of basic needs, as well as two highly respected hospitals and countless other medical centers, including the state's largest VA center. So the connection between Billings and the fuel industry is the same as the connection between Billings and any other industry in Montana. Shipping, finance, production in the form of the refineries, and much of the supplies come from Billings.

To put it simply, Billings is more about commerce than any other city in Montana. And it shows.

Another reason I left Billings for last is that it is where I live, and it is where I grew up, starting at the age of twelve. We moved here after my dad quit his job managing a ranch between Billings and Sheridan for construction magnate Peter Kiewit. Kiewit was a nice man, but he was an absentee owner, spending most of his time in Omaha tending to his multi-billion-dollar business. He hired my dad, who was a schoolteacher at the time, to manage a crew consisting of men who had worked for Kiewit for many years, and of course they resented it. And took it out on Dad by simply ignoring most of what he asked them to do. Or doing a half-assed job.

After two years the pressure got to my dad, and my folks decided to move to Billings, where my mother's sister and her family had lived for almost twenty years. My mother attended Eastern Montana College just out of high school as well, so she knew the city a little.

When we moved here in 1969, Billings was still considered a cow town. Although the refineries were here, oil wasn't quite the presence it would later become. In 1969 Billings was still mostly populated with family-owned businesses. Hart-Albin was the largest department store in town, offering what seemed like a massive amount of clothing, household goods, makeup, and shoes. Today that building looks quaint compared to the behemoths on the west end of town. It has been broken up into offices, like most of the buildings downtown.

When I returned to Billings in 2007, the most troubling thing about it was that most of the best restaurants in town had been converted to casinos. Gambling was at one time made illegal in Montana, in 1889, the year Montana became a state. When Prohibition was repealed, gambling resurfaced, although it was still officially illegal. In 1937 the legislature legalized several table games in various locations, if licensed by the county, and from there gambling slowly found its way into the Montana culture, at least legally. By most accounts, it was always a huge presence even when it wasn't legal. In 1973, the legislature passed the Card Game, Bingo, Raffles and Sports Pool Act, and twelve years later, they passed the Video Poker Machine Act, allowing five machines per liquor license, opening the door for the influx of casinos.

Today there are almost one hundred casinos in Yellowstone County. And although the businesses bring in untold tax revenue, the number of stories I've heard of broken families, lost businesses, not to mention broken spirits, is heartbreaking. In just a matter of years, a close family friend of ours gambled away his wife's parents' family business, which they had spent decades building into a local institution. The effect on the family is impossible to measure.

Billings also offers religion. At last count, there were about 150 churches listed in this town of just over 100,000 people. The churches range from the Korean American Community

Church to the Montana Southern Baptist Fellowship, to the St. Nicholas Greek Orthodox Church. A massive Mormon temple, affectionately known as the wedding cake, sits just below the rims, and an impressive old house on Clark Street has been converted to a Buddhist Center. It's interesting to note that of all of the states west of the Mississippi, only Alaska, New Mexico, and Wyoming have more churches per capita than Montana. We are a church-going people, and I can't help but wonder whether the uncertainty inherent in our economy has played a large role in that dynamic. The three largest denominations are Catholic, at 23 percent, Mormons at about 5 percent, and Evangelical Lutherans at about 3 percent.

Despite the occasional history of racial intolerance in Montana, which has generally always been motivated by the political climate of the country, and aside from the constant of the Native American situation, Montana has almost always shown considerable tolerance toward religious groups. Evidence of this tolerance includes the presence of the Hutterites, the Hmong community in the Bitterroot Valley, a strong Muslim community in both Missoula and Bozeman, and perhaps most dramatically, the Church Universal and Triumphant, a large religious community (some have called it a cult, although they and many scholars reject that label) that moved to a ranch just outside Livingston in 1986. The latter has never released membership numbers but they were a strong presence during the 1980s when they attracted national attention by predicting nuclear war by the end of that decade.

The general attitude toward religious groups in Montana seems to be fairly consistent with our attitude toward many groups, which is that if they mind their own business and don't try to push their wares onto us, we'll leave them alone.

One thing I've come to admire about my mother is her innate desire to find some real human comfort from her experience with religion. So whenever we moved to a new town, which we did often during my childhood, my mother would go church shopping. And her search was not centered on ideology. She was not as concerned with whether or not the church shared her views, as much as whether or not she made a personal connection with the minister. So during the course of my childhood, we started out as Episcopalians, but by the time we arrived in Billings, we had become Presbyterians. So my mother sought out the Presbyterian Church where she felt most comfortable, and she found it not far from our first home in Billings. And although we had a good experience in that church, especially with an immigrant minister named Mike Repka, who had escaped from the Czech Republic during the communist occupation in the 1960s, Mom soon fell out with the other ministers there, and the next thing we knew, we were Methodists.

Our new minister happened to be the father of one of my friends in junior high, Steve Klingman. Steve's dad, Vern, looked like he'd stepped right out of a barbershop quartet, with his hair deftly parted almost but not quite down the middle, and his neatly trimmed mustache. He even wore white shoes. But man, could he preach. He had a folksy style, but he also projected an air of certainty and humanity that was infectious. I came to adore that entire family, and Steve Klingman, whom I mentioned earlier as the man who introduced me to Richard Brautigan, remains to this day among my best friends. I also give Steve credit for turning me on to great literature when we were just out of college. If not for Steve, I may have never become a writer.

There is perhaps no better symbol of the duality of Montana than Billings, with its abundance of churches and casinos. Billings is a place that is conflicted. For most of its history, Billings could be counted on as a bastion of small-town values, despite its size. For the most part this is still true. But as with many other towns I've mentioned in my story, Billings has shown that same spirit of solidarity and open-mindedness when one of their own has become the target of bigotry.

For example, in the 1980s, one of the local Jewish doctors, a man named Brian Schnitzer, became the victim of vandalism by some local white supremacists who had been doing minor damage for several months. The supremacists started by spreading racist literature around town. They disrupted the services of an African-American church, and spray painted swastikas and racial slurs onto the home of a Native American family. Finally, a brick came through the window of the Schnitzer house. Schnitzer had a menorah in the window for Hannukah. By this time, Billings had seen enough, and several community leaders from all faiths gathered and, as a sign of solidarity, decided to post menorahs in their own windows. Soon menorahs were showing up in windows all over town.

The act attracted national attention, in large part because of its catchy name, "Not in Our Town," which eventually inspired a documentary, then a feature film (called *Not in This Town*, probably to avoid copyright infringement), starring Adam Arkin and Kathy Baker. Not in Our Town eventually grew into a national organization based in Oakland that uses film and media to call attention to similar situations all over the country.

So that's one side of Billings.

This is also where a man like Max Lenington, who was the county assessor as well as the county superintendent of schools, could get away with saying that Obama was re-elected because "there are more lesbians, queers, Indians, Mexicans, and niggers than the rest of us," without paying any consequences for it. This is also where Judge Baugh, as previously mentioned, could sentence a Billings high school teacher to only thirty days for raping one of his fourteen-year-old students.

The point is that this is the underlying mentality of much of Billings, Montana. It is a place where racist and sexist jokes still fly without protest, and where an effort to call this to people's attention often inspires a roll of the eyes, or an accusation of being too politically correct.

Sadly, people like Lenington, who later published a letter claiming he wasn't a racist (his main argument being that he has a black son-in-law...oh, and that he *said* he wasn't a racist), are missing a larger point. And a pretty simple one, really. If you are separating people according to race, that is racism. We all do it. I have been pretty appalled at how often I do it since coming back to Montana. I see a Native American downtown who is clearly drunk, and I jump right into the old narrative that I heard growing up. I see a black person in Billings and I wonder why they're here. I have racist tendencies, whether I like it or not. When I lived in San Francisco, most of that stuff went away.

I have to stop myself all the time from letting those thoughts go to the next level, which would be jumping to the conclusion that "these people" aren't worth starting a conversation with or getting to know. Each of these individuals becomes part of the greater "they," a shapeless lump of people with fixed values and personality that will never evolve into the singular, unique people they are. And of course, the step after that would be to act on those thoughts, a step that is probably much closer to where I am than I would like to think. A few drinks, a bad interaction with one of "these people," and you have the perfect formula for an ugly situation.

ONE OF THE MOST striking things about Billings is how much it continues to grow. The census for Billings in 1910 showed a population of about 10,000. By 1960, it had grown to 80,000 including the surrounding communities. By 1980, the population had grown to 110,000, and it now stands at around 140,000 with surrounding communities, which include Lockwood, a town that houses 8,500 of its own. It is this rapid and steady growth (Billings is predicted to be the second most rapidly growing city in the state behind Bozeman) that makes Billings the least Montana town in Montana in my eyes. The influx of chain stores and restaurants, and huge financial institutions, has overwhelmed much of that small-town charm that Billings still had when I first moved here in 1969.

But still, it *is* Montana. And I can't help but think back to that year, and how things changed for our family once we moved here. My father used to tell the story of something that happened toward the end of the two years we spent on the Kiewit Ranch. The stress of the situation had pushed him to the edge, and one day he decided to drive into Sheridan, to the VA hospital. He told the receptionist he needed to talk to someone.

"What seems to be the problem?" she asked.

"I don't know…I just need to talk to someone," he told her.

"Well if you don't know what's wrong, I'm afraid there's nothing I can do for you," she told him.

My father was not an assertive man under the best of circumstances, and this was obviously not one of his stronger moments. He walked out of that building and sat on the steps, where he broke down and cried.

So when he and my mother decided to move to Billings, my father's confidence was shattered. My parents' marriage was on shaky ground, and the stress in our house was constant. When Dad wasn't able to find a decent job for the first year we were here, things just got worse. But about a year after we arrived in Billings, Dad heard about a program offered at Eastern Montana College (now MSU-Billings) called Teacher Corps. The concept was similar to the Peace Corps, except in this case they would send teams of graduate students to the Indian reservations to work in the schools there. My father was selected to be a team leader for the team that went to St. Labre Indian School, and I think that experience saved him from plunging into a deep place.

He loved the Northern Cheyenne people, as well as the people on his team. It was a transformative experience for him. He got the acceptance there that he had never received on the ranch.

But this continued to be a trying time at home, as the school was 125 miles from Billings, and Dad spent the week living on the campus there, leaving Mom with us three kids. She also went back to school at the time, so money was tight.

For me, it was both exciting and scary. Attending the one-room school near the Kiewit Ranch had been a very interesting experience. Because my parents were not accepted by the neighbors, I got a taste of what it's like to be an outcast in a rural community. The kids were never mean, but they had their own subtle ways of letting us know we would never be part of their world. Parties that we weren't invited to, subtle comments. My second year there, when I was one of two fifth graders and we were the oldest of the thirteen students, the other boys persuaded me that when we played soccer at recess, the only fair teams would be me and all the first, second, and third graders against the rest of the school. I went along with it because I didn't have a choice, but we got beat every single day, and of course I got teased when I lost my temper day after day. There is no greater isolation than having an entire community push you aside, with no other options to turn to for friendship and comfort.

So when we moved to Billings, I was thrilled to go to a school where there would be an entire classroom of kids my age. As it turned out, the grade school I attended that year also shipped in three classes from a school that was being remodeled, so I went from being one of two fifth graders to being one of five sixth-grade classes of about twenty-five kids each. It was both overwhelming and exhilarating. I loved it and I was scared to death.

I RETURNED TO BILLINGS in 2007, after being gone for twenty-five years, and the experience was completely different this time. I moved here from San Francisco, after living in several other cities as well, so the shock was the opposite this time, moving from a city of several hundred thousand people to one where I could be anywhere I wanted to go in less than a half hour. I felt a sense of calm and peace that I hadn't experienced in years. San Francisco is one of my favorite cities in the country, but I haven't had a single moment in which I regretted coming home.

The house I live in was built in 1948, and at that time it was surrounded by fields. It is now in the very center of town. I recently met a woman who grew up here as a child, and she told me stories of playing down at Spring Creek, which runs just fifty yards from my house, and seeing nobody all day. Her family owned the home for twenty years, until her parents were killed in a plane crash, at which point it was sold to a family called the Hupps. One of the Hupp daughters would go on to marry an ambitious young soil scientist who eventually became governor of Montana. His name is Brian Schweitzer.

It's a typical Montana story, in which a modest family home can be connected to the history of our state by just a degree or two. Montana is still a place where you or someone you know well can have a personal relationship with one of the most powerful people in the state.

The more it has grown, the more Billings has attracted a more progressive population. Today there are more artists and writers here than there have ever been. Other than Will James, I don't remember hearing about a novelist from Billings until Terry Johnston—who wrote serial Westerns. But it is in the visual arts that Billings has developed a strong foundation. Lyndon Pomeroy has been creating stunning metal sculptures for decades, and although most of his works have found a home in Montana, there have also been several commissioned from as far away as Wisconsin. His works include: a beautiful depiction of pioneers hefting a log onto an unfinished log cabin wall; a mural of two mechanics, about 20 feet tall, that adorns one of the local repair shops; and several miners surrounding a sluice, painted in the middle of the walking mall in Helena. Pomeroy is a Montana native, raised on a sheep ranch up in the northeast corner of the state. He met his wife, Lenore, when he was supposed to retrieve her and deliver her back home for a date with his brother. "When I saw her, I decided I wanted her for myself, and we've been together ever since." I'm not sure how that affected his relationship with his brother, but Lyndon and Lenore Pomeroy are two of the nicest people I know... good friends of my parents for many years, and parents to four remarkable children.

But perhaps the greatest persona among the Billings artists is Mr. Ben Steele. Ben Steele was raised on a ranch near Roundup, in a town that no longer exists, Musselshell. Ben was of the age when it was expected that he would join the military when World War II broke out. Ben had the great misfortune of ending up in the Philippines, where he was among the many soldiers who were captured and forced to endure the famous Bataan Death March. Ben survived that horrific event, only to spend the next four years in various prison camps. According to Michael and Elizabeth Norman's excellent account of the lives of many of the survivors of Bataan (*Tears in the Darkness: The Story of the Bataan Death March*), Ben was among those who were shipped to Japan in 1942 to serve as slave labor in one of about 160 labor camps set up to utilize the nearly two hundred thousand prisoners of war held by the Japanese.

Part of what got Ben through this whole experience was his art. He started sketching while he was in the Philippines, and at one point turned his entire collection of sketches over to a priest who promised to get them into safe hands. Unfortunately, the person this priest handed the drawings over to was on a ship that went down in the Pacific, where the drawings were lost forever. But Ben eventually picked up a pencil and brush when he was freed, and his renderings of his experience in the camps are haunting and superb in their craftsmanship. Ben taught at Eastern Montana College for several decades and experienced a heartwarming experience of healing when he was faced with his first Japanese student, a young man from Hardin named Harry Koyama.

When Koyama first showed up to Ben's painting class, Ben had a hard time. It was the first Japanese person he'd seen since the war, and just looking at Koyama, "my heart hardened and filled with hate." But Ben soon learned that Koyama's family had been imprisoned themselves in one of the internment camps. Although it made it somewhat easier, it wasn't until he was able to sit down with Koyama and talk that they began to find some healing.

I recently attended Ben Steele's ninety-seventh birthday party, and Koyama presented him a painting at that party, still wet with oil, of the two of them with their arms around each other.

THERE ARE MANY OTHER great artists in Billings, but I wanted to mention these two because they are such state treasures, and close friends. When Billings recently laid plans for a new middle school, Steele was among the names suggested for the school. I went to the hearing, and it was a tense affair, as a vote had already been taken approving a different name. But after several impassioned speeches extolling Ben's many good virtues, including his boisterous, infectious laugh, the motion passed, and Ben Steele Middle School is scheduled to open in the fall of 2016.

TODAY BILLINGS PROVIDES the best health care services in the state, including services for mental health. But we still struggle with a large homeless population and problems with how to deal with the mentally ill. In June of 2014, while I was early on in my travels, one of the most popular and well-respected people in Billings was knifed to death in broad daylight by a young meth addict who had stalked him for three days preparing to rob him. Michael Sample was a nature photographer and the vice president of the Sample Foundation, which provided philanthropic services to many organizations in the state.

Sample was known to be generous to the homeless population near his downtown office, to the point that they would sometimes gather and wait for hours for a handout. The young man who killed him was apparently among those who felt entitled to take advantage of Sample's kindness, and for reasons beyond comprehension, stabbed him three times in an exchange that happened right after Sample met his father for lunch.

CHUCK TOOLEY WAS THE mayor of Billings when the incident with Dr. Schneitzer took place and the community rallied to form Not in Our Town. Even all these years later, Tooley becomes animated when he talks about the period following those events.

"There was such a positive energy around here after all that happened, and we used that energy to organize a downtown association and make big plans to revitalize the city." Tooley pulls out a book filled with architectural drawings of the downtown, and many of the buildings have since become a reality. "That whole sequence of events really brought people together," Tooley says. "And even people who didn't necessarily agree politically could see that we had something special going on that we needed to capitalize on."

Chuck Tooley is a tall, slender man with a theatrical voice and a perfect smile. He looks like an actor that would always get the role of the family doctor or, well, the mayor. He grew up in Red Lodge. His father was a diplomat. While Chuck was living in DC for a few years, he met his wife Joanie, who was the managing editor of the *New Republic* at the time. The Tooleys laugh easily, and are always dressed to the nines even for casual affairs. I'm not sure I've ever seen Chuck in a pair of jeans, and to be honest, I don't think it would suit him.

Chuck and Joanie are as passionate about the affairs of Billings today as they were when he was the longest-serving mayor in the history of Billings, thanks in part to a legislative decision. A two-term limit was imposed on the mayor's office while Chuck was serving his first term, but that was a two-year term, so when his first four-year term ended, it was determined that he was still eligible for another term. So he ended up serving ten years.

Chuck also served on the Montana Arts Council for ten years, and has taken on various other duties in the fields of the arts.

"We were able to open up about one hundred businesses as a result of that whole situation with the skinheads," Chuck told me. "It was such a great example of how you can turn something like that toward a positive outcome if you gather as a community and work together to not let it take things in the other direction."

You can still see signs of that spirit in downtown Billings today. There are only a few empty buildings downtown, and some of the areas that were once considered very sketchy have been developed to feature hip little art galleries and quality restaurants. Just across the railroad tracks that run south of Montana Avenue, an old building that used to be one of the worst bars in Billings, The Arcade, now houses a Subway sandwich shop. Further down that same block, a building that used to be a meat packing plant is now high-end lofts, Swift Building Lofts. Next to that is one of the best organic restaurants in the state, the Fieldhouse Café, owned by Chef Ben Harman, the son of Steve and Joni Harman, who developed the Swift Building Lofts. There are now many excellent restaurants in Billings, including several sushi bars, an Indian restaurant, several Thai restaurants, and a French restaurant, Enzo, which has been producing amazing food for about thirty years now. But of course, the most popular restaurants in town, aside from the franchise restaurants, are still the ones that serve up a good Montana steak.

In 2011, Billings passed a $16 million bond, including an anonymous $2 million donation, to build a new library. The old library, the second building to house the facility in Billings, was an old hardware warehouse that had been converted in the late 1960s at a cost of just over a million dollars. This new library was designed by noted Phoenix architect Will Bruder, and it opened in January 2014. Circulation has more than doubled since it opened its doors.

Billings continues to grow and develop into a more metropolitan city by the year. But in its heart, Billings is still more rural than most of the larger towns in Montana. Art and literary events still draw crowds that can be counted on two hands. And the ones that draw larger crowds often do so because they are an event where people are anxious to be seen, not because they are particularly interested in art or literature. It says a lot that the largest town in Montana does not have an independent bookstore. It says a lot that, until a year ago, there were only two movie theaters in town, both owned by a huge conglomerate that only shows big-budget films. Finally last year someone opened a small theater, Art House Cinema, that features more independent films and even documentaries. After moving here from San Francisco, where I developed a taste for good movies, I was starved for this stuff, and I know I wasn't alone.

All in all, Billings is going through some growing pains. Our city council struggled with a recent non-discrimination ordnance, a piece of legislation that really should have been a no-brainer. Every other major city in the state passed this ordnance, which simply stated that no business can discriminate against people because of their race or sexual orientation. Billings decided not to pass it. Some people in Billings still struggle with the concept that equal rights is not the same as special rights.

The truth is, I want to like Billings much more than I do. And that has a lot more to do with me than it does with Billings. I am not a church-goer, nor do I drink or gamble. I have never owned a gun or a fishing rod, or a pair of skis. I haven't hiked since...well, ever. So in many ways, I don't fit the stereotype of Montana. But I've slowly become aware that this stereotype is not as true as I always believed it to be.

So I've taken several actions to meet people who appreciate the things I like. A couple of years ago, along with my friend Connie Dillon, an excellent painter and photographer, I started a salon, where we invite fellow artists to meet once a month to talk about the arts and what we can do to generate more interest in them in Billings. It has led to many interesting discussions, as well as a much stronger sense of community among those who have decided to join us.

But the thing I am most proud of is the Native American Race Relations and Healing Symposium I started with Adrian Jawort. After our initial symposium, which brought over one hundred people to the public library, we have organized a monthly lecture series to bring in people to discuss various Native American issues. It feels as if we're making a small dent in the hard shell that has prevented these discussions from taking place for so long. And I've met some incredible people, many of whom have been mentioned in earlier chapters.

In 2009, *Fortune Small Business* magazine named Billings the best small city in the United States in which to start a new business. Likewise, a couple of years ago *Kiplinger's Personal Finance* magazine named Billings among the ten best places to live in the United States. I'm always shocked by things like this, because when you live someplace, you tend to notice things about it that you find annoying or problematic.

Perhaps this is the best time to employ Gary Gannon's method of measuring wealth, by taking into account the four major categories: economic, social, natural, and human resources.

The economy here is strong and getting stronger. But it's hard to argue that this is one of our biggest strengths. Socially, Billings has a great deal to offer, with two major hospitals, a decent-sized college, and just about any of the basic services a person could need. As far as nature goes, you can't go wrong with anyplace in Montana. Billings is an hour's drive from amazing hunting, fishing, hiking, skiing, and rafting. Whatever you want to do. And the people. Well, they're Montana people.

THE MORE I THINK about it, what I finally realize about Billings is that it probably symbolizes the relative youth of our region better than any city in Montana. As a culture, the West is still in its infancy compared to most of the world. In many ways, we are still trying to find our identity.

Most of the people I know in Billings have barely a passing relationship to the narrative that was foisted on Westerners all those decades ago by John Ford and Zane Grey. Although there are several excellent Western-wear stores in Billings, as well as booteries and saddleries, if you see someone wearing that kind of outfit in downtown Billings, it is likely they are from somewhere else.

Perhaps the most symbolic recent story from Billings was an incident from about a year ago, when a bull broke loose from the local auction yard and ran amuck through the middle of town for about four hours. In a town of 100,000, they couldn't find anyone with a horse who was close enough, or perhaps willing to risk their safety, to capture the bull, so after chasing it with a four-wheeler and other vehicles, probably scaring the poor frothing animal half to death, the police shot the bull. It was a source of great amusement and ridicule, but also some anger, as people wondered how a Montana town would not be equipped to handle a single head of livestock.

But there is still an attachment to Western culture here that is hard to shake. For one thing, it sells. The West draws crowds, and one look at Deadwood, South Dakota, or Red Lodge or Virginia City will tell you that it can even be very lucrative. So like every other resource in Montana, the arts are also susceptible to the carpetbagger who rides into our region, wraps a kerchief around his neck and tugs a big felt hat on his head and perpetuates every myth about the West ever created. These guys make me crazy because they keep people believing that everyone in the West still talks like John Wayne and solves every problem with a punch in the head or a gun. And although many of these artists make good money, the chances that they will make a mark on the world of art are slim, because they make so little effort to explore what's really happening here.

Billings is full of this clash between the old and the new, with galleries packed with paintings of wildlife and landscapes. Some beautiful work. On the other hand, we also have a growing cultural scene with two strong theater companies: Billings Studio Theater, which has been producing plays and musicals, featuring local talent, for over sixty years. We also have a newer company called NOVA, formerly the Venture Theater, and they have made their mark presenting more experimental and contemporary works, as well as plays by local writers and directors. We also have the Yellowstone Art Museum, which features a nice blend of classical western art along with progressive contemporary artists. The museum just recently learned that it has been accredited by the American Alliance of Museums, an honor that only 2 percent of art museums in the US achieve.

Billings also has a theater downtown, the Alberta Bair Theater, which brings in nationally recognized acts, such as Garrison Keillor, the Beach Boys, and traveling productions like *Mama Mia!!* A few years ago, they surprised most of us in Billings by bringing in Eddie Izzard, a British comedian who is known to perform in drag. But he brought the house down, and it was absolutely packed. The Alberta Bair was founded by the daughter of a wealthy rancher in Meagher County, and it also houses the Billings Symphony Orchestra, which actually performs at an extremely high level of talent, and the Billings Opera, which I have to admit I have not attended since high school.

So Billings is trying to become urban, and in many ways succeeding. For one thing, it has grown so large now that a good percentage of the people who live here were not raised in Montana. The hospitals here have provided good jobs, and of course the financial institutions here provide more good jobs, so that there are big housing developments spreading out to the west end of town, with houses priced much higher than we're accustomed to in Montana.

But there will always be that element, the people who come to town with manure on their boots to shop for the month's groceries. But more importantly, there will always be that pressure to somehow relate to our role as Westerners. It's a very subtle pressure, but it's always there, in a snide remark from friends about why you don't like hunting, or the freedom people have using racial slurs as long as there's nobody around who might call them on it. It's the pressure to not be a burden to anyone, no matter how badly you're hurting. And it's not that the people here are intentionally applying this pressure. It's just what they know. It's what they grew up with, and it's what they have lived with their whole lives.

AFTERWORD

"Time only changes the outside of things.
It scars the rocks and snarls the trees,
but the heart inside remains the same."
—Charles M. Russell

When I began this project, I had no idea what the final product would look like, or what themes would emerge. The only thing I knew for sure was that I wanted to get to know Montana and its people in a more meaningful way. I didn't consider myself an expert on Montana, and I still don't, even after nearly two years of immersing myself in its rich history, and talking to people from all over the state, and reading dozens of books about it.

What I do believe is that I had the great opportunity to learn about the effect this place has on its people. I decided early on that there were two ways I could approach this. If this was to be a serious historical record of our state, it would have required years of research, and part of me wanted to do that. There were counties where I *wanted* to spend years doing research, some because of their beauty, some because of the incredible history, but mostly because the people made me feel so welcome there.

But I didn't have the resources or the time for that kind of project. Besides, a part of me felt more inclined to make my trip around this state in more of a whirlwind fashion so that I could experience it instinctively. I wanted to feel as if I was tapping into the spirit of Montana rather than getting lost in historical facts. I wanted to explore its heart rather than its chronology.

So now that I've reached this point, and I feel as if I haven't talked to enough people, or read enough books, I have to take comfort in the fact that this would probably be the case no matter how many people I talked to, or how many books I read. Because this place is that big, and that complicated. I barely touched on the amazing hunting and fishing in Montana. People save up money and vacation time for years to come out here and spend two weeks on our rivers, or trekking into the wild with a rifle slung over their shoulder. I haven't talked enough about the complicated issues of water and mineral rights, or access to public lands. People will no doubt point out several other issues that I missed. I hope so, anyway. Because that's how complex this place is. There's no way I could cover a fraction of what's important to everyone.

My writing students often ask, "How do you know when your book is finished?" and in this case, I would have to say it's because I reached my deadline.

WHICH BRINGS ME TO what I've found. The main thing I found is that Montanans live in a place that inspires fierce devotion. Whether their town or their county is thriving or falling into deep ruin, Montanans will stand in the middle of the street and take a bullet for their community, their state. Okay, maybe not a real bullet, but you know what I mean.

And this determination to defend ourselves has led many of us to fall victim to a certain kind of tunnel vision when it comes to recognizing that some of the things we and our ancestors have done for decades are not really working any more. In fact, some of them probably never did.

So we have been faced with the task of finding some balance between the myth and the reality of what it means to live in Montana. The narrative that was created early on about the West came about for a reason. People needed to believe it to justify certain events, and perhaps to survive. So those myths served their purpose. And they are part of who we are. But some of them are no longer useful.

It probably sounds as if I believe that Montana needs big changes. But that's not what I've come to believe at all. I think there are a few small things that could and should be changed sooner rather than later. Things like giving women a bigger role in policy-and-decision-making, finding some kind of healing with the Native American community, and paying closer attention to the entities that come into our state, the ones that have taken advantage of our resources for decades. But overall I discovered that most of the things that are hurting us as a state could be corrected with a slight adjustment in the way we look at ourselves and our history. And I know human nature just enough to realize that this kind of change—the change in attitudes and values—probably comes more slowly than any change you can possibly make. It can be a glacial process.

For decades, we have been led to believe that self-sufficiency is the ultimate goal of the strong and successful. We have been led to believe that we should be the strong, silent type, and that if we aren't, we need to work hard to become stronger and more silent. The ultimate result of this philosophy is that it leaves many of us very much alone. These qualities can be fabulous when things are going well. Or when we feel great about ourselves and our purpose in the world. But when we question ourselves, or feel vulnerable—when we become overwhelmed with fear or uncertainty—being silent and self-sufficient is the worst possible response.

So we drink. We kill ourselves. We throw our sinking self-image out onto those around us, sometimes in violent, ugly ways, and we decide that our problems are everyone else's fault, and that if *they* would go away, or act more like we do, or learn to think more like we think, then *we* would feel better. This attitude leaves little room for healthy human relationships, and more importantly, it leaves almost no room for reaching out and asking for help.

But I haven't met very many people who don't need help at some point in their lives. Anyone who claims otherwise is living in some kind of strange, frightening fantasy world that can be extremely dangerous. I know that place too well to deny that it exists. I lived there for a short while myself. And the only way out was to realize that I was stuck and needed help. But it was scary how hard that was, because I had been trained like so many of us to believe that I should work it all out for myself.

Montana has so much beauty. One look at some of the splendor that exists in this place and you find yourself searching for words. And it's not just the landscape. But what is most beautiful about this place is the spirit of it. The way the people here love so hard and so thoroughly, whether it's the land or their families or their country. They love until it makes them blind, until they feel the need to barricade themselves against anything that threatens that love. They love with hearts so full that the blood can pump up and swell their view of themselves.

The vast openness of this place can inspire your imagination until you believe you can accomplish anything. I have often driven along the eastern part of this state and thought about how riding across this country on a horse for weeks at a time could have given the imagination of someone like George Armstrong Custer so much time and room to grow that it blew up beyond the boundaries of any rational mind. Many people don't realize that part of what inspired Custer to make his harebrained charge on that fateful day was his growing ambition to become president of these United States. He had many people urging him to run, based in large part on his previous conquests in battle. So he was hoping to add one more big victory to his resumé, to boost his chances of attaining our highest office. Despite the fact that his company had a desertion rate well over 50 percent, he was living in a world where he was invincible, an unconquerable hero.

Montana is a place that will not let go of you. I moved away from Montana in 1996, and for many years after that, I kept renewing my Montana license plates, even though I moved around to several different states. I was always so proud when someone asked me about it, or gave me a thumbs up from their own car. When I was living in San Francisco, someone once left a note on my windshield, saying he was from Bozeman and he'd like to meet this other Montana person in the neighborhood. So I dropped by his house, and he really grilled me about the license plates. He wouldn't let it go, and I eventually realized he was jealous. He wanted to have his own Montana plates.

SOME OF THE BEST quotes about Montana capture this idea, and they're not wrong. The most famous is that of John Steinbeck, who said in *Travels with Charley*, "I'm in love with Montana. For other states I have admiration, respect, recognition, even some affection. But with Montana it is love. And it's difficult to analyze love when you're in it."

But my own personal favorite Steinbeck quote about Montana is "Montana seems to me to be what a small boy would think Texas is like from hearing Texans."

Over time, Montana has inspired writers and artists to honor not only the myths, but also the truth. It makes for an interesting dynamic, bouncing back and forth between Louis L'amour and Bill Kittredge, Zane Grey and Debra Magpie Earling.

Montana inspires artists like Clyde Aspevig and Dale Livezy and Russell Chatham, their oils spread in a way that might capture just a fraction of the beauty of this amazing sky, the watercolors blending together to project a hint of the colors that push their way through this crusty earth.

So I GUESS THE final question becomes whether or not I found what I was looking for on this journey. Did I find an idea of what Montana represents, what it means, to me or to anyone, for that matter? And to answer that, I turn to two final stories.

When I was working on my grandfather's ranch that summer when I was sixteen, my uncle and I were moving a flock of sheep when one of the lambs broke free. This was early in my time there, so I was ready to prove my worth as well as my skill on a horse. I quickly took off after the little guy, digging my heels deep into my horse's flanks. But when I caught up to the lamb, he abruptly stopped, ran behind the horse, and then broke off on a run again.

I caught up to him two more times before I finally got it through my head that this wasn't working. I probably yelled something nasty at him, then turned my horse around and started trotting back toward the flock. And of course when I turned around to see whether he was still running, he was following me back to the flock.

A COUPLE OF DAYS before I finished this book, I watched an eighty-year-old woman fall and land hard on the back of her head. She was using a walker, and when she landed, the walker flipped over and hit her in the face. It was a horrific sight, unfolding just ten feet from where I stood, and it brought up the worst feelings of helplessness and fear.

The hardest part of the experience, though, was that this woman was my mother. We had just finished running some tests at the hospital, where we had spent about three hours shuttling from room to room. They fit her with an IV, and gave her some kind of drug to simulate physical activity so they could take pictures of her heart and determine whether she was physically strong enough to endure surgery on a hernia. The tests seemed to have gone well, and they took less time than we had anticipated. But she was tired and a little weak from walking more than she usually does in a day. Just before she fell, a man had picked up a form that had fallen from her walker. She was in the process of putting the form into the fold-up seat on her walker when I showed her where to sit in the waiting room while I went for the car. This combination of things led to her losing her balance, doing a slight pirouette, and falling straight backwards, and landing flat on her back. Her head smacked against the marble floor, and I was just one of many who shouted and ran to her.

My mother and I have sometimes had a difficult relationship. We have often gone for long stretches without talking. But it has always been me that initiated this silence. She never once stopped talking to me, and each time I decided to talk to her again, she replied without the slightest hesitation.

Perhaps because of this past, this incident affected me deeply, and as I left her at the hospital that night—where they had admitted her again to make sure there was no internal damage—I broke into tears thinking about the look of terror on her face as she fell. And I couldn't stop crying.

I felt as if there were so many things I could have done to prevent this from happening. If I had recognized how tired she was, I would have asked for a wheelchair, or if I had just stayed with her for those ten more feet that she needed to walk into the waiting room, but mainly if I had just had the presence of mind to slow down and to *notice* what was happening.

Mothers are amazing in the way they forgive, and still offer what they can, and I can't help but think about the fact this place we live is referred to as Mother Earth. And I can't help but wonder whether we don't take enough time to slow down and notice how forgiving she can be, no matter how much we ignore the warnings.

LIKE MOST ANIMALS, WE are fairly simple beings when it comes right down to it. Some food, a place to lay our heads, a sense of usefulness. It's the world around us that complicates these things. And there are few places that are as complicated as Montana. There are also few places that provide as many opportunities. And when you think about the things we do to utilize these resources, just the verbs themselves indicate a sense of abuse, even violence. We plow, we corral, we break, we excavate, we herd, we cut, and we drill. We cultivate, thresh, dam, pluck, and hobble.

There are so many things that happen every day, hour after hour, that prove in some small way that we have very little control over what happens in our lives, but when the health and safety of someone we love is directly affected by this kind of powerlessness, it brings home the most basic rule of life on this earth, that we are small, insignificant dancers in a very complex and chaotic ballet.

But when you live in a place like this, you also eventually learn the futility of trying to tame the elements. You learn that a lamb running from the flock isn't the end of the world. That you aren't going to stop it from doing what it wants to do. You learn that no matter how hard you try to protect the ones you love, they will sometimes fall. And finally, you learn that the best way of getting what you want is by recognizing that we are only temporary guests here—stewards of this place—and that by treating it and its inhabitants with the respect they deserve, we improve our chances of having them come to us.

SUGGESTIONS FOR FURTHER READING

Abbott, Teddy "Blue." *We Pointed Them North*. Norman: University of Oklahoma Press, 1939.

Allen, Frederick. *A Decent Orderly Lynching: The Montana Vigilantes*. Norman: University of Oklahoma Press, 2004.

Alt, David, and Donald Hynman. *Roadside Geology of Montana*. Missoula, MT: Mountain Press Publishing, 1986.

Black, George. *Empire of Shadows: The Epic Story of Yellowstone*. New York: St. Martin's Press, 2012.

Brooks, David. *Restoring the Shining Waters: Superfund Success at Milltown, Montana*. Norman: University of Oklahoma Press, 2015.

Brown, Dee. *Bury My Heart at Wounded Knee*. New York: Henry Holt, 1970.

_____. *The American West*. New York: Touchstone Publishers, 1995.

Carrels, Pete. *Uphill against Water: The Great Dakota Water War*. Lincoln: University of Nebraska Press, 1999.

Clay, John. *My Life on the Range*. N.p.: Antiquarian Press, 1961.

Clayton, John. *Stories from Montana's Enduring Frontier: Exploring an Untamed Legacy*. Charleston, SC: The History Press, 2013.

Connell, Evan. *Son of the Morning Star: Custer and the Little Bighorn*. New York: North Point Press, 1997.

Davis, Mary Lou. *Life on the High Plains* and *Come Ride with Me*. Published by author, 2012.

Del Grosso, Robert, and John Coy. *Montana's Marias Pass: Early GN Mileposts and BNSF Guide*. Amazon Digital Services, 2012.

Dimsdale, Thomas. *The Vigilantes of Montana*. Norman: University of Oklahoma Press, 1953.

Dissly, Robert, ed., *History of Lewistown*. Lewistown, MT: News-Argus Printing, 2000.

Dunbar-Ortiz, Roxanne. *An Indigenous Peoples' History of the United States*. Boson: Beacon Press, 2014.

Egan, Ken, Jr. *Montana 1864: Indians, Emigrants, and Gold in the Territorial Year*. Helena, MT: Riverbend Publishing, 2014.

Fanning, T. J. *Looking Back on the Front: A Bridging of Historical Perspectives*. New York: Stonesong Press, 2011.

Fraley, John. *Wild River Pioneers*. Libby, MT: Big Mountain Publishing, 2008.

Frazier, Ian. *Great Plains*. New York: Picador Press, 2001.

Fuller, Emeline. *Left by the Indians*. Amazon Digital Services, 2013.

Garfield County Historical Society. *100 Years Trailing Through Time*. Jordan, MT: Garfield County Historical Society, 2013.

Gibson, Richard I. *Lost Butte Montana*. Charleston, SC: The History Press, 2012.

Glasscock, C. B. *The War of the Copper Kings*. Helena, MT: Riverbend Publishing, 2002.

Gloege, Marvin. *Survival or Gradual Extinction: The Small Town in the Great Plains of Montana*. Middletown, CA: Meadowlark Publishing, 2007.

Gray, Donna. *Nothing to Tell: Extraordinary Stories of Montana Ranch Women*. Guilford, CT: TwoDot, 2012.

Hargreaves, Mary Wilma. *Dry Farming in the Northern Great Plains*. Cambridge, MA: Harvard University Press, 1957.

Harris, Ethan E. *Left by the Indians: Story of My Life*. Amazon Digital Publishing, 2013.

Howard, Joseph Kinsey, ed., *Montana Margins: A State Anthology*. New Haven, CT: Yale University Press, 1946.

Howard, Joseph Kinsey. *Montana: High, Wide and Handsome*. New Haven, CT: Yale University Press, 1943.

_____. *Strange Empire: The Story of Louis Riel*. N.p.: Swann Publishing, 1965.

Hurdle, Joan. *Every Dam Place*. Published by author, 2011.

James, Will. *Lone Cowboy: My Life Story*. New York: Charles Scribner and Sons, 1937.

Josephy, Alvin. *The Nez Perce Indians and the Opening of the Northwest*. New York: Mariner Books, 1997.

Kauffman, Gladys, ed., *As I Remember: Stories of Eastern Montana's Pioneers*. Helena, MT: Sweetgrass Books, 2006.

Kittredge, William, and Annick Smith. *The Last Best Place: A Montana Anthology*. Seattle: University of Washington Press, 1990.

Kohrs, Conrad. *Conrad Kohrs: An Autobiography*. Polson, MT: Gull Printing, 1977.

Krakauer, Jon. *Missoula: Rape and Justice System in a College Town*. New York: Doubleday, 2015.

Lambert, Lois. *In My Dreams I Can Walk*. Published by author, 2010.

Leeson, Ted. *Inventing Montana: Dispatches from the Madison Valley*. New York: Skyhorse Publishing, 2009.

Libby, Orrin. *The Arikara Narrative of Custer's Campaign and the Battle of the Little Bighorn*. Norman: University of Oklahoma Press, 1997.

Limerick, Patricia. *The Legacy of Conquest: The Unbroken Past of the American West*. New York: Norton Publishing, 1987.

Linderman, Frank. *Plenty Coups, Chief of the Crows*. London: Faber & Faber Ltd., 1930.

MacKay, Malcolm. *Cow Range and Hunting Trail*. Midland, MI: MacKay Press, 2013.

Malone, Michael, and Richard Roeder. *Montana: A History of Two Centuries*. Seattle: University of Washington Press, 1976.

_____. *The Montana Past*. Missoula: University of Montana Press, 1969.

Mandler, Lou. *This Storied Land*. Greybull, WY: Pronghorn Press, 2002.

Marquis, Thomas. *Memoirs of a White Crow Indian*. Lincoln: University of Nebraska Press, 1928.

McGinley, Patrick. *A Special Place in Hell. Stories on life in Butte, Montana*. CreateSpace Independent Publishing Platform, 2014.

McLaughlin, Ruth. *Bound like Grass*. Norman: University of Oklahoma Press, 2010.

Meikle, Lyndel, ed., *Very Close to Trouble: The Johnny Grant Memoir*. Seattle: Washington State University Press, 1996.

Mercier, Laurie. *Anaconda: Labor, Community and Culture in Montana's Smelter City*. Champaign: University of Illinois Press, 2001.

Mineral County Historical Society. *Mineral County History*. Superior, MT: Mineral County Historical Society, 2004.

Montgomery, David R. *Dirt: The Erosion of Civilizations*. Berkeley: University of California Press, 2007.

Myers, Rex C., and Harry F. Fritz, eds., *Montana and the West: Essays in Honor of K. Ross Toole*. Boulder, CO: Pruett Publishing, 1984.

Niehardt, John G. *Black Elk Speaks*. New York: William Morrow, 1932.

_____. *A Cycle of the West*. New York: Macmillan, 1949.

Parrett, Aaron. *Montana Then and Now*. Bozeman, MT: Bangtail Press, 2014.

_____. *Literary Butte: A History in Novels and Film*. Charleston, SC: The History Press, 2015.

Raban, Jonathan. *Bad Land: An American Romance*. London: Picador, 1997.

Roe, Frances M. A. *Army Letters from an Officer's Wife, 1871-1888*. N.p.: Hard Press, 2006

Rostad, Lee, ed., *Grace Coates, Honey Wine and Hunger Root*. Helena, MT: Falcon Press, 1985.

Sager, Catherine. *Across the Plains in 1844*. Whitefish, MT: Kessinger Publishing, 2010.

Shover, Charlotte Rosenquist, ed., *The Diary of Ichobod Borror: Gold Prospector around Virginia City, Montana*. N.p.: Charlotte Renquist Shover, 2013.

Smith, Adam, *An Inquiry into the Nature and Causes of the Wealth of Nations* (London, 1776).

Smith, Henry Nash. *Virgin Land: The American West as Symbol and Myth*. Cambridge, MA: Harvard University Press, 1950.

Strange, Mary Zeiss, *Hard Grass*. Albuquerque: University of New Mexico Press, 2010.

Stegner, Lynn, and Russell Rowland. *West of 98: Living and Writing the New American West*. Austin: University of Texas Press, 2011.

Stegner, Wallace. *Beyond the 100ᵗʰ Meridian; John Wesley Powell and the Second Opening of the West*. New York: Penguin Books, 1992.

Stewart, Elinore Pruitt. *Letters of a Woman Homesteader*. New York: Houghton Mifflin, 1988.

Swartout, Robert, ed., *Montana: A Cultural Medley*. Helena, MT: Farcountry Press, 2015.

Swibold, Dennis. *Copper Chorus: Mining, Politics, and the Montana Press, 1889–1959*. Helena, MT: Montana Historical Society Press, 2006.

Toole, K. Ross. *Twentieth-Century Montana: A State of Extremes*. Norman: University of Oklahoma Press, 1972.

Tooley, Chuck. *An Offering: My Reflections on Public Service*. Billings, MT: BCC Incorporated, 2005.

Walter, Dave et al., *Speaking Ill of the Dead: Jerks in Montana History*. Helena, MT: TwoDot, 2000.

Weaver, Kenneth L. *Governing Montana at the Grass Roots: Local Government Structure, Process and Politics*. Bozeman: Montana State University, 2002.

Western, Samuel. *Pushed Off the Mountain, Sold Down the River*. Jackson, WY: Homestead Publishing, 2002.

White, Richard. *Railroaded: The Transcontinentals and the Making of Modern America*. New York: W.W. Norton, 2012.

Whithorn, Doris. *Paradise Valley on the Yellowstone*. Mt. Pleasant, SC: Arcadia Publishing, 2001.